Pious Persuasions

Early America: History, Context, Culture

Jack P. Greene and J. R. Pole, Series Editors

Pious Persuasions

Laity and

Clergy in

Eighteenth-

Century

New England

ERIK R. SEEMAN

The Johns Hopkins University Press

BALTIMORE AND LONDON

This book has been brought to publication with the generous assistance of the Julian Park Publication Fund of the College of Arts and Sciences, State University of New York at Buffalo.

The Johns Hopkins University Press
2715 North Charles Street
Baltimore, Maryland 21218-4363
www.press.jhu.edu

An earlier version of chapter 1 appeared in *Religion and American Culture: A Journal of Interpretation*; a portion of chapter 2 appeared in the *Proceedings of the American Antiquarian Society*; a portion of chapter 4 appears in *Sex and Sexuality in Early America*, edited by Merril D. Smith (1998, New York University Press). Grateful acknowledgment is made to the editors and publishers of these publications.

Library of Congress Cataloging-in-Publication Data will be found at the end of this book.

A catalog record for this book is available from the British Library.

ISBN 0-8018-6208-6

Frontispiece: Rachel Weeping (1772–76), by Charles Willson Peale; courtesy of the Philadelphia Museum of Art, given by the Barra Foundation, Inc.

Contents

Preface ix

Acknowledgments xv

Introduction: Lay-Clergy Interactions in Colonial
New England 3

One The Spiritual Labor of John Barnard
A Boston Housewright Constructs His Piety 15

Two "She Died Like Good Old Jacob"
Deathbed Scenes and Attitudes toward Death 44

Three The Performance of Piety
Religious Rituals and Their Contested Meanings 79

Four Alternative Practices
Magic, Heterodoxy, and the Margins of Religious Culture 116

Five Earthquakes and Great Awakenings
The Continuity of Revivalism 147

Six The Piety of Experience Richardson
Religion, Politics, and Gender 180

Conclusion: Religious Culture and the Origins of the
American Revolution 204

Notes 211

Note on Primary Sources 249

Index 257

Preface

LAYPEOPLE IN eighteenth-century New England, as one might expect, relied on their ministers to explain obscure biblical passages and to aid them
in cultivating their piety. At the same time, some laypeople took their ministers' words and interpreted them in novel ways. Others went wholly outside ministerial teaching to formulate beliefs or engage in practices deemed
heterodox by their pastors.

The many examples of original lay ideas I found as I researched this book
have led me to reconsider how historians have described the workings of
culture in early New England. David Hall writes that culture is "ambivalent": it provides people with choices even as it limits the range of choices
available to them. Culture works as a series of scripts, and people must choose
among the scripts presented to them when interpreting their world.[1] This is
an elegant way to answer the very old question, to what extent is human
agency structured by culture?[2]

But while culture may be ambivalent in all societies, culture is not equally
limiting in all times and places. For this reason I have borrowed and adapted
a metaphor used by T. J. Jackson Lears, which allows me to discuss the differences among societies generally and between seventeenth- and eighteenth-
century New England in particular. Lears positions societies along a spectrum from "open" to "closed" cultures. In a society with a purely closed culture
it is not possible to add cultural scripts to those that elites deem appropriate,
while in a society with a purely open culture there is no barrier to adding
new scripts and people act unrestrained by previous scripts.[3] This formulation's advantage is that it is sensitive to historical specificity: it does not
posit one universal model for the way that culture is created, negotiated, and
reproduced.

To make the discussion more concrete, one can describe seventeenth-
century New England's culture as nearer to the closed end of the spectrum,

with some but not a great deal of room for adding new scripts. Ministerial interpretations of religion—with a few notable exceptions—largely prevailed. Eighteenth-century New England's culture, as a result of the institutional and cultural changes that I will outline in the introduction, moved more toward the open end of the spectrum. Laypeople had a greater (though not complete) ability to add new scripts to the culture. Thus, in the years after about 1700, ministers played less of a role in determining the scope of available beliefs and practices. Take, for example, millennialism. New England ministers did not invent this belief, of course, but they were deeply concerned with the arrival of the millennium.[4] If this culture were closed, laypeople would have followed their ministers and spent a great deal of time thinking about the Second Coming. But, in fact, the vast majority of laypeople chose to ignore millennialism as they practiced piety, seeing it as too esoteric in lives filled with more pressing concerns.

In addition, seeing eighteenth-century culture as more open helps account for that period's heterodox individuals. For example, in 1753 Sarah Prentice declared that she had died and returned in immortal form. Prentice clearly did not choose this breathtakingly heterodox assertion from among the cultural scripts approved by the clergy. Indeed, a cultural model that privileges elite creation cannot fully explain religion's gendered dimensions. The movement led by Sarah Prentice was deeply concerned with the relation between evangelical piety, sexuality, and the body, concerns that the range of ministerial options did not adequately meet. Thus, in certain instances, women found it easier in the more open eighteenth century to bring their own ideas to religious culture, thereby expanding and shaping that culture.

Recognizing the eighteenth century's relative cultural openness puts one more nail in the coffin of the declension model of New England religious history, which traces the supposed decline of spirituality from New England's first generation of colonists through the so-called Glacial Age prior to the Great Awakening. In contrast to the declension model, this cultural openness resonates with the process of Christianization that historians have more recently described, with a wider and deeper attachment to religion in the eighteenth century than in the seventeenth.[5] In the later period's more open culture, ministers played a diminished role in circumscribing the parameters of available beliefs. Religion became more "popular," both in the sense of consisting more of lay-inspired cultural scripts and in the sense of appealing more to ordinary people.

My theoretical ideas about culture spring directly from the wide range of lay sources upon which this book is based. While most studies of religion and culture in early America largely use sermons and ministerial diaries for evidence, I have taken seriously lay ideas about doctrine and belief. To uncover these lay beliefs I have relied on a careful reading of hundreds of lay diaries, letters, conversion narratives, and published poems and broadsides. Because these literary sources tend to have been left by the most pious laypeople, I also analyze lay rituals and other religious practices. This examination of practice has allowed me to understand those on the religious culture's margins who often did not leave written records. Finally, I have studied ministers' sermons and diaries to ascertain what laypeople heard weekly in their meetinghouses and what clergymen hoped their parishioners learned.

My model of culture and attention to lay sources are put into practice in chapter 1, "The Spiritual Labor of John Barnard: A Boston Housewright Constructs His Piety," which is based on a carpenter's spiritual journal kept between 1716 and 1719. Barnard (1654–1732) was a pious man—he was, in fact, a deacon in Increase and Cotton Mather's church—and it is possible to show how his ministers' cultural scripts played a large role as Barnard fashioned his piety. But though he agreed with his pastors on many doctrinal points, he found some of their teachings—on the impending millennium and Satan's pervasive power—uncompelling. As a result, Barnard read the works of other ministers, including the Mathers' longtime nemesis Solomon Stoddard, searching for alternatives. However, ministerial writings and sermons did not circumscribe Barnard's religious horizons. He read and interpreted the Bible on his own, attended prayer meetings and discussed Scripture with pious friends, and led family prayers. Barnard's concerns, typical of many laypeople, were part of the process of shaping culture that occurred as laypeople brought their own interests to bear on religion.

Chapter 2, "'She Died Like Good Old Jacob': Deathbed Scenes and Attitudes toward Death," focuses on the variety of lay reactions to death. Historians have written as if there was a single Puritan way of death, when in fact they have merely outlined the ideal type the clergy constructed in sermons. Of course, the ideal deathbed scene, with the dying person expressing a guardedly optimistic hope to arrive in heaven, was a powerful cultural norm and many people died just so. But some people infuriated their ministers by dying in a state of perfect assurance, convinced they were going to heaven. Others died in complete anguish, revealing the limits on people's abilities to manipulate religion to provide comfort. Finally, on the deathbed ordinary power relations of lay/clergy and female/male could be momentarily inverted. Women took advantage of their position at the center of an emotionally charged scene to "command" like the biblical Jacob.

In chapter 3, "The Performance of Piety: Religious Rituals and Their Contested Meanings," I examine the three most important church rituals: reading conversion narratives, baptism, and the Lord's Supper. Although historians have seen ritual as preserving social order, ritual could result in disorder as well. These three rituals were sites where alternate interpretations of religion could be performed. For example, many laypeople—especially women—believed that baptism protected their children, as opposed to ministers, who declared that it was merely a seal of the covenant with Abraham. Moreover, ordinary people interpreted communion as a ritual of reconciliation. They would therefore not partake if the community was rent with discord, even when their ministers pleaded with them to come to the Table.

The strongest challenge to a cultural model that privileges ministers is found in chapter 4, "Alternative Practices: Magic, Heterodoxy, and the Margins of Religious Culture." Historians have seen magic in the eighteenth century becoming "folklorized," that is, confined to the lower classes, and being seen by elites as "quaint" and powerless. While the class aspect of this analysis is correct, ministers continued to inveigh against magical practice throughout the eighteenth century. Therefore, people who practiced divining, fortune-telling, and even maleficium, or black magic, did so in direct opposition to well understood ministerial teachings. Heterodox individuals such as Richard Woodbury and Sarah Prentice reinforce this interpretation. Woodbury, Prentice, and the magical practitioners of eighteenth-century New England did not rely on clerically approved cultural scripts to shape their practices.

In chapter 5, "Earthquakes and Great Awakenings: The Continuity of Revivalism," I question the Great Awakening's status as a turning point in New England's history. One historiographical tradition holds that the Awakening of the 1740s allowed laypeople to challenge authority for the first time and therefore provided a model or an inspiration for the American Revolution. However, the Awakening was only the largest and most contentious of the four major revivals that swept New England between 1727 and 1764. These four revivals did not foster individualism, but occurred within the context of communally oriented lay piety.

I return to an intensive examination of one individual's beliefs and practices in chapter 6, "Religion, Politics, and Gender: The Piety of Experience

Richardson." A resident of Sudbury, Massachusetts, Richardson (1705–1782) kept a lengthy spiritual journal that has never been analyzed. Her writings reveal someone who experienced rapturous highs at the Lord's Supper and devastating lows when fearing that her recently deceased son was not in heaven. Richardson's piety demonstrates the limits of people's abilities to pick and choose among different cultural options for comfort. Furthermore, Richardson displayed the sort of emotional piety that worried ministers and led to their gendered critique of emotionalism. Richardson also participated in an important shift in popular piety in the 1760s and 1770s: the politicization of religion. War with France and then England caused many laypeople to link religion with politics to an unprecedented degree.

Finally, in the conclusion, "Religious Culture and the Origins of the American Revolution," I show how lay independent-mindedness helped facilitate the revolutionary movement in New England. Although not the primary impetus for breaking from Great Britain, religious culture was one element that helped lead to confrontation. Rather than focusing on the Great Awakening as the crucible in which lay challenges to authority were created, I see the entire sweep of the eighteenth century fostering ideas that could challenge hierarchy and patriarchy. As New Englanders prepared to defy English rule, they built on a tradition of ordinary people questioning authority when they felt it went against their beliefs and interests, culminating a process begun almost a century before.

To give the reader a sense of the amount of formal learning of the laypeople and ministers who appear in this book, I have chosen not to modernize spelling. To make long quotes more readable, however, I have occasionally supplied missing punctuation. I have also spelled out the thorn "y", changing "ye" to "the" and so forth. Though rarer in the eighteenth century than the seventeenth, the archaic uses of "i" for "j" and "u" for "v" have been modernized. I have spelled out common abbreviations such as "wch" for "which" and "chh" for "church." Other editorial insertions appear in square brackets. Biblical citations are from the King James Version. All dates are New Style.

Acknowledgments

IT IS A PLEASURE TO THANK those who have aided this project financially and intellectually. For monetary support I am indebted to the Peabody
Essex Museum, the Massachusetts Historical Society for a Dowse Fellowship, the American Antiquarian Society for a Hiatt Fellowship, the University of Michigan's Rackham Graduate School for a Regents Fellowship, the
Mellon Foundation for a Candidacy Fellowship and a Dissertation Fellowship, and at the State University of New York at Buffalo, the Julian Park Publication Fund and the History Department.

Numerous people have read portions of this book, and their suggestions
have improved the final product. I thank Andy Achenbaum, Keith Arbour,
Anne Brown, Richard D. Brown, David Hall, Brooks Holifield, Peter Laipson,
Jill Lepore, Michael MacDonald, Mark Peterson, J. R. Pole, and Stephen Stein.
Several commentators on conference papers deserve credit for their insights:
Patricia Bonomi, Richard D. Brown, Patricia Cline Cohen, Robert Daly, Sue
Juster, Bryan Le Beau, and Patricia Tracy. Richard Godbeer read the entire
manuscript and offered invaluable suggestions at a crucial stage. Charles
Cohen, the reader for Johns Hopkins, went far beyond the call of duty and
supplied dozens of insights for improving the manuscript. I am grateful to
Ross Beales, Anne Brown, Annette Laing, and Ken Minkema for generously
sharing sources and unpublished research. Martin von Wyss of Hybrid De-
signs in Somerville, Massachusetts, produced a first-rate map. My editor,
Robert Brugger, has helped steer this project toward publication.

My graduate school advisors—Sue Juster, Ken Lockridge, Gerry Moran,
and Maris Vinovskis—offered models of the historian's craft that I can only
hope to imitate. I am indebted to them for their unfailingly perceptive readings of my work.

Victoria Wolcott has been my partner in love and scholarship since before
I began this project. To her I owe more than words can express.

Pious Persuasions

© Martin von Wyss

Lay-Clergy Interactions in Colonial New England

*T*RUMPETS HERALDED the eighteenth century's arrival in Boston. For the price of five pieces of eight, influential layman Samuel Sewall commissioned a suitably conspicuous way to mark the "Entrance of the 18th Century," and on the morning of January 1, 1701, "just about Break-a-day Jacob Amsden and 3 other Trumpeters gave a Blast with the Trumpets on the common near Mr. Alford's. Then went to the Green Chamber, and sounded there till about sunrise."[1] Unfortunately for historians, a new century rarely announces its break from the previous century so clearly—broad historical changes do not pay attention to humanly constructed divisions of time. Nevertheless, this study takes as its starting point the trumpet blast on Boston Common that cold January morning, not because anything changed when the brassy notes rang out, but because it conveniently demarcates two centuries that were, in fact, quite different from one another.

My research indicates that the eighteenth century witnessed greater cultural distance between laypeople and their ministers than the seventeenth, which led to greater conflict. This change, however, was not sudden or complete: it developed gradually, and there remained large areas of overlap between ministerial prescriptions and lay belief and practice. Most lay religious practice continued to be quite orthodox. Moreover, ordinary people did not become "secularized" in eighteenth-century New England; rather, the vast majority remained strongly committed to reformed Protestantism.[2] Indeed, in some areas the eighteenth century ushered in a firmer attachment to orthodox religion.[3]

But compared to the earlier period, the eighteenth century saw increasing tensions between ministers and their parishioners.

Although some disputes centered on economic concerns such as ministerial salaries and parish taxes,[4] laypeople were concerned with more than the economic costs of their religion. Consequently, this book focuses primarily on doctrinal and theological issues. To cite just one example, laypeople became more willing in the eighteenth century to voice interpretations of baptism that differed from their ministers' views. Clergymen universally declared that baptizing a child could not guarantee its entrance into heaven should it die suddenly, while some laypeople quietly asserted the contrary.

This growing contention contrasts with the dynamic that had prevailed earlier. Most historians of seventeenth-century New England describe a "shared culture" between laity and clergy.[5] Although seventeenth-century New England included some dissenters, laypeople and their ministers largely agreed about the fundamentals of reformed Protestantism. According to David Hall in his important *Worlds of Wonder, Days of Judgment,* laity and clergy were united in many of their beliefs, including the power of prayer, the necessity of godly behavior, and the visibility of God's hand in the "world of wonders" (natural and supernatural occurrences that served as portents). It should be emphasized that Hall does not argue that there was only harmony between laity and clergy. Hall makes it clear that in the seventeenth century there was a "current of resistance" engendered in part by near-universal literacy and a marketplace of print. Some issues, such as participation in the Lord's Supper, remained contentious throughout the century. But for the most part "lay men and women exercised their freedom to accept the same ideas" as the clergy.[6] This dynamic would change by the eighteenth century.

The New England churches founded in the 1620s and 1630s—first in Plymouth, then in Massachusetts Bay, in Connecticut, and in New Haven—remained in a state of flux in their early years. Laypeople and ministers needed to decide on basic matters of church governance, such as the standards for admitting new members. Orthodox New Englanders had to address challenges offered by dissenters such as Anne Hutchinson, Roger Williams, and the Quakers. But by 1648 and the drafting of the Cambridge Platform, which outlined orthodox belief and practice and attempted to unite disparate groups around a compromise "Middle Way," ministers and their congregations settled into a pattern that would define religious experience for the rest of the century. The Congregational system that developed in these decades proved flexible and responsive to local needs. Variations from church to church in matters of ritual, discipline, and ecclesiastical procedure signaled strength rather than weakness, as laity and clergy negotiated at the local level fine points not outlined in the Cambridge Platform. On most issues, the shared culture of laity and clergy served as a foundation for amicable relations between the two groups.

In the process of negotiating religious culture, ministers had a great deal of authority in the seventeenth century. Migration to New England had been largely self-selecting. While some colonists placed economic motives first, it seems that most of those who migrated in the peak years of 1630 to 1642 were the "godly sort" who left England primarily because of their objections to the religious policies of King Charles I and Archbishop William Laud.[7] Most of these migrants had great respect for their ministers: Richard Mather, John Cotton, John Davenport, Thomas Hooker, and other towering figures. These first-generation ministers used their charisma and standing to broker the compromise embodied in the Cambridge Platform.

Further buttressing their authority, the early ministers had a great deal of control over the availability of print. Until 1675 the only printing press in New England was located at Harvard College and it churned out uniformly orthodox books and pamphlets. England supplied a greater variety of titles than were printed locally in the seventeenth century, but the long distance from London increased these books' cost and limited the number of titles that made the transatlantic journey.

Even if ministers had been united on all fronts in the seventeenth century—which they most certainly were not—they could not have avoided all conflict between themselves and their parishioners. The reformed Protestant movement was simply too dynamic and placed too much emphasis on believers reading and interpreting the Bible for themselves to allow for uniformity of belief and practice. The controversy that erupted in the 1660s over the Halfway Covenant is instructive. This issue, about who could receive baptism, demonstrates the potential for disagreement between ministers and laypeople; it also shows how the clergy were able to keep this conflict from spinning out of control. A 1662 synod offered a solution to the problem of full members' children who sought baptism for their own children, proposing that people baptized in the church who had not yet had a conversion experience should be allowed to have their children baptized. While most ministers supported the Halfway Covenant (with a few notable exceptions, including John Davenport), in many congregations a majority of members were opposed. Numerous laypeople worried that this innovation would dilute the purity of the gathered faithful.[8] This conflict foreshadowed a number of eighteenth-century controversies, in that ministers and laypeople were found on both sides of the debate, but in the eighteenth century even a strong majority of ministers on one side of an issue would not be able to convince many of their parishioners of their views. This was not the case with the Halfway Covenant: most churches eventually adopted the plan, with about three-quarters of New England's churches using some form of expanded baptism by 1690.[9]

Ministers' ability to overcome lay resistance in matters like the Halfway Covenant diminished in the eighteenth century as a number of cultural and institutional changes toward the end of the seventeenth century began to widen the distance between the two groups. These developments did not have an immediate impact but eventually attenuated the shared culture that characterized the seventeenth century. One change, though largely symbolic, was a harbinger of a wider variety of ideas available in print in the eighteenth century: the cessation of Harvard's monopoly on printing in 1675 when John Foster opened his press in Boston. It was not coincidental that this new press offered the first almanacs in New England to include astrology that predicted human affairs.[10] Universally denounced by ministers, such almanacs found a market among some laypeople. Although this particular breach in the wall of orthodoxy was only temporary—ministers succeeded in getting predictive astrology out of almanacs by the century's end—this signaled a greater range of ideas available in the eighteenth century. Likewise, whereas New England's first newspaper, begun in Boston in 1704, hewed close to the orthodox line, the *New England Courant* started by James Franklin in 1721 sounded positively anticlerical at times.

In part as a result of the first of these developments, some ministers in the latter part of the seventeenth century began to feel as if they were under siege. The jeremiad (a sermon that mourned the decline of piety since the founding generation) was not an empty literary convention but an expression of sincere clerical concerns. To help counteract the ills outlined in the jeremiads, ministers called the Reforming Synod of 1679. There, Increase Mather joined with fellow ministers in a campaign against such perceived lay sins as covetousness, Sabbath breaking, and contention.[11] This synod indicated that many ministers were unhappy with the state of religion and sought to alter matters for the better. The response to this perceived decline of lay piety and to a perceived loss of clerical power was an attempt during the 1680s and 1690s to shore up ministerial authority with a number of institutional innovations. These changes increased the distance between lay and clerical religious cultures.

The first alteration in the religious culture involved a symbolic change in the ordination ritual. For most of the seventeenth century, ministers were ordained in a simple ceremony where laymen (usually church elders) performed the laying on of hands, symbolizing that power originated with the congregation. Beginning in the 1680s, ordination was "clericalized": other ministers performed the laying on of hands. This shift symbolized the clergy's desire to set themselves off as a separate professional class, which culminated in the early eighteenth century with ministers arguing that their power derived from the ordination ritual itself, not from the election of the congregation.[12]

A second institutional innovation aimed at increasing the clergy's power was the ministerial association. By the end of the century many ministers had become frustrated with Congregationalism's atomizing tendencies, with individual churches able to make their own decisions on matters of polity. Therefore they sought to create bodies that would allow them to pool their influence and mete out discipline to straying individuals and congregations. Their solution was the ministerial association, a group of clergy who met occasionally to discuss disciplinary questions and to offer one another support. Boston-area ministers formed the first association in 1690 and the idea quickly spread. The Saybrook Platform (1708), which joined Connecticut's churches in disciplinary matters, formalized this system in law.[13] Though never very powerful, these associations represented the clergy's attempts around the turn of the century to form themselves into a distinct, more professionalized class with interests different from many laypeople.[14]

In addition to these institutional alterations, several social and cultural changes furthered the distance between clergy and laity. Ministers were much more likely than their parishioners—especially outside of Boston—to be aware of the latest philosophical ideas emanating from England. New England ministers, influenced by early Enlightenment writings, began around 1700 to move away from an emphasis on providentialism.[15] While most laypeople maintained their belief in the "world of wonders," the new ministerial focus on greater rationality widened the cultural gulf between ministers and all but their most educated parishioners. Indeed, clergymen (along with a few genteel laypeople) were the most eager participants in "anglicization," elite Americans' unabashed imitation of English culture.[16] This turn toward English models prompted ministers to move away from the "plain style" of writing and preaching that had been crucial in transmitting clerical messages to untutored laypeople. In its stead arose a style that was self-consciously "literary" in imitation of English wit and wordplay.[17] Thus, by 1700 or so ministers were institutionally and culturally distanced from the majority of their parishioners to a degree unknown during the previous century.

Meanwhile, most laypeople in the eighteenth century maintained a tradition of communally oriented piety that allowed certain concerns to develop less through interactions with their ministers and more through interactions with other laypeople. People prayed more often with their families than in the meetinghouse and heard more religious discourse from their friends and neighbors than from their ministers. Communal piety was not necessarily oppositional; in fact, clergymen urged their parishioners to love their neighbors and to practice piety with them. But in the particular setting of the eighteenth century, such communal religious practice could distance laity from clergy.

Popular religious culture in colonial New England was enacted within a matrix of personal ties, with family and pious friends. Even when engaging in secret or "closet" devotions, laypeople concerned themselves with family and peers.[18] More to the point, people often practiced piety outside their churches, in prayer meetings and in family reading and prayer, usually with their minister's support but almost always without his presence. In 1706 Cotton Mather reported in his diary that he had visited a women's prayer group for the first time: "I visited a Society of devout Women, who were keeping this, as a Day of private and solemn Thanksgiving unto God . . . It may be, I am the only Man in the World, that has preached unto such an Auditory!"[19]

This kind of separation from ministers had significant gender implications, as women chose the topics and nature of their prayers without pastoral interference. Likewise, during family prayer and Bible reading, humble men and women gave voice to their feelings and offered their own interpretations of Scripture, focusing on the issues that seemed relevant to them. In such settings, for example, people rarely voiced the millennial themes that so fascinated their ministers but seemed to most of them too esoteric and otherworldly. Furthermore, people observed their neighbors in spiritual distress during religious revivals and became caught up in the excitement. And only in the home and neighborhood would people utter ideas too dangerous to whisper in front of their ministers: "Perhaps God has offered us universal salvation, and we are not implicated in Adam's original sin," or, "I believe I have achieved a state of perfection, and my body shall not be corrupted," or even, "If you write these symbols on a piece of paper and hang it around your neck, it will cure your canker." Such were the possibilities with ministers ever further away from their parishioners culturally and institutionally.

Despite the increasing distance between laity and clergy, the actual practices of lay piety were not strikingly different in the eighteenth century than in the seventeenth. Prayer, alone and with others, remained the central devotional practice. The sacraments of baptism and the Lord's Supper continued to mark significant moments in people's lives. Deathbeds remained arenas for enacting important religious questions. And people continued to attend church and hear their ministers preach. Nonetheless, laypeople (as individuals, not as a unified group) were increasingly likely to interpret these practices differently than their ministers.

This separation between certain laypeople and clergy was not a linear historical development. Beginning with the American Revolution and increasing with the Second Great Awakening of the early nineteenth century, the gap between these two groups would narrow again as some ministers became more responsive to lay demands.[20] Nineteenth-century ministers paid a great deal of attention to their audience's desires, a stance in contrast to that of most eighteenth-century ministers, who were deeply concerned with professional prerogative. At the same time, greater denominational rivalry in New England allowed people more choices about worship and forced ministers, in effect, to compete for parishioners.[21] The personal experience of religion also changed after the Revolution. In contrast with the communally oriented lay piety of the eighteenth century, nineteenth-century religion (at least among evangelical Protestants) focused on "personal, interior, self-conscious experience" for both ministers and parishioners. Furthermore, the Romantic style of religious experience—with its emphasis on "withdrawal from the social world"—which had just begun to attract Boston's lay elite immediately prior to the Revolution, flowered in the nineteenth century.[22] Finally, laity and clergy both participated in creating a popular American civil religion, in which the new republic's political and religious missions were seen to be intertwined.[23]

But these nineteenth-century changes are outside this book's purview. Instead, I focus on the eighteenth century and uncover beliefs and practices that demonstrate New Englanders' independent-mindedness throughout that century. One of this book's goals is to illuminate patterns of lay-clerical interactions that have previously been seen to arise from the Great Awakening but, in fact, were present long before.

The Great Awakening was predated by the sort of independent thinking and questioning of authority that historians have usually ascribed to the revival itself. This pre-Awakening questioning of ministerial authority was not limited to the impious. In fact, most challenges to the clergy came from godly laypeople who found themselves at odds with their minister's interpretations of a religious ritual or scriptural passage. For example, in 1726 Rev. Samuel Dexter of Dedham, Massachusetts, called for a fast day in his church. Dexter, consonant with the early eighteenth-century ministerial campaign to consolidate power, wanted as great a clerical presence as possible on this solemn day, so he invited five ministers to join him in the fast-day service. This large contingent of outside ministers angered some of Dexter's parishioners, who "went about their worldly Occasions & had Us'd their Utmost Endeavour to prevent other Peoples attending on the Fast." These were not ungodly men and women; they returned to church the following week. But when they came back they were surprised by the anger of their minister, who reproved them "sharply" for absenting themselves from the fast. According to Dexter "this Reprehension was taken very heinously, one said I abused them—Entreated them abominably. Another, I told a Devilish Lye in saying Father forgive them they know not what they did."[24]

Here was the crux of the problem: Dexter believed that the men and women who stayed away from the fast knew not what they did, when in fact they knew precisely what they were doing, which was in direct response to Dexter's attempt to solemnify a fast day with a phalanx of outside ministers. In such exchanges laypeople expressed ideas about rituals that differed from ministerial interpretations, long before the Great Awakening supposedly gave laypeople the power to challenge authority.

As in the dispute with Dexter, women often participated in these pre-Awakening challenges to authority. For example, in 1735 in the Westborough Church, "Mary Bradish offered a Confession for having composed a paper of Verses of a scandalous and calumniating Nature respecting the Committee appointed by the Town (some time since) to search out who it was cut the pulpit cusheon, & tending to defame others also."[25] In this case the church had been doubly assaulted, first by a rogue who cut the pulpit cushion, perhaps as an unsubtle manifestation of a disagreement with Rev. Ebenezer Parkman, and second by a woman using the popular tradition of parody to mock the godly men investigating the incident. Thus, women did not always maintain the high standards of the "vertuous women" celebrated by Cotton Mather and other ministers.

Because this book examines women's actual practices and writings, rather than simply ministerial images of female piety, it is able to show areas of slippage between clerical injunctions and female practices.[26] In fact, many tensions between laity and clergy in the eighteenth century had to do with images of women. Ministers, trying to reconcile themselves to an increasingly feminized church membership, created an image of the idealized female saint who sought God early, prayed, fasted, attended church, and submitted to her minister and God.[27] But in many spaces, especially the contested arena of the deathbed, women asserted their prerogative to speak and to be heard.

If ministers were supposed to have authority in any arena, though, it was in the meetinghouse. Indeed, throughout the eighteenth century, ministers preached and people attended their sermons. Between 1700 and 1785 in Essex County, Massachusetts, for example, only fifty-three people were charged (and only twenty-one convicted) for absence from Sabbath worship, a charge that could be initiated when a person missed four Sabbaths in a row.[28] Despite having something of a captive audience, ministers occasionally had to avoid preaching on certain subjects, or alter the tenor of a sermon, in fear of their parishioners' negative response. For example, Ebenezer Parkman shaped many of his sermons to avoid his flock's criticisms. Amidst some contention in 1747, Parkman described how he decided what to preach: "Design'd to have preached on Song [of Solomon] 1:7–8, but perceiving that Some of the people were so very wavering and not able to bear at present the least Severity I drew up a Conclusion to treat them with great Gentleness and therefore preach'd a.m. on 1 John 17 and p.m. on Rom. 6:13."[29]

Likewise, in 1766 Parkman tried to avoid controversy regarding justification by faith alone. He reported, "I am engag'd on the Difficult subject of Good Works, from Titus 1:8. *Difficult,* because people are so prone to charge ministers with *Arminianism,* even if they preach most Evangelically."[30] Ministers wanted to preach about good works: as self-appointed upholders of morality, the clergy made obedience to God's commands an integral part of their teachings. But throughout the eighteenth century many laypeople objected to any interpretation of Scripture that seemed to deny the doctrine of justification by faith alone (even if such denial was not the ministers' intent).[31] On this issue and many others, ministers had to accommodate their parishioners' doctrinal interpretations, at least as the clergy understood them.

When ministers angered members of their flock about doctrinal matters the result was contention, often protracted and painful. Such disputes were not limited to the post-Awakening period. In 1712, for example, Rev. Joseph Green of Danvers incurred the wrath of some of his parishioners for a sermon he preached. Green wrote in his commonplace book, "I met with Great temptations from some of the chief of my people contending with me for teaching them from the 3 Prov 10 that Men should ordinarily honour God with one tenth of their Increase or clear gain."[32] It was not the impious fringe that challenged Green's authority, but the "chief" of his people, the most substantial farmers. They rebutted Green's interpretation of Proverbs 3:9–10, which the minister had glossed as demanding one-tenth of the farmers' profit in support of the church, but which in fact reads that one should honor the Lord with "the first fruits of all thine increase." Clearly, the laypeople in Danvers felt "first fruits" meant much less than one-tenth of their profits.

But even if people did not approach their minister with objections, it did not mean they agreed with everything he said. Numerous differences of opinion never turned into disputes because laypeople sometimes chose to keep their beliefs to themselves. In this way the distance between laity and clergy sometimes, ironically, worked to smooth over differences that otherwise might have caused contention. Evidence for these disagreements is difficult to unearth, but may occasionally be found in colonial New England in lay sermon notes, notes that many pious men (and a few women) kept of the sermons they heard. These notes ranged from one-line entries recording the sermon's text to verbatim shorthand transcripts of the entire sermon.[33] Historians have used these sources to show how closely laypeople followed their ministers' preaching.[34] Indeed, that conclusion can be drawn from most sermon notes since few contain any editorial commentary. But sometimes the notes reveal active listeners, fond of good sermons but critical when the preacher offered an interpretation that differed from their own. Joseph Brewster, a shoemaker in Portsmouth, New Hampshire, attended church faithfully every Sabbath. With equal diligence, this artisan recorded in his diary the text of the sermons he heard. But in several cases, Brewster subtly showed his distaste for a sermon. After a trip to Maine in 1757 he noted, "went to Berwick, [John] Rogers Preach'd, Text I forgot, well I might."[35] Perhaps Rogers delivered a particularly somnolent sermon that Sabbath, leading Brewster to doze instead of paying attention. Sometimes laypeople were less subtle. One Sabbath Joshua Green, a Bostonian who usually took very careful and extensive notes, recorded nothing but the sermon's text. Where he usually summarized the main themes of that week's discourse, Green simply scribbled, "An harangue."[36] This layperson recognized the difference between good gospel preaching and a clerical diatribe.

Perhaps the best example of active lay reception of sermons is in the diary of Abraham Fitts, blacksmith of Chester, New Hampshire.[37] Fitts rarely failed to add some editorial comments to his notes, reporting after a sermon in 1764, "I thot as good a sermon as ever I heard from him," referring to his pastor Ebenezer Flagg. Likewise when he heard "2 remarkable sermons to me I thot." Fitts could also be bluntly dismissive, declaring that his minister's performance one Sabbath included "two weak sermons." Even more interesting than these comments are when Fitts disagreed with Flagg on doctrine. One such instance occurred in 1763, when Flagg preached on Luke 4:1–2, which tells the story of Jesus' temptation in the wilderness. According to Fitts, the "improvement," or significance Flagg drew from this text, was that "Satan could but tempt and if we resisted or yealded it was our act." But Fitts disagreed with Flagg's interpretation, writing, "I thought if we yealded it was our act or sin but if we resisted it was by the Spirit of God."[38] This seemingly minor point relates to a crucial issue about which laypeople were ever vigilant: human free will versus God's omnipotence. In his sermon Flagg argued that people are culpable for their sins since Satan can only tempt and not force people to sin. But Fitts worried that this formulation denied God's power, so he asserted that if people resisted sin it was only through divine intervention.[39] Pious laypeople did not enter the meetinghouse as empty vessels waiting to be filled with the minister's words, but as critical and even sophisticated thinkers.

This independent-mindedness could lead laypeople to question some of hierarchy's most fundamental tenets. Gordon Wood, in his Pulitzer Prize–winning book on the radicalism of the American Revolution, describes pre-revolutionary America as an extremely hierarchical society.[40] There is no doubt that eighteenth-century New Englanders recognized distinctions in rank as an important component of an orderly society. Nevertheless, their tradition of active lay thinking in doctrinal matters could lead, in certain situations, to a critique of hierarchy and the patriarchal foundations of ministerial authority.

A revealing incident along these lines occurred in Westminster, Massachusetts, when in 1747 William Baldwin and other townspeople became embroiled with their minister in a heated dispute. Once again the issue was free will. The aggrieved faction of the church insisted that Rev. Elisha Marsh preached that "every one under the Light of the gospel might be saved if thay wo[u]ld do what thay co[u]ld."[41] Baldwin criticized Marsh in a letter that maintained all the trappings of a hierarchical society. In every instance, Baldwin referred to Marsh as "Rev'd Sir," and he declared that he did not want to speak in a manner unbefitting his rank: "I chose to write to you Because I am hasty of Spirit & knowing that you would not allow me liberty to spake all my mind without Braking in apon me & so will provoke me to spake unadvisedly which I was not willing to do." But at the same time, Baldwin offered a devastating critique of patriarchy. The minister had told

Baldwin to "come to you as a Child to a father & you wold give me Correction." Baldwin's response to this condescension illuminates the limits of patriarchal authority before the Revolution:

> in answer to that I shall take notis of Several things in that Relation, first some fathers are unfaithful in the Instruction of their Children, 2dly some fathers teach their Children bad principles, 3d some fathers use a grate deal of Rashness in Correcting their Children whereby they do more hurt than good.[42]

He continued in this vein for another five points. Baldwin did not reject all distinctions of rank, just as he did not entirely reject a father's prerogatives. But within a hierarchical framework and using the language of hierarchy, Baldwin asserted his ability to know when he was being mistreated and taught "bad principles" by his spiritual father. This passage is an apt metaphor for eighteenth-century lay-clergy relations, which were ordinarily marked by lay respect of ministerial learning and ability but often became contentious when ministers preached in opposition to their parishioners' desires. Thus, ordinary people's tradition of thinking for themselves, and not merely the Great Awakening, helped prepare the way for the rejection of authority entailed in the American Revolution. In the relatively open culture of eighteenth-century New England, laypeople had become accustomed to contesting and negotiating elements of their religion. Standing on New England's battlefields, with war trumpets sounding the beginning of a new historical epoch, laypeople engaged in a revolution against patriarchal authority that had some of its roots in the process by which religious culture had been shaped during the previous century.

CHAPTER ONE

The Spiritual Labor of John Barnard

A Boston Housewright Constructs His Piety

*J*OHN BARNARD (1654–1732) was a carpenter. While he constructed houses for his fellow Bostonians, he constructed a spiritual edifice, too. As a carpenter, Barnard used the tools and materials available to him and, within the architectural conventions of his day, built homes according to his individual judgment as a craftsman. Similarly, though in a less self-conscious manner, Barnard fashioned a cosmology out of the varied building blocks available to him in colonial Boston's religious culture: sermons, godly books, pious conversation, and prayer. As is evident from the 184-page spiritual journal he kept between January 1716 and October 1719, Barnard actively constructed a personal piety.[1]

Barnard's piety partook of both the seventeenth century's more closed culture and the eighteenth century's more open culture. Born in the middle of the seventeenth century, Barnard lived long enough to watch Boston grow from a sleepy provincial backwater to a bustling metropolis. During this period, print became increasingly available to ordinary readers like Barnard, as the number of books, pamphlets, and broadsides grew dramatically. This printed material, though largely authored by ministers, allowed ordinary readers like Barnard to tap into a fairly wide range of ideas. As several historians of European popular religion have demonstrated, laypeople took from ministerial injunctions ideas they found relevant.[2] Different readers took different things away from the same texts, just as listeners did from oral injunctions.[3]

In addition, Barnard participated in an important religious development of the last decades of the seventeenth century: the sacramental renaissance.[4] This ministerially sponsored movement placed greater emphasis on reformed Protestantism's sacraments, baptism and the Lord's Supper. Ministers urged their parishioners to pay more attention to the Lord's Supper, especially by preparing themselves for the ritual through rigorous introspection, ideally in a spiritual journal. Barnard's journal, exactly the sort his ministers championed, demonstrates the ironic effects that this clerical campaign could have when taken up by a clever, if not formally educated, layperson. The journal gave Barnard the space to work out his ideas on his own, in a more concrete form than would otherwise have been available to him. True, laypeople had kept diaries before the sacramental renaissance, but not journals like Barnard's, which consisted mostly of religious musings before fifty communion Sundays over the course of nearly four years. The space his journal provided, along with the social context of Barnard's religion—his practice of piety with family and friends outside the meetinghouse—accounts for those beliefs and practices that were compelling to Barnard, even if they were not his pastors' major emphases.

This is not to imply that Barnard's journal documents radical dissent from orthodoxy or the creation of an oppositional religious world in the tradition of Carlo Ginzburg's Menocchio.[5] In fact, most of Barnard's beliefs and practices were consonant with the prescriptions of his ministers, Increase and Cotton Mather. But it is precisely Barnard's place within the mainstream of orthodox belief and practice that makes his writings so interesting, for they paint the portrait of a deeply religious man, a deacon and a member of the Mathers' Old North Church, who took an active part in the construction of his piety. By one calculation, a godly layperson like Barnard listened to some fifteen thousand hours of sermons in his lifetime.[6] In Barnard's case the Mathers delivered the large majority of these sermons. Indeed, the influence of these many hours of oral sermons can be found throughout the journal, as Barnard occasionally used his journal to take sermon notes and often cited passages from the Mathers' sermons to make appropriate points. Barnard also read the Mathers' publications, distributed gratis to him and his fellow parishioners, and he wrote about these books in the journal. But Barnard's reading material also included the Bible, a work subject to multiple and conflicting interpretations; a book by Solomon Stoddard, the Mathers' nemesis; and several works by English authors, written in a different social and religious context. Furthermore, Barnard's social roles as father, husband, and housewright shaped his piety outside of the walls of the church. Barnard's cultural horizons were not circumscribed by the sermons he heard every Sunday, and as a result he chose to emphasize some personally meaningful ideas his ministers did not stress.

So was Barnard representative of his era's laypeople? Certainly not of all laymen and laywomen. Barnard himself noted, "I read more then many of my Ranke."[7] In addition, his age, sex, and occupation generated concerns that were not universal. Finally, Barnard's participation in the communion ritual placed him among a minority of New Englanders. But lay piety ranged across a broad spectrum, from those whose infrequent church attendance was punctuated by Sunday snoozes to those like Barnard for whom praying, reading godly books, spiritual discussions, and churchgoing were serious matters. For this group of godly laypeople, Barnard's piety is broadly representative—but only broadly so, because Barnard's journal demonstrates the degree to which lay piety was personal. Each layperson emphasized certain beliefs or practices and gave other doctrines a novel application. The relevance of John Barnard's piety lies both in the particulars of his case and in the illumination of the process whereby an individual built his spiritual edifice out of timbers gathered from diverse sources.

Sacramentalism

Near the end of the seventeenth century, New England underwent what E. Brooks Holifield has termed a "sacramental renaissance." Seeking to bring more people into their churches and hoping to foster a more vital piety, ministers increasingly emphasized the importance of regular attendance upon the Lord's Supper.[8] Although David Hall correctly points out that only a minority of laypeople in early New England took communion, he has underestimated the power of the Lord's Supper for participants.[9] In his otherwise incisive analysis of Samuel Sewall's diary, Hall's brief discussion of the Lord's Supper focuses on Sewall's fear of approaching the Table for the first time, omitting an exploration of the ritual's meaning during the rest of his life.[10] Barnard's journal demonstrates that for communicants the Lord's Supper was a source of empowerment, in addition to being a ritual that could engender awe and fear.

The Mathers were the leaders of the sacramental renaissance; Cotton Mather's handbook *A Companion for Communicants* was the earliest of the American communion guides that proliferated at the turn of the century. For the Mathers and other clergy sponsoring the sacramental renaissance, diligent participation in the Lord's Supper involved more than receiving bread and wine: rigorous self-examination was also necessary before approaching the Table. "There is indeed a Threefold *Self Examination* which we are to labour in," urged Cotton Mather. "We are to look *Forward,* or to see whither we are *going;* to look *Backward,* or to see, what we *have done;* to look *Inward,* or to see what we *do.*"[11]

Barnard almost definitely owned a copy of Mather's *Companion.* Mather noted in the records of the Old North Church in 1690, "This Day, at the Lords Table, I endeavoured to furnish every communicant with my Companion for Communicants."[12] In many ways Barnard was an exemplar of the sacramental renaissance. For the nearly four years covered by his spiritual journal, he never missed an opportunity to partake in the Lord's Supper, a string of fifty consecutive appearances at the Table. Even more impressive is Barnard's commitment to self-examination. The day before each of those fifty communion Sundays was filled with introspection: the looking forward, backward, and inward that Mather prescribed. Although at least one historian has wondered whether laypeople found time for such extended introspection,[13] Barnard went out of his way to make the time: "my time is short, & my sperit somthing exhausted, by reson of a Jurny from Marblehed, ariving late in the evening, yit I desire to improve what time & strenth I have ... in order to prepaire for Communion with my blesed saviour in his house & at his table on the morow" (122).

Though it might seem that Barnard got his piety straight out of Mather's *Companion,* the reality is much more complex. Mather's influence is evident in many ways: Barnard's concern with searching for evidence of saving grace, his continual desire to "do good," even the fact that he kept a sacramental journal. But through the very keeping of his journal Barnard provided himself with the space necessary to construct his piety in a more concrete fashion than would otherwise have been possible. As a result of the mental space created by his journal and the influences of his social roles, Barnard's piety parted company with the emphases of the Mathers on two crucial issues. Whereas Cotton Mather emphasized an individualistic experience of the Lord's Supper, Barnard's journal evinces a more corporate conception of the ritual. And while the Mathers almost never mentioned the direct presence of Christ in the Supper in their sacramental guides, Barnard's piety centered on direct and immediate communion with Christ at the Table.

The Mathers' parishioners must have had little doubt about what their ministers saw to be the most pressing duty in preparation for the Lord's Supper. Cotton Mather incessantly reminded his flock that prior to communion all participants must ask themselves whether they had experienced a saving change. As Mather plainly stated, "for a man to be mistaken about his own *Good State* is a thing of the *Illest Consequences* in the World." Sometimes people who had been saved did not perceive it, but the real problem came when people believed they were saved when in fact they were not. Mather warned his readers to imagine a man "to be not in a *good State; Suppose* him to be, *in the Gall of Bitterness, and the Bond of Iniquity;* for this man to be now misled by a false Assurance, *This* undoes him Totally, Finally, and very Terribly."[14]

These warnings had one of two effects on godly laypeople. Some were scared away from communion, to the clergy's great chagrin. Keeping in mind warnings like those from Mather, as well as the biblical injunction that those who eat and drink unworthily at the Lord's Table eat and drink "damnation" to themselves (1 Cor. 11:27–29), these laypeople thought it better to avoid the Lord's Supper rather than risk eternal damnation.[15] Other pious people, however, were spurred by ministerial cautions to examine themselves rigorously for signs of conversion. Barnard took this path. Every four weeks for almost four years, Barnard's self-examinations aimed to determine whether he had been saved and if he was fit to participate in communion.

The process of examining himself for sin made Barnard rather fearful at times. His doubts and fears the night before communion reveal why some laypeople were scared away from the ritual. Meditating on sin before the Lord's Supper, Barnard, having absorbed many years of teaching about the wages of sin, worried because "the punshment which the law of god thretins for sin is exeding dredfull, the law of god thretins death for the least sin, the wages of sin is death, death temporall, sperituall & Eternall, death both of body & soule" (20). At times this sense of sinfulness created in Barnard a feeling of self-loathing. "I have great cause to morne," Barnard lamented, "for the unhollynes of my heart & life, sin has made me a loathsum Cretur, I abhor my selfe before the lord" (30). Although he sometimes found "unbelefe so strong in me" (11), Barnard's fears and doubts did not keep him away from the sacrament. Nor, however, were these expressions of fear merely formulaic. Having accepted the sacramental renaissance's emphasis on self-examination, Barnard found that process painful but overcame his doubts through his faith in the "lov of god to por sinfull man" (10).

Barnard linked this orthodox desire to examine himself with participation in the sacrament. He noted that "some are intruders when thay come to the holly table of the lord, & not welcom to him, thay com unwort[h]yly, O with what trembling of soul, have I need to Inquire, *lord, is it I?*" (21). Barnard admitted that the visible church of professed believers could never be pure. Concerned that he might not be saved, Barnard prayed in the manner that the Mathers recommended. "O help me I hope thou doest help me," he begged God, "senserly to examin my selfe, & makest me to Indevor to be very thoughtfull, prayerfull, & sollom in my preparations, & my main arant [errand] thear, I hop[e] is to injoy Christ & to be delivered from all sin" (110).[16] Painfully aware of his own sinfulness and of the potential for polluting the sacramental table, Barnard placed his fate in the hands of God.

In addition to communion, Barnard's sacramental piety focused on baptism and its relation to saving grace. This issue had divided Protestants since the Reformation, with some seeing baptism as an efficacious means of grace and others believing that it was merely a covenant seal.[17] Barnard believed that baptism alone did not infuse grace. He noted that "thear are many Baptized over whose Baptism will not save them, but will agravat[e] thear confusion in the end." As usual, Barnard worried about his state: "I desire with a greaved heart for my short comings to inquire *lord, is it I?*" (110).[18] This sentiment reflects what Holifield has called "the new baptismal piety," which ministers promoted in the early eighteenth century. In this movement, part of the sacramental renaissance and a result of the Halfway Covenant's logic, clergy urged baptized people to live in a way consistent with their baptismal obligations. Ministers asserted that this applied to all aspects of life: "the *Baptized* are to observe all the Laws of *Jesus*." Even more insistently, they applied this to communion. Cotton Mather railed at his readers that "you that are Baptized most horribly violate your *Baptismal Vow,* while you wittingly and willingly neglect any Institution of the Lord Jesus Christ."[19] Barnard showed the influence of Mather's teachings when he prayed, "O *help me to improve my Baptisme,* as an obligation to a godly life, *let me* be afrade to wallow in any filthynes of flesh & sperit, *help me* to keep a good conchenc" (110). He interpreted his participation in communion as flowing directly from the obligation he incurred when he was baptized as a child, a sentiment congruent with the new baptismal piety.

Barnard and Cotton Mather were in substantial, though not total, agreement on the importance of good works in glorifying God. They also expressed similar ideas about good works as evidence of conversion. Mather's best known exposition of these points is *Bonifacius: An Essay upon the Good,* though he expressed these ideas throughout his writing. The reputation of this essay notwithstanding, Mather made it clear that good works could not cause one to be saved, that they were only the result of justification. "It is in the first place, to be taken for granted," asserted Mather, "that the *end* for which we do *good works* must not be, to afford the matter of our *justification.*" To make the point even clearer, Mather addressed the reader directly: "Sir, all your attempts at *good works* will come to nothing, till a *justifying faith* in your Saviour, shall carry you forth unto them."[20]

Throughout his journal, Barnard referred to the importance of good works in language reminiscent of Mather. Barnard wrote of his "desire to be a laborious, active Christian, & to abound in good workes, workes of pyety, Charity, & Equity, Indeavoring to doe all the good I am Capable of, to all with whom I may be Conserned" (7).[21] Mather offered several concrete recommendations to increase good works, including holding private days of thanksgiving, thinking about piety when work was slow, and convening religious meetings.[22] Barnard performed each of these piety-inducing actions. Like his minister Barnard did not think that by abounding in good works he would be able to insinuate his way into heaven. Still, Barnard agreed with Increase and Cotton Mather and felt that salvation demanded some preparation. As he wrote prior to one Lord's Supper, "Thear are sumthings nesisary to be dune by men, in order to thear salvation, god will not save man, without his doing sumthing, not that men are, or can be saved by thear owne doings, no it is the Infinite mercy of god, & merits of Christ, whearby any are saved" (16). Barnard understood the complex ministerial line on the relationship between preparatory actions and salvation.[23]

In orthodox fashion, Barnard consistently gave God credit for these preparatory actions. No believer in pure free will, Barnard saw the spirit of God working in him to create the desire to do good works. "Belevers are led & acted by another sperit then that of the world," Barnard prayed, "thro grace I hop[e] the good sperit of god . . . dus Inclin[e] me to the things that are holy Just & good" (3). Barnard had a clear conception of the doctrine, emphasized by the Mathers and others, that conversion was prior to, and indicated by, good works.

Barnard, putting good works in a slightly different light than Cotton Mather did, linked his sanctification to his sacramentalism. Nowhere in *Bonifacius* did Mather discuss the role of the sacraments in doing good, nor did he expound upon doing good in his communion guides. But at the end of each of his fifty precommunion examinations, Barnard concluded with a brief note about what he expected to experience at the Lord's Table the following day. These passages often resembled the following: "I desir to come to the sup[p]er of my lord, that from him I may reseve new suplys of grac[e] & strenth, to forsake all sin, & to be holly in heart & life" (18). In this passage Barnard linked participation in the Supper with godly behavior. Similarly, three years later he wrote, "I desire to come to my dearist lord at his table, that I may grow in grac[e], be frutfull in good workes, take care I may have nothing to doe but to dy, when death comes, & in the mean whil that I may walke close with god" (168). As a result of his communion with Christ at the

Table, Barnard felt he would be better prepared to imitate his spiritual father's positive qualities, demonstrating that Barnard saw the sacraments as inextricably bound up with godly behavior. On the link between good works and sacraments, the writings of Barnard and Cotton Mather reveal slight differences of emphasis.

On other issues, however, the gulf between Barnard's and his pastors' interpretations of the Lord's Supper was wider and more fundamental. These issues, involving Christ's presence at the Supper and the ritual's social aspects, show a godly layperson whose piety contained elements somewhat at odds with that of his ministers.

Whether Christ was present at communion had long been controversial among Protestant theologians. In the sixteenth century, John Calvin and Ulrich Zwingli represented the two ends of the spectrum of learned opinion. While Calvin emphasized Christ's spiritual presence in the sacrament, Zwingli saw the Lord's Supper as a memorial or symbol of Christ's death.[24] Cotton Mather was closer to the Zwinglian interpretation. According to Richard Lovelace, "Mather nowhere refers to the direct presence of Christ in the Supper."[25] Cotton Mather's language in describing communion "could sound flatly Zwinglian," argues Holifield.[26] Consider the following passage, in which Mather compared the Lord's Supper to a memorial: "Our Lord is gone from us, and as we do by some Token keep up the Remembrance of an Absent Friend; so do we in this Ordinance Retain and Revive the Remembrance of an Absent Lord."[27] Likewise, Increase Mather focused on preparation for the Lord's Supper in his sermons, discussing the presence of Christ only in his private diary.[28] One would not want to take this line of argument too far: Cotton Mather did occasionally mention Christ's presence in his publications. In his *Companion,* he told readers that "you are now coming to a Table which the *King* of Heaven is peculiarly and eminently present at."[29] But this was not his main emphasis. Significantly, in this 167-page guide to communion Mather mentioned Christ's presence only twice while nearly half the book discussed preparation for the ritual.[30] For the Mathers, communion's chief importance lay in its ability to dispose the laity toward pious introspection prior to the sacrament.

Barnard had a rather different conception of why he participated in the Lord's Supper. Certainly he believed in the importance of self-examination; most of his spiritual journal consists of such introspection. But Barnard also experienced Christ's direct and immediate presence in a way that infused the ritual with a powerful meaning.[31] Prior to partaking in the sacrament every four weeks, Barnard evinced a strong desire to experience Christ's spirit. The day before one communion Sunday, he prayed, "help me in obedienc[e] to that Comand *this doe,* to draw near to the[e], at thy holy table" (23). Sometimes he felt despair because he did not wish to be with Christ, as when he bewailed that "I have cause to be deeply humbled that I have so few longings after Communion with Christ, yit I hope I may truly say I long for more of Communion with Christ in his ordenances, it greaves me I have so litle, yit the tast[e] I have had of it makes me long for more" (52). Despite this, his desires usually took a more positive tone.

Barnard had reason to be positive, for his wish to experience Christ's presence at the communion Table was usually granted. "Att the Table of the lord," Barnard wrote, "I with an Ey of faith beheld a Crucifyed Saviour in the Sacriment of his holly Super, not spared, but given to Death, for me" (21). He often pinpointed the exact moment when he felt the divine presence: "I had sweet Comunyon with Christ in the second prayer, it broke my heart to consider the love of Christ to me, & he drew out my soule to him" (59). These experiences often led Barnard to consider the importance of a holy life. He reported that "I came to him . . . beging him, whom I aprihended gratiously present at his table, that I might feal the blesed effect of a true fa[i]th, even love to god, repentanc of sin, & hollynes in heart & life" (107). At the Table, these experiences were often sensual, as when Barnard "*laboured* to looke to my dear saviour, with a *beleving,* a *loving,* a *penitent,* an *admiring,* an *adoaring* Ey" (157). With such immediate sensations of the holy spirit, it is no wonder that Barnard wrote rapturously of his desire to participate in the sacraments: "The holly *Institutions & Ordenances* that god hath apoynted in his word, I hope I delight in them, as means of Comunion with god . . . I count one day thear better than a thousand els where" (126). His interpretation of the Lord's Supper, though never outlined in a theological treatise, is apparent in these passages. Taken together they depict a man with a sacramental piety that differed in emphasis from that of his minister.

In addition, Cotton Mather and Barnard had differing interpretations of the social implications of the Lord's Supper. Although this ritual brought together all the members of the gathered church, Mather chose to emphasize the individualistic side of the experience.[32] This formulation flowed directly from Mather's concern for preparation—as noted above, a concern that filled almost half of his *Companion for Communicants.*[33] Throughout the *Companion,* Mather addressed the reader as an individual and described in exquisite detail the process of self-examination. Only twice did Mather ask the reader to consider his or her social ties while at the Table.[34]

As is evident in his journal, Barnard did not share this interpretation.

Though Barnard was concerned with preparation and self-examination, his understanding of the rite also involved a corporate dimension. Like early modern German peasants and Puritan artisans in seventeenth-century England, Barnard brought community concerns with him to the communion Table.[35] Mather would have liked his parishioners to concentrate their attention "wholly toward God in spiritual self-concern,"[36] but Barnard could not. As a result of Barnard's participation in a tight-knit community of saints, he turned his attention at least partially in their direction during the ritual.

Barnard continually returned in his journal to the theme of his love for "godly men." In one representative instance at the Lord's Table, Barnard "pleaded hard . . . that I might have such a love to the bretherin, as might Evidenc[e] it to me that I am pas[s]ed from death to life" (21). In other words, Barnard saw sincere love of the saints as evidence of conversion, and thus a reason to be admitted to communion. Similarly, in his preparations for communion, Barnard emphasized his corporate conception of the Supper. One morning he asked himself, "doe I love other men, espeshally godly men, allas [alas] my love is litle worth, I can do but litle to expres it, yit I hope I may truly say I . . . take a speshall delight in the children of god, & to make their condishon my one [own], O that I might so love my brother" (57). Usually in his self-examinations, Barnard linked his corporate vision of participation in a community of saints directly to his sacramentalism. He queried, "doe I love my bretheren with a singular love, . . . indeed the saints are thay in whom is all my delight, I caire not to be intimately familiar with any others" (61). Later in the same examination, when concluding with the reasons he participated in communion that day, he wrote, "I com this day to my saviour that the grac[e] of *lov* . . . may be increased in me" (64). In each of these passages Barnard saw his love of other visible saints as an important reason to participate in communion. For him, the Lord's Supper accommodated both individual and corporate religious cultures.

But all was not love and happiness within the community of saints. Barnard knew that "in near relations natural tempers Jare [jar]" (75), and in such situations the Lord's Supper had an even more important function: as a ritual of social integration. Barnard found communion an appropriate setting for forgiving those who had injured him. Again, Barnard went beyond Mather's individualistic interpretation of the sacrament to a conception more attuned to social interactions. In a self-examination before communion, he asked himself, "dus the grac[e] of love, cause me to forgive & forgit Injurys reseaved from my neighbour?" This was a difficult question for Barnard, who felt he had to balance the Christian model of meekness with his own desire to stand up for his rights: "I have been . . . apt to thinke, if I dont resent it, I shall be trampled upon, but I hop[e] this fear dont hinder my atempts to overcom evel with good . . . I desire to com to the table of the lord, that his love may be brought whom [home] to my soul." The sacrament the following day convinced Barnard that forgiveness was the proper response to his unkind neighbors. "Att the Table of the lord," he reported, "I Indevered from my heart to forgive them that have wronged me, becaus god has I hope forgiven me my many sins, I beged of my hevenly father . . . that I might never reveng them, but doe all the good I could to them that have wronged me, . . . & that I might know that I am pas[s]ed from death to life becaus I love the bretherin" (15).[37] The power of sitting before Christ's presence convinced Barnard of the importance of social harmony. It was easy for ministers to prescribe otherworldly thoughts when their parishioners came to communion, but a world of joys and troubles led laypeople to concern themselves with more earthly topics. Thus, Barnard's sacramentalism provides evidence of a godly layperson emphasizing certain beliefs and practices—corporatism and the presence of Christ—that were somewhat different than those of his pastors, while remaining largely within the framework they had articulated.

Social Sources of Piety

What were the sources of Barnard's particular piety? Why did his sacramentalism have a personal cast, and why did it differ somewhat from his ministers' prescriptions? Since so much evidence about colonial New England religion is in the form of manuscript and published sermons, it is tempting to equate the extant body of sermonic literature with lay religious culture. But when one examines a godly layperson's life experiences, other, extraministerial sources of piety become evident. For Barnard, these experiences included a wide variety of social roles. As a housewright he spent most of the daylight hours six days a week planing and nailing together boards for new homes. He was the patriarch of a large family: with two wives he had eight children who lived into adulthood. Consistent with his role as patriarch he led family prayers and offered instruction. Sundays, Barnard spent in the Mathers' Old North Church, which he joined in 1678 and where the members elected him deacon in 1695. There he prayed, listened to sermons, and watched baptism rituals. These various social roles were among the building blocks of Barnard's piety, and they were among the sources of lay contributions to the religious culture.

Family concerns do not take up as much space in Barnard's journal as they do in the diaries of some other New Englanders. Partly this resulted from his age: in his early sixties, he was beyond the roller-coaster emotions of the years of births and infant mortality. Partly this was due to the genre of his reflections: not a diary of daily occurrences but a journal of sacramental piety and extraordinary happenings. Nonetheless, from the journal emerges a man whose place within his family shaped his piety.

In his private devotions, Barnard always—without exception—prayed for the protection of his family. During one typical day of prayer, he "indevored to spred the case of every one of them before the lord, & to implore his mercy & grac[e] for them" (90).[38] Not only did Barnard pray *for* his family, he prayed *with* them, probably twice daily. The evidence for this point, however, is only indirect. Several times he noted what he did before private fasts or thanksgivings with an offhandedness that suggests a daily occurrence: "I began the day as usally in secrit, & with my famely" (90). In another entry, Barnard seems to refer to family prayer. On a noncommunion Sunday, he wrote, "in evening prayer bewailling the hardnes of our hearts & the blindnes of our minds, the sperit of god helpt me to bring them to Christ, to break & inlightin, & at the same time touched & broke my heart" (81). It is likely that by "our" and "them" he meant his family. That he brought others "to Christ" suggests one important aspect of family worship: it was an opportunity for Barnard to be a leader rather than a follower. In family prayer he was the active one, the one formulating prayers. This contrasted with his more passive role within the church as one who listened to prayers composed by the minister. As when he put his pen to his sacramental journal, within his home Barnard authored his piety.

This leadership role may be linked to his position as his family's patriarch. Old enough to be granted respect, young enough still to be gainfully employed, Barnard was the undisputed head of his family. In terms of gender relations, this raises tantalizing questions that the journal does not fully answer. It is probably no coincidence that Barnard never specifically mentioned his wife in his entire journal. Steeped in a religion replete with images of "father" and "master," Barnard may not have been able to conceive of a significant role for a woman in his piety. One hint of this is found in Barnard's only mention of a woman. In April 1718 he noted that "my wiffs mother Hanah Long, formerly Ballintine, dyed between elleven & twelve a clocke in the night, in the 83rd year of her age, I hope she was one that truly feared god, & is now at rest in the bosome of her saviour" (101). Unlike the four other death notices that Barnard wrote in his journal, all about men, this is the only one that contains no eulogy, no list of Christian qualities, merely a vague hope that she truly feared God.[39] On the other hand, there is evidence that, at least for imbuing their children with religious scruples, Barnard and his wife shared equal duty. As one of Barnard's sons noted in his autobiography, though his father alone used his carpentry skills and "made a little closet for me to retire to for my morning and evening devotion," both his parents "took special care to instruct me themselves in the principles of the Christian religion."[40] And certainly Barnard's journal only partially reflects the time and love he gave his wife. Ultimately, though, Barnard's patriarchal role shaped his piety, giving him the power to lead family prayer and the means to omit his wife from his religious musings.[41]

If he left his wife out of his journal, he did not omit his thoughts about his male children. One incident in particular—his twenty-six-year-old son Jonathan's voyage to England—shows how fears for the safety of his children shaped Barnard's piety. In January 1719, Jonathan left for England. One month before he departed, Barnard was already getting nervous and invoking the image of God as a substitute father: "my son Jonathans intended Voige for England, calls for humble prayer, for direction, protection, & desired sucsese, but espeshall, that god would bring him near, & keep him neare to himselfe, that he may not be led away with the workers of Eniquity, but honour his profision, by a holly, & upright heart & life" (132). As Barnard would do if he were near enough, he wished for God to keep his son near to himself and protect him from evildoers. This passage also relates to the sacramental renaissance, when Barnard prayed that Jonathan would "honour his profision," or keep the covenant he made when he joined the church. After Jonathan set sail, Barnard continued to pray for his son during his preparations for the sacrament. Plaintively he prayed that "senc [since] my god has gratiously heard prayers hethertoo, I trust in his mercy, he will stile [still] doe so, however I commit him to the conduct of our gratious redeemer, & know he wont hurt us, but doe us good" (140). The welfare of his children motivated Barnard, like almost all pious laypeople, to pray and seek God's favor.

Another part of the social matrix that shaped Barnard's piety—and was a source of his corporate interpretation of the sacraments—was his circle of pious friends.[42] The importance of these relations is demonstrated in Barnard's brief eulogies marking the deaths of companions. When his "dear frind Deacon Thomas Baker" died in May 1719, Barnard wrote that he had lost "a faithfull friend & companione," a man who was "to all apearanc, a plaine, senser [sincere], harmles man, & an upright Christian, one that feared god above many, very usefull in his plac[e], and served his generation according to the will of god" (153). The importance of such godly men for

Barnard is clearer still in the tribute to William Robey. Robey was, like Deacon Baker, "a dear Christian frind of min[e]," a person "with whom I hav often had, comfortable, sperituall conversation." Even more importantly for shaping Barnard's piety, Robey was "one of our family meatting." Barnard explained the purpose of family meetings:

> Deacon Bakers hous, was the last hous, that he visited, before his sicknes & death, whear he with foure or five more of us his Christian frinds, meet together, as we had used to doe at one anothers houses by turnes, for sume time before, onc[e] a fortnight, on no other busnes, but to pray together, & to cary on sume sperituall discourses, for our owne edyfication, & prepairation for a dying houre. (89)

Here was yet another extraministerial source of Barnard's piety: the private meeting. These meetings' potential for subversiveness was highlighted during the Antinomian Crisis of the 1630s when Anne Hutchinson used private meetings to air heterodox opinions. In contrast, Barnard's meetings were by no means subversive; the Mathers strongly encouraged them.[43] But this was yet another site where Barnard was exposed to the religious ideas of people other than his ministers and a place where Barnard could take an active role in formulating his own piety. Barnard had these people in mind as he constructed his corporate interpretation of the Lord's Supper.

Of course, not all Bostonians were as pious as Barnard, Baker, and Robey. In fact, some people seem to have scoffed at Barnard for his intense religiosity. These people affected Barnard's piety, intensifying a tendency toward martyrdom. In his examination of May 19, 1716, Barnard noted, "I . . . have suffered reprotch, & contempt, & in my busnes too Doubtles, for my fathfulnes to the Cause of god, his Churches, & servants" (13). It is tantalizing to speculate: did some less pious people refuse to hire Barnard because of his religious scruples? Did they have to put up with religious lectures as he shored up their retaining walls? One might think piety made sound business sense in colonial New England, but Barnard's writings suggest that this was not always the case. Barnard's response to these perceived slights was to take a tone of slightly self-righteous superiority:

> I had rather loos any thing in the world than the frindship of god, tho fear of being scofed at, & mockt, for a strict adhearanc to Religion, . . . for all that I suffer for god hear shall hearafter be rewarded, I may suffer Joyfully the spoyling of any thing I have hear because . . . the sufferings of this present time are not worthy to be compaired with the glory that shall be reveled. (14)[44]

Experiences such as this caused Barnard to develop a piety that at times seems to revel in martyrdom. Furthermore, these slights led Barnard to use communion as a ritual of social integration, for the next day at the Table he endeavored "to forgive them that have wronged me" (15).

Another influence on Barnard's piety was his calling as a carpenter. The vicissitudes of being an artisan in his early sixties in an economy subject to severe downturns helped reinforce his providential outlook. Providentialism, which held that God's will could be discerned in extraordinary occurrences, was not unique to Barnard; rather, it was one of the most commonly invoked cultural scripts in early New England, accepted by ministers and laypeople alike.[45] The significance of Barnard's case lies again in its demonstration of extraministerial influences on one layperson's piety.

Occasional, dramatic incidents at work furnished Barnard with evidence that God's hand was protecting him. In the spring of 1719, Barnard noted one such "mercyfull providenc":

> As my man William Loaring & my selfe & Georg wear together shoaring up a lintow [lintel] of a barn, of Coll Hutchinsons, the Ruffe & Sid[e] sudinly slipt & fell downe upon us, only as god mercyfully ordered it, a fenc post stopt it so, as one corner of the Ruff board against the sid[e] of the barne, & a short jack stud at the other end, which prevented its falling flat upon us, which if it had, it might have crusht us to death, but god has been pleased to spaire our lives a litle longer, let his name have all the glory, & lord help me so to number my days & to aply my heart to wisdom, & to quicken my pac[e] in the Right ways of the lord, that whenever death comes it may be safe & joyfull. (154)

Barnard's providentialism is evident in several parts of this passage. That "god mercyfully ordered" the fence post to stop the roof from crushing him is a classic expression of seeing God's hand at work in one's life experiences. So is the moral he drew from the story: it was a sign from God to pursue holiness.

In far less dramatic fashion, Barnard's craft provided him with evidence of God's pleasure and displeasure. The four years covered by his journal were a series of cycles of ample employment followed by maddeningly slow periods. Unlike pious farmers who mostly had the weather to contend with, Barnard's material well-being was influenced by confounding business cycles and the boom and bust periods inherent in the building trades. "For about a month past I have had very litle to doe at my trade," Barnard reported sadly in July 1718, "& it is stil a ded time, I have no prospect of a full Imployment, only some small Jobs to doe." He tried not to second-guess God: "I acknowlidg the Justis, & Rightiousnes of god in it." But this providence was hard to understand: "I deserv nothing, but I hope to se[e] the goodnes of god in it too." Barnard's answer both reinforced and derived from his providentialism: he decided to submit to the unknowable will of God. He prayed "that I may have a heart cherfully & thankfully, & patiently to submit to what ever his holly providenc orders for me or mine, . . . lord all is wel because of thy ordering, only give me an heart to conform to thy will" (115). In this early modern world of daily difficulties, it took a deep faith to see a divine order in the problems that could beset an old carpenter.

The hardships associated with aging point to a link between piety and the life course. Barnard saw his calling as an integral part of his piety: hard labor was a way to glorify God with good works. Every night before he went to sleep he asked himself, "Had my worke a labouriouse hand?" (67). But as he got older, Barnard occasionally found himself too ill to work. In the fall of 1717 he noted, "I have been a weake [week] for the most part confind to my house, because of a windy paine in my bowells, that I could not bare to walke or stand many minits at a time" (68). Two and a half weeks later he was still unable to "walke without paine" (73). Perhaps when Barnard could not labor with his hands he felt compelled to increase his spiritual labors. This period of sickness witnessed an increase in Barnard's devotions. In ordinary times Barnard observed occasional days of fasting and prayer, but the month of September 1717 saw Barnard engage in an unprecedented four such days. He made the link explicit when he noted that, "being indisposed for my worldly Imployments I desir[e] to improve this day in recounting the mercys of god" (65). Because labor was a spiritual matter, growing old and infirm made Barnard even more concerned with his spiritual state—and gave him the time to increase his devotions.

The final social source of Barnard's piety was his encounters with death. Although colonial New England was actually remarkably healthy for its time, death still seemed a constant threat to most people.[46] In his sixties, Barnard was beginning to witness his friends and family dying—as many as three in three cruel months in 1718—and he was often ill. These circumstances made him think his death was imminent, even though he would live another fifteen years. In his journal he occasionally noted, "mortality is advancing on me" (33). This preoccupation with death had two effects: it reinforced his providentialism and it provided an incentive to greater religious scrupulosity.

His response to his brother's death in 1716 reflects both of these tendencies. He saw God's purposeful hand when he wrote, "it is a loude Call from heven unto me." Because he had "lived two years longer in the world" than his brother, this was a sign that he needed to be increasingly pious and watchful, and "to quicken my pac[e], & to make Redy" (8). Similarly, when his friend Edward Marin died at age fifty-three, Barnard interpreted it as having divine meaning. "I looke at it a loude call to me, that am about 10 years older, to prepair for my owne death," he wrote, echoing his earlier statement, "& I hope thro grac[e] god will in mercy sanctyfy his & the death of some others, to me & help me by his sperits grac[e], that I may be not only habitually, but also actually prepaired" (94). In this way Barnard strove to make meaning out of his confrontations with death.

Barnard's daily rituals of piety incorporated his fear of death and his desire to live as if death were imminent. In a precommunion examination, he asked himself, "doe I take caire that if death come upon me sudenly, I may have nothing to doe but to dy, & to go to heven?" In other words, he wanted to know if he would be able to die with a clear conscience. To that end, he noted that "I doe Indevor to set death before me, every day" (167). This ritualized confrontation with death was best expressed in his nighttime ritual of three questions, the last of which was, "if I dy this night is my soule safe?" His rhymed response to that question began,

Soule what if ase the morning come
Death sumons me to heare my doome
Say, may I bravely looke thro grace
The King of Terrors in the face. (67)

Although it has the cadences of a children's rhyme, this nightly ritual expressed deep and powerful sentiments. Barnard confronted his own death and how he should behave given his mortality. Daily he sought to abound in good works to prove his conversion to himself. As with the other social sources of Barnard's piety, the deaths of friends and family did not *cause* him to be deeply religious; others in colonial New England encountered death without ever cultivating an intense piety. Rather, these deaths served as building blocks for Barnard's particular piety.

Lay interpretations of death, work, and parenthood did not occur in isolation from ministers; a notation in Barnard's journal illuminates the complexity of the social sources of piety. Barnard wrote that the death rhyme and others were "all composed, & given to me by Doctor Cotton Mather when he was a young man, which are stil in my memory" (67). Though written by Mather, it is significant that Barnard prepared himself for sleep each night with this particular verse. One can only imagine the number of pious poems Mather gave his parishioners, but this one most resonated with Barnard. In this way the social sources of Barnard's piety interacted with the words he heard in the meetinghouse each Sunday. Barnard used his experiences as a father, husband, housewright, and bereaved friend—in conjunction with the doctrines delivered by his ministers in church—as tools for building his piety. These various social roles were therefore among the sources of the distinct emphases of laypeople's piety and of lay contributions to New England's religious culture.

Reading Religion

By candlelight late into the night and by the light of the rising sun, John Barnard read religion. He read the Bible, the Psalter, and books of piety and theology. He read books by his ministers and tracts composed thousands of miles away in England. Barnard's reading material greatly influenced his piety.[47]

The books available to Barnard provided a range of ideas that any literate person with some spare cash could appropriate; even those without money could borrow books from friends or their minister. That Barnard lived in the colony's center of bookselling and printing only increased the availability of books. These books carried ideas that sometimes contradicted those espoused by a person's minister; even when they did not, there was no telling how a person might use a particular passage. In the cognitive moment when readers processed the words on a page, laypeople could fashion their own piety out of readily available building blocks.[48] The wider availability of books was one factor that helped make eighteenth-century religious culture more open than that of the seventeenth century. In this context Barnard used his literacy to build his personal piety.

Because he was not formally educated, however, reading did not come easily to Barnard. "I read the Scriptures, & other good bookes often, I believe I read more then many of my Ranke, but allas I soon forgit what I read, am not able to give any tolerabl account of it, I am ashamed of my barannise [barrenness], & have been tempted to read lese [less]" (124). Barnard placed such importance on reading skills that in his brief eulogy to his friend William Robey he mentioned that Robey was "well red in the Scriptures, & other good bookes, & was able to giv a good account of what he red" (89). Unlike Barnard, Robey was able to give a "good account," quoting from books at meetings of their private religious society. Even though his reading was somewhat labored, Barnard was not a passive reader. Instead, he read in the following way: "it is my Usial Custom, in reading the Scriptures & other good bookes, to looke inward, & compair my heart with the truth, or dart my heart to god imploring that the things I read may be found in my soule, & I may be conformed to the truth as it is in Jesus." He was also an active reader in that he picked and chose among what he read for material to apply to his piety. In the end, because "reading many times keept me from wors[e] Imployment" he persisted in reading "as much as I am able, when fair opertunitys presents, as well as at my stated times every day" (124). Every day, at least twice a day, Barnard encountered the printed word.

Although Barnard read more than most of his "Ranke," his literacy did not set him apart from other New England men and women, who almost universally could read.[49] Furthermore, one item on his reading list put him on common ground with most other people: the Bible. Significantly, the Bible is multivalent, speaking to the reader in many voices, depending on the section being read and the reader's preconceptions. Where literacy is widespread, elite groups cannot hold a monopoly on biblical interpretation. But while Barnard focused on those parts of the Bible most relevant to him, he did not interpret specific passages outside the orthodox fold. Barnard's use of the Bible would have been considered entirely appropriate by his pastors.

The section of the Bible that most interested Barnard was the book of Psalms, from which he took almost all his direct biblical quotations. Perhaps this book appealed to him because it was easier to remember, with its strong rhymes and cadences, especially as translated in the Bay Psalm Book. Indeed, Barnard suggested that he found some parts of the Bible difficult to understand: even though he endeavored "Dayly to Consult [God's] word" in the Bible, he sometimes felt his efforts were only a "poore Mesur [measure]" and he occasionally admitted that he was "ashamed of my Ignorance" (6). Hence the appeal of the tuneful Psalms.

The rhythmic rendering of these ancient hymns in the Bay Psalm Book allowed Barnard to sing them. For example, in a day of secret devotion, "to reforme whats amise [amiss], I sang 1st part 51 psalm" (59). This quote hints at one of the chief ways Barnard employed the book of Psalms. When times were difficult, as when work slowed, he selected comforting passages to read. "It is a very scarc[e], & ded time with respect to busnes & suplys," Barnard wrote in the spring of 1719, and "I se[e] nothing but straits, & dificultys before me, & know not what to doe." Seeking an answer to his worldly trials, he found an appropriate passage in Psalms: "I live on that promis 37 ps[alm] 3, trust in the lord, doe good, thou shalt be fed, I bles god I dont as yit dispond [despond], but submit to any thing my father orders for me" (157). Though he said that he would submit to God's will, the Psalm offset that passivity by affirming that he could take an active role, by trusting and doing good.

Barnard used Psalms as part of his ritualistic devotions. Consistent with Cotton Mather's directions, Barnard kept days of fasting and thanksgiving as often as he could. The structure of these private devotional days revolved around the Psalms. Typical was the day of fasting and prayer he kept on December 27, 1718. Times were hard for Barnard and his family that winter: he noted that "thear are severall ocasions for me to humble my selfe before the lord, & to cry unto him for mercy." After cataloging each piece of evidence of God's displeasure with him, he cited an appropriate Psalm. When he prayed "that I who am on the very brinke of eternity may be made meet for the inheritanc of the sa[i]nts in light," he cited Psalm 51. This was an appropriate choice since it starts with the lines, "Have mercy on me, O God, according to thy loving kindness; according unto the multitude of thy tender mercies blot out my transgressions." Barnard's logic is less immediately apparent when he read Psalm 101 in conjunction with noting "the anger of god against this towne, in that he thretins us with the spreding of the small pox, that has long hovered over us" (132). This Psalm, after all, describes a king pledging to rule justly. Barnard's connection between a coronation psalm and smallpox in Boston is comprehensible in light of Barnard's corporate interpretation of piety and his providentialism. Psalm 101 includes the line, "I will early destroy all the wicked of the land." In Barnard's providential outlook, smallpox was not a random occurrence in Boston: it was a clear sign of the "anger of god." As suggested by his choice of Psalms, Barnard believed God was destroying the wicked by sending the scourge of smallpox. This is one of many examples of Barnard's creative—though entirely orthodox—interpretations of scripture.

Even more significant, though, is Barnard's discussion of the books he read other than the Bible. It is rare to know what books a layperson owned, much less his reactions to them. Although his journal does not contain a complete catalogue of his library, it sheds enough light on a godly layperson's mental world to show that literacy was one of lay piety's fundamental building blocks.

The journal reveals how books could reinforce a minister's teachings among his parishioners. In *Bonifacius,* Cotton Mather told other ministers that "an incredible deal of good may be done, by distributing little *books of piety.*"[50] Barnard's writings bear this statement out. Except on a few small issues, Barnard's uses of Cotton Mather's *A Midnight Cry* were very similar to what its author had hoped. For reasons like this, some theorists see the acquisition of literacy not as liberating, but as instilling discipline and social control.[51] But Barnard's journal paints a more complex picture since Barnard's acceptance of Mather's dicta was voluntary, outside his pastor's purview. In addition, Barnard used books by other authors to expand the range of available ideas.

In form a classic jeremiad, *A Midnight Cry* ended with a covenant renewal that included sixteen "acknowledgments," which if "often Read over in a year, both publickly at our *Meetings,* and privately when we are *Humbling* of our selves before the Lord," would help effect a spiritual reformation.[52] This suggested use of the book greatly appealed to Barnard. Three times in private devotions between October 1717 and January 1719, Barnard picked up the book his pastor had given him and compared his behavior to its sixteen points. One day of prayer Barnard used the book in the following way:

> Oh holly sperit of god help me, I have been looking over the sixteen acknowlidg-ments in the Midnight Cry, & find that I am in sume degree guilty of all of them, but thro grac[e] I hope I may truly say I acknowlidg them to be great evells, & desir[e] & hope heartyly to Indevor to confes them, bewayle them before the lord & beg his pardon. (74)

That Barnard would find himself guilty of all sixteen points is revealing. Mather's list contains some items, including a denunciation of not preparing oneself before accepting the Lord's Supper, of which Barnard was clearly not guilty. How to explain this seeming contradiction? Mather did not intend his sixteen points to be a checklist for people to look over and declare themselves innocent on all counts. As noted above, Mather wanted parishioners to use the list when they were "humbling" themselves, when they were "utterly Despairing of any Strength" to avoid the stated evils. Barnard accepted this construction, stating that he could only understand his sinfulness "thro grac[e]," that is, with the help of God. The sixteen acknowledgments provided Barnard an opportunity to humble himself in the way prescribed by his minister.

Other themes in the *Midnight Cry* resonated with Barnard. Barnard and Mather agreed that during old age spiritual concerns were more pressing than usual. Mather seemed to speak directly to Barnard when he wrote, "To *you* that have *Hoary Heads found in the way of Righteousness,* . . . the God of Heaven is very shortly sending for you to be brought unto himself in Heaven . . . O be not now sound *Asleep.*"[53] This sounds very much like Barnard's continual refrain about standing "on the very brinke of eternity." Similarly, Barnard accepted and implemented Mather's advice that "every *Night* before we *Sleep,* we should settle Accounts betwen our God and our selves, even as if before to morrow morning we were to appear before Him."[54]

Some themes in the *Midnight Cry,* however, were not assimilated into Barnard's piety. Millennialism was one of the most common subjects in Cotton Mather's writings; *Midnight Cry* was no exception.[55] Mather spent much time explaining that Christ's return to Earth was imminent. He told his parishioners, "we are to *watch* by a constant *Expectation* of, and *Preparation* for, the Coming of our Lord . . . We ought so to behave our selves as if our Lord were immediately to break in upon the World."[56] In addition to the *Midnight Cry,* many of Cotton Mather's works contained millennial expectations, especially around 1715 and 1716, just as Barnard began his sacramental journal. Joseph Mede, the highly respected English scholar of prophecy, had picked 1716 as the year for Christ's return to Earth and Cotton Mather believed the prediction. In *Bonifacius,* published in 1710, Mather had announced with anticipation that "M.DCC.XVI is a-coming."[57] Likewise, in *Shaking Dispensations* (1715), Cotton Mather trumpeted millennial themes in expectation of the events of 1716.[58] According to Reiner Smolinski, "it is hard to read any of Mather's writings without finding some reference to the imminence of Christ's Second Coming."[59]

Increase Mather shared this concern for the Last Days and preached on the subject every year after 1707.[60] In 1709 Increase Mather wrote of his expectations of the impending conversion of Jews that would mark the onset of the millennium.[61] Similarly, the following year he urged his parishioners to be fervent in prayer since the "Glorious Kingdom" was "Now Approaching." Increase Mather chastened his flock, arguing that people "fall under Reproof, who will be Earnest in Prayer for other matters, but not for the Enlargement of Christ's Kingdom in the World."[62]

But Barnard, though earnest in many spiritual matters, was not inclined to follow the Mathers' concern for the impending millennium. Only once in 184 pages did Barnard hint at millennial ideas, and then only obliquely and ambiguously in 1717. During a day of fasting he noted, "I Indevored to praise god for . . . the near aproatch of hapy days to the Church of God" (59). Not once in 1716 did Barnard suggest that he expected the Reign of Christ to begin that year. This is not to imply that Barnard would have taken issue with the prevailing interpretation of the book of Revelations or that he did not believe in the eventual return of Christ to Earth. Rather, Barnard read *A Midnight Cry* and its references to millennialism, heard the sermons of both his millennially oriented pastors, and yet did not incorporate chiliasm into his piety in any significant way. As an active reader and constructor of his own piety, Barnard chose to deemphasize this issue, not finding it personally relevant.[63]

Likewise, Barnard's piety did not assimilate Cotton Mather's focus on Satan's power. According to Richard Godbeer, "Cotton Mather showed little reluctance to blame Satan for his own misfortunes and failings." Typical of Mather's writings were "remarks that verge on the Manichean in their evocation of the Devil as an independent force, rather than as the subordinate instrument of God's just wrath."[64] *A Midnight Cry,* written in 1692 against the backdrop of the Salem trials, contains several statements on the independent power of devils. Mather casually noted that "'tis well known, that the *Devils* make a Compact with some *Witches,* to be the Masters of their *Souls* upon their Departure hence."[65] Barnard did not give Satan such agency in his writings. He mentioned Satan only four times in his journal, mostly when acknowledging "my slavery to Satan, the flesh, & the world" (64).[66] Again, this was a difference in degree, not in kind, from Mather, for despite these differences, Barnard used *A Midnight Cry* in ways very close to what Mather had hoped: as an adjunct to private devotions and a spur to humble himself before God.

If literacy could reinforce the teachings of one's ministers, it could also expand one's horizons beyond the boundaries of the parish, into a world of differing and contested ideas about religion. Barnard, in his quest for the assurance of whether he had experienced a saving conversion, turned to Solomon Stoddard's writings. There he found an interpretation of conversion that differed from the Mathers' and gave him the assurance he desired.

Like most ministers of their era, the Mathers believed that conversion "took time—often a long time."[67] In contrast, Stoddard had a somewhat unusual interpretation of the moment of conversion, seeing it as "a cataclysmic flash, a convulsion." According to Stoddard, "This change is made at once on the Soul, it is wrought in the twinkeling of an eye."[68] This had important ramifications for Stoddard's view of assurance. Because conversion was such an unmistakable event, Stoddard argued that people could easily discern their own saving change: "Conversion is the greatest change that men undergo in this world, surely it falls under Observation."[69]

In *Three Sermons* (1717), Stoddard sought to comfort those who wanted to come to the Lord's Supper but feared they had not had a saving change. When Stoddard wrote, "it is a pain to a Man to be between hopes and fears about his Conversion, for his eternal Salvation doth depend on his Conversion," Barnard would have heartily agreed: one dominant tension in Barnard's journal was between his hopes and fears about conversion. Barnard may have read Stoddard as criticizing the Mathers when Stoddard reasoned, "when [an unsure man] reads threatnings to Unconverted Men, he has an awful sence of the doleful condition of such Men . . . then it turns in his thoughts, that may be he is one of them, and he is frighted least they should be executed upon him."[70] Stoddard hoped to bring such scrupulous people into the church by arguing that one's conversion was relatively easy to detect and should not be a source of anguish.

Several times in his journal, Barnard excerpted out of books passages that he found to be especially pertinent. Neither copying outright nor simply summarizing, Barnard condensed passages, leaving some sentences intact while omitting others entirely. His omissions and alterations are therefore significant, for they reflect his conscious decisions. The first section of *Three Sermons* that Barnard condensed was about conversion, headed "It may be wrought by Gospel promises." In this section, Stoddard quoted such reassuring biblical passages as John 6:37, "He that cometh unto me, I will in no wise cast out," and Stoddard used very positive formulations to interpret these passages: "These promises are a great security to all that come to Christ, they give an assurance that Men shall be accepted."[71] Barnard copied the following positive-sounding passage almost verbatim from this section: if "in this or such like promises, god has made descoverys of his grac[e] & fathfullnes, & the sufficiency of Jesus Christ, to the soul, so that you are bold to cast your selfe upon him, then [you are] converted" (131). Stoddard was not saying that all people are saved, nor did Barnard interpret him in such a way. But from a range of statements about assurance that Barnard could have chosen to copy, either from books by the Mathers or other books he owned, this was among the most optimistic.

The remainder of Barnard's summary included similar passages that he wanted to apply to himself. Stoddard wrote about several invitations in the Gospel to come to Jesus, from which Barnard copied, "if you have seen the truth of the gosple in those Comands, that it must needs be a safe thing to trust in Christ, & from the Incouragement of gods word venter [venture] on Christ, then [you are] converted" (131). Why did Barnard leave out the "you are" that appeared in the original sentences? Perhaps he found such a direct formulation a little too positive even for his taste. In *Three Sermons*, the following statement appeared: "God has shewed you the truth and glory of the Gospel, it is a *sure* sign that *you are* Converted."[72] Barnard rendered it, "god has shewed you the truth & glory of the gosple, its a sign of conversion" (131). He seems to have backed away a bit from Stoddard's positive interpretation of Gospel promises. Having actively sought a more reassuring for-

mulation than his own ministers put on assurance, Barnard may have re-
coiled against going too far in that direction.

Not only did Barnard look to the writings of other New England ministers to supplement his pastors' teachings, he also read books written in
England. Not all English books stood in opposition to New England's ministerial teachings. But the particular books Barnard chose emphasized some
issues—most notably assurance—and downplayed others—free grace and
the inscrutable will of God—in comparison with the New World books he
read. In addition, the authors of Barnard's English books reflected the diver-
sity of English religion: William Beveridge (1637–1708), was an Anglican
bishop, while John Flavel (1630?–91) and Richard Steele (1629–92) were non-
conformist pastors.

On September 6, 1717, during the month when he was so sick that he missed
several weeks of work, Barnard noted that he had been "reding in Doct
Bevridgs thoughts of Religion, about the glorious Mistery of the trinity, &
the incarnation of Christ" (68). The timing of this entry suggests a link between his feelings of mortality and the subjects he chose to read, for the
chapter on the incarnation of Christ contained a number of reassuring passages about the benefits of Christ's death for all believers. The first half of
Beveridge's highly popular book, *Private Thoughts Upon Religion*, consisted
of twelve articles of belief, the fifth of which was "I believe the Son of God
became the Son of Man, that I, the Son of Man, might become the Son of
God." In this chapter, Beveridge discussed the "New Covenant" signified by
Christ's crucifixion, by which "if I perform the Conditions therein requir'd,
I shall not only be retriev'd from the Bondage and Corruption that is inherent in me, as a Child of Wrath, but be justified and accepted as the Son of
God, and be made a Joint-Heir with Christ." Similarly, Beveridge argued, in
the incarnation of Christ, the "Divine Person" did not assume the nature of
a particular man, but of human nature in general. As a result, "all that partake of that Nature, are capable of partaking of the Benefits He purchas'd for
us, by dying in our stead."[73] These passages, generous in their formulation,
profoundly moved Barnard: they "affected my heart, & drew out my soul to
a ferm belef in my dear saviour" (68). In a time of sickness, wondering if he
would ever get back to work to support his family, Barnard did not read
books that threatened sinners with hellfire and brimstone. Rather, he chose
books that emphasized reassuring aspects of Christian doctrine.

Barnard also read Beveridge's third chapter, on "the glorious Mistery of
the trinity." This section's theme was denying rationality, as when Beveridge
wrote, "I ever did, and ever shall, look upon those apprehensions of God to

be the truest, whereby we apprehend him to be most incomprehensible; and that to be the most true of God, which seems most impossible unto us." This element of mystery was related to Beveridge's use of ecstatic, almost mystical language. He reported that "I cannot set myself seriously to think of it, or to screw up my Thoughts a little concerning it, but I immediately lose myself, as in a Trance, or Extasy."[74] Barnard would have been hard pressed to find such language in the Mathers' writings, for they reserved such discussions of pious passion for their private diaries. These words impressed Barnard, who carried the ideas he had encountered in his reading with him the next day during his precommunion examination, noting ruefully that "I know but little of the misterys of Christ" (68). Barnard used his reading to fill such gaps in his spiritual knowledge.

When Barnard read John Flavel, he again was concerned with whether he had been saved. Out of Flavel's massive, 467-page treatise *On the Soul of Man*, Barnard copied two passages that somehow seemed more personally relevant than the rest of the work. The first related to Barnard's concerns about death. Flavel wrote a great deal about what happened to a person's soul upon dying and what people could expect on their deathbeds. That Barnard counted himself among the saints is suggested by his copying of a passage that dealt with the deathbed experiences of the saved. Barnard, paraphrasing Flavel, wrote about "the diferanc of go[d]ly souls in dying," that "sume have a hard, streight, dificult enteranc into heven." The three reasons for such difficulties, as copied by Barnard, were "the weaknes of thear faith," the "vyolenc of temtations," and "the hidings of gods face." Contrastingly, other saints "have the privilidge of an easy death." Their more positive experiences resulted from several actions under their own control: "a heart weaned from the world, . . . a fervent love to Christ, & longings to be with him, . . . purity, & peace of conchenc, . . . [and] the worke of obedienc[e] faithfully finished" (145–46).[75] Saints could perform all four of these activities themselves, which would have been important for Barnard. Early New Englanders had inherited a Protestant version of the medieval European tradition of "Ars Moriendi," or the art of dying well, which specified that people should be composed on their deathbed, able to answer questions about their spiritual state with equanimity. Those who did not die well disappointed themselves and their families. Thus, Barnard found it empowering to read about concrete steps he could take to help insure proper deathbed behavior.

Flavel's other passage on assurance that Barnard quoted shows how this material could, on occasion, reinforce the teachings of his minister. Sounding a great deal like Cotton Mather, Barnard transcribed the following: "whilst your hearts put off & neglect gods calls, you can by no means arive to the evidenc[e] & ashuranc[e] of your Ellection." Mather's doctrine of "do-good" could hardly have been expressed better than when Barnard, following Flavel, prayed, "*lord, let me* but find my heart complying with thy calls, *my will obediently* submiting to thy comands, *sin my burden, & Christ* my desire; I never crave a fairer or shurer evidenc[e] of thy ellecting lov to my soule" (174).[76] It is even possible that Barnard borrowed this book from the Mathers, since its sheer size—six by eight inches, 467 pages—would have made it an expensive purchase. In any case, when Barnard read and copied this passage on assurance, he reinforced his minister's teachings on the issue of works.

Barnard read other books in his library in a slightly different manner: rather than copying passages that struck his fancy, he read them over and over. Richard Steele's *Upright Man* was one such volume. As Barnard noted in his journal, "I have been reading off [of], & *very often* have red, the Characters of an upright man, in Mr Steals upright man" (177).[77] This was in keeping with a "traditional," or intensive, style of reading. In an era when books were relatively expensive, people had a tendency to read their books many times.[78] This style was also marked by active reading, as recommended by Steele in his preface: "Read and think, and read and pray, and then through his Grace [this book] shall be useful to you."[79] Barnard followed such a pattern of reading and thinking, as he reported, "I have laboured to looke into my owne heart & life, & thoughts, & examined, as I went allong [reading], with a hearty dessire not to be deceved" (177).

Not only did Barnard's reading style mark him as a man of his time, but his reading material did as well. *Upright Man* was a very popular book, easily purchased due to its small size (three by five inches), and it went through many editions. Steele's message was relatively simple, with homely metaphors directed at uneducated lay readers. For example, when discussing saints and sinners Steele wrote, "an upright Saint is like an *apple* with *rotten specks*, but an hypocrite is like the *apple* with a *rotten core*."[80] The popularity of this book links Barnard to other godly laypeople in his affinity for books of piety and his tendency to read them intensively.

Some of the ideas to which Barnard was exposed in *Upright Man* differed in emphasis from those of the Mathers. Steele's book catalogued actions that distinguished saints from reprobates, including ways for people to show their devotion to God through their behavior, and in this it resembled much of the Mathers' writings. Increase and Cotton Mather, however, always included in their discussions of good works a countervailing discussion of the free and unmerited grace of God.[81] Steele, on the other hand, could leave the reader with the impression that good behavior could affect one's conversion. Nowhere in his book did he caution his readers against believing that upright behavior will cause them to be saved. Nor did Steele include participating in the Lord's Supper as one of the characteristics of an upright man. Ultimately, Barnard did not include either of these emphases in his piety, remaining strongly Calvinist in his views on free grace and interpreting communion as one of the most important aspects of piety. Barnard did not incorporate everything he read into his piety.

On other issues, however, Steele's book seems to have influenced Barnard. Steele was deeply concerned with laypeople's written and spoken words, several times noting that "the Upright man is sincere in his words . . . The upright man perhaps cannot speak *elegantly* but he can speak *truly*."[82] Barnard, who considered himself someone who spoke truly if inelegantly, interpreted words as an indicator of conversion. He noted that a person with "a pure heart[,] his *words* will be pure." For all that this chapter has focused on literacy, Barnard lived in a highly oral society, a place where one's reputation was based on word of mouth and where slander was a frequent court action. "O that I could always so speak as to minister grac[e] to the hearers," Barnard prayed, "I would always keep a gard upon my lips, that I sin not with my toung" (127).

Ultimately Barnard took Steele's more general lessons with him as he composed a precommunion examination. "It is a hapy & Joyfull knowlidg, for one to know that, he is senser [sincere] & upright in all his dealings with god & man." Echoing Steele, he prayed "that I may more fully know whether *I am senser & upright or no*" (116). Having read Steele many times, Barnard knew the importance of upright behavior. As he did with all his reading material, Barnard engaged with ideas that increased the variety of tools available to him to construct his piety. Barnard used some of these tools over and over again, while others gathered dust. In all cases, though, Barnard decided which tools to employ.

During the last years of his life, when John Barnard stepped out of his house in Clark Square and ambled across Fish Street into Shingle Alley, he could survey with pride the numerous monuments to his craftsmanship: Colonel Hutchinson's barn, Captain Pitts's coffeehouse, and even the wooden sidewalk lining the street. Similarly, Barnard's sacramental journal bears witness to years of spiritual labor. Although the construction of his piety was a less self-conscious process than the construction of a house, both acts included the addition of personal touches within certain constraints. These constraints resulted from the availability of tools and materials in one case, the accessibility of religious ideas in the other. Barnard's spiritual edifice was not precisely typical of those constructed by other laypeople, but this does not lessen its significance. To illuminate the complexity of early New England's religious culture demands analyzing a wide variety of lay sources. For this book's purposes, Barnard stands closer to the orthodox end of the spectrum of lay religious culture; he borrowed from both the more closed culture of the seventeenth century and the more open culture of the eighteenth.

Although many of Barnard's concerns seem to come directly from his ministers' words, the Mathers' sermons did not circumscribe Barnard's religious horizons. On numerous issues Barnard and the Mathers agreed completely, but Barnard was an active thinker and declined to concern himself with some issues about which the Mathers regularly preached, including the imminent millennium and Satan's power. Furthermore, Barnard put different and more personally relevant emphases on some other ideas, most notably, sacramentalism and conversion. In his sacramentalism Barnard stressed a corporate notion of the Lord's Supper over the Mathers' more individualistic formulation, and Barnard was also more concerned with Christ's presence at the Table. Regarding conversion, Barnard accepted an essentially Stoddardean interpretation of one's own conversion being relatively easy to detect, an interpretation that gave Barnard a degree of assurance about his final state. Barnard stands as an example of a layperson disagreeing with his ministers on doctrinal points years before the Great Awakening.

But these theological concerns were not formulated solely from material provided by ministers in the meetinghouse and in godly books, for Barnard spent the vast majority of his time outside the church, with friends and family or at work. A man like Barnard, continually thinking about religious matters, used his worldly experiences as building blocks for his piety. Although his literacy skills were not at the same high level as his facility with a plane and adz, Barnard spent his free time reading the Bible on his own terms, which shaped and reinforced his beliefs. As we will further see in the next chapter, in which ordinary people interact with ministerial models of proper deathbed behavior, laypeople both drew from their culture and contributed to it as they constructed their piety.

CHAPTER TWO

"She Died Like Good Old Jacob"

Deathbed Scenes and Attitudes toward Death

*E*XPECTING ISAIAH PRATT'S death at any moment, Rev. Ebenezer Parkman of Westborough, Massachusetts, and the young man's family gathered around Pratt's bed in February 1742. The mourners wept as Pratt seemed to die, when Parkman noticed that "by Degrees he came to," and those present "were astonished." They were even more astonished as Pratt related a deathbed vision of extraordinary vividness. He reported beholding "the Devil who met him as he seem'd to be in the way towards Heaven & told him that there was no room for him there." Pratt remembered "seeing Hell & hearing the most dreadfull noise of roaring & crying." These disturbing images were countered by a vision of "Christ, . . . who had a great Book before him, and in turning over the Leaves of it told him that [Pratt's] name was there & shew'd it him." Pratt's assertion that he had seen his name in the Book of Life, which implied that he knew he was saved, grieved Parkman. Because reformed Protestantism held that people could not be sure whether they were saved, Pratt's assurance was subversive. In rebuke, Parkman declared that the young man's visions "were not to be depended upon, . . . that we have a more sure word of prophecy to which we should do well to take heed."[1]

Since development of the Ars Moriendi (art of dying well) in late medieval times, clergymen have constructed models of proper deathbed behavior.[2] In eighteenth-century New England, the ministerially sanctioned model death included resignation to God's will, a well-grounded (but not overly confident) hope that one was saved, and temperately offered final counsels. Transgressions of this script, as in Isaiah Pratt's death, revealed cultural tensions. Within New England's religious culture—and not just between laity and clergy—existed a tension between people's predestinarian beliefs and their desire for assurance that they were saved. Consequently, Pratt's hope for assurance was countered by Parkman's insistence that such knowledge was not possible. Likewise, this culture contained an ambiguity about the significance of dreams: their predictive possibilities were acknowledged, but they were not to be interpreted too literally. Again, this caused pastor and parishioner to disagree about the significance of Pratt's deathbed experience. Thus, the dying scenes of Pratt and many others demonstrate that laypeople's deathbed behavior was informed by beliefs and experiences sometimes at odds with their ministers' sermons and exhortations. Laypeople drew on the broader culture of death and dying and at the same time contributed to it.

This point modifies the traditional interpretations of death and dying in early New England. Historians have written as if there were a single "Puritan Way of Death."[3] In their descriptions of deathbed scenes and attitudes toward death, these historians have outlined an "ideal type": the expected norm as formulated by the culturally dominant group. Relying largely on ministerial sources, these interpretations overlook the complexity of lay attitudes and lay contributions to the culture of the deathbed.[4] The ideal type's cultural power is apparent in that many deathbed scenes conformed closely to the prescribed model; others, however, differed in important ways.

Moreover, historians of death in early New England have largely ignored the unique experiences of women, claiming a lack of documentary evidence.[5] In fact, numerous manuscript sources exist that were written by or about women and their experiences of death. These sources demonstrate that during the deathbed scene power relations of all sorts, including minister/layperson and male/female, could be temporarily inverted, or at least altered. Like Isaiah Pratt, who voiced his assurance in the face of ministerial cautions, dying women often spoke with an authority they otherwise found difficult to claim. Though fleeting, the power these women appropriated was real and challenged clerical authority. This chapter will examine lay attitudes toward dying, death, and mourning and then show how those ideas were expressed in deathbed scenes.

Attitudes toward Death

The relationship between religion and death has long been noted by anthropologists and historians; in colonial New England, laypeople's repeated encounters with "strokes of God's wrath" often awakened a latent piety. Conversion narratives demonstrate this strong link between death and piety: of 159 eighteenth-century narratives examined, 39 (25 percent) explicitly linked the death of a family member or neighbor with a period of heightened piety.[6] For some laypeople, this period of death-inspired piety occurred quite early in their lives. Esther Bissell of East Windsor, Connecticut, related in 1700 that "when I was about eleven years of age it pleased the Lord by the death of my brother more to awaken me than I had been before."[7] In many cases, family members' deaths triggered conversion. During the heat of the Great Awakening in 1741, Eleazer Beeman of Westborough, Massachusetts, did not say that his conversion was brought on by George Whitefield's preaching or his awakened neighbors' urgings. Rather, in his conversion narrative he offered that "God's holy Dealings & Dispensations towards me have greatly awakened me," specifically "what an holy God was pleas'd to do to and with me in the Course of the last winter, in my own & my wifes sickness, and the Death of Three of my Dear Children."[8] For Beeman and others like him, the deaths of loved ones were often the proximate cause of becoming full church members.

Perhaps the most vivid example of this link between death and piety was described by Hannah Wadsworth of Grafton, Massachusetts. In a society where death was literally palpable, handling a corpse could provide a powerful incentive to increased piety. Wadsworth testified in a confession to her church that "by the Death of a Person in this Neighbourhood where I was Called to cast the winding Sheet Round, it Pleased the Lord By his holy Spirit to awaken me more Powerfully, and Give me a Great Sence of Eternity."[9] The typically female activity of preparing the body for burial awakened Wadsworth's latent piety; the records are silent about whether other women experienced similar transformations.

If Wadsworth was somewhat atypical, Lydia Prout's experience of the connection between death and piety was closer to the norm. Prout's writings reveal the extent to which the deaths of relations and children often increased the religious fervor of the bereaved. Prout, born in Boston in 1686, belonged to the church in Scarborough, Maine. The three years she kept a spiritual journal coincided with a grim period when five children and her mother died. Her journal shows that for those who were already church members, death still increased their piety, as evidenced by greater attention to such ritual practices as communion and covenant renewals.

In 1714 Prout buried one of her children; the following year Prout's grief continued due to the death of her mother and another child. At first, this terrible providence was disorienting: "I found the afflictions so heavy that I could not tell what to do." But Prout eventually took comfort in her interpretation of God's design: she saw the deaths as a signal to increase her piety, noting that "I thought I could be contented to bear the affliction if I might but glorify God thereby." Her reinvigorated piety manifested itself in an increased reliance on religious rituals. As a church member for many years, Prout had long participated in the Lord's Supper. But her recent grief made this ritual even more powerful than usual. In the sacraments "I never had such longing after communion with God & christ in heaven, that I can remember as I have had ever since" these deaths.

Her other ritual response to grief was to write and sign a covenant. Exhibiting the common lay belief in the power of writing, Prout put pen to paper to signify her sincere desire to increase her piety:

> Though I have been Join'd to the church these many years I never have written & sign'd the Covenant which I have been uneasy at but now think it proper to do. I call heaven & Earth to record this day that I do here take the lord Jehovah father Son & holy Ghost for my Portion & Cheif good & do give up my self Body & soul for thy service promising & vowing to serve thee in holiness & righteousness all the days of my life by thy grace strengthening me. L. P.
> The Covenant that I here made on Earth let it be ratified in Heaven.[10]

Having previously been "uneasy" about signing a covenant, Prout now assumed the formal tone of a minister in order to highlight the seriousness of her task, even affixing her initials to the covenant within her own journal. In a time of grief, Prout created her own ritual of giving herself "Body & soul" to God's service, modeled on the ministerially promoted covenant renewal ritual.

Laypeople's reactions to loved ones' deaths varied. Some people could not channel their grief into piety, as Lydia Prout did. Many such people were disconsolate, despite their ministers' warnings against excessive grief. This is not to say that New England clergymen tried to suppress all grief; in their model of correct mourning people were supposed to shed tears for the deceased. Cotton Mather wrote that when someone dies "we must not be Stocks and Stones."[11] Similarly, Samuel Willard opined that "those who part with their Friends without sorrow, are guilty of a trespass both against nature and Religion."[12] But the clergy demanded that mourning be moderate and that people experience feelings of "resignation" and "submission" to God's will. As Henry Gibbs warned, "Our Mourning should be exercised with Christian Moderation."[13] Later in the century, Jonathan Parsons wrote that "if it be the Lord that takes away our Friends by Death, then we should watch against *Impatience* under such Losses." Faced with the loss of a loved one, Parsons argued, "We have no Reason at all to murmur."[14] Indeed, ministers asserted that a family member's death should prompt thanks to God rather than a questioning of his will. Rev. John Barnard (son of the first chapter's carpenter) urged that "we are to Bless God even when He takes away."[15] Cotton Mather, ever demanding of those who would live in a godly fashion, addressed his readers: "Christians, under all your *Afflictions,* labour to say stedfastly, to say joyfully, not, 'All these things are against me,' but rather, 'Thanks be to God for his unspeakable Gifts.'"[16]

Many laypeople did their best to adhere to this ministerially propagated norm of correct mourning. As Rev. Samuel Chandler noted with approval in 1746, "Mrs Prebble seems submissive under her Bereavement of a son."[17] Laypeople understood the standards for correct mourning and in many cases consciously set out to grieve in accordance with the ideal. After his son's death in 1729, Joshua Lane tried to live up to cultural expectations, imploring "that I may so behave myself under my present affliction that God may be glorified by me, and so that I may have occasion to say in the end that it is good for me that I have been afflicted."[18] Even more explicitly, Ebenezer Storer on several occasions begged in his journal, "O that I might mourn in a right manner."[19] Sometimes laypeople urged resignation and submission on others who grieved. Sarah Osborn of Newport wrote to her friend Mrs. Oliver Prentice on the death of Prentice's husband that Osborn, herself a widow, knew "how hard it is to flesh and blood the Parting with ones other self." Because she knew the pain involved, Osborn was in a position to write, "may He now bestow on you resignation to his holy will which is His peculiar gift."[20]

But some laypeople found certain aspects of the culturally dominant model unappealing. Specifically, people occasionally resisted ministers' calls to thank God during hard times. One example of this occurred in 1726, after Rev. John McKinstry of Sutton preached a sermon from Ephesians 5:20: "Giving Thanks always for all things unto God and the Father in the name of our Lord Jesus Christ." In this sermon McKinstry "maintained that we ought to give Thanks to God not only for Prosperous but Even Adverse Dispensations." This doctrine caused an uprising among some of McKinstry's parishioners, who felt it overlooked the pain of grieving. "One Putnam (and Sundry others Combining) had been Set Against, and Still manifested uneasiness at Such Doctrine and this man was Resolute to make a stir about it." Putnam and his allies proceeded to charge McKinstry with being "inorthodox." Rallying around their besieged colleague, eight ministers of the Marlborough Association signed a letter supporting McKinstry. The pastors proclaimed that "we judge said Doctrine to be agreeable to the Sacred Scriptures and Sentiments of the most Judicious Expositions of Orthodox Divines."[21] Such a confident pronouncement, however, could not mask the tensions that arose from ministerial attempts to regulate lay emotions. For many laypeople, familiar with the grief of parting with a loved one, it was simply unrealistic to require thanks in the wake of a painful loss.

When laypeople were unable or unwilling to be moderate in their grief, this usually proceeded from an inability to understand God's will. After his son's death, John Gates did not understand why he was being punished. Several times in his months of grieving Gates asked "that I and my Famaly may understand the meaning of the Holy and Righteous anger of God against us."[22] In 1713, John Paine went even further in the direction of heterodoxy, questioning God's will in his son's death: "O cruel Death what can nothing Satisfy but the life of So pleasant and desirable a comfort, why couldst thou not have Seized on Some older infirm person whose life is Even a burden to them Selves and they them Selves a burden & a trouble to all about them."[23] Instead of being resigned to his son's death, Paine questioned the reasons for it. Daniel King was also provoked by a child's death—perhaps the most difficult kind of death to understand—to question the reasons for his misfortune. In his anguish King wrote, "I know we deserve thy rath but Lord thou hast made precious promises in thy Holy Word to repenting sinners."[24] In this passage, King expressed what no minister considered correct: that those who repented deserved some special protection for their families.

The consequence of not understanding acts of providence was incorrect mourning. People unresigned to God's will had difficulty reining in their grief. Four months after her son's death, Experience Richardson was still grieving. Aware of the injunctions against so long a period of grief, she worried that she thereby sinned: "I fear I have sin[n]ed against God in destreesing myself about the state of my child that is dead but I pray to God to give me a right sperit about this thing."[25] Similarly, John Gates wanted to temper his grief so he would "not Displease God nor provoke Him," while Lydia Prout was "afraid of dishonouring God by my unruly passion."[26] Pious laypeople, continually told by their ministers to mourn moderately, worried that their emotions were dangerous.

Ministers actively sought to bridle these emotional tendencies, as when John Cotton wrote a letter to Mary Hinckley of Plymouth, Massachusetts, in 1683 attempting to "allay that excessive grief that hath taken hold of you."[27]

Ministers were particularly vigilant because in this state of intense grief, some laypeople were apt to utter heterodoxies. Rev. Samuel Chandler visited in the fall of 1749 a certain Mr. Phillips, who had "Buried his only Daughter last Sabbath." Chandler reported that he tried to comfort Phillips: "I told him that the due consideration of Gods Sovereignty would calm & quiet the Spirit under all troubles, he said he had something more than meer Sovereignty to comfort him."[28] Although the meaning of Phillips's cryptic comment remains ambiguous, it is clear that grief drove Phillips to voice the heterodox opinion that God's power would not comfort him, but some earthly means (drink?) would.

Laypeople did not grieve forever. At some point in the mourning process, whether one hour or one year after a loved one's death, the bereaved began to concentrate more on living and finding comfort. One broad group of actions from which people took comfort was memorializing the dead. Gravestones, with their deathly visages and monitory verse, allowed the deceased to speak to the living. Naming practices further reflected a conscious effort to remember the dead.[29] People also recalled the memory of the deceased in the common practice of marking the anniversaries of deaths, as when Experience Richardson noted in her diary that "this Day three years my oldest son died . . . O that I may be prepared to go where I think he is."[30] Richardson was comforted by invoking her son's memory and by assuming that he had gone to heaven. Likewise, Benjamin Lyon of Woodstock, Connecticut, noted in his diary in 1764 that "this Day two year ago my Sister Bowen departed this life, and I, wretched I am here yet." Lyon's concern focused less on the ultimate destination of his sister than on this memory's effect on his own preparations for death. Hence he prayed, "O lord, prepare me for the cold, grim Messenger, Death."[31] Although Lyon used less overtly comforting language than Richardson, he nonetheless kept the memory of his sister alive as he prepared for his ultimate end.

If remembering others comforted colonial New Englanders, so did the thought of how they would be memorialized by their survivors. Sarah Prince of Boston picked the text for her funeral sermon at the age of twenty-seven! As she confided to her diary, "I desire if ever a sermon be made on my death, It may come from there, Most Lovely Words, Rev. 7:14: 'These are they which came out of great tribulation, have washed their Robes and made them White in the Blood of the Lamb.'"[32] Prince enjoyed imagining her death inspiring a sermon that implied that Christ's blood purified her soul. In another gesture to posterity, Prince wrote a letter in 1755 and sealed it "Not to be opened till after my death." Speaking from beyond the grave, this letter addressed her young acquaintances and warned them to prepare for death. Prince emphasized the power of her words, reminding her friends, "I speak as from Eternity, won't you believe me?"[33]

Others who did not go to the same lengths as Prince still desired to be remembered by posterity. Seth Metcalf, a farmer from Rutland, Massachusetts, indicated this in a bit of doggerel on his diary's flyleaf:

> Seth Metcalf is my name also New England is my Station
> Rutland is my Dwelling Place and Christ is my Salvation
> When I am Dead and in my Grave and all my bones are rotton
> If this you See Remember me Let me not be Forgotton
>
> Rutland March 15, 1758.[34]

The act of writing could be an attempt to overcome death's finality. Metcalf knew that even if he died the day after writing this, he would continue to speak from beyond the grave. Similarly, Hannah Heaton kept an extensive journal throughout her adult life in order to live on after death, though the image she chose was slightly more ghostly: she hoped her children would envision her countenance when they read her words. At the end of a volume of her journal in 1772, Heaton wrote:

> My dear Children
> I leave you here a little book for you to look upon
> that you may see your mothers face when she is dead and gone.[35]

In another stab at verse, John Gates contemplated the reactions of others to his death: "My Grave and Coffin are at hand my Glass hath but Little sand, I am now a writting but annon they will say of me that he is gone."[36] For many laypeople, keeping a diary in which they recorded local deaths reflected not an obsession with death but a desire to remember and be remembered.

Through their various attempts to keep alive the memory of friends, family members, and themselves, laypeople achieved two ends. First, they rekindled memories of people no longer alive, evoking the comforting presence of someone now dead. Second, they convinced themselves that they too would be memorialized by their survivors and would live on in their loved ones' memories. In these ways laypeople symbolically overcame death and achieved an earthly immortality of sorts.

But this did not always suffice, for laypeople needed to come to terms with some of their religion's difficult doctrines. One of reformed Protestantism's most important tenets was predestination. The orthodox accepted that God had determined before history who was saved and who was damned.

Furthermore, they assumed that only a small fraction of people were destined for heaven, which held true for infants and young children.

This misnamed doctrine of "infant damnation" has caused early New Englanders to be ridiculed, especially by nineteenth-century observers who saw infants as the purest of all beings.[37] Later caricatures notwithstanding, ministers were indeed adamant about "infant damnation," repeatedly stressing that children who died were not automatically saved. Cotton Mather, in a sermon directed toward parents, told his audience that "You can't begin with them *Too soon*." He warned that "Satan gets them to be proud, profane, reviling and revengeful, as *young* as they are."[38] Mather stated that children were not simply bad or mischievous, but liable to be damned. "Your Children," he asserted, "are Born Children of Wrath. Tis *through you*, that there is derived unto them the sin which Exposes them to infinite Wrath."[39] Along these lines Samuel Willard held that "the innocency of Children cannot save them . . . It is then a very poor Hope that is built upon this Consideration."[40] Jonathan Edwards asserted that "all are by Nature the Children of Wrath, and Heirs of Hell," going so far as to say that "as innocent as Children seem to be to us, yet, if they are out of Christ, they are not so in God's Sight, but are young Vipers."[41]

Laypeople, however, were less explicit about "infant damnation," and they certainly did not agree that their children were vipers. If they believed in the theory of "infant damnation," they almost never applied those beliefs in practice.[42] Lay men and women simply assumed that when their infants or young children died, they had gone to heaven. I have never come across a layperson entertaining thoughts that his or her child might be in hell, while there are countless examples asserting that a child is in heaven. For example, Lydia Prout took comfort from her offspring's ultimate resting place. After her three children died at once, she professed that "I do beleive they are in Heaven shining among the saints in Glory which is a great Joy to me in the thoughts thereof in the midst of all my trouble."[43] Amidst all her troubles, Prout could not bear to consider what ministers held: that her three children might be in hell. Later in the century, Experience Richardson had a similar response to her four-year-old son's death. Nine months after little Luther had died, Richardson thought about the boy as she rode to Sunday meeting and began to feel disconsolate. After some melancholy thoughts, she cheered herself by thinking, "I do beleve he is gone to rest."[44] The similarity between Prout's and Richardson's thoughts bears remark: both wrote "I *do* believe" my child is in heaven. Their use of the word "do" in both cases makes sense only as a response to the contrary assertions of ministers, who in their sermons promulgated the doctrine of "infant damnation."

Although laypeople expected their children to go to heaven, this did not mean that parents were above using examples of sudden death to heighten their children's piety. In 1755 Aaron Bull, a wealthy sea captain living in New London, Connecticut, left his family for a voyage to Barbados. While aboard ship he wrote a letter back to his family, instructing his children to be sure to pray, read the Bible, and obey their mother while he was away. Behaving well was imperative, he informed his children, because "you will one Day give an Account and it a[i]nt improbable that that Time will be very soon, for you know you have lost two brothers and one sister and which God will call for next we cant tell." Repeating this sentiment later in the letter, Bull urged his children to contemplate death before they went to sleep, "remembring your Dear brother Aaron who had little or no time after he was takein sik to prepare for Eternity . . . and it is not unlikely you may have as short time to prepare for it as he had."[45] When parents addressed their children they sometimes assumed the tone of ministers warning their parishioners to keep thoughts of death close at hand. This is unsurprising since ministers sometimes viewed themselves as the "spiritual fathers" to the "children" of their flock, and parents often imitated this role within their own households.

As with "infant damnation," some laypeople differed from what their ministers advised by ascribing meaning and power to dreams, visions, and divination. Occasionally (though it is difficult to know how often) laypeople consulted with those who practiced divination. One case, recorded by Cotton Mather in 1694, involved "two young women" who were "guilty of consulting an ungodly Fortune-teller, in the Neighbourhood, with desires to be informed of some secret and future things."[46] Perhaps these women and others like them consulted the fortune-teller about romance, but perhaps the "secret and future things" they were interested in related to death and dying: whether they were headed for heaven and when they would die.

An act probably more common, but still frowned upon by ministers, was interpreting dreams to learn about death or one's final estate. In her 1757 collection of poems, Martha Brewster of Lebanon, Connecticut, recorded a dream she had shortly after her father's death. In this dream her father returned from heaven to answer her questions. "I Dreamed," wrote Brewster, "I saw him standing in the Room where I was, and none else present; he was in good Habit, with a healthful and pleasant Countenance." This was a comfort when contrasted with her last images of her father as a sick and dying man. In this dream her father's first words were surprising. "He chearfully said to me, Child, I am a Glorified Spirit, and am come to make you a Visit!" Brewster, sensing a rare opportunity, proceeded to quiz her father about heaven. When asked what heaven was like, he answered, "it is full of Glory, perfect Happiness, and Eternity crowns it." Remembering his last moments on earth, Brewster asked her father about the "Pains of Death," to which he asserted that "it was little or nothing, I was immediately transmitted into Glory." This interrogation continued for some time, until Brewster finally awoke. As she lay in bed she thought about her dream "without any Fear, or uncomfortable Awe of Ghastly Death, but as though I had had a real Visit from a dear deceased Father, and Saint from Heaven."[47] Having a dream of her father in good health and happiness comforted Brewster in the same way a real visit from her father would have. For her, the dead's secrets were partly revealed through her nocturnal vision.

Dreams, however, could also bode ill. Jane Billings of Westborough, having just buried one of her children, dreamed "that She Saw a man bring the Coffin of her youngest Child into the House, upon which she took on [i.e., wept]; but presently there came in another Man with a large Coffin, and said to her that She had not need to take on for her Child for here was a Coffin for herself also, for she Should die next." This dream, combined with another man's vision of "a large Coffin (as well as a small one) in the air just over the Burying place last Tuesday Evening," was interpreted by Billings's neighbors to be an ill omen. As Ebenezer Parkman noted, this "story much fright people about Mrs. Billings Death." Expressing the typical ministerial injunction against putting too much stock in dreams, Parkman assured his parishioners "that we have a more Sure word of Prophecy etc."[48] It is clear, however, that Parkman's words did not prevent these people from interpreting the visions as revealing future truths about life and death.

In a way similar to dream interpretation—though generally not suspect in ministers' eyes—some laypeople took notable events or coincidences to reveal God's will and to shed light on death. One night in 1713, Susanna Thayer, a young domestic servant in Samuel Sewall's home, came to Sewall afraid she was going to die. Comforting the girl, Sewall reflected on the day's events, thinking, "I was the more startled because I had spilt a whole Vinyard Cann of water just before we went to Bed: and made that Reflection that our Lives would shortly be spilt."[49] Such a coincidence was meaningful in a providential world view that saw God's hand in the everyday world. An anonymous diarist of the late 1750s provides a touching glimpse into this providential mind-set:

And there is another thing which we have taken Notis of in respect to all our first Creatures for our very hen that my wife brought with her was killed by the hens Picking her to death our Hogg was so near Dead by being choaked or by eating too much that we were forced to kill him our first Cat was killed by a Backlog being flung on her our first dog was killed for Taking after the sheep our first Horse died by being cast in the Barn our first Cow that we raised dropt down dead in the yard as we thought by the murrin [murrain] our first swarm of bees went away and also our first Child Died & the wife of my youth.[50]

This man's diary title helps explain why he recalled such a string of coincidences. He called his journal "A book of Remarkable Providences which are to be kept in Remembrace by us & our Children after us that so we & they may Remember that God Over Rules all things in his wise Providence according to His own Sovereign will & Pleasure." To such a person a pattern of deaths acquired meaning from the way it revealed God's will.

This is not to say that people did not fear their own deaths, or entertain the possibility that they might be headed for hell. In fact, people were much more apt to think about their own potential damnation than about the same possibility for others, even though for most laypeople thoughts of their own damnation evaporated while they were on their deathbed. Nonetheless, before they reached that point, many people found terrifying the prospect of their death and the possibility they might wind up in hell. Conversion narratives are filled with references to lay worries that they might be damned; people often cited fear of hell as one spur to conversion. In some cases, ministers planted the seeds of fear in their parishioners' minds. A minister asked Ruth Hassock of Ipswich in 1764 "whether I was afraid I should roar in hell to all eternity? This struck me with Distress, sometimes greater and sometimes less, till this work [i.e., the religious revival] began so powerfully in Chebacco, when my concern increased."[51] More conventional was Abigail Giddinge, who said in her distress that "I tho't if I went to sleep I should awake in hell."[52] For these pious women, the terrors of death were inextricably bound up with fears of hell.

The most significant consequence of a fear of hell was the overwhelming desire most pious laypeople had for assurance of their final state. Like Isaiah Pratt at the beginning of this chapter, most people could bear only limited thoughts about the possibility that they would go to hell. People found it much easier to contemplate hell when they were young and healthy—like the two women quoted above—than when they were old or on their deathbeds. As housewright John Barnard phrased it in 1719, "to hope in the Mercy of god, & in the merits of Christ for Etternal life, is what most that live under the gosple norishe in them selves, or else thear dispare would drive them to destraction."[53] In other words, people would go crazy if they could not comfort themselves with the prospect of going to heaven. This is not to say that laypeople rejected ministerial teachings about predestination; in fact, as we have seen, laypeople were sometimes more vigilant on this issue than their ministers. But within the parameters of predestinarian teachings, laypeople sought signs that they were saved.

This final example points to another of the many complexities of lay attitudes toward death: life-course changes affected the way people thought about their own deaths. John Barnard was sixty-five when he wrote those wise words describing people's tendency to hope for mercy. A similar case occurred in 1767 when Experience Richardson visited "Mrs Brigham an aged women [*sic*] a hundred years old." Brigham was a rather remarkable woman, for despite her advanced age she "had hir Reason very well and was Netting [knitting] and made good work." Eventually the conversation got around to death (as well it would with a hundred-year-old woman), and Richardson recorded that Brigham "seemd to be exceding willing to die if she could have a full assurance." Brigham expressed this desire despite the theological reasoning that deemed full assurance impossible. Richardson herself noted that as she grew older her fears of death and hell increased. In 1753 at the age of forty-eight she recalled how at the age of "fifteen or sixteen" she "was so afected with a spiritual vew I thought I had of my sav[i]our that I Longed to die to Go to him but now I am afraid to die for fear I am deceved."[54] If children and young adults sometimes opined that death held no terrors for them, older people were less likely to do so.

In addition to age, gender differences prevented laypeople from holding one monolithic attitude toward death. On the simplest level, men did not experience women's fear of childbirth. There is evidence that fewer colonial women died in childbirth than we might expect,[55] but colonial New England's women were not privy to such statistics. Instead, they saw childbearing as one of the most dangerous moments of their lives. Mary Noyes of New Haven, nearing the time of her childbirth, wrote to her friend Sarah Osborn that "God only knows what is before me, whither this is not the last time I shall converse with you after this Manner."[56] Similarly, Cotton Mather's sister Jerusha Oliver linked childbearing and death in her spiritual journal. Writing in 1710, Oliver remarked that "I am (I think) above five Months gone with Child," a fact that caused her some unease. Oliver turned to private devotions to combat her fear, setting aside a day of prayer: "I would in a very special manner this day prepare for my Lying-in, and would therefore prepare for Death. I am of a very fearful disposition naturally, and am much afraid of Death, and therefore afraid of what will be the issue of my being with Child."[57] Similarly, Hannah Heaton wrote in 1754 that pregnancy "was always satans time to try to tempt me to sin against god by holding up gastly death before me." This image of death in childbirth especially horrified women because, as Heaton asserted, "it is the hardest of all deaths."[58]

While all women feared childbirth, their responses to this fear varied widely. Some women, like Elizabeth Phelps of Hadley, Massachusetts, were submissive to God's will. Several days after delivering a child in 1772, Phelps remembered, "I think I was enabled to resign myself entirely to the Disposal of Providence."[59] Others, like Lydia Prout, faced childbirth with less equanimity. For Prout childbirth meant the possibility of death, which meant the possibility of hell: "I have been concern'd about being with child & sometimes very melancholy for fear I should dye to think what would become of me, reading the last chapter of Revelations, where it is said the faithless & unbelieving are to have their part among the Liers in hell, & I knowing myself to be full of doubts & fears."[60]

It is possible that childbearing, with its attendant fears, contributed to the skewed sex ratio in early New England churches. Throughout the colonial period, with some variations over time, women made up 60 to 70 percent of full church members.[61] While fear of childbirth was not the only reason for this, the connections are suggestive. For those women who survived childbearing, looking back on the experience tended to convince them of God's goodness and the efficacy of prayer. The most common expression of God's mercy was his "appearance" to these women in their hour of need. The sources are filled with such references: Margaret Cary of Charlestown recorded that "this day God was pleased to appear to me in a wonderfull manner, in a time of great difficulty and distress," while Elizabeth Phelps thanked God that "thou hast passed before me in a great deal of mercy Since last I wrote; Gladness is put into my heart and a song of praise in my mouth."[62] In addition, many women were convinced of the power of prayer by their deliverance from danger. Cary, quoted above, expressed such a sentiment after her next birth, when she wrote, "I called upon him, and he heard and answered me in a way of mercy. Lord, grant that a sense of thy goodness may always abide upon me."[63] Women's piety and attitudes toward death were shaped in part by pregnancy, which brought with it fears of death, and the survival of childbirth, which brought a reaffirmation of religious belief.

In addition to differences in age and gender, laypeople experienced their children's deaths in a variety of ways, making it difficult to describe a single model of lay attitudes toward death. The age, sex, and birth position of a child who died—not to mention the age and sex of the parent—influenced the parent's grieving. Because there are too many permutations of this dynamic to allow all to be studied, I will focus on the especially intense grief of fathers whose eldest sons died on the brink of manhood. These deaths were particularly hard to accept because they were usually unexpected—few people died in their teens and twenties—and they dashed long-planned goals of property and cultural transfer. A man's sense of himself as a man was bound up with passing an inheritance (property as well as religion) to his eldest son.

In 1749 Daniel King was a forty-five-year-old church member in Marblehead who in the previous twelve years had experienced the deaths of two of his young sons and one of his daughters. Nothing, however, could have prepared him for the death by a violent fever of his eldest son, Nathaniel. Part of King's grief stemmed from the suddenness of the death: "my dear son went well to bed Thursday night Dead the next Wednesday morning." But much of his anguish stemmed from the fact that this was his eldest son, the one on whom King had pinned the greatest hopes of passing on the family name and spirit. "Oh wretch that I am to deserve such things at Gods Holy Hands," King castigated himself in his spiritual journal, "to have my son almost arrived to mans years being a few hours above 19 years old . . . to have him I say at this Time of life taken aw[a]y and in so sudden a manner oh how awfull." After "mans years" King had originally written "and so great a help to me" but crossed those words out, realizing that they went against the tenets of correct mourning. King understood that in the culturally dominant model it would not have been proper to be upset because he lost not only a son but a young helper. But later King allowed himself to express his material worries, admitting that "by this my worldly schemes are disapointed."

Because of Nathaniel's age, sex, and birth position, King was far more upset than he had been at the deaths of his three other children. His grief can be measured in sheer literary output: he wrote some 1,650 words on Nathaniel's death, compared to an average of only 300 words for the others. But quantification does not begin to capture the intensity of King's grief and self-loathing when Nathaniel died. King blamed himself, asking his savior to "pardon and blot out my many heinous Iniquities that have provoked Thee to come out against me and my family in this dreadfull Judgement." More dramatically, King saw his neglect of family worship as a cause of his son's death: "oh humbling thought, what a stupified besotted Creature to doe so little as I all along have done for his precious soul, how few serious and close applications in Love and affection have I made to him about spiritual and Eternal things, most dreadfull neglect and even hatred." As a result of this abdication of spiritual duties, King blamed himself for "murdering and destroying my family." Nearing the edge of sanity as the result of self-blame and self-hate, King implored God "to have Mercy on me or I am under for ever."[64]

We do not know how long Daniel King mourned since this entry was his last for seventeen years, until his wife died in 1766. With John Gates, however, it is possible to trace the year-long period of grieving caused by his eldest son's death. A forty-four-year-old farmer from Stow, Massachusetts, Gates was also taken by surprise by the death of his eighteen-year-old son, Josiah. Unlike King, Gates's diary entry on the death of his son in March 1757 was relatively brief, acknowledging his "inexpressable Grief and sorrow." The real pathos of Gates's grieving is revealed slowly in subsequent entries, where it becomes clear that for a very long time by early New England standards, Gates could not get over this death. Throughout this period, he used the language of Job to express the depth of his pain.

Gates experienced a great deal of anguish on public ritual days, which served to remind him of the change that had occurred in his life since the previous ritual. Three weeks after Josiah's death, the colony held an anniversary fasting day. On that day Gates prayed, "O Holy and Righteous God . . . thou hast Greatly increased in my Tabernacle Lamentation, mourning, and woe in the course of thy Providence since the last annaversary Fast by removing the Flower of it by Death for which I weep, mine eye mine eye runneth Down with tears."

Much of Gates's grieving centered around his house and how his son would never share that space with him again. On the day of the anniversary fast, Gates lamented that "man is carried to the Grave and Returneth to this House no more and this place shall see him again no more for ever." Several days later he again noted that "the places that Did know him shall know him no more for ever," echoing Job 7:10. Gates's sense of home centered to a great extent on his eldest son's presence. While living, Josiah embodied all his father strove for in establishing a productive and loving domicile.

Unlike the stern Puritan parent of lore,[65] Gates waxed poetic about his son, referring to him most commonly as a "flower." One month after Josiah's death Gates wrote, "he faded away as a flower that is plucked of[f] as soon as it apear'd." Seven months later his imagery had become more morbid: "I had a pleasent Famaly a year ago the Flower of which is now Rotting in the Grave." About this time, six to nine months after Josiah died, Gates realized that his period of lamentation was lasting longer than it should, at least according to the culturally dominant script. On a day of thanksgiving in November Gates noted that "these Days of thanksgiving have been much esteemed by me as Days of Rejoycing but God hath so broken in upon my Famaly the year past by Death that my Heart is sad and heavy. But o that I may not Displease God nor provoke Him." Gates realized that others considered his grieving excessive, which translated into a lack of support he received from his friends, who "Drink wine in Bowles and Chant to the sound of the viol and are not Grieved for the afflictions of the afflicted." His companions began to tire of Gates and his inability to shake his depression. "Friends forsake me," lamented Gates, "and many that I have shewed much kindness to now take occation to speak evil." In part because his society disapproved of his intense grief, Gates neared the end of his tether and used the words of Job 17:11 to express his sense of suffering: "my Days are past, my purpose is Broken."[66] Ultimately Gates got over his eldest son's death, but only after nearly a year of sadness and increasing distance from his friends.

Thus, lay attitudes toward death and dying were complex in early New England, influenced by one's age, sex, and the circumstances of the death in question. Nonetheless, some generalizations can be made. Most people feared death and hell, and as a result they spent much of their lives searching for assurance that they were bound for heaven. This fear of death was continuous throughout the period: the Great Awakening did not mark a divide between an earlier period of terror about death and a later period of equanimity. Another constant in the eighteenth century was an independence of thought among laypeople. Though many adhered to ministerial models of correct mourning, others did not, choosing not to embrace all their ministers' prescriptions. These laypeople's search for comfort upon the deaths of loved ones led them to overlook some of reformed Protestantism's more difficult doctrines, including "infant damnation." Finally, a search for knowledge about their future estates led some people to rely on dreams and divination, in opposition to their ministers' directives.

Deathbed Scenes and Inversions of Power

The countless deathbed scenes played out in early New England were potential sites of contestation, places where laypeople expressed their heterogeneous attitudes toward death through conscious actions. While some scenes conformed closely to the ministerial model, others differed in important ways. Variations occurred because during the deathbed scene the usual power relations were inverted or at least temporarily altered—especially along axes of male/female and minister/layperson. As the center of attention in a highly charged scene, the dying person often gained the power to speak and act in ways unthinkable in a more workaday setting. As a result, deathbed scenes provide a lens for examining some of the tensions both among laypeople and between laypeople and ministers.

People on their deathbeds occupied a classically liminal position, seen by observers as straddling two worlds. From this liminality dying people accrued the power momentarily to reverse roles with their superiors: "Liminality implies that the high could not be high unless the low existed, and he who is high must experience what it is like to be low."[67] During these moments of power inversion, tensions within New England's religious culture were illuminated as if by a flash. For a moment women were like men, laity were like clergy, assurance was possible, and visions revealed the realities of heaven and hell.

MODEL DEATHBED SCENES

So that variations from the ideal may be understood, I will describe a model deathbed scene, using the fictional Elizabeth Dyer.[68] The scene began when Dyer's sickbed was transformed into a deathbed, a change not so much physical as interpretive. At some point in her long illness, Dyer and her family realized that her malady was likely to be fatal. After this, the family made an effort never to leave Dyer unattended, in case she suddenly grew worse. The appointed "watcher" was in this case a female family member, but if financial circumstances had permitted, Dyer's family may have relied on a midwife or domestic servant. Throughout her sickness neighbors and friends had been paying visits, and when she took a sudden bad turn, they were called to be present at her end, along with her family members. The minister, who had already visited with Dyer, was called in to pray with her one final time. When the minister arrived, he prayed with Dyer and questioned her about her beliefs (though he had known her for many years) and asked whether she had good hopes for going to heaven. Since all was going according to plan, Dyer answered that she believed in God's mercy through Christ and hoped (but was not overly sure) she was going to heaven. Ultimately, Dyer gave a final blessing to her husband, her children, and her gathered friends. Shortly, death arrived and Dyer's husband performed the practical and symbolic act of closing her eyes. Weeping, which up to this point had been controlled, commenced more loudly. A few hours later Dyer's daughters and female friends washed her body and wrapped it in a shroud.

From the clergy's viewpoint, the most crucial part of the deathbed scene was the interaction between the dying person and the minister. During this questioning, the minister and other observers could discern how godly the person really was. Because of the high stakes, ministers outlined what people should think, what they should say, and how they should behave on their deathbeds. Cotton Mather offered a list of expressions appropriate out of a dying person's mouth:

> Vain World! False World! Oh! that I had minded this World less ...
> There is no Evil so Odious, or Dangerous, or Damnable, as our Sin.
> Oh! my vain Company, it has undone me: I wish I had never seen the face of such and such young people; Their company hath been the Damnation of my Soul!
> Christ is the most precious Thing imaginable.
> Alehouses *are* Hellhouses![69]

In ministerially sanctioned expressions, the dying person reflected on his or her life, repented for sin, and put faith in mercy through Christ. As Benjamin Colman argued, the goal in death was "to die in a *pardoned, justified, and sanctified State,* having our Peace made with God, reconciled to God thro' the Death of His Son." But in no case were people to be absolutely sure that heaven was their final destination. Although ministers encouraged hope, certainty betrayed complacency and lack of rigor in one's self-examination. The ministerial model's "well-grounded Hope" was meant to give the dying person the power to be resigned to God's will.[70]

Laypeople were exposed to the ministerial model of proper dying through oral and printed sermons. Many pious men and women enjoyed reading about triumphant deaths; they found no shortage of books to sate this desire. Benjamin Lyon of Woodstock, Connecticut, kept a massive spiritual journal between 1763 and 1767, writing often about his reading material. Among his favorite genres were collections of good deaths. It is possible in Lyon's journal to witness one pious layman imbibing the ministerially propagated cultural scripts regarding deathbed behavior. In 1763 Lyon reported that "this Day I have read about 100 pages in Mr Willison Afflicted Mans Companion with much Delight, Especially the Dying Speeches of the Saints." Reading these speeches caused Lyon to pray "that I might be enabled to live such a life as these heavenly men did & die such a triumphant Death." Specifically, Lyon hoped to "leave this world Joyfully & glorifying his blessed & glorious name."[71] Lyon had similar reactions to reading "Mr Baxter's Dying Thoughts," "Edward Pierse's Great Concerns of Every one to prepare for

Death," and "a Sermon of Dr Watts, stiled the watchful Christian Dying in peace."[72] Ministers did not need to coerce their parishioners into learning about proper deathbed behavior; such reading material proved exceedingly popular among pious New Englanders.

Because of these scripts' deep penetration into New England's religious culture, many lay deathbed scenes conformed to the ministerial model, especially regarding resignation to God's will. The model's power is apparent in the dying scene of Elizabeth Foxcroft, who expressed her resignation to God's will that she suffer. In 1721, the fifty-seven-year-old Foxcroft lay dying and in a great deal of pain. Her reaction to her physical discomfort demonstrates the power of the cultural norms: "when a very shocking Turn sometimes forced Her to lisp out a Complaint of, 'Pain, Pain!' She wou'd instantly correct Her self, and rebuke Her (seeming) Impatience; saying, 'But 'tis my heavenly Father, who is thus chastning of Me, and I deserve it.'"[73] Foxcroft's desire to adhere to the cultural norm was even more powerful than her desire to express pain. Whereas Foxcroft expressed her willingness to suffer, Cotton Mather's sister, Jerusha Oliver, spoke of her willingness to die. So exemplary were Oliver's words that Mather published a long description of her dying days. Particularly worthy of emulation, Mather felt, were expressions such as this, uttered by Oliver when she realized she was dying: "Here is a Strange Thing! when I was in Health, Death was a Terror to me. But now I know, I shall Dy, I am not at all afraid of it."[74] Oliver's fearlessness derived from her trust in God's will.

Many people's willingness to die grew out of their anticipation of a union with Christ. Sometimes the desire to part with this world could be taken too far, at least in the clergy's opinion. When Jonathan Dayly's wife said upon her deathbed that "her Husband, & Children & all seems no more to her than Dirt in comparison of Christ," Rev. Samuel Chandler felt compelled to differ gently with her. As he phrased it in his diary, "it was mentioned to her it would be a tryall to part with them."[75] More often, however, ministers noted with approval a willingness to die, as when Ebenezer Parkman recorded the "Remarkable Declaration" of the dying Susé Rogers in 1740. "As to dying," Parkman wrote, "She hop'd she was ready, and was willing because she hop'd she had not sought God in vain (for He is a Mercifull God)."[76]

Laypeople as well as ministers recorded many such instances of model deaths in which the dying person expressed a willingness to die. When Abigail Cleaveland of Canterbury, Connecticut, wrote to her sons describing their father's death, she emphasized the dying man's knowledge of his approaching end, his resigned solemnity, and his desires to be with Christ:

Your dear and tender and careful father the ninth day of february [1751] I trust
fell a sleep in Jesus, the mor[n]ing before he dyed his heart was greatly inlarged
to call in all the Christians to sing and pray with him, . . . he was asked what
they should pray for, he said, that I may touch the hem of Christs garment and
be made whole.[77]

The communal aspect of the deathbed is apparent in this scene, with the
dying man's wish to be with "all the Christians" as he died. Another letter
bearing the grim news of a family member's death illustrates the significance
some laypeople attached to a person's willingness to die. In 1763 Tarrant
Putnam of Sutton, Massachusetts, faced the task of writing to his son, Elijah,
to inform him of the death of his sister Molly. The elder Putnam wrote,

> a few Days before her Death she seem'd wonderfully resin'd to the will of God
> whether in Life or Death. Two Days before her Death I asked her if she was
> willing to part with us, she said with a great zeal & earnestness, O Father said
> she I am willing to leave Father & Mother & Brothers & Sisters & Everything to
> go to Christ.[78]

Putnam interpreted Molly's resignation to God's will as cause for hope that
she was in heaven.

This sort of model death provided both the dying and the survivors with
an optimistic view of the dying person's final estate. In the case of Molly
Putnam's death, her father opined that "she gave very good ground to hope
she made a happy change."[79] Putnam expressed this despite frequent ministerial injunctions against such beliefs, such as when Mather Byles argued
that "it is a vain arrogance to judge a man's estate in the *other world*, by the
manner of his expiration *here*." Byles decried as "daring pride" the tendency
of people to "judge of their neighbours uprightness, by the events that befall
them" on their deathbeds.[80] Similarly, Samuel Willard argued that "Death
gives us no rule of judging whether men be good or bad."[81] Warnings like
these had little effect on laypeople, however, who found comfort in their
loved ones' model deaths.

For example, in October 1712 two of John Paine's brothers died. Five
months later, on his own fifty-third birthday, Paine reflected that "I have
cause with sorrow of heart to bewail and lament the awfull Stroakes of the
rod of god upon me in taking away two of my natural breth[r]en who were
dear unto me." Despite this sadness, Paine had reason to hope because of
their model deaths: "there was mercy mingled with this affliction & honey
with this gall in that they both departed under comfortable circomstances
as to their Eternal Estate, glory be to god."[82] An explicit example of the con-

nection that laypeople drew between people's final words and their final estate was recorded by Jonathan Willis of Medford, Massachusetts. In 1744 Willis noted the arrival in town of his kinsman, one Mr. Parks. According to Willis, Parks "com to town last night & before this morning he departed this Life and we cant doubt but it is for a better, for I hear that a day or 2 ago he did exspress his joyfull hope & his undaunted ferelessness of dying."[83] Despite the warnings of ministers against inferring so much from a person's dying words, Willis received comfort from his relative's lack of fear. Thus, ministers and laypeople interpreted model deaths somewhat differently: ministers argued that they demonstrated the *possibility* that a person was saved, while most laypeople regarded them as *proof* that a person was saved.

Perhaps the most vivid account of a person's dying demeanor providing comfort to the survivors is in the diary of Sarah Prince of Boston. In July 1744, when Sarah was only sixteen, her sister Deborah lay on her deathbed after seven weeks of a painful illness. When it became apparent that Deborah was going to die, Sarah was anguished because Deborah did not seem to be dying with the comfort one expected of a saved person. "When we found she was evidently struck with death," reported Sarah, "she was in extream agonies of soul." Deborah's display of moaning and crying was "eno' to melt the hardest heart," causing Sarah and her brother to retire to another room where they could weep more loudly without fear of disturbing their sister. When her sister Mercy told Sarah to compose herself a little, Sarah replied that her tears were "for her soul which is worth 10,000 worlds and I can't bear it shou'd go out of the world in Uncertainties." For Sarah, her sister's dying demeanor was extremely significant as a sign of whether she was saved. This began to worry her brother, who nervously asked, "do you doubt of her state?" But before this debate could continue, Mercy returned to the room weeping joyful tears and asking her siblings to hurry to the deathbed. They witnessed the glorious sight that "every cloud was scattered and God had lifted up the light of his Countenance on her . . . The Chamber which a minute before was full of distress and anguish now fill'd with Joy, Praise, Love and Admiration." Deborah's peaceful demeanor had a powerful effect on the observers: "we to whom she was dearest were the most willing to part with her—for my part I was intirely willing."[84] A model death made all the difference to many pious observers. Although ministers warned that people's final estates could not be judged by the circumstances of their deaths, lay survivors often took comfort when a loved one died well.

These examples begin to hint at the importance placed on a person's dying words. A person who died without being able to speak left survivors worried about whether the person was saved. When Elizabeth White's husband of three years died in 1770, he left her without any final words of comfort. Caleb suffered from a terrible fever that "deprived him of his senses, so that he was never himself not long together to his dying day." This made his death difficult for White to accept. "O its dreadfull! beyond Expression," lamented White, "to Lose ones dear freinds; without one ray of hope that it is well with them." She would have much preferred a death in which he could have spoken to her and comforted her: "If he had died upon a sick bed, I should have some Peace concerning him, but now I have none. He is gone & I know not how it is with him."[85]

Even when the dying person was not a loved one, final words carried a great deal of weight. While serving in the French and Indian War, Benjamin Glasier of Ipswich witnessed a soldier hanged for theft. Inspired to compose a poem, Glasier commented at length on the condemned man's last words:

> the twentyfifth Day of July
> a man for theft was Judged to Dye
> and when he Died on the Lad[d]er hold
> he Cried Lord have mercy on my Soul.
>
> he Spoke to the Sold[i]ers grate and Small
> to mind in time on god to Call
> and not goo [sic] on as he had Dune
> Least to the galows all Should Come
>
> and mind [h]onesty more than their purse
> Not Steall nor Ley Sware Nor Curse
> Least to the galous them Selves they Brang
> and with a holter their to Swing.[86]

This was the only occasion in a lengthy diary when Glasier copied someone's spoken words. Uttered on the verge of death, these words appeared to Glasier as especially noteworthy.

Thus, the liminal position of the dying person, poised between the worlds of the living and the dead, gave his or her words greater power than they ordinarily had. Samuel Sewall seemed to believe that a dying person's blessing was especially efficacious. On one occasion in 1691, Sewall sought the power of a deathbed blessing as protection for his children. After visiting a man so sick that he had missed two consecutive church meetings, Sewall wrote, "Had my four children to Mr. Robert Saunderson to receive his Blessing as he lay on his Bed." In 1698 Sewall paid a visit to the dying Charles Morton. After prayers and pious conversation, Sewall prepared to leave.

"When I took leave, He said, 'I wish you well and all your family.' I told him I doubted not but that I should fare the better for his Blessing." Similarly, ten years later Sewall attended the deathbed of another man and "ask'd his Blessing for me and my family." At first Sewall was disappointed in his request because the dying man felt that Sewall was already blessed. But at his departure Sewall got his wish: "Yet at my going away He pray'd for a Blessing for me."[87] In these examples words of a dying person seem almost to have an incantatory power for Sewall. Even those aspects of deathbed scenes that conformed to the clerical model—a willingness to die, resignation to God's will, offering blessings and counsels—could signal the potential for dissonance between laity and clergy on matters of death.

UNORTHODOX DEATHBED SCENES

But not all deathbed scenes adhered to the model. The differences between the ministerially sanctioned script and the actual performance of deathbed scenes illuminate the tensions within New England's religious culture. For example, laypeople occasionally did not die with equanimity; not everyone could be as optimistic as the model encouraged.[88] People commonly had fears of death in the days leading up to their mortal hour. Dozens of examples of this dynamic survive, such as the case of "Old Mr Randall" of York in what is today Maine. Like many laypeople, he had once been relatively sure of his future state, but the trauma of an imminent death caused him to have doubts. As his minister noted, Randall "says that he has had such a Love to Christ that he could have parted this life for the next but now he has not clear evidences."[89] Although no record survives of his dying moments, if Randall was like most people his doubts evaporated shortly before he died.

But perhaps Randall was among the small group of people who felt no comfort even as they passed out of this world. This was not the typical lay response to dying, but it happened often enough to demonstrate that laypeople could not always appropriate aspects of religion in order to gain comfort. Isaac Backus noted several such distressing cases in his diary. A particularly upsetting example occurred in 1753 when Backus received a report of the sickness and death of his sister Eunice. His brother's letter was "shocking" since Eunice was "in great distress of mind 'till the last." In a case in which he was not so personally involved, Backus reported that Priscilla Eddy "had no strength to trust in Christ" even as she died. Likewise, when Backus preached at the house of Richard Gridly in 1766 he learned that

Gridly's wife had died a month before "in great terror of mind."[90] Ebenezer Parkman also occasionally noted instances of people dying without comfort. "I am told by the Deacon's [John Fay's] Son James," reported Parkman in 1748, "that they could not discern that he was any clearer about his Spiritual state till he dyed, than he was when I was with him."[91] Israel Loring recorded a case in 1728 when a man had "fallen into a Distraction" on his deathbed as a result of worries about his sinful life. "In this Condition he lay till his death," Loring noted sadly.[92] Although it would seem that there was a great incentive for people on their deathbed to find assurance, they did not always do so. Religion could not always be so self-consciously manipulated to provide comfort.

When they occurred, breaches in the model deathbed scene signaled tensions in the relationship between laity and clergy. Rev. Ebenezer Parkman recorded an illustrative lapse of bedside decorum in 1727. Called to the deathbed of Samuel Forbush's wife, Parkman commenced with his role in the scene, asking the dying woman if she had repented of her sins, if she had found the Lord's Supper a comfort during her life, and if she truly loved the godly. The dying woman was answering all the questions correctly when one observer, "Old Mr. Forbush," in a "sad passionate manner" intoned, "Sir, We are grown folks." This breach in the model deathbed scene shocked Parkman: "I turned about in great Surprize." A lengthy debate followed between the learned minister and the disputatious observer, who argued that "we understand these things already have read in the Bible and Some other Books, and ourselves know these things being grown folks and come into years."[93] Old Thomas Forbush held firm to his point that the model deathbed scene enacted unequal power relations, with the dominant clergyman leading the scene and asking unnecessary, condescending questions. By speaking up in this highly charged moment, Forbush registered his displeasure with such an uneven arrangement.

More common than an observer committing a breach in the model deathbed scene, however, was for the dying person to act in opposition to the script. A person's final repentance was an issue that lent itself to dispute. Ministers expected laypeople to tread a narrow path regarding deathbed confessions. On the one hand, clergymen wanted laypeople to repent for individual sinful acts and other isolated transgressions. Rev. John Ballantine, minister in Westfield, Massachusetts, visited Samuel Johnson and asked him the usual questions, including if he was sorry for his sins. "I asked him if his striking an officer, who was in the discharge of his duty seemed a sin, he said no. People are convinced now adays without having any knowledge of sin."[94]

Ballantine's editorial comment reveals that he believed Johnson's answer to be typical of a lay tendency, not an unusual aberration. Similarly, Ebenezer Parkman found the Widow Pierce to be unrepentant on her deathbed. According to Parkman, "She is very bad, yet no great Signs of Repentance. Her Case very Deplorable! God be Mercifull to her!"[95] In all likelihood Johnson and Pierce did not believe they had sinned and consequently would not repent on their deathbeds.

On the other hand, ministers were wary when laypeople attempted to repent for a sinful life, as opposed to isolated sinful acts. Stressing the need for godliness throughout one's life, clergymen did not want people waiting until their dying moments to realize the consequences of living a life in sin. Cotton Mather summed up the prevailing ministerial view when he wrote that "a *Repentance* at the Last, if there be any *Space* for it, is mostly an *Insincere*, but always a *Suspitious* Repentance." Noting that the terror of the deathbed could lead people to false conversions, Mather argued that the "*Change of Mind*, which takes men upon a Death bed, is usually no more than a *Conviction* upon them; there is no Real *Conversion* in it."[96] Similarly, Thomas Foxcroft warned against "the great but too common Folly of depending on" a "Death-bed Repentance."[97] Despite these cautions many laypeople persisted in these breaches. Confessions for avoiding the Lord's Supper were common, such as when Ebenezer Parkman visited Lieutenant Maynard's father. On this visit he found him "in a very low Condition, and it was very doubtful whether he would recover." Parkman reported that the old man "had his Reason in a Considerable Measure while I was there, & freely & bitterly lamented his neglect of attending on the Lords Table. He said if it should please God to recover him, he would by no means neglect it any longer."[98] Such promises occurred frequently, even when the dying person realized the potential for insincerity. When Daniel King's son Nathaniel was dying, the boy repented his sins but also mentioned "the great hazard of a Death bed repentance and named a person he knew in Salem that in his late sickness had made great promises that he would reform and never sware any more that now was as bad or worse than before." The elder King's response, however, was not to avoid such a fragile support for one's hopes, but to "convince him and my self that his [Nathaniel's] repentance was true."[99] In these liminal moments, tensions within the religious culture emerged.

These repentances were well-meaning gestures, but they angered ministers nonetheless. When John Hambleton was dying, he called Ebenezer Parkman to help him repent. Hambleton seemed sincere; he "was very humble and broken for sin, full of passionate and repeated Crys to God and

Christ, Sent for his Companions to ask their forgiveness, and to call 'em to repentance and to charge 'em to turn from sin to God." But Parkman cast a pall over the tearful proceedings: "I warn'd him of the Danger of trusting to [these actions] and how rarely a late Repentance was true, proceeding so much from the present Extremity, which forc'd it."[100] Ministers wanted their parishioners to live every moment as if they were about to die. Many laypeople, conscious of their inability to maintain such a standard, opted instead for the solace provided by a dying repentance.

Likewise, ministers found it troublesome when a dying person desired assurance too strongly. Although no minister was present to be offended, the deathbed scene of Daniel King's son differed from the model scene in this respect. When asked by his father if he was willing to die, Nathaniel replied that he was willing, but only "*if* he was prepared for it." The prospect of being unprepared for death left Nathaniel only conditionally willing to die. In this vein he responded to his father's admonition that despair about dying was sinful, saying that "he knew despair was wrong and that he hoped in Gods Mercy and did not dispair of it but wished for assurance, oh if he could be assured of the Love of God he should be willing to Die."[101] In a manner similar to a number of others, Nathaniel King's deathbed desires contradicted the clergy's warnings that no one could have full assurance as they died.

Some laypeople went beyond a mere desire for certainty and proclaimed themselves to be saved with a self-confidence that irked ministers. Ebenezer Parkman recorded a number of these cases. In 1745 Parkman visited a dying deacon who "answer'd me with great readiness respecting his state, and said he had such Hope, and such scripture ground for his Hope that he was not afraid." This dismayed Parkman, who "gave him some Cautions,—Strait the Gate—few etc.—the many deceiv'd—the Heart deceitful—the wiles of Satan."[102] Similarly, one man named Williams was "in Danger of Death by the threatning mortification of his Hand." Parkman tried to get Williams to show some humility and fear as the result of his sinful life, but Williams remained optimistic about going to heaven. Parkman reported in his diary, "Visited Neighbour Williams and desiring I might be alone with him, all left us, and I dealt in some plainness with him as to what I conceived to be his particular sins, but he entertains a great Deal of Hope concerning his Spiritual Welfare."[103] Some laypeople's fears of hell and dying led them on their deathbeds to the unscriptural belief in the certainty of their sainthood.

Isaac Backus, the Baptist minister of Titicut in southeastern Massachusetts, also reported a number of dying people overly assured of their final estate. In 1755 Backus visited John Sambon, an "apprentice who complains of being poorly." To Backus's surprise Sambon opined that he was "not afraid of being damned because he thinks he has such views of Gods goodness that [God] won't cast him off if he goes on to do as well as he can: and he said he should be glad if he should be taken with the Throat distemper and die!" This view perturbed Backus, who "found need to rebuke him sharply, and tell him the danger of these snares."[104] Likewise, in 1764 when Backus visited John Cole's wife, who was dying of consumption, she offered her belief that she was going to heaven. According to Backus, "Sister Cole said 'Wearisome nights are appointed unto me, but I trust I'm going where 'tis all day,' and more to like purpose."[105]

Sometimes laypeople reached this unorthodox conclusion through even more unorthodox means. In keeping with the lay tendency to attach significance to dreams and visions, a deathbed dream could provide powerful grounds for assurance. The example of Isaiah Pratt that opened this chapter demonstrates a layperson receiving assurance through a deathbed vision. Ministers did not consider such visionary assurance orthodox, and Ebenezer Parkman asserted that "these Things were not to be depended upon but that the Apostle Peter has caution'd us, saying that we have a more sure word of prophecy to which we should do well to take heed &c."[106]

Despite such ministerial injunctions, many laypeople continued to accept their visions, which, like Pratt's, usually involved the presence of Christ. One person comforted by a deathbed vision was Hannah Heaton's daughter-in-law. As this young woman lay on her deathbed in 1778, just a few days after delivering her first child, she reported to those around her that "she had been to heaven and had seen god and christ and that god bid her be gone for she was a sinner but she said christ bid her come and take of the water of life freely." In this vision a loving and personal Christ helped soften the fearsome and distant figure of God. As with others who saw Jesus on their deathbed, this woman gained perfect assurance from her vision: "she said she knew if she dyed she should go to heaven."[107] Likewise, in 1766, Isaac Backus recorded the case of Samuel White, a young man who was dying and in great distress for his soul. White expressed the model idea that a deathbed repentance risked insincerity. "I have delayed my soul concern," lamented the youth, "but, o, a sick bed is a poor time to prepare!" White behaved like this until the next morning when he cried out, "O what have I seen." When the observers pressed White for a description of his vision, "he said he had seen Jesus, who appeard so lovely that he couldn't help loving of him, and went on to praise him and to warn and invite others in a wonderful manner for some hours."[108] White was thus released from his earlier torment by a dying vision.

These deathbed visions were so comforting that people sometimes asked their friends to pray that they would have one. In 1738 a young woman of twenty-one named Abigail Upham was dying in Malden, Massachusetts. On her deathbed she requested a vision of Christ. When a friend of hers visited one evening, she urged him, "Pray for me, that I might recover, if it be the Will of God; but especially that Christ might be revealed to me." The next morning the young man returned to find Upham in a peaceful frame of mind. "O our Prayers the last Evening were graciously answered," she said. "I have seen Christ, and he smil'd upon me: and now I am going." When her friend asked her where she was going, Upham, buoyed by her deathbed vision, optimistically replied, "I am going to Mount Zion, and unto the City of the living God, the heavenly Jerusalem, and to an innumerable Company of Angels, &c."[109] People on their deathbed did not worry whether such visions were "scriptural" evidence of being saved. Rather, on the brink of death, they took from these visions what comfort they offered.

A smaller number of laypeople, usually but not always those deemed "irreligious" by their more pious neighbors, went so far in their opposition to the model deathbed scene as to reject altogether the prayers or even the presence of a minister while they died. When Rev. David Hall of Sutton, Massachusetts, visited a man who was sick with a terrible fever, the man's behavior was so uncongenial that Hall suspected that he was "Possessed with the Devil." Hall noted that the man "refus'd to speak till asked if I should pray when he said no."[110] Another impious man who had a similar reaction to his imminent death was George Hacket of Raynham, Massachusetts, described by Rev. Isaac Backus as a "ringleader of frolicking." After nearly two weeks of sickness Hacket approached his end, lamenting his sinful life. But Hacket apparently gave up any hope of reaching heaven, for "at last he said 'he didn't want any body to pray for him, for' said he 'I shall be in hell before morning. The devil has got hold of me now and he'll soon have me there.'" In the model deathbed scene the dying person's hope for reaching heaven was crucial; hence Hacket's breach angered Backus, who "endeavoured sharply to check" Hacket's sentiments.[111]

Occasionally this type of breach, with a person declining the minister's prayers, occurred as a result of the minister's actions. In 1756 Ebenezer Parkman paid a call on Noah How's dying wife. After Parkman asked some "very close and trying" questions, as was the norm, the woman responded tartly that his "Discourse worry'd her desperately." Because of this she decided she no longer wanted the minister's presence at her deathbed. In Parkman's words, "Upon this I desisted, & bid her farewell, nor did either of them ask me to pray with them."[112] An extreme example of this sort of transgression can be glimpsed in Samuel Sewall's report of the death of a sea captain named Crofts in 1702. According to Sewall, "for Debauchery and Irreligion [Crofts] was one of the vilest Men that has set foot in Boston. Tis said he refused to have any Minister call'd to pray with him during his Sickness, which was above a fortnight."[113] Sewall's remark that "tis said" that Crofts refused to have a minister with him demonstrates that this was considered such a breach of the model as to be the subject of gossip. Though rare, these cases reveal certain laypeople finding greater comfort on their deathbeds without the potentially meddlesome presence of ministers. The significance of all these unorthodox deathbed scenes lies in their demonstration of some of the fissures in lay-clergy relations, specifically in the areas of assurance, repentance, and the validity of dreams and visions.

INVERSIONS OF POWER

Ordinarily, ministers held the lion's share of the power in their face-to-face interactions with laypeople. Though laypeople were not silent in their dealings with clergymen, ministers' speech was privileged, with time set aside several times a week when the ministers dominated the dialogue. Women in particular, due to cultural strictures against challenging their "superiors," were less likely than men to confront ministers outside ritualized settings. These usual power relations were altered, and sometimes wholly inverted, when a person lay dying. Surrounded by supportive neighbors and family, faced with little prospect of earthly retribution, in a liminal position between this world and the next, dying laypeople often found the power to speak their minds. As he lay dying in 1741, one unnamed man summoned his courage and confronted his minister with an issue long troubling him. According to the clergyman, "one thing I shall not forget I hope, [was] his observing to me that I had not for sundry years given him any perticular word of exhortation or inquir'd into the state of his soul from his mouth."[114] For years this pious man had felt silenced in his dealings with his minister, waiting for the time when his pastor would ask him about his spiritual state. On his deathbed he could wait no longer; he was finally empowered to offer criticism. Not all deathbed words were based on such pious desires, though. Sometimes the torrent of words that flowed out contained an undercurrent of heterodoxy: "Capt Whipples wife is in a Strange condition, don't speak much nor don't care to see any Body. She says that she & her Husband & Children are all doom'd to damnation, & that the servant of the Family & all the Worlds Heathen & Mahomitans will be saved."[115] This woman's deathbed scheme included not only the inversion of clerical/lay power, but Christian/non-Christian privilege.

Whipple's words reveal one additional inversion: that of typical male/ female power relations. Significant alone is the fact that an observer listened to Whipple's words and carefully wrote them down, for in this period women's speech was devalued. Aside from conversion narratives, instances of recorded female speech are rare indeed, with one exception: examples abound of dying women's words. Men who ordinarily did not record female speech in their diaries often wrote down the dying words of female family members and friends. Sometimes these words were even printed and distributed widely. When Grace Smith of Eastham, Massachusetts, died in 1712, her dying words were given greater power than her ordinary speech, for the speech she uttered on her deathbed was copied down and published as *The Dying Mothers Legacy*. The subtitle of this small book was, "Left as a Perpetual Monitor to her Surviving Children; as it was taken from her own Mouth a little before her Death, by the Minister of that Town where She Died." Even if these words were strictly conventional, with such advice as "Dearly Love and Prize the Word of God," their female source was highly unconventional.[116]

Not only did society pay more attention than usual to women's dying words, women felt themselves empowered to speak on their deathbeds in ways not typical of their gender. When Mary Clarke Bonner of Cambridge languished on her deathbed in 1697, the observers were surprised that she spoke with "so Loud a voice." In addition to speaking more loudly than her family expected, Bonner spoke more firmly. In response to one of the observers, who "Spoke to her to forbare and not to Spend her Self," Bonner replied forcefully, "I must Speak and tell of the Mercy and Goodness of God."[117] Likewise, Cotton Mather reported that as Sarah Frothingham of Charlestown lay dying "she address'd a Room full of Spectators, with as plain & free & audible a *Speech* as ever she had in her Life, and such as threw them all into an Astonishment."[118] Another woman chose a different tactic when she wanted to make a point on her deathbed: Mrs. Grice of Boston, because she was "averse to hearing anything about her Soul, her sins, or another World," grew impatient with her minister and "us'd indecent Language."[119]

Elizabeth Price, also of Boston, was described by Charles Chauncy as rhetorically engaging in male speech—of a holier sort than Grice—on her deathbed. For a long time Price had been too sick to venture to the meetinghouse, which greatly upset her as her mortal hour drew near. Price's eloquent speeches from her deathbed about desiring a meeting with God compelled Chauncy to link her with a male biblical figure: "With holy *David*, her *soul thirsted for God, the living God:* and that was her complaint, 'O when shall I come and appear before God!'"[120] And although we do not know her name, when Lieutenant Dewey's wife died in Westfield in 1762 she left a memory of typically male speech. "Her life was exemplary and her end peaceful," wrote her minister, John Ballantine. "She died like good old Jacob when he had made an end of commanding his Sons. Though she had been scarcely able to speak audibly for some time, yet the morning she died, she continued speaking to admiration for an hour and a $^1/_2$."[121] Observers were not used to women "commanding" and "speaking to admiration" for such extended periods. Buoyed by the liminal power of her deathbed and its temporary inversion of gendered power, Dewey found a legitimacy attached to her words that previously had eluded her. Like Elizabeth Price, Dewey's words impressed her minister as suitable for a male biblical hero.

This dynamic is also apparent in the deathbed scene of Bethiah Walley of Ipswich. Perhaps during her lifetime Walley had difficulty commanding respect for her speech. In contrast, on her deathbed observers found her words highly important. This was demonstrated partly by her brother, a minister, when he copied down her words for posterity. He reported that "she told a Friend a few Days ago to this Purpose, that she hoped she had not got the great Work of preparing for Death to do now, but that it was done some years ago." Even more telling, as Walley spoke her final words her friends engaged with her speech and demanded a clarification. "The last Words, which she was heard to say, which were in the Night past, were these: 'Oh! redeem me,' being asked by one of the Watchers, what she would be redeemed from, she answered, 'From Sin.'"[122] Those who observed Walley's death wanted to be sure of what she meant by her dying words, for the deathbed transformed ordinarily marginalized female speech into the center of male and clerical attention.

Isaac Backus also recorded several cases of women's words being accorded great respect as they were spoken from their deathbeds. In 1755 Backus visited Elizabeth Deans, a young woman who had been ill for quite some time. On this day her friends gathered around her while Backus prayed. Despite her sickness Deans "talked in a moving manner to her companions around her." Commanding attention from her deathbed, Deans was able to affect those about her with her spoken words. Similarly, Backus found conversing with his eighty-eight-year-old grandmother on her deathbed to be a powerful experience. Despite her advanced age, Backus's grandmother had clear recollections of "her Conversion (which was above 60 years ago) and Several revivals since." These religious stories, "together with her parting councils and advice did much overcome my mind." Finally, Backus described the deathbed eloquence of Mary Eaton, who after a long sickness described for those gathered the wonders of God's grace. As Backus wrote, "And thus she went on for an hour or 2 praiseing God and admireing his goodness, and warning and inviteing others. I haven't heard a person talk more blessedly this long time."[123] Significantly, Backus remarked that he had not heard another *person* speak so blessedly in a long time. Having acquired the power that accrued from her liminal position on the deathbed, Eaton's speech was no longer marginalized as distinctly female, but was accepted by those around her as the powerful words of a religious *person*.

Though hardly a model deathbed experience, one example from the Great Awakening lays bare the intertwined elements of death, gender, and power. Durham, New Hampshire, under the pastoral care of the radical New Light Nicholas Gilman, witnessed many unusual occurrences during the Great Awakening. Unlike most ministers, Gilman gave credence to his parishioners' religious visions. A young woman named Mary Reed had had several such visions when she announced to Gilman on March 26, 1742, that she believed she would die that night. Rather than fearing such a fate, Reed displayed an extraordinary equanimity: "She was well content to bid the world and all Friends farewell. She directed Me that if she returnd No More to life I shoud Send for Her Cloaths and dispose of them to the Poorest persons in Town." That evening, after retiring to bed, Reed "fetchd many deep Sighs as tho' Her soul was departing, after which she lay Some time to appearance Breathless." Shortly Reed's breath returned and she lay in a deep sleep the rest of the night.

After Reed's encounter with "death," she assumed the power of a religious prophet. Women in this period had an incentive to put their words in a style associated with prophets, which helped them gain attention and increase their power.[124] Rather than being instructed by her minister, she used the power she gained through her near-death experience to offer him advice. Gilman was respectful in her presence:

I asked her—whether I ought to mind what men said of Me? She answered—No, No, Mind what the Spirit of Christ Says—Take Him for your Guide, and his Word for your Rule. He has a Great Work for you to do, but don't be afraid[,] He will carry you through it—after Some time when I was in My Study, She Sent to Me desiring Me to read the First Chapter of Jeremiah. Upon enquiring whether I was to read it to My Self she replied Yes, it is Sent to him and it is his Case. Afterwards she lay Blessing and praising God in whispers, in the Language of a Soul actually in Heaven.

Ministers in this period—radical New Light or not—did not generally ask women for spiritual guidance. Contact with death, however, increased the respect accorded to women's spiritual pronouncements. Reed, in fact, managed to escape the ironic bind of other women who accrued power on their deathbeds. While Mrs. Grice, Grace Smith, and women like them gained power on their deathbeds, it was power of the most fleeting kind: within hours they were dead, unable to reap the benefits of their momentary inversion of traditional power dynamics. Mary Reed, on the other hand, experienced the best of both worlds. Granted power and respect due to her immediate contact with death, she lived to exercise that power. For at least nine months (and probably longer) after her experience, she continued to advise her minister about religious matters, going so far as to suggest biblical verses on which Gilman should preach.[125]

The deathbed transformed ordinarily marginalized female speech—and lay speech and actions more generally—into the center of male and clerical attention. Although Mary Reed's experience was unusual, her use of the deathbed to invert ordinary power dynamics was typical. Deathbed scenes were contested in early New England, with laypeople asserting their various and occasionally unorthodox attitudes toward death. Thus there was not a single "Puritan Way of Death"; there were many ways of death, and they expressed the range of lay attitudes toward the religious culture's most important elements: the possibility of assurance, the importance of resignation to God's will, the meaning of dreams and visions, the importance of prayer, the proper goals of repentance, the significance of a good death, and the relationship between superiors (men, clergy) and inferiors (women, laity). Laypeople did not have a monolithic position on any of these issues, but when individuals disagreed with their ministers, those differences could be aired on the deathbed.

Ministers developed patterns of mourning and dying that many people followed; model deaths represent laypeople choosing from the range of available ministerial ideas and the power of this clerical culture. We can see these cultural scripts' power in moments when laypeople countered their initial responses to death and dying with more "appropriate" sentiments, as when Elizabeth Foxcroft explained away her cries of "Pain!" or when Lucinda Howe wrote of "the suden & awful Death" of her Brother but then—to avoid seeming to question God's will—went back and crossed out "& awful."[126] We can also see the strength of these ministerially approved patterns when laypeople hoped to grieve or die correctly, as when Ebenezer Storer repeatedly prayed, "O that I might mourn in a right manner."[127]

But laypeople did not merely draw on the ministerially approved culture of death and dying. They also contributed to this culture, adding their own ideas about such practices as the interpretation of deathbed visions. In this way some laypeople helped create alternatives to the ministerial model. This process was aided by the deathbed's liminality and observers' beliefs that dying people straddled two worlds. As a result, when dying people disagreed with their ministers, they gained the power to speak with a stronger voice than usual since in liminal moments resistance to orthodoxy more easily emerged, as low could become high and high could become low. Although not precisely a ritual in the anthropological sense—as were reading conversion narratives, baptism, and the Lord's Supper (the subjects of the next chapter)—the deathbed scene was indeed a liminal moment. As such the deathbed symbolizes the possibility of lay contributions to the relatively open religious culture of eighteenth-century New England.

CHAPTER THREE

The Performance of Piety

Religious Rituals and Their Contested Meanings

I
N 1743, Mercy Cary of New Salem wanted to have her children baptized. She could not, however, because the minister of this town in north-central Massachusetts suspected that she had conceived her first child before she was married. In an era when perhaps 20 percent of all first births were conceived out of wedlock,[1] this was not an extraordinary occurrence. Typically no more than a pro forma confession before the church was needed to have one's child baptized. Cary duly confessed to fornication, but angered her minister when she had the audacity to remark that "she had rather Confess that she had been guilty of the Sin tho' she was Innocent then [*sic*] not have her Children Baptized."[2] Cary's statement reveals that some parents—and, as we shall see, mothers in particular—felt baptism's protection was so important for their children that they would rather confess falsely than leave their children vulnerable. Cary's interpretation of baptism set her apart from the prevailing ministerial view, which held that the ritual was not an efficacious means of protecting against damnation and was merely an outward sign of Abraham's covenant, akin to the mark of circumcision.

This example points to a problem with historical understanding of ritual. Historians are too apt to interpret rituals as "constitutive of community," according to anthropologist Nicholas Dirks.[3] The tendency to interpret ritual's function as the creation of community is reflected in studies of seventeenth-century New England.[4] These works accept the functionalist view that rituals "'are intended to preserve and strengthen the established order.'"[5] In Dirks's opinion, this interpretation overlooks the degree to which ritual can create disorder and facilitate resistance to dominant power structures, as when Mercy Cary asserted her beliefs about baptism in opposition to those of her minister, Samuel Kendall. By following Dirks I do not mean to argue that ritual was nothing more than staged conflict; ritual practice often brought the godly members of a community together in a setting that enhanced their feelings of shared goals and desires. And the previous interpretations of New England's rituals may have greater credence for the seventeenth century, with its relatively closed religious culture and less cultural and institutional distance between ministers and laypeople. But in both the seventeenth and the eighteenth centuries a number of factors occasionally allowed rituals to become sites for performing alternative interpretations of religion.

Most importantly, the signs transmitted by ritual are never stable. If one understands ritual as a text, with certain words and actions inscribed in its performance, one can see how rituals are as open to multiple and conflicting readings as any written text.[6] Laypeople in New England, for example, could sometimes "read" the "sign" of a minister pouring water on an infant's head differently than the clergy did. A second factor allowing for conflicting interpretations of rituals is that gender tensions beneath the surface of the religious culture can emerge during a ritual. In eighteenth-century New England this was most common in baptism, as women, to their ministers' chagrin, were more likely than men to believe that baptism protected children by guaranteeing them entry into heaven if they died. The liminality of participants in ritual is a third factor that can lead to conflicting interpretations. As with the dying, participants in ritual were sometimes emboldened by their liminal position to question their ministers' interpretations. Finally was the early modern belief in the efficaciousness of speech. Although most people could read and books were common, colonial New England remained a largely oral culture. Words were not seen as evanescent, disappearing into thin air upon being spoken, but as having very real power. To early New Englanders, speech "seemed inherently more mysterious, dangerous, and 'real' than it does today."[7] Ritual, since it combined speech with stylized gestures, was understood to be particularly efficacious. This occasionally led to disputes over ritual's meaning since much was at stake in interpreting such powerful acts. Conflicts over rituals were more vituperative than other disputes—over ministers' salaries, for example—because people believed rituals were efficacious.

Furthermore, several factors specific to eighteenth-century New England promoted conflicting interpretations of ritual. While the forms of baptism, the Lord's Supper, and reading conversion narratives were roughly unaltered since the seventeenth century,[8] the context in which these rituals occurred had changed. A growing cultural and institutional gap between laity and clergy added to the distance between the two groups. In addition, because the Halfway Covenant debate had been more or less settled, conflicts began to focus more on the nature of baptism and less on the ecclesiastical questions of who should be admitted to the ritual. Likewise with the Lord's Supper: many laypeople maintained a communally oriented interpretation of the ritual, while ministers, through the sacramental manuals that proliferated around the turn of the century, increasingly sought to focus attention on individual preparation.[9] Thus, the ritualized performance of piety sheds light on how New England's religious culture was negotiated. Laypeople participated in clerically approved and conducted rituals and often chose to interpret the rituals along ministerial lines. But there were occasions, resulting from the particular combination of speech, liminality, gender, and power embodied in these rituals, where laypeople asserted their own interpretations and thereby added scripts to the religious culture.

In this chapter I examine three rituals in which pious New Englanders took part: reading a conversion narrative in order to gain admission into a church, baptism, and the Lord's Supper. These rituals fell along a spectrum between community creation and community disruption. On the end of community creation was reading conversion narratives, which served to demarcate a religious community. This ritual engendered little conflict. In the middle of this spectrum lay baptism, which even within the pro-pedobaptism ranks created a degree of conflict. Laypeople and their ministers agreed on the ritual's importance, but laypeople tended to stress baptism's efficacy over the interpretation of their ministers, who saw the ritual merely as a covenant seal. Finally, the Lord's Supper created the most conflict, as laypeople and ministers time and again clashed over communion's meaning. Clergymen repeatedly lamented the low turnout at the ritual. In addition, ministers were frustrated by full church members who chose to absent themselves from communion during sometimes frivolous disputes. Lay writings about these three rituals show that they were open to varied interpretations. Thus, religious rituals both created community and were a stage on which laypeople could play out alternative interpretations of their religion.

Reading Conversion Narratives

In 1764, a woman in her thirties named Sarah Eveleth stood before her Ipswich congregation and opened her heart to her fellow parishioners. Taking part in a 130-year-old ritual, she stood while her pastor related to her peers her account of conversion, so the congregation could judge whether to accept her testimonial as sincere. Eveleth's account began by looking back to her first religious stirrings. She noted that "the first real conviction I had was a Sermon I heard Mr Ebenezer Cleaveland preach some years ago, but when I got home, those words came to me with power, awake those that sleepeth and arise from the Dead and Christ shall give thee Light." Moreover, she related that she had felt completely humbled by God's power: "I saw God might justly cast me off forever; and I could plead nothing but mercy, mercy." The most humbling aspect of the testimonial, however, still remained. One can only imagine the dramatic hush that greeted these words: "And I do now acknowledge my sins in the Breach of the 7th Commandment in having my first child too soon."[10] Upon hearing this intensely personal account, the male congregants voted to accept Eveleth as a member in full standing.

What significance did the reading of a conversion narrative hold for Sarah Eveleth? What significance did this ritual hold for the congregation and the community? This ritual marked a key moment—perhaps *the* key moment—in its participants' religious creation of self. This effect emerged from the narrativity of the ritual's structure.[11] Furthermore, on the group level, this ritual helped unite individuals into a community, especially when compared to baptism and the Lord's Supper. These powerful and important results derived from ritual's ability to transmit messages both about the present social and psychological state of the participants as well as about notions of the divine.[12] Unlike baptism and the Lord's Supper, very little controversy surrounded reading conversion narratives. There is no evidence that lay-people interpreted this ritual in a manner at all different from their ministers.

First, the sources upon which this section is based should be introduced.[13] The early reformed Protestant emigrants to New England located the conversion experience—the moment when a person realized that he or she was a member of the elect—as one of religion's central experiences. Only those who had a conversion experience could become full members of the church. In most congregations, having an experience was not enough: the potential member also needed to give a relation of conversion to the members of the congregation, who would then vote whether to accept the account. This system was firmly in place by the end of the 1630s.[14]

Later in the century, however, the practice of admitting only "visible saints" waned. Following Solomon Stoddard's lead, a number of churches in Massachusetts and Connecticut began admitting to full membership anyone whose behavior was not scandalous, reasoning that it was impossible to determine the sincerity of these relations.[15] The Great Awakening of the 1740s reversed this pattern, as New Lights again emphasized the centrality of conversion. Many New Light congregations, including the Fourth Church in Ipswich, demanded that a conversion testimonial be read in front of the congregation.

The testimonials on which this section is based are not from the Great Awakening itself, but from the smaller Seacoast Revival of 1763 to 1764.[16] Fifty-three testimonials survive, thirteen by men and forty by women. I have chosen to examine this group of narratives, instead of those extant from all of New England, in order to focus on the dynamics within one community. These documents, however, conform to the patterns of other eighteenth-century conversion narratives, and the conclusions drawn in this section may be applied elsewhere.[17]

The pastor of the Fourth Church, John Cleaveland, described the procedure for preparing the accounts: "The Pastor and Ruling Elders shall examine the Candidates, as to their Knowledge, Principles, and gracious Experience, and if they have no Objections against them, take down in Writing the Relation of their Experience . . . which is read to the Church in the public Congregation."[18] Significantly, this ritual occurred within a framework of ministerial control, with the minister both asking the questions that framed the narrative and filtering the words of his parishioners' responses. Some ministers went so far as to recast the narratives laypeople wrote to fit better what the clergy saw as the ritual's didactic mission.[19] This is not to say that these narratives do not reflect lay religious thought. Rather it is to point out how this ritual was under greater ministerial control than either baptism or the Lord's Supper, a fact that accounts for this ritual's relative lack of controversy.

When exploring the meanings of having these accounts read before the congregation, some historians do not take this ritual seriously enough, arguing that the ritual's invariance indicates the participants' unthinking attitude. One scholarly account of this batch of testimonials notes that "the relations followed a set formula" and proceeds to dispatch of them in two pages.[20] But ritual's formulaic nature should not be a reason for its dismissal: ritual's invariant structures communicate messages about "the divine," while its variant aspects indicate "the current states of the participants."[21]

The ritual of reading conversion narratives had a number of more or less invariant aspects[22]: the pastor read the prewritten account, the congregation listened while remaining seated, and afterwards the congregation voted whether to accept the relation. This always took place in the meetinghouse. The testimonials themselves followed a more or less invariant format. The participant described his or her early sinful days, then the first stirrings of religious faith, and finally the conversion experience itself. These more or less invariant aspects of the ritual transmitted vital messages about the divine. That the ritual always occurred in the meetinghouse was crucial to its efficacy. Merely telling a friend over a fence about one's conversion experience would not qualify one for full membership in the church; it had to be done in a specified location (unlike baptism, which could occasionally take place outside the church in a private home). The participant's location in front of the congregation signaled to all involved that the candidate, by reason of relating a sacred occurrence, was the center of attention. That the relation was read instead of being delivered extemporaneously signaled an important message about the canons of the religion: it stressed reason and deliberation. Even this, one of the most evangelical congregations in the colony, one that had been castigated by Old Lights during the Great Awakening as unduly "warm," was not about to leave the description of the conversion experience to the heat of the moment. This testimonial had been approved by the pastor and elders. Finally, the congregation's vote to accept the relation signaled the acceptance of the participant into a distinct social group.

The form of the ritual and the pattern of the testimonials were not the only invariant aspects of the ritual. The words themselves were highly stylized and phrases were repeated in many of the testimonials. Almost all end with some form of the following: "I desire to be humbled before God and Man for it and desire you and all people to forgive me." Or from another: "I hope you will pray for me that I may never dishonour Christ but shew forth his praise and Glory." Many begin with the phrase, "What first bro't me under concern," and then relate the first religious stirrings. These stock phrases served to signal that an important event was taking place. These phrases were reserved for the solemn occasion of testimonial reading. Other phrases that appeared in many of the testimonials were part of the broader religious culture. For example, Phillis Cogswell, a slave, related that "it would have been just with God to cast me into hell." Similarly, Elizabeth Ingersol, a young white woman, noted that "it was just for God to cast me off." This similarity of phrasing signaled that these people shared a common experience, despite their differences in social status.[23] This ritual's invariant aspects connected the participant and congregation in a shared cosmology in which God was justified in sending people to hell and in which people were seen as inherently sinful, yet in which there was the opportunity for redemption. This shared cosmology was central to the creation of community.

Invariance was only one side of the coin, however. This ritual demanded a great deal of variance since each participant related the account of his or her unique conversion experience, within the genre's conventions. This variance allowed the transmission of self-referential messages to the congregation.

This ritual was first of all an act of self-effacement and a display of humility because this was a performative act and the observers were as important as the participants. The ritual began with some sort of recognition that the participant had been in "a lost and perishing state." The participant then related the exact nature of that sinful state. Jeremiah Kinsman noted that he had been stirred by the Great Awakening of 1741, but soon after fell away into sinfulness: "But not long after this I entered into a married state and soon got intangled in the cares of the world, and became very cold in Religion and in a great measure neglegent of my Duty, which I speak to my shame, and which has caused me much grief." Some of the sins that people related seem relatively inconsequential by modern standards, but it is apparent that the participants took them seriously as marks of a sinful character. The gravity with which people described some of these "minor" sins is striking. Rachel Low confessed, "I saw my sins to be numerous, but Sabbath-Breaking and telling lyes for sport lay weight on me." And some sins that people confessed were much more serious, such as Sarah Eveleth's confession to fornication.

This self-effacement was significant both on the personal level and the community level. Individuals were in effect cleansed by relating their sins to the congregation. In some respects this group confession was even more purging than a solitary confession would have been since all the members of the community got to hear everyone else's sins. It took a certain degree of humility to admit to one's minister that one had fornicated, but it took an exponentially higher degree of courage and humility to confess the same thing in front of an entire congregation. Participants in this ritual felt that they had shared the burden of their sins with the congregation. In a cosmology that considered people inherently sinful, confessing before one's peers united the participant and the congregation in acceptance of sin.

The ritual's variant aspects also transmitted information about social status. This is apparent in the narrative of the congregation's wealthiest man, Abraham Choate. At first glance it might seem that, in fact, there are no differences between this testimonial and the others, that this was a classless ritual. Choate began with a ritual self-effacement similar to all the other parishioners: "I desire to present myself before thee with the deepest Humiliation and Abasement of Soul, sensible how unworthy such a sinful Worm as I am, is to appear before the holy Majesty of Heaven, the King of Kings and the Lord of Lords." But key distinctions can be found underneath the layers of stylized language. Choate used a phrase that none of the other participants employed, expressing religious ideas in the language of the emergent merchant class. Addressing God, he asked to "enter into a covenant-Transaction with thee and thy People." The congregation may have noticed that this man transacted business with them as well as with God. Furthermore, Choate described how his class position actually hindered his salvation. He noted that because "I cannot serve God and Mammon," he desired that "I may be enabled to take up my Cross daily and persevere to the End in following Christ." Mammon, the personification of money as a false god, was a barrier between Choate and true grace. He signaled to his fellow parishioners that his previous attempts to serve God and Mammon were in vain. He would now have to take up his cross—the burden of his wealth— and strive to worship none other than God. Thus, this ritual sent a number of messages about Choate's current state. Choate made clear that he was a man of more substantial means than the rest of the congregation, but at the same time he indicated his willingness to join with the others in a community of sinners attempting to serve God. This ritual's variance allowed him simultaneously to distinguish himself from and unite himself with his fellow parishioners.

These two effects of the self-referential signals sent by reading conversion narratives—the acknowledgment of the omnipresence of sin through ritual self-effacement and the simultaneous union/differentiation of individuals— are a subset of this ritual's most important office: the creation of self through the legitimation of personal history. In effect, when Rev. John Cleaveland and the Elders of the Fourth Church sat down with potential converts and asked them to relate their conversion experiences, they asked these people to construct a personal history. Granted, they only asked for a narrow slice of their personal history. Candidates did not respond with aspects of their history that were considered tangential to their conversion experience. But therein lay the importance of this request. The participant was asked to describe his or her seemingly ineluctable march toward conversion in a thousand words or less. The significance lies not merely in the events upon which each person focused, but in the fact that this ritual legitimized that particular construction of personal history.

Candidates constructed their past histories differently, with many people ordering their lives around the vicissitudes of early modern life. Hannah Sergeant drew on a natural metaphor to signal her past sinful state: "In the Time of the Drought, Summer before last when I saw the ground was parched,

I saw my soul was as parched and barren and God might destroy me." A strong earthquake in 1755 proved to be a signpost along the road to conversion for several participants. Rachel Low noted that "I was never under much convictions till the Friday after the Earth-quake in 1755." Another recalled that "in the time of the Earth-quake, I was bro't under new-concern." As discussed in chapter 2, death played a prominent role in marking periods of intense religious concern. Bethiah Foster made sense of her past by recalling that "the first that seem'd to bring me to any real concern about my soul, was the death of my two brothers William and Aaron Bennet." Sarah Eveleth also saw death as an important aspect of her religious development. She found it worthy to order her conversion narrative, and in effect her personal history, into three periods. First came her early sinful days. Then came a period of trial, when "my Children were taken sick of the Throat-Distemper." Despite her prayers, "soon after three of my own and a fourth of my husband's died of that distemper." Her conversion experience soon followed.

It might be objected that this sort of construction of the past occurs continuously. A woman who leans over the fence and tells a neighbor of her four children dying of the throat distemper is also constructing her past. This is certainly true. But ritual is imbued with an efficacy that ordinary speech does not have. Anthropologists make a distinction between two types of speech: perlocutionary and illocutionary. The former, of which ordinary speech consists, depends on the words' persuasiveness for its efficaciousness. A person who says, "You should get your hair cut," has not caused anything tangible to transpire. Illocutionary speech, on the other hand, is contained in ritual and effects change through the very utterance of the words. A minister in a wedding ritual who says, "I now pronounce you husband and wife," is not merely talking about marrying a couple, he has married them as a result of the power invested in his words by ritual.[24]

The conversion ritual contained illocutionary messages. Participants who narrated their histories did not merely describe events that had taken place long ago. They related these occurrences to their current religious condition in a way that gave those events the appearance of being determinative. At that moment their sense of self was created anew: participants declared that their past was purposeful and that it had pointed in the direction of religious fulfillment—that it had been legitimate. When the congregation's male members raised their hands to accept the narrative, they signaled that the community agreed with this assessment. The community's imprimatur was the final act in this ritual process of legitimation.

Ultimately, this ritual was a rite of passage for the participants. Whatever their previous doubts about their religious state, the reading of those words obviated most misgivings. The participant, by the ritual reading of the conversion narrative, had passed into a new social state, into the realm of the converted, into the realm of the religiously legitimate. The reading of the conversion narratives provided a clearer demarcation of life stages than even the conversion experience itself. The conversion experience had an indeterminate beginning and end, and one might even be fooled into believing that another emotional or physical sensation was the conversion experience. But the ritual reading of the conversion narrative occurred at a specific time and could not be mistaken for anything else. Its status as an irrefutable occurrence allowed this ritual to legitimize personal history and to help create a religious sense of self.

In the end, Sarah Eveleth was a changed person for having her conversion narrative read in front of the congregation. Quoting from a hymn, she provided an apt metaphor for religion in her life:

> The Door is shut but is not barr'd
> And he that is within
> Bids me to ask and seek and knock
> And strive to come in.

> Then will I ask and seek and knock
> Untill the Door be open
> I will not stir one step from hence
> It is a Door of hope.

Earlier in Eveleth's life, the door to heaven would have indeed seemed shut. She began her married life under the cloud of fornication and felt herself to be an unworthy sinner. After her conversion experience, however, she was able to see that there was hope, that her striving had not been in vain. Following her participation in the conversion narrative ritual she saw that her early days of sin were a necessary precursor to her present days of happiness. By having her testimonial read and having her personal history accepted by the community, she was able to see that her life had been purposeful and legitimate.

Baptism

At age twenty-five, one year after marrying Hannah Hull and one month before becoming a father, Samuel Sewall had his first serious thoughts about joining a church. After wrestling with the issue for a few weeks, Sewall decided to come forward. The reasons he offered for the timing of his decision are illuminating: "through importunity of friends, and hope that God might communicate himself to me in the ordinance [of communion], and because of my child (then hoped for) its being baptised, I offered myself, and was not refused."[25] With fatherhood impending, Sewall sought church admission in large part so his child would be baptized. This pattern was broad and not limited to the most orthodox, like Sewall. Anne Brown has found a strong link between church admission and baptizing children: fully 75 percent of the parents who entered the Beverly, Massachusetts, church from 1702 to 1765 either were expecting their first child or brought a child for baptism within a few weeks.[26] For many laypeople, one incentive to join the church was to receive baptism for their children since laypeople in general and women in particular believed that baptism offered their children protection against damnation. This belief helped make baptism a more contentious ritual than reading conversion narratives.[27]

Since the Reformation, baptism had been one of only two sacraments performed by Protestants.[28] In the 1510s Martin Luther initiated a sacramental revolution and declared that confirmation, penance, ordination, marriage, and extreme unction were not sacraments. And even though baptism remained a sacrament, Luther denied the Catholic doctrine that baptism imparted its grace *ex opere operato,* or by the power of its own operation. Shortly thereafter Ulrich Zwingli and John Calvin described the chief purpose of baptism as a seal of Abraham's covenant, similar to the function of circumcision among the biblical Israelites. Seventeenth-century New England theologians inherited this tradition and argued that people who were not visible saints could not have their children baptized. By the eighteenth century, however, as a result of the Halfway Covenant and other less restrictive policies, baptism became available to all believers, as long as their behavior was not scandalous, and to their children.[29]

Ministers widened the sphere of eligibility for baptism partly because they saw the ritual as an opportunity to call for good behavior from their flocks. John Graham, like many other ministers, urged his readers to renew their covenant with God, arguing that "they are bound to this by their *Baptism.*"[30] Benjamin Wadsworth focused more explicitly on the behavioral effects of baptism: "By receiving Baptism, he doth devote and consecrate, bind, ingage and oblige himself; to live unto, and obey God the Father, God the Son, and God the Holy Ghost, as long as he lives."[31] Because so many laypeople sought baptism for their children, ministers saw this pool of baptized people as a potential source for later converts to the church as well as a group that might be more open to calls for godliness. The important point is that, despite these attempts to use the lure of baptism to get people into the meeting-house, New England ministers followed Luther and declared that baptism was not efficacious; that is, baptism did not cause a person to become a member of the elect.[32]

For the most part, laymen in eighteenth-century New England accepted this formulation. Because they believed that baptism was an outward seal of the covenant, laymen focused on the public nature of the ritual when they wrote in their diaries about baptism. For example, Joseph Goodhue of Newbury reported that March 23, 1746, "was the first Day that the ordinance of Battism was Administred by Mr Parsons in the New meeting Hous[e] & the Number [baptized] was Eaight."[33] Men like Goodhue believed that the ritual marked an important milestone in the public life of the church and of the children baptized. This was even more evident when their own children were baptized. Ebenezer Storer of Boston repeatedly emphasized the ritual's public nature in his prayers after his daughter's baptism. Storer wrote in 1756, "O blessed be his Name, that . . . he has given me an opportunity pub-licly to devote it [his daughter] to him in Baptism." He continued, "I bless Thee that I have this Day had an opportunity publicly & solemnly to devote this Child to Thee in the Way of Thine own appointment."[34] In typical phrases, Storer shows that the ritual's importance for laymen was intertwined with its public performance.

Similarly, Samuel Sewall commented on baptism's public nature in a sug-gestive manner. When describing the baptisms of his children and grand-children Sewall often noted the child's reaction to the baptismal water. At the baptism of one of his sons in 1687 he reported, "Child shrunk at the water but cry'd not." When a daughter was baptized in 1690 he noted, "She cried not at all, though a pretty deal of water was poured on her by Mr. Willard when He baptized her." And after his granddaughter's baptism in 1704, he wrote, "though the Child had cry'd before, [she] did not cry at Mr. Colman's pouring on the Water."[35] Sewall may have interpreted a child's lack of crying as a sign that the child accepted the seal of the covenant. Since the child's reaction to baptism was so public, Sewall was grateful when his off-spring seemed to accept the ritual.

Women, on the other hand, seem to have been less likely to focus on the ritual's public nature and more likely to believe that baptism provided their children with protection against damnation. This was not an absolute dif-ference from men's interpretations, but a difference of emphasis.[36] Most women would have agreed with Ann Fiske when she wrote about baptism's protection of children: it "delivered from *Death* & restored to *Life*" those who participated.[37] Likewise, this chapter's opening example reveals that Mercy Cary felt it was worth lying to her pastor to obtain baptism's protection for her children. Other women revealed baptism's powerful lure when they attempted to have their child baptized in a church with which they were not on good terms. After a church meeting in Stow, Massachusetts, a member noted that Hannah Randal "had a Bastard Child born of her Body the 22 of July last" and that she "offered it to Baptism." The (male) members of the church, who felt that baptism was not appropriate, thwarted Randal's desires: "The Church voted that they ware not in Charity with said Hannah Randal so as to have Mr Gardner Baptize her said Child."[38] Randal, who must have realized that her child's baptism was not likely, nonetheless went out on a limb and faced the scrutiny of the church.

Women risked so much because they saw baptism as an act by which they gave their children to God, thereby gaining protection for them. Mary Cleaveland of Ipswich wrote in her journal thirteen times in the thirteen years from 1750 to 1762, and seven of those entries noted the births of her seven children. In each entry after a birth she recorded a brief prayer asking for the child's safety, usually mentioning baptism as playing a key role in ensuring safety. After the birth of her son Parker in 1751, she wrote, "I trust the Lord enabled me to give it to him in Baptism." When Nehemiah was born in 1760, Cleaveland pleaded, "I hope I was in sum mesuer enabled to give him to God in baptism."[39] Rev. Benjamin Colman's funeral sermon about his daughter, Jane Turell, reveals a similar dynamic. Colman described Turell's reaction to her child's baptism and its death only eleven days later: "all the family remember the many tears of Joy and thankfulness she shed at the presentation of this child to God in holy Baptism, and her more than common composure of mind and quietness at its death and funeral."[40] The child's baptism comforted Turell when the child died, for in her interpretation, baptism was more than a seal of the covenant. Rather, in Turell's view baptism was an efficacious means of insuring her child's entry into heaven.

Less literate and less elite women shared Cleaveland's and Turell's belief in baptism's power. In 1745 Ebenezer Parkman reported that "Mr. John Oakes Wife here again in Order to her being propounded and having her Child baptiz'd, but [I] am oblig'd still to delay gratifying her, not finding her acquainted with what is necessary to be known and understood of the main Principles of Religion."[41] Parkman was no stickler when it came to examining people before joining the church; he rarely found people deficient in their religious knowledge. Here, then, was a woman who was not very pious, and probably not a regular church attendant, who still believed in baptism's power and desired the ritual for her child.

This analysis should not be taken to mean that women had (and always have had) an inborn instinct that made them want to protect their children through baptism. But when one focuses on women's words and actions rather than on ministers' images of women, it becomes clear that ministers did not wholly control the discourse of how women should behave and how they should worship. Baptism was thus a moment when women's alternative interpretations of ritual added scripts to the religious culture.

Women, like men, sometimes expressed other ideas about baptism that were at odds with the prevailing interpretations. Isaac Backus reported one such heterodox view when a church council was convened to look into irregularities concerning baptism, including charges that an unordained man had performed adult baptisms. In this case a woman expressed her view that the ritual itself was more important than the person who performed it. According to Backus, John Finney's wife said that "if persons did but obey the command of God in baptism their baptism was good if the devil had been the administrator."[42] Hyperbole notwithstanding, Finney's wife expressed the view that the power of the ritual derived from its very occurrence and not from the sanction and participation of the ministerial elite. Her interpretation was radically antiministerial, moreover, in its insistence that the behavior of the person baptized, as commanded by God, legitimized the ritual. This example shows the greater potential of baptism relative to reading conversion narratives for facilitating individual interpretations: although ministers performed baptism, laypeople could put their own emphases on the proceedings, even to the extent of denying ministerial privilege. Most laypeople, however, did not go as far as Finney's wife in repudiating the minister's role. As we shall see, laypeople were often quite concerned with the qualifications of the person who performed the ritual.

A rather more orthodox expression of the belief that baptism's power derived from its participants' godliness (and not necessarily from sacred space, as with reading conversion narratives) is demonstrated by the practice of home baptism for sickly infants. Occasionally (though not often) an infant was so ill that it could not be taken to the meetinghouse or it could not wait until Sunday for baptism. A church vote was usually required to sanction the ritual. Home baptisms show that the performance of the rite was of primary importance because the sacred space of the church was not required to legitimize the ritual. In some ways, performing baptism in the family's home was very appropriate since the home (in addition to the ritual) was associated with protection.[43]

Because baptism was public, even when it occurred in a private home, most laypeople were concerned with the presiding minister's qualifications. At a Worcester Association of Ministers meeting in 1756, Rev. David Hall of Sutton asked his colleagues for advice regarding an allegedly ineffectual baptism. Ezekiel Cole, a radical New Light with a small but devoted following during and shortly after the Great Awakening, had baptized a child during the period when he claimed the authority of a standing minister. Cole had subsequently "acknowledg'd his sin and folly in presuming to be ordain'd & to act as a Minister." As a result, "the Father of the Child desires it might be baptiz'd notwithstanding all that was done by Cole."[44] This father worried that Cole's lack of a lawful ordination invalidated the ritual, thereby expressing his belief that a clergyman required the imprimatur of the standing ministry, ritually expressed through a valid ordination, in order to protect his child. The ministers agreed with this father; Parkman opined that he would baptize the child if the case were his.

A similar case shows that laity and clergy were not always in such accordance on this issue. Rev. John Ballantine of Westfield reported in 1769 that "Gerard Pratt's Wife of Granville desired me to baptize their child because they were offended with Rev. Mr. Smith for preaching half the time in the West part of the Town, according to vote of inhabitants." Mrs. Pratt thus evinced an even more stringent test than the father in the previous example: she would not have her child baptized by a minister with whom she was angry. Although this sort of action was much more common regarding the Lord's Supper, it also is explicable for baptism. As a ritual of cohesion, according to Mrs. Pratt, baptism might be invalidated by conflict between the minister and the child's parent. Ballantine, however, did not agree with Mrs. Pratt's logic. He tersely noted, "I refused to baptize it."[45] Clergymen felt that baptisms performed by unordained ministers were illegitimate, but they were not willing to extend that reasoning to ministers quarreling with their parishioners.

Laypeople could be very strict about the rules of baptism, occasionally vexing their ministers in the process. One Sabbath in 1739 Ebenezer Parkman heard from William Pierce, a resident of Southborough, that he did not want his child to be baptized by the town's minister, Nathan Stone. According to Parkman, "Pierce had excepted against Mr. Stones form of baptizing because of his using the word [into] instead of [in] the name, etc. and therefore entreated me to baptize his youngest Child." Stone had alerted Parkman of this impending request, saying that he consented to the man's desire to have his child baptized by Parkman, who nonetheless "demanded of him [Pierce] whether he had any Disgust with Mr. Stone on any other, etc."[46] Parkman felt that Pierce's worries about a very minor deviation in wording were unwarranted, but Stone's consent mollified him, and Parkman performed the baptism.

Laypeople were also apt to maintain strict standards about admitting others to baptism. People may have wanted baptism for their children, but that did not necessarily lead them to deal charitably with others who were trying to get their own children baptized. Ministers sometimes found laypeople unnecessarily stubborn on this point. However, these conflicting views merely reflected these groups' differing agendas: ministers stressed baptism's importance in order to inculcate piety, while congregations had an interest in keeping the ritual as pure as possible to maximize its protective powers. On October 28, 1770, Rev. John Ballantine exchanged pulpits with the minister in Sheffield. During the course of the church service, Ballantine "proposed to some of the members of the Church to baptise 2 Children of Capt Ashley's, one by his former Wife, one by his present one, on the right of the present Wife." Ashley hoped to have his children—including one by a previous wife—baptized based on his present wife's right as a member of the church. The church members, however, "objected that no one but the natural offspring of a professor had a right to be baptized on the professor's own account." In order to buttress their claim, the members cited 1 Corinthians 7:17, which they interpreted as meaning that "if neither of the Parents were believers, the children were unclean and had no right to ordinances." This aggravated Ballantine, who offered half a dozen reasons why the children should be baptized, including the fact that "the unbelievers referred to in the text were pagan Idolators." In exasperation, he asked the members, "Is there not a difference between a Pagan and one educated by Christian Parents who has heard the Gospel?" Ballantine could not convince his antagonists, however, and the children remained unbaptized.[47] Thus laypeople could be stricter than their ministers about admitting people to baptism.

A short postscript to this unhappy pulpit exchange occurred when Ballantine returned to Westfield and found some of his parishioners upset at him. In response to some of his church members, who did not want to wait another whole week to have their children baptized, Ballantine assented to an unusual Tuesday service, in which he preached and "baptized the children, some of the Church having expressed their uneasiness that it was neglected on the Sabbath." But Ballantine could not win for trying, as "Deacon Smith went out when the children were brought forward."[48] Laypeople had very clear ideas about baptism, how it should be worded, and when and where it should take place—though they did not always agree among themselves about these particulars. A breach of any of these expectations could lead to dissent and division; in this case, Deacon Smith was angered by the unorthodox Tuesday baptisms.

In general, ministers and laypeople agreed on baptism's importance, although occasionally this agreement hid differing interpretations. Where ministers saw a ritual seal of the covenant and a chance to bring a new generation under the watch of the church, laypeople in general and women in particular saw an efficacious means for protecting their children against damnation. The ritual lay in the middle of the spectrum of community creation and disruption. Although, like reading conversion narratives, baptism brought members of the community together in a celebration of their religion's fundamental doctrines, it also occasionally disrupted that community with disagreements over the ritual's meaning. This resulted from ministers' merely partial control over the ritual: though ministers performed baptism and directed what was said, they did not control lay interpretations of the ritual's symbolic significance.

Lord's Supper

At the conflict end of the ritual spectrum lay the Lord's Supper. In terms of both individual piety and social integration, the Lord's Supper had ambivalent meanings for New Englanders. As the most important public ordinance, the communion ritual engendered powerful and sometimes conflicting responses within laypeople and their society. A morning spent receiving bread and wine at the hands of one's minister could invoke feelings of both love and self-loathing, both desire and fear. Thoughts of life and death intermingled with feelings of empowerment and weakness as pious saints approached the Table. On a societal level, the communion ritual helped manifest both peace and conflict. Protestant ministers had long stressed the importance of introspective preparation for the Lord's Supper. John Calvin led the way for this movement in the early sixteenth century, focusing on the necessity for rigorous self-examination before partaking in the ritual. Reformed Protestants in England followed this doctrine and carried it to New England in the seventeenth century. By the early eighteenth century, a spate of sacramental manuals published both in London and Boston attested to ministerial concern with preparation for communion.[49]

Although ministers focused on laypeople's preparation for the sacrament, laypeople were principally interested in the ritual as one of social integration. This is not to say that laypeople did not prepare for the ritual as their ministers prescribed; indeed the sources on which this section is based are in large part the written records of lay preparatory exercises. For most laypeople, though, communion held another important purpose: gathering the community of saints in worshipful harmony. But lay theory was not always consonant with lay practice. Not only did the Lord's Supper serve to divide saints from nonsaints, it could also create divisions within the godly community.

"LOVELY IN SUFFERING": AMBIVALENT EXPERIENCES

When Sarah Prince Gill wrote in 1764 that Christ "appeared Lovely in suffering"[50] during the Lord's Supper, she captured some of the tensions of lay emotions during the ritual: these feelings are well described as "lovely suffering." As the spiritual journals of pious laypeople confirm, participation in the Lord's Supper could produce the highest of highs and the lowest of lows. Alongside the potential for meeting with Christ's actual presence and tasting the sweetness of his blood existed the chance that one partook unworthily. As all New Englanders knew, the penalty for such sinful participation was no less than eternal damnation (1 Cor. 11:27–29).

Appreciating this ambivalence requires taking seriously godly laypeople's writings. The self-flagellation that was part of preparing for the Lord's Supper may sound like reflexive cant to modern ears. But when historians write that popular religion served to create safe havens in an early modern world of dangers,[51] they fail to engage seriously with the expressions of fear and self-loathing in lay journals. Perhaps these interpretations are meant to counter the popular images (and views of earlier Progressive historians[52]) of early New England religion as fraught with terror. Though it is useful to correct the excesses in the popular images, fear should not be erased from our understanding of early American religion. Not simply conventional, fear was as bound up with the experience of communion as was joy. Lay writings also show that people were not merely consumers of ministerial ideas about the ritual. Rather, laypeople contributed ideas about the sacraments to New England's religious culture.

Ministers urged their parishioners to prepare themselves fully before approaching the Table. Those godly people who heeded this advice looked forward to the ritual with a mixture of anticipation and worry. As pious men and women peered into their souls, they often found much that made them uncomfortable. Because being unprepared for receiving the sacrament was a sin, this was one of their chief concerns before the ritual. In April 1752, four days before the scheduled communion, Experience Richardson worried that "next Sabbath Day is Sacrament Day and I am not prepared for it. O if God does not asiste me I cannot do it." Like many people, Richardson felt a sense of powerlessness due to her inability to ready herself for the Lord's Supper. Similarly, in the next year Richardson connected her sense of worldly troubles to her inability to prepare for the ritual. She wrote, "This day boore down with new and old affliction and cannot trust in God I think nither, nor cannot prepare for sacrament which is next Sabath."[53] Several days before the event, Richardson was already trying to prepare herself to come to the Table solemnly and piously. To her deep regret and concern she could muster no better effort.

When worldly cares interfered with preparing for the Supper, it led to a great deal of worry. In 1744 Jonathan Willis was a sixty-year-old merchant living in Medford, Massachusetts. Willis's spiritual journal contains a number of entries in which worldly cares interrupted his attempts to prepare for communion. On a Saturday evening before the sacrament, Willis beseeched, "O lord I pray thee to pardon my unpreparednesse for thy holy Day & table & blesse me & my family, compose my mind being ruffled by my Negros absenting him selfe from me without leve." In another case, again the night before the Supper, Willis noted that "the clutters of the world & a bad hart has grately belated me tonight that I have only an hour or two to cumpose my selfe for that solemnity before me on the morrow, though it may be it is the most sollom act of Devotion that a saint is ever call'd to in this world."[54] Significantly, Willis considered an hour or two to be insufficient to get ready for the sacrament.

Clearly, preparation was important to pious laypeople—occasionally too important, according to some ministers. Many clergymen realized that the scrupulosity of those like Richardson and Willis could lead people to avoid the Lord's Supper out of fear of eating and drinking unworthily. When Jane Turell, daughter of Rev. Benjamin Colman, wrote during a period of doubts that "I was exceeding dull and heavy, and ready to go away from the Sacrament,"[55] it troubled her minister, in this case her father. In his funeral sermon on her death in 1735, Colman rebuked his daughter not only for delaying joining the church, but for preparing too scrupulously for the Lord's Supper:

> She early gave her Self up to God, but her *timorous* Disposition restrain'd her from proceeding early to the *Lord's Table;* nor was it without much Conflict of Soul and great Distress, thro' Fear of coming unworthily, that she at last came into full Communion. She afterward *exceeded,* to her *own* and her *Consort's* great Discomfort, in her Preparations for Communion Days; which was her *Infirmity,* and I do not praise her for it. Good Christians should take more the Comforts of Religion in their Way to Heaven, in their Obedience to Christ, and in the Observation of his special *Institutions.*[56]

Keenly aware that if people stayed away from the sacrament every time they felt dull and heavy it could lead to mass absences, Colman publicly scolded his deceased daughter for preparing too carefully. In contrast to the interpretations of popular religion as a safe haven in a dangerous world, here we have a minister complaining about a layperson's inability to find refuge in her religion.

This, however, is not to imply that Jane Turell or any pious layperson found nothing but terror in their communion preparations. Rather, at times this preparation could be powerfully uplifting. Most anticipated, and most often cited in their preparations, was the chance of union with Christ during the sacrament. This union could take a number of forms. Turell looked forward to the moment when she would meet Christ "in thy *House,* and at thy *Table.*"[57] Moses Abbot, a young man living in Boston in 1728, prayed, "there meet with me, O my dear Saviour! and bless me, and speak peace to my soul."[58] Preparing for the Lord's Supper in 1733, Sarah Pierpont wrote ecstatically of the possibility of union with Christ, "I chuse[,] I prize[,] I lay hold on this Christ as he offers himself to me in the Gospel, O my Jesus make me thine be thou mine & that forever."[59] For Pierpont and other pious laypeople, preparation for communion could lead to intense expectations for a meeting with Jesus.

This preparation was at its most intense before a person approached the Table for the first time. Numerous diarists record careful accounts of their first communion, seeing it as a turning point in their lives. A person's first communion often coincided with important life-course changes such as marriage or the birth of a child and also served as an unmistakable signpost on one's spiritual pilgrimage. For people like John Gates, acceptance to the Lord's Table offered the promise of spiritual improvement. "Oh that it might be a Day much Remember'd by me," proclaimed Gates after his first communion, "and hence forward that I may get myself to Reform and mend every thing that is amiss."[60] Likewise, Daniel King hoped his first communion would mark the start of a new attention to holiness. In 1730 he prayed, "help me (as I have solemnly sworne) to forsake every Evil way I hope I Desire to hate and forsake sin and walk worthy of My high Profession."[61] Mary Dodge of Ipswich most succinctly expressed this desire to make a new start. Twenty-one years old and riding the Great Awakening's crest of religious enthusiasm, Dodge noted in April 1743 her reactions to her first communion: she "thought that his fru[i]t was swe[e]t to my tast[e] and thought I would lead a new life."[62] In the conventional language of newly acknowledged saints, the first appearance at the Table marked the start of a new spiritual life.

But the Lord's Supper was associated not only with images of life and rebirth for pious New Englanders. Many approached the Table thinking of death, linking this most powerful ritual with mortality. As Moses Abbot noted in 1728, "by commemorating my Lord's death" he would "be prepared for my own death."[63] John Barnard also contemplated death when he thought about the Lord's Supper. Preparing for the ritual one day in 1716, he began to have thoughts of his impending death. But he was solaced to remember the pleasantness of communion with God that was in the ritual. According to Barnard, "the thoughts of having an uninterupted Comunyon with my dear saviour, & of being wholy freed from sin, dus sumtimes sweeten the thoughts of death to me."[64] The Supper reminded Barnard of death, but it also reminded him that the communion possible in the ritual would be even greater in heaven.

A person in mourning could also find comfort in the ritual. Lydia Prout, having recently experienced the death of "all my Children at once," approached the Table full of thoughts of her children, worried that her faith was being tempted and hoping for comfort. Prout was not disappointed: "I never met with more from god in my Life," she wrote after the ritual.[65]

Others were not so lucky. In one case, a woman hanged herself shortly after receiving the sacrament, perhaps not finding the solace she hoped. According to a contemporary account, this woman, a certain Mrs. Marion of Boston, was

> a Pious woman who on a Sabbath came home after meeting P.M. and went into her Closet (I think after she had receiv'd the Sacrament) (as was her frequent practice) to read and pray and not coming out after frequent calls at 12 at night her husband (Mr Samuel Marion) broke in and found her hanging (which to all apearance was done by her own hands) Stone Dead.[66]

Clearly the Lord's Supper did not bring Marion the relief it brought Prout. This diarist felt that Marion's possible participation in the ritual was significant because people associated the Lord's Supper with forces of life and death. Marking their savior's death with a ritual holding out the possibility of eternal life created ambivalent and at times conflicting feelings.

Similarly, people gained power from communion even as they ceded power to Christ. Before approaching the Table, Lydia Prout often listed the benefits she expected to gain there. In one typical example she wrote, "I hope my design in going to the table of the lord is not out of any other ends but to glorify to meet with christ, and to have communion with him, that my doubts may be resolv'd, my sins mortified, my faith & other graces strengthen'd."[67] Like Prout, Experience Richardson also hoped to gain strength and freedom from temptation through communion. "I have a deceitful heart," lamented Richardson, "but I have been telling God that I design to Go to the Lords supper that I may have more grace & strength to over come this sin & all other temtations which I am troubled with."[68] Like many pious laypeople, Prout and Richardson expected a great deal of empowerment from communion.

Often these people found the power they craved. After partaking one sacrament day in 1757, Richardson reported that she received strength. She noted, "I told God I would receve these elements as a token that he would give me more strength to over come my pride both of a spirittual & temporal & my uneasyness under my deffeculties." She also made clear that the Lord's Supper could be more rewarding than an ordinary Sabbath day. After receiving the sacrament she reported, "I had more power over my thoughts then I have had in time of publick worship. I desire to prais God for it."[69] The Lord's Supper offered Richardson the power to gather her thoughts and conquer her temptations.

Typifying the same dynamic, the life of Benjamin Bangs of Harwich, Massachusetts, provides a case study of the empowering possibilities of the Lord's Supper. Born in 1721, Bangs spent his life tied to the sea. A whaler as a young man and a merchant as an older man, Bangs recounted in his journal both his economic and spiritual growth. A remarkable change takes place in his journal precisely on May 18, 1760, the date of his first participation in the Lord's Supper. Before that day, the spiritual entries in his journal were simple and straightforward, a typical example being "O God that my Soul also may Increase in grace." After he was accepted into full communion with his church, however, Bangs appropriated pious language. After his second communion, for example, Bangs displayed his newfound facility with the rhetorical conventions of the godly. "O my God may I be more watchfull & carefull to depart from all Iniquity," Bangs pleaded, "begging for an Interest in Christs precious blood & that thy Holy Spirit may flow into my Hard & Obdurate Heart: so that I may come unto thee with more Love & less fear."[70] The Lord's Supper empowered Bangs to speak in the language of the godly.

In a seeming paradox, though, communion involved relinquishing power: professing to serve Christ and to give up one's will to him. In a very common formulation, Ebenezer Storer of Boston declared after the ritual to have "solemnly given myself up to thee, & engaged to be thine & thine only." Storer also expressed the common sentiment that a person could do nothing without God. After the ritual he prayed, "Grant me the gracious Influence of thy blessed Spirit to assist me, without which I cannot do anything to purpose in the ways of religion."[71] Sarah Pierpont of New Haven also described ceding power to Christ. In a section of her spiritual journal entitled "Meditations and Reflections after the Ordinance," Pierpont wrote, "I was enabled to receive Jesus Christ my sweet savior & to give my selfe to Him."[72] This paradox—of an empowering ritual that also brought forth professions of powerlessness—perhaps can be resolved by considering the ritual's ability to convince its participants of Christ's power, as when Sarah Prince Gill hoped that "at his Table . . . he wou'd come as a *Conqueror* to destroy sin in me and . . . I beg'd that I might feel his mighty Powers in bearing down my Lusts—subduing my Enmity to his Laws—and disa[ti]sfaction to his Providence and Will."[73] If people ceded power to Christ during communion, they were also aware that they were ratified as members of the community of saints and thereby able to receive Christ's power, which, of course, was unparalleled.

This influx of Christ's power led people to raptures, visions, and even to cry out. Especially during revivals, crying out in ecstasy during the Lord's Supper was fairly common. On one of his peregrinations to dispense the Gospel to Baptists without ministers, Isaac Backus reported that when he administered the Lord's Supper, "many did shout for joy and these exercises took up all the afternoon."[74] Similarly, Rev. Samuel Chandler once noted that "Mrs S-w-l was much affected, seem'd much melted, & many others in a sweet frame."[75] With the ritual generating such passion, it is unsurprising that some participants reported having visions. Rev. Nicholas Gilman, not one to discount reports of visions, recorded this case during the peak of the Great Awakening: "Hubbard Stevens just before Lords [Supper] declard he saw a bright Light like and exceeding [a] bright star about as big as a Mans fist come down out of the Turret and lighted on one of the Beams aloft till after noon time it disappeard."[76] Though occasionally condemned by ministers less tolerant of emotionalism than Backus, Chandler, and Gilman, some laypeople experienced such power at the Table that they could do little to control their outbursts. This fervor provides evidence of the empowerment gained from the Lord's Supper, as anthropologists have noted that ecstatic religious behavior is a sign of direct infusion of the holy spirit that bypasses ministers' authority.[77] Though a ritual conducted by ministers, communion allowed the unmediated reception of the holy spirit. The diminished ministerial control compared to reading conversion narratives helped account for the Lord's Supper's potential for greater conflict.

In contrast to these emotional moments, laypeople sometimes experienced little if any spiritual power during the ritual, which caused intense worry. In 1696 Samuel Sewall had been a member of his church and receiving the sacrament for nearly two decades. Still, he intensely examined himself after the ritual and occasionally found himself lacking in piety. These were occasions for great lamentations, as when he prayed, "O, Lord God forgive all my unsuitable deportment at thy Table the last Sabbath-Day, that Wedding Day; and if ever I be again invited (Invite me once again!) help me entirely to give my self to thy Son as to my most endeared Lord and Husband."[78] Sewall used marital imagery to highlight his feelings that he had betrayed a loved one with his lack of spirituality. Likewise, Elizabeth Phelps used imagery of separation when complaining of her lack of passion at the Table. After the ritual she recorded in her diary, "O my Soul mourn that thou hast been so Little effected this day, surely the Lord is departed—Laboured under much confusion and discomposure of mind."[79] When Jonathan Willis had a weak experience at the Lord's Supper he catalogued a whole range of negative sentiments that he felt. "O the worth of one more quiet Sabbath & Sacrament opertunity," wrote Willis after the ritual, "but ahlasse how poorly improved & Oh how little soul advantage how little growth if indeed any how little peace or joy in beleiving or rather how much fear darknesse unbeleif impenitence inward disquiett least I eat & drink unworthylie."[80] If we take Willis's words seriously—and we must in order to understand the complexity of lay belief—we see that after this spiritually flat Lord's Supper he felt "little peace of joy in beleiving." At the same moment that some of his fellow worshippers experienced rapturous joys as they took the bread and wine, Willis was wracked with fears. He saw his dullness at the Table as a sign that perhaps he was not truly saved, and therefore he might be eating and drinking damnation to himself.

This, then, was why laypeople associated the Lord's Supper with feelings of fear and awe. After John Gates participated in the Lord's Supper he hoped to maintain the godly fear induced by the ritual, praying, "keep me in thy

Fear all the Day Long."[81] Before the ritual Lydia Prout was "very much afraid I should set about it in my own strength & so should be deceiv'd at last."[82] After the ritual Daniel King reported his "doubts and fears and uncomfortable feelings" at the Table. Benjamin Bangs summed up the feelings of many pious New Englanders when he wrote, "I must confess that my fears of unworthyness are great and I go to it [the Lord's Supper] with Greatest awe and fear as a most solemn Ordinance."[83] The lengths to which recent historians have gone to see early New England religion as more than a religion of terror sometimes err on the side of safety and comfort. Many pious New Englanders felt "Greatest awe and fear" as they approached the Table, a fact that must be recognized to appreciate the religion's complexity.

Whereas fear resulted when the heart and mind were unreceptive to ritually induced piety, the senses were the route to an infusion of the spirit: a way to overcome fear, at least partially. Participants in the Lord's Supper often remarked on the physical aspects of eating and drinking, in particular noting the power of Christ's blood. William Cooper of Boston connected the physical taking of the bread and wine with an increase in spirituality. After the ritual he wrote that he had been "made partaker of his Body and Blood to my Spiritual nourishment and growth in Grace . . . O my Soul! thou hast opened thy Mouth to the Lord and must not go back."[84] Cooper analogized opening his corporeal mouth to receive the elements with opening a figurative mouth to his soul to receive Christ's spirit. Benjamin Bangs prayed to have "one Drop of the Blood of the Cross fall to my share," as did Jonathan Willis, who noted that "one drop of thy Blood aplyed too [to] by faith would wash me white as snow as white as wooll."[85] Samuel Sewall described an incident where he was brought to tears contemplating the power of Christ's blood:

> I sit down with the Church of Newbury at the Lord's Table. The Songs of the 5th of the Revelation were sung. I was ready to burst into tears at the word, *bought with thy blood.* Me thoughts 'twas strange that Christ should *cheapen* us; but that when the bargain came to be driven, he should consent rather to part with his *blood,* than goe without us; 'twas amazing.[86]

Like other laypeople, symbolically eating the body and especially drinking the blood of Christ most clearly brought home to Sewall the power of the Lord's Supper.

This focus on the physical aspects of eating and drinking led to a profusion of sensual imagery in lay descriptions of the event. For some, participation seemed to heighten their awareness of their senses, again a way to reduce their fear of the ritual. Many laypeople used language similar to that employed by Sarah Prince Gill to describe her feelings after the ritual. On one typical occasion Gill reported, "At the Lords Table I was refresh'd, his Fruit was sweet to my Taste."[87] The connection of the ritual with eating led many laypeople to formulations like those Daniel King used when he noted, "I have had some hungring after Christ."[88] Likewise, Sarah Pierpont wrote, "My Soul Hungers & thirsts after the[e] as a Hart pants after the water Brooks so pants my soul after thee O God." In straying from the imagery of eating and drinking, Pierpont dramatically displays the tendency to extremely sensual conceptions of the ritual when she prayed: "let me go to thy Table and there behold my crusified Jesus and be able to put my Finger into the Print of the Nails & thrust my Hand into his side and to say feelingly my Lord & my God."[89] Although this sort of imagery was rare for New Englanders and much more like the ecstatic language of German-American pietists such as the Moravians,[90] Pierpont's words are significant nonetheless: this powerful image relates Pierpont's desire to speak *feelingly* to her god. Deeply connected with the lay ability and desire to feel the spirit was the wish to feel and taste the physical elements of the ritual. The body could be a site of empowerment through the Lord's Supper.[91]

These sensual images were only a short distance from a sexualized view of Christ and the ritual.[92] Pierpont, for example, described her desire "that my soul may be ravisht with love to thee."[93] Jane Turell quoted the passionate love poetry of the Song of Solomon when she triumphantly noted after participating in the ritual, "My beloved is mine and I am his! All things are mine!"[94] But this sort of passionate and even sexualized desire for communion with Christ was not the province only of women. Men shared these feelings. Ebenezer Storer, ordinarily quite reserved in his journal, proclaimed that he desired to "kiss the Son with a kiss of Homage & Subjection."[95] While preparing for the Lord's Supper in 1731, Moses Abbot desired "a more flaming love to him!"[96] In a very common formulation, Jonathan Willis described himself as the bride of Christ. Preparing for the Lord's Supper on January 3, 1747, he wrote,

> Satirday eve before the Sacrament & a kind of New Years feast to be attended on the morrow. God help me to sanctifie my selfe for the Lord will com down & o that I may have on the wedding garment ready for the Lords coming that I may be made wellcomb at the wedding, amen.[97]

For Willis, the Lord's Supper represented a feast celebrating the joining of himself and other saints to Christ.

As with Willis, the emphasis on sensuality and even sexuality seemed to prepare laypeople for meeting with the literal presence of Christ in the meetinghouse during the ritual. Though somewhat controversial in its day, a number of godly laypeople believed that while at the Table "the Lord will com down." This was the ultimate, though not always effective, antidote to the fear generated by the ritual's power. As discussed in the first chapter, John Barnard found Christ's literal presence to be one of the most significant aspects of the ritual. Similarly, Hambrick-Stowe uses Samuel Sewall to demonstrate the "popular belief in the literal presence of Jesus Christ in the meetinghouse during the Sacrament." Early in his life Sewall feared he did not have the requisite faith to approach the Table. He therefore worried that "for the abuse of Christ I should be stricken dead; yet I had some earnest desires that Christ would, before the ordinance were done, though it were *when he was just going away,* give me some glimpse of himself; but I perceived none."[98] A number of other New Englanders also spoke of Christ's literal presence during the Supper. To cite just two examples, Experience Richardson recorded a particularly pious day at the Table when she wrote, "I thought I had more of the presents [presence] of God then I use to have Such days."[99] Likewise, after a sacrament day Sarah Prince Gill wrote that she "had reason to think I had Experienced Communion with God—the ordinances of God were more Precious. I cou'd not be contented without the Presence of Christ in them."[100] This sort of view sometimes troubled New England's ministers, who, as David Hall demonstrates, had a policy of "rejecting out of hand" the doctrine of Christ's real presence at the Table.[101] Thus, some laypeople used the physicality of the ritual as the basis for a belief that could set them apart from their ministers.

Of course, not all full church members took the Lord's Supper so seriously. The story of one Barter of Boston, related by Rev. John Comer in 1730, illustrates this nicely. Barter, a member of Boston's New North Church with a penchant for drink, was suspended from communion after a particularly inebriated incident. Having sincerely repented for his sin, the congregation in a spirit of Christian charity restored Barter to his right to communion. Perhaps as a reminder that he needed to keep his spiritual house in order, the congregation assigned Barter the tasks of keeping the meetinghouse clean and ringing the bell. This arrangement worked well until one day when

the deacons of said church having set the sacramental vessels on the table in the meeting house for communion, between the ringing of the 1st and 2d bell, before the congregation came together [Barter] went to the vessels and drank so excessively that he with difficulty got into the belfry, but was incapacitated upon the operation of the drink to perform his office, and lay there *dead drunk* all sermon and sacrament time.[102]

Although an unusual occurrence, Barter's abuse of the holy wine suggests an attitude toward the Lord's Supper among some laypeople that was not as reverent as most examples in this section. While I have focused on pious partakers, it is important to remember that the less pious were not likely to record their thoughts on paper, and therefore their beliefs are inaccessible unless they committed some gaffe like drinking all the communion wine.

But even pious laypeople experienced the Lord's Supper in an ambivalent fashion. This ritual was extremely powerful, not only because it was the central symbol of membership in the community of saints on Earth, but because of its associations with mysterious otherworldly forces. At the same time that laypeople took the symbolic body and blood of their savior they participated in a ritual that, if they were sinful, would lead them to damnation. The Lord's Supper therefore fostered feelings that ranged the spectrum of human emotion.

SOCIAL COHESION AND SOCIAL CONFLICT

The Lord's Supper was more than an individual experience, however. In addition to being mindful of their personal experience, laypeople were very concerned with the ritual's social aspects. This social focus flowed from the lay tendency toward a communally oriented piety. As they approached the Table, laypeople felt the power of the ritual multiplied as they contemplated the gathering of saints, for the aggregation of the holiest members of the community was a physical sign of the ritual's importance. Similarly, at the Table people thought of their loved ones and companions, especially if those people were absent from the ritual. Because it was a social ritual, laypeople often expressed their disputes in this arena, to their ministers' chagrin. When a clergyman and some of his parishioners engaged in a dispute, whether over doctrine, salary, or other issues, the aggrieved members often signaled their displeasure by refusing to accept their minister's administration of the Supper. And despite ministerial calls to come to the Table regardless of their differences, laypeople often abstained from communion even when engaged in a dispute outside the church with other laypeople. Ordinary New Englanders felt that the Lord's Supper was a ritual of social integration; it should not be performed if threatened by the pollution of discord.

Because laypeople saw the Supper as a social ritual they emphasized its performative aspects.[103] The performance of the ritual could make a space more holy, as when Joseph Goodhue of Newbury noted the significance of the first performance of the ritual in a new meetinghouse. In April 1746 Goodhue wrote, "Was the first time the sacrament of the Lords Super was Administred By Mr Parsons in the New Church in the New meating house— A blesed Day it was to many souls."[104] Laypeople even used the term "performance" to describe their part in the ritual, as when William Cooper lamented, "O how imperfect are my best performances."[105] This conception of the Lord's Supper as a public performance led laypeople to emphasize the power of watching the ritual. The members of the Second Church in Ipswich thus voted in 1769 "that the Congregation be informed on Sacrament Day, that it is agreeable to the Church—such as are dispos'd tarry in the Galaries during the Administration of the Lord's Supper."[106] These people expressed their view that watching the performance of the Lord's Supper was a profitable exercise for those who could not partake. And although the vote does not explicitly say so, the wording—that it was "agreeable" to the church—suggests that the impetus for this came from those who wanted to tarry in the gallery for their own edification. Even those who could ordinarily partake occasionally expressed the desire to watch. In 1761 Benjamin Bangs was on a short overnight trip away from his Harwich home. When he went to the meetinghouse in the town he was visiting, he found that the "Blessed Sacrament of the Lords Supper was here administred: I did not know it would be." According to Bangs, "I longed to partake thereof but know not how to make my self known unless by going out publickly which through fear & Bashfullness I did not." This led him to pray during the ritual "that although I did not taste outwardly of the Elements, I might have the sweet Influence shed abroad in my Soul."[107] Bangs knew that one important social aspect of the Lord's Supper was as public performance, and so he desired to partake implicitly by watching.

Bangs expressed a similar social conception of the ritual on another sojourn. For Bangs and other regular participants in the ritual, thoughts of the Lord's Supper accompanied thoughts of the other Saints with whom they ordinarily partook. While Bangs was away from Harwich he often felt out of place, his pious demeanor at odds with the merriment favored by other travelers. He worried, "I had great Intemptions [temptations] with being with Loose Company at my Lodgings yet I keep alone as much as possible." He was comforted, however, thinking "the Sacrament of the Lords Supper I suppose to be administred at Harwich." As a result he "Begged that the Dear partner of my Joy & Sorrow in this Life might partake of more uninterrupted

Joy this Day than I have."[108] Although he would have preferred to participate, Bangs gained peace through the implicit experience of communion
derived from imagining his wife at the Table. In the reverse situation, William
Cooper thought of his wife while he was at the Table when she could not
join him. "On the Sabbath," Cooper wrote, "my Wife was suddenly seized
with a pain in the Bowells which tho' it went kindly off yet prevented her
accompanying me to the House & Table of the Lord."[109] The Lord's Supper
was something Cooper and his wife did as partners in holiness, not something he considered only in relation to his individual experience. As a result
her absence was noteworthy. More unusual was Jonathan Willis's affection
for his wife's servant, Mary Dill, who died after twenty years of service in
January 1747. Although his feelings for her could sound sexual, as when he
cried out "O how I misse her at home at meeting in the week & at the Sabbath,
in the day & in the night," Willis's affection for Dill was based primarily on
her great piety. At the first Lord's Supper after her death Willis lamented,
"but ahlasse Mary Dill that yous'd to be so constant at such seasons & yous'd
to com at Sacrament time in to my Pew, she was missing."[110] Laypeople interpreted the Lord's Supper as a ritual of social integration; when their partners in holiness were absent it changed the tenor of the experience.

The ritual's social nature was also apparent during conflicts between clergymen and their parishioners.[111] Disputes could cause laypeople to absent themselves from the Lord's Supper, which frustrated ministers.[112] I will now examine four cases when laypeople expressed their consternation with their
minister by avoiding communion. These laypeople used their power to absent themselves from the ritual to display their concern with such highly
charged issues as whether loved ones were in heaven or hell, the performance of baptism, and the unholy mixture of drunkenness and communion.[113]

In 1739 Samuel Veazie was ordained minister of the church in Duxbury,
though not without some dispute. In fact, dispute would haunt Veazie's entire eleven-year tenure as minister in Duxbury, for shortly after his ordination the Great Awakening began and Veazie metamorphosed from a quasi-
Arminian into a New Light supporter of the revival. His new views set him
at odds with a majority of his parishioners, though it is significant to note
that a large minority of the town supported Veazie. One of the minister's
most grievous statements, in the eyes of the aggrieved faction, came when
"we asked him what was become of our fathers, and good Christians as we
had reason to call them, and he said they are gone to Hell!"[114] Although this
probably exaggerated Veazie's actual words, he may well have said that it was
impossible to know whether they had gone to heaven or hell. This would

have been disconcerting to those who had gained comfort from the model deaths of "good Christians."

These concerns led a group of parishioners to absent themselves from the Lord's Supper and seek to receive it elsewhere. The leader of this dissident group was Samuel Alden, who in 1742 was instrumental in having a council called to examine these issues. During the council Alden stated that "he could not accept [Veazie] for his pastor" and as a result he could not "with a quiet Conscience submit to his Administrations" of the Lord's Supper. This forced Alden to "go to some other Church for the benefit of Special ordinances." The church asked him his reasons for withdrawing from communion, and Alden replied that "he feared he should Sin against God, if he received the Elements at Mr Veazie's hands."[115] Alden believed that if his minister was corrupted with improper doctrines, it corrupted his administration of the Lord's Supper. For Alden, communion was not merely about his own private preparation for the ritual. The meaning of the ritual depended on its social circumstances, which in this case included tension between a group of parishioners and a minister voicing what seemed to Alden to be mistaken doctrines on two sensitive subjects: death and the final resting place of one's ancestors. The importance of this ritual created desires for consensus within the community before people partook, which ironically led to more conflict when there were disagreements. In this way the Lord's Supper sometimes magnified disputes between laypeople and their ministers.

In 1750 a similar dispute broke out in Ashford, Connecticut. Rev. John Bass was accused by a group of his parishioners of not believing strongly enough in Original Sin. Ten angry church members sent Bass a letter indicating their grounds for suspicion: "When you baptize Children you don't so much as mention one Word of the Child's being Guilty of Sin ... or of any other Words that represent the Child being guilty of Original Sin." Bass then fanned the flames of controversy when in a sermon he directed his flock to receive their understanding of God's will from the Bible, and "not to content themselves with a Religion at Second-Hand."[116] Bass said, in effect, that those who had reservations about how he performed baptism did not base their concerns on a biblical foundation. This sort of condescension infuriated his parishioners. For the aggrieved, no alternative remained but to absent themselves from the Lord's Supper. Bass narrated these events as follows:

> Now it was, that some were too uneasy to sit still any longer; and as the Administration of the Supper was to be on the next Sabbath, something they thought must be immediately done ... They apparently became more confirmed in their Suspicion of me than before; and to such a surprising Length did some

carry their groundless Resentment, that on the next Lord's Day they withdrew from the Ordinance of the Supper, thereby proclaiming abroad their Discontent; which spread among the People, as they became acquainted with the Grounds of it.[117]

Withdrawing from the sacrament revealed to Bass the "surprising Length" to which the aggrieved would go. Bass would have preferred that the dispute remain outside the realm of ritual, and for good reason. Lay disruption of ritual norms attracted a great deal of attention, publicizing the cause and helping to gain supporters. A conflict that originated with differing interpretations of a ritual—in this case, baptism—resulted in laypeople using their power to remove themselves from another ritual in order to galvanize the opposition to their minister. These people used their power to walk away from the Lord's Supper as a way to "vote with their feet," to show their displeasure with their minister and to assert their power to disagree with his doctrine. These tactics succeeded: Bass, who would not change his position regarding Original Sin, was soon dismissed.

The conflict that simmered for at least five years between Captain Dwight and Rev. Justus Forward in Belchertown, Massachusetts, is yet another example of this dynamic. Unfortunately, the only evidence of this dispute is in Forward's partisan diaries and some issues remain shrouded in ambiguity. Still, it is possible to get a sense of the symbolic uses to which the Lord's Supper was put in the dispute. In January 1762, having been ordained about six years before, Forward despaired over the difficulties he was having with some of his parishioners. During an evening of quiet contemplation Forward "mused seriously on my case as a Minister in Belcher-Town, & the Rage and spite which Capt Dwight evidently shews against me." In April of that year, Forward noted that Dwight and his wife, who had been present during the sermon, "went out" when he administered the Lord's Supper, although the cause for Dwight's dissatisfaction was not recorded. At this point Forward's diary breaks off for three years, but when it resumes in 1766 the antagonists were still in disagreement, with Dwight having separated himself completely from the church and not just from communion. After a few years of separation Dwight wanted to return to the church, but he stated that "if he came he should not hold Communion with me or any of the Party adverse to him." In the next few days, however, Dwight softened his views, apologizing in front of his fellow parishioners, stating his desire to take communion with them, and offering that "if any Body objected he would not come."[118] When no one objected the controversy ended. Again, the Lord's

Supper was a flash point in a controversy that originally had little to do with the ritual.

A final, more complicated example stretched from the late 1760s to the early 1770s and was unique in that it involved several ministers and their congregations in a dispute over the symbolic meanings of the Lord's Supper. Thomas Goss had been the minister in Bolton, Massachusetts, since 1741 and had made some enemies by evincing Old Light tendencies during the Great Awakening. These tensions simmered until 1768 when some of his parishioners charged that he "had in sundry Instances appeared as if he were overcome with Spirituous Liquor . . . in Time of public Worship . . . and particularly in the Afternoon, Sacrament-Day." In the eyes of his parishioners this was a grievous breach of the decorum associated with the Lord's Supper. Unable to get Goss to confess in anything but the most ambiguous terms, the people of Bolton called several ecclesiastical councils but still did not receive satisfaction. As a result they took the unusual step of dismissing Goss without the advice of a council. In response, a group a clergymen issued a proclamation that the aggrieved members of the church in Bolton should be boycotted. This clerical contingent ruled that anyone who "shall either preach the word, or dispense the ordinances to them, in their present state, is chargeable with supporting schism."[119]

At this point what had been a small argument over a pastor's drunkenness after the Lord's Supper and his unwillingness to apologize exploded into a power struggle over who was the source of authority in New England churches: laypeople or clergy. When six members of the aggrieved Bolton faction sought to receive communion at the Second Church in nearby Lancaster (now Sterling), the pastor of that church, John Mellen, refused to accept them. But the members of the church in Lancaster "voted not to have the Bolton members withdraw, who offer'd themselves at the Communion."[120] The Bolton faction, emboldened by this show of support from a sympathetic group of laypeople, refused to leave. Mellen therefore "declin'd administring the ordinance & withdrew himself." Mellen later expressed his opinion that the deacons would have taken the laypeople's side in this dispute, arguing that "I had Reason to think in that Situation, no Charge of mine however solemn would have hindred the Deacons from giving them the Elements which I thought would be a Profanation & Prostitution of the Ordinance of Christ."[121]

This conflict dragged on for a number of years and ended ambiguously. But the dispute's significance is captured in a speech by Mellen that illuminates the differences between the clerical and lay interpretations of the Lord's Supper. During an ecclesiastical council in 1773, Mellen addressed his parishioners:

> Several of you, Brethren, mentioned several true & serious things, relative to the Ordinance, by which it might be inferred that Christian Communicants should be heavenly in their Carriage, in preparing for the Heavenly Feast & Kingdom of which this is an Emblem, that they should be peaceable & not schismatical & the like ... If any feel implacable Malice at their Hearts & wicked Passions they cannot conquer, let them absent themselves, or rather take up with the Apostles advice in the like care if they will not with mine, viz not to neglect the Ordinances, but to keep the Feast, yet not with the old Leaven of Malice & Wickedness, but with the unleavened Bread of Sincerity & Truth.[122]

Mellen's heartfelt address reveals that on one level, minister and laity agreed about the Lord's Supper. Both felt that participants must be "heavenly in their Carriage" and not come with enmity against anyone, whether minister or fellow layperson. But there the congruence ended. While for Mellen the solution was merely to embrace "Sincerity & Truth," the pious laypeople knew that demanding such a path denied human nature. Both groups had as their goal the same end: peaceable participation in the ritual. But laypeople understood that "implacable Malice" was not so easily forgotten, and thus the ritual was apt to be tainted by the pernicious influence of all-too-human malice and distrust.

Laypeople also expressed this interpretation of the ritual in their disputes with other laypeople.[123] These upset ministers even more, in a way, than cases involving lay-clerical disputes, for it seemed unjustifiable to ignore the Lord's Supper over a dispute that had no apparent religious ramifications. But the lay interpretation of the fragility of the ritual, unwittingly described by Mellen, led to such instances.

Ministers were frustrated by what seemed to them the petty disputes between laypeople that could keep the antagonists, and sometimes their supporters or kin, away from the Table. Seemingly minor quarrels took on greater significance when their ritual significance was at stake. Although all the issues are not clear, a case from the early 1720s in Norton, Massachusetts, illustrates this connection between the ritual and the mundane. The Leonard family was the most influential in Norton, and in the early 1720s Mrs. Leonard and her son were involved in a dispute over tax abatements. For two years another member of town, John Skinner, persisted in "Charging Scandalous Lying upon them." Skinner felt that the Leonards provided untruthful testimony at a court in Bristol, Rhode Island. As a result of this tension between himself and the powerful Leonards, Skinner registered his unwillingness to have the Lord's Supper sullied by "renouncing and abstaining from the Communion of the Church at Norton [for] about 2 years." Skinner was so enraged that he "declared His Resolution not to return to the Communion except they would Censure madam Leonard for Lying." A ministerial council, called in to settle this dispute, looked with extreme disfavor on Skinner's abstention from the Lord's Supper, which the council saw as merely "making trouble among them."[124] The council did not see, in fact could not see, that Skinner's remove from the Table represented not a desire to make trouble, but an interpretation of the Lord's Supper as a ritual of social integration. A lack of harmony among the participants profaned the ritual. Until his quarrel with Leonard—which originated in a secular tax court—could be settled, Skinner would remain separated from the church.

Similarly, in Ipswich in 1754, an earthly dispute became a rent in the holy fabric of the community. Jane Barnum, involved with her sister in a name-calling quarrel, withdrew from the Lord's Supper on April 14. This unsisterly controversy arose because Barnum's sister, the Widow Ruth Belcher, called Barnum the "Whore and Strum" of John Cogswell, Jr. In this case, unlike that in Norton, those passing judgment on the propriety of this withdrawal were Barnum's fellow lay members of the church. They voted "that the Reasons which Jane the Wife of Benjamin Barnum has given for absenting her self from the Sacrament of the Supper the 14th of last April so far good that the Church judge her excusable."[125] In this case laypeople agreed that a person should not attend the Lord's Supper when involved in a bitter family controversy.

Another conflict between laypeople that had ramifications for ritual practice occurred in Isaac Backus's Titicut parish between two church members, John Hayward and Esther Fobes. This ugly dispute lasted for almost three years and was conducted with a rancor that belied its petty beginnings. In October 1756, Hayward was called to a church meeting to explain why he had withdrawn himself from communion. His reason, on which he refused to elaborate, was that he was involved in a dispute with Fobes. After a few more meetings Hayward finally explained the problem: his wife had lent Fobes "a thimble, some pins, needles, thread, etc." and they had not been returned. Hayward did not see this as merely an oversight on Fobes's part; he accused her of being under the "government of a Covetous and dishonest principle." Fobes denied the charges, and the controversy continued in like fashion for almost three more years.[126] Significantly, a minor affair, centering on some needles and thread, could disrupt the ritual practice of a congregation. To the anguish of Backus, the three years during which this controversy simmered were times of spiritual difficulties for his church. Despite numerous meetings and even a day of fasting and prayer, Backus could not heal the divisions in his church. For laypeople, coming together at the Lord's Supper necessitated Christian fellowship; in its absence, they preferred to disrupt ritual practice rather than profane the feast.

Usually the Lord's Supper helped cement the ties of religious community. But conflicts did occasionally arise over the meaning of communion. When this happened, the dispute often revolved around the ritual's performative aspects. While ministers believed in the importance of participation in the ritual, they stressed equally the preparation for the ritual that occurred in the days prior to a sacrament Sunday. Like their ministers, laypeople felt that participation in the ritual was important, but they also believed that the Lord's Supper gained significance from the performance of community integration on the stage into which ritual transformed the meetinghouse. When there was conflict within this religious community, laypeople sometimes used the Lord's Supper symbolically to dramatize their dispute. Instead of using the ritual as a means of reconciliation, as their pastors wished, laypeople used the ritual to seal a reconciliation already gained. Thus, the Lord's Supper was the religious ritual most likely to generate contention.

Rituals could both bring a community together in a moment of social integration and serve as the stage on which community tensions were played out. Likewise, people interpreted a ritual both as a zone of comfort and a zone of danger. In the reading of conversion narratives, people found their religious self-constructions legitimized, both individually and collectively. This ritual was generally not controversial, partly because of the degree of ministerial control. It therefore was the ritual most constitutive of community. In contrast, baptism occasionally served to engender conflict within the pedobaptist community. For laypeople in general and women in particular, baptism protected children from damnation. Baptism's implications were subject to interpretive disputes among laypeople and between laypeople and their ministers, largely centered on the ritual's efficacy. Finally, participants considered the Lord's Supper the most powerful ordinance of the church. This power caused ambivalent feelings and led to a number of quarrels over the ritual's meaning, making it the most contentious religious ritual. Communion's power also presented laypeople with a potent weapon when they wanted to dramatize their anger with their minister. With so much at stake in the realm of social integration, most laypeople refused to attend the Lord's Supper when their community's fabric was torn. Although ministers urged them to mend the rent as quickly as possible, most laypeople felt that their disputes were not so easily patched. While ministers hoped to use the Lord's Supper as a means of reconciliation, laypeople insisted on using it only as a seal thereof. If reading conversion narratives was a way to create community, with optimism and high hopes, and baptism a source of protection for the religious community, then the Lord's Supper reflected the hard work of community and the potential for differences over fundamental and powerful issues.

Religious rituals were a volatile combination of liminality, multivalent text, and efficacious speech and gesture. Combined with the gender tensions of the period and the growing distance between laity and clergy, rituals embodied the potential for disruption. Although pious laypeople—as opposed to those heterodox individuals examined in the following chapter—participated in rituals that their ministers approved and conducted, they occasionally chose to interpret these rituals in their own way. If ministers controlled some ideas about ritual, laypeople added others, most notably about the protection of their children and Christ's real presence in communion. Ultimately, religious rituals in colonial New England were more than arenas for creating and maintaining community. They were, in addition, sites where alternate interpretations of religion could be ritually performed.

CHAPTER FOUR

Alternative Practices

Magic, Heterodoxy, and the Margins of Religious Culture

*I*N THE SPRING OF 1755 Robert Keyes's young daughter disappeared without a trace. Despite the efforts of "Hundreds of men" who searched forest and field in Westborough, the girl could not be found. Sympathetic to the terror of losing a child, Keyes's neighbor, Thomas Smith, went to a "Wise-Man," one "Williams Wood a blacksmith in Scituate nigh Providence," to find out where the girl might be. When Ebenezer Parkman found out about this recourse to magic he was extremely upset. Four days later, on the first chance he had, Parkman preached a sermon "against the foolish and wicked practice of going to Cunning Men to enquire for lost Things."[1]

This example demonstrates both lay use of and ministerial response to magic in the eighteenth century. In this period it seems that most lay magical practice was "white magic," which aimed to discover lost articles or tell the future rather than injure an enemy. These practices were embedded within people's ordinary activities. We can imagine that Smith did not make the sixty-five-mile round trip to Scituate merely to visit the "Wise-Man." More likely he had business that took him in that direction anyway, and like a person on a sojourn delivering a letter for a friend, Smith used the opportunity of his journey to consult a man he had perhaps visited before or whose reputation he had learned of from neighbors. In any case, Smith would have understood, even without Parkman's lecture, that ministerial opinion squarely opposed such practices. In the eighteenth century there was no ambiguity on that score, as was reflected in Parkman's sermon. Significantly, Parkman was not content with privately admonishing Smith, but found it necessary to devote an entire sermon to the wickedness of consulting wise men. Parkman believed that Smith was not an isolated example, but rather reflected a tendency all too common among his parishioners.

This chapter examines those beliefs and practices that fell completely outside the eighteenth-century ministerial definition of orthodox. These included on the one hand magical and quasi-magical behaviors and on the other religious views that ministers considered heterodox. These beliefs and practices, more than any others, show the space available in colonial society for the creation and maintenance of alternative (and in some cases resistant) world views. When laypeople consulted fortune-tellers or became followers of charismatic heterodox leaders who claimed to be immortal, they participated in activities that ministers would have banned if they could. The examples in this chapter demonstrate that some laypeople contributed clerically condemned ideas to the religious culture.

Magic

Historians have generally paid more attention to the rise of Enlightenment ideas in the eighteenth century than to the persistence of magical beliefs.[2] Those scholars who do examine the occult in the eighteenth century demonstrate that magical practice retained numerous adherents, though the number of participants may have declined from earlier periods. Studies of magic, and especially witchcraft, in seventeenth-century New England are much more common.[3] Richard Godbeer argues that reformed Protestantism's ambiguous doctrines allowed for widespread use of magic in the seventeenth century. Furthermore, the clerical opinion that permitted astrology so long as it did not predict human affairs was a distinction too fine for some to make. According to Godbeer, the affinities between orthodox religion and magic enabled laypeople to switch from one to the other "without any sense of wrongdoing."[4]

This was no longer true in the eighteenth century. As the result of a late-seventeenth-century ministerial campaign against magic and the increasing acceptance of Enlightenment rationality among more educated classes, those who used magic in the eighteenth century were aware that their social "betters" considered their practices wrong. Indeed, practitioners of magic understood that their actions were resistant to the dominant religious culture.

This point modifies Jon Butler's concept of the "folklorization" of magic. Butler argues that in the eighteenth century "colonial magic and occultism did not so much disappear everywhere as they disappeared among certain social classes and became confined to poorer, more marginal segments of early American society."[5] This was largely true.[6] I do not agree, however, that magic's confinement to "people of minimal importance" made it seem "quaint" to "magistrates and ministers."[7] In fact, magic continued throughout the eighteenth century to be a source of power struggles between the clergy and some laypeople. The attention ordinary people paid to magic in the eighteenth century reveals not their powerlessness but rather their ability to shape religious culture. With such great social pressures urging people to abstain from magic, magical practice was not merely a colorful vestige of an earlier age. Rather, it was opposition to ministerial teachings in its most obvious form.

In the history of magic since the Reformation, such a situation did not always obtain. At least some magical practice in sixteenth- and seventeenth-century England resulted from inadequate penetration of clerical teachings into the culture of uneducated laypeople.[8] Ministers sometimes had difficulty reaching all the people of rural England with the message that magical practice and orthodox religion were incompatible. But Tudor-Stuart England was a very different place than eighteenth-century New England. From its beginnings, New England had been both more literate than England[9] and more religiously fervent. One can say with assurance that no laypeople in New England were ignorant of the clergy's stand on magical practice, especially after the increased ministerial attacks on magic in the 1680s and 1690s.[10]

There were, however, activities that were less clearly problematic, which I have labeled quasi-magical. This term denotes beliefs and practices on the boundary between magic and science. In the eighteenth century this encompassed the fears of sounds and natural events that seemed to be the work of spirits, and the nonmagical (or not strictly magical) remedies used to combat these fears. These cases were borderline because they were rooted in the "world of wonders," the belief that unusual occurrences in the natural world had supernatural significance. Laity and clergy shared these beliefs (though clerical belief in the world of wonders declined in the eighteenth century); indeed, Increase and Cotton Mather were two of the most dedicated interpreters of wonders in colonial New England.[11]

Laypeople often interpreted extraordinary meteorological and astrological events as signs of heavenly displeasure. Typical was lay reaction to the comet that appeared in night skies in January 1744. As Ebenezer Parkman noted, "the Thoughts and Conversation of People Seem to be very much engross'd by the Appearing and Continuance of the Comet in the West." This attention paid to the comet was not limited to laypeople: Parkman wrote in his diary, "I desire it may put me in Mind of the Greatness, Glory and Power, and the wisdom and So great Dominion of the infinite God whose works these are." But sometimes ministers felt that laypeople could become overly obsessed with these phenomena. Later that month Parkman received a letter from his brother Samuel relating that Samuel's wife was "destracted about the Comet."[12] The word "distracted" had connotations of madness; Parkman used it to indicate he felt his sister-in-law's reaction was excessive. Similarly, in 1734, when Hannah Heaton was thirteen, she viewed the northern lights for the first time. This dramatic natural phenomenon frightened Heaton: "About half the orrisen [horizon] loockt red like blood, I was in dreadful distress of soul, I was afraid christ was a coming to judgment, my flesh burnt as if I were in a scorching fever."[13]

By the mid to late eighteenth century, men of science became increasingly skeptical about the world of wonders as experienced by people like Hannah Heaton. These men, influenced by and part of the Enlightenment, opined that ordinary people's reactions to natural occurrences reflected an unhealthy superstition. John Perkins, a physician born in Boston and educated in London, reported the case of one Meeds of Lynnfield, a young man who in 1773 was "melancholly & greatly Nervous at the New Moons for a long Time."[14] This struck Perkins as a strange belief since new moons occurred regularly and were clearly an ordinary part of the natural world. In a similar manner the self-described "gentleman" Nathan Bowen of Marblehead looked down upon ordinary people's quasi-magical beliefs. In 1742 he reported that "we are now full of apprehension about a High Tide which Some body has given out to be many feet higher than Common on the 25 Instant. Alas how prone are the Common people to Superstition, its in the power of any designing man to Turn their heads as he pleases." Fifteen years later, on the date of an expected solar eclipse, Bowen noted that the eclipse did not cause a great deal of darkness and must have been rather slight. Nonetheless, this extraordinary occurrence, which took place on a Sunday, caused "an alarm, in time of Afternoon Service, to the greate Terror of the Old Women of both sex's."[15] In both of these instances Bowen displayed the newly fashionable upper-class contempt for ordinary people's quasi-magical world view, in the second example gendering his criticism rather unsubtly. For the rational gentlemen of Enlightenment New England, belief in the portentous character of natural phenomena marked one as "common" and "old": uneducated and hence effeminate vestiges of an earlier benighted period.

Even more frightening to many laypeople than natural phenomena were seemingly unnatural events. For example, in 1753 Elisha Brown of Gloucester hanged himself in his house. A week after this suicide Rev. Samuel Chandler visited with the widow because the whole family had "quit'd the House by reason of some noises &c & fears of Spectres &c."[16] It took all of Chandler's persuasive powers to convince Widow Brown and her family that their fears were unfounded. Strange noises were the root of another woman's fears in Westfield. In 1762 Rev. John Ballantine wrote in his diary that "Esq. Moseley informs me that he heard 3 distinct raps of the West end of the house. They were heard by himself and Wife 3 nights in succession, his Wife was very much terrified."[17] Perhaps Esquire Moseley underplayed his own terror when relating this incident to his minister; certainly he felt it important enough a story to confide in his clergyman. Again, these were borderline incidents. Whereas Chandler expressed consternation at the credence the widow and her family gave to the noises, Ballantine was less dismissive, perhaps due to his own personal demons.[18]

Thus, quasi-magical activities sometimes had the support of orthodox New Englanders. Nine times in his diary Samuel Sewall reported driving a nail or pin into a corner beam of a new building.[19] Although he never explicitly stated why he did this, presumably it offered the new structure some degree of protection. But though it had "roots in pagan folklore,"[20] this custom did not seem to arouse the ire of ministers. In fact, most of the buildings Sewall thus protected were meetinghouses, and in one case in 1716 it seems that Sewall drove his pin next to that of a minister: "I went over to Charlestown in the morn, and drave a Pin in Charlestown Meetinghouse, in the Corner-post next [Rev.] Mr. Bradstreet's."[21] Although the phrasing is ambiguous, it seems that Sewall's nail was next to Rev. Simon Bradstreet's nail. In any case, evidence survives of at least one minister driving a nail for good luck. In 1759 John Ballantine recorded that he "went to the Meeting house to see the repairs, drove a nail, as they phrase it."[22] Ballantine's words "as they phrase it" suggest he did not customarily perform this act but did not frown upon it. Perhaps in the eighteenth century ministers and laypeople agreed that driving a nail was a harmless vestige of an earlier tradition, like an atheist today saying "Bless you" when a person sneezes.

More troubling than driving a nail for luck was the use of religious forms in an incantatory, quasi-magical way to protect a new building. Parkman reported in 1747 that a woman hoped to use a sermon for protective purposes: "Mary Bradish here, about having a Sermon at her House when she first goes into it. But we agree that the Private Meeting which is appointed to be at her Fathers next week be at her House, which is close by, to avoid Superstition and Ostentation."[23] Parkman was troubled by this woman's desire, apparently based on a folk belief in the protective powers of a minister's formally intoned words, to have Parkman deliver a sermon to protect her new house—perhaps from the kinds of noises that so terrified Widow Brown and Esquire Moseley's wife. Parkman convinced Bradish that a private meeting of church members would more suitably signify the community's collective recognition of her new abode.

If these fears and remedies were on the border of ministerially sanctioned practices, other practices were more clearly magical and roundly condemned by the clergy. Despite clerical admonitions, some people persisted in magical practices as a relatively simple and seemingly effective way to gain power. The use of astrology to predict human affairs was one such practice, one that probably declined in the eighteenth century. In general, ministers' position regarding astrology was ambivalent. Learned opinion accepted "natural astrology," the very common use of the position of the stars and planets to help determine weather and planting information, but frowned upon "judicial astrology," the belief that heavenly bodies controlled the actions and decisions of individuals.[24] Thus, the large number of astrological almanacs bought in early New England were generally not heterodox, since these popular and inexpensive little books were essentially compendia of natural astrology.

More disturbing to ministers would have been the judicial astrology performed by Joseph Stafford of Tiverton, Rhode Island, from the 1730s through the 1760s. Stafford, who used his divining powers to bring in extra income, kept receipts of the money locals owed him for his magical activities. These practices included divining whether someone's "sea Voyag" was going to be safe, telling three men's fortunes, and hunting "for treasures hid by Indians."[25]

Further evidence of judicial astrology is found in the family record kept by Christopher and Elizabeth Champlin of Westerly, Rhode Island. The Champlins' record was probably kept in an almanac:

> The ages of their children
> Christopher was born Nov the 30th 32 min past 7 in the morning 1707. ♂
> Joseph was born Aug the 4th: 1709 at 8 o'clock in the morning. ☉
> Elijah was born July the 20th 1711. Died Feb the 18th 1712–13.
> Ann was born March the 29th: 1714. Planetary hour ♂
> George was born Feb 15th 1716. Planetary hour ☿
> Elizabeth was born Jan 10th 1718–19. Planetary hour ♀
> Thankful was born March 27th 1721. Planetary hour ♂ Died Oct the 22nd 1725.
> Lydia was born Nov the 19th 1723. Planetary hour ♀ Died Oct the 10th 1725.
> Elijah was born May the 23–1726. Planetary hour ♃ Died March the 10th 1729.

Jabez was born Aug the 31st 1728 on the 7th day of the week.

Oliver was born May the 12th 1730 on the 3rd day of the week.

Mary was born June the 29th 1731 on the 3rd day of the week at 6 o'clock in the morning.[26]

The only reason the Champlins could have had for noting the planetary hour of the births of their children was a belief in judicial astrology. Given such detailed records it seems likely that they brought their children to local astrologers to get a horoscope or "nativity," in which the child's life course was mapped out through an analysis of planetary alignment at the child's moment of birth. Interestingly, the Champlins did not record their last three children's planetary hours. It is tempting to speculate that the ministerial campaign against judicial astrology finally induced this family to abandon magic. But it is also possible that the family found their local astrologer to be unreliable, maybe after he or she predicted long lives for Thankful, Lydia, and Elijah, all of whom died before the age of four.

Questions of life and death were inextricably bound up with lay magical practice. As a result, some of the most common magical practices concerned healing. In *Angel of Bethesda*, a treatise on medicine finished in 1724 but never published, Cotton Mather described and condemned lay magical healing practices. According to Mather, some people believed in a magical power derived from birth order: "We have a Fancy among our Common People, That a Seventh Son, among Brethren that have not had a Sister born between them, is endued with I know not what, *Power of Healing* Various Distempers, with a Touch of his Hand upon the Part affected." While some laypeople relied on a magical touch from a specially endowed person, others found written words to be effective. Mather complained, "How frequently is *Bleeding* Stancht, by writing of Something, with Some Ceremonies, on the Forehead! How frequently is a *Toothache* Eas'd, and an *Ulcer* Stop'd, and an *Ague* Check'd, by Papers, with some *Terms* and *Scrawls* in them, sealed up and worn about the Neck."[27] Though Mather decried these resorts to "Unlawful Fellowship with the Invisible World," he was unable to stop them. Laypeople understood ministerial contempt of such practices but some chose to persist in them, probably because standard medicine was often ineffective.

The other common forms of white magic unraveled mysterious secrets, both of the present and future. As in the example that began this chapter, people went to cunning men and women to learn the location of lost items and to find treasure. In a 1729 satire of popular magic, Benjamin Franklin wrote about astrologers, "with whom the Country swarms at this Time." Treasure seekers consulted these people "about the critical Times for Digging, the Methods of laying the Spirit, and the like Whimseys, which renders them very necessary to and very much caress'd by the poor deluded *Money-hunters.*"[28] These magical practitioners were not all of equal repute; Nathaniel Ames warned in his 1752 almanac "that Cunning Men are not always honest; trust them as you have tried them."[29]

Though the target of frequent clerical attacks, fortune-tellers remained popular throughout the eighteenth century. When Increase and Cotton Mather learned of two women who consulted a medium in 1694, they moved quickly to question the women in front of the church. According to the church records, "Two young Women, belonging to our Communion, to wit, Re-beckah Adams, & Alice Pennel, having been found guilty of consulting an ungodly fortune-teller, in the Neighbourhood, with desires to be informed of some secret & future things, this Day in public made a penitent Acknowledgment of that miscarriage, & so their Church reconciled unto them."[30] Coming so soon after the Salem witchcraft episode, this incident must have seemed like a greater threat than usual. Someone with even more cause to worry about the aftermath of Salem was Rev. Joseph Green, the minister in Salem Village who began his tenure in 1697. Twice in 1702 Green felt it necessary to preach against divination.[31] Although it is not known if this divination involved an African-American conjurer, ten years after the witchcraft in which a woman of color, Tituba, played such a large role, another case a few years later did: "A Boston justice of the peace, John Clark, committed an African servant girl to the house of correction for fortune-telling in 1709."[32] This hints at a dynamic largely invisible to historians but likely common at the time: white laypeople seeking knowledge of the future consulted slaves and free blacks who practiced African forms of divination.[33] One historian has argued that "almost half" of the diviners in New England before 1850 were "African Americans, Native Americans, or those of mixed ancestry."[34]

These examples from the period shortly after Salem were repeated throughout the century. In fact, Salem Village was again the site of a dispute over fortune-telling as late as 1746, when a group of church members reported that several people in the parish had "resorted to a woman of very ill reputation, pretending to the art of divination and fortune-telling, &c." These pious laypeople asked their minister to preach about "their disapprobation and abhorrence of this infamous and ungodly practice of consulting witches or fortune-tellers, or any that are reputed such."[35] Not all laypeople were attracted to magic; those who considered themselves godly church members generally disapproved of such activities. Practitioners of magic were often marginalized people: women, people of color, the elderly. Such was the opinion of Rev. Ezra Stiles, who believed in 1773 that magic was a thing of the past, except that "some old Women (Midwives) affect it." Stiles's example was seventy-year-old Granny Morgan of Newport, Rhode Island, who accustomed herself "to a hocus pocus, & making Cakes of flour and her own Urine and sticking them full of pins and divining by them."[36] Thus, eighteenth-century magic revolved around the desire for power. Those laypeople who consulted the Granny Morgans of New England attempted to learn the secrets of the future, a practice strictly forbidden by their ministers that nonetheless held great allure; the practitioners of white magic thereby gained power, in the form of respect, attention, and money.

This dynamic was yet more apparent for those who practiced the more feared arts of maleficium, or black magic. Unfortunately for the historian, since there were no witchcraft convictions in eighteenth-century New England, there are no court records to document black magic; extant evidence is mostly rumor and suspicion. For example, Rev. David Hall reported in his diary in 1745, "I have a strange account of some appearance of witchcraft in Woodstock & some places."[37] Hall did not elaborate on the rumors he heard. Likewise, John Perkins, a doctor in Maine, remembered some years later that "the common people that way [i.e., Maine] haveing been seiz'd with such things were a little too whymsical, they told of of a place or two that were ha[u]nted."[38]

Despite their brevity, these rumors could reveal how marginalized people used maleficium to gain power. In 1723 Rev. William Waldron related the following account in a letter to his brother:

> There is a story started in Town of a certain woman who is suspected of witchery. Tis certain that there are Two Men that have been unaccountably harrassed and disturbed in their Business att Sea, by cross winds, and unsuccessfull attempts, one man they putt a shore at Marthas Vineyard, he was strangely taken with a Deadness on one side of Him, they dispaired of his Life, but when they had ridded the Vessell of him they sett sail with a pleasing Gale but it was observable that all the time this man was on board the wind was right ahead so that they determined that he was the action that troubled the Sloop, he is since come to Town. The occassion of the suspicion is some Threatening speech which the old woman used when this mans wife dismissed her from their House for she was a boarder with them . . . Now you may believe if you please or may lett it alone.[39]

Whether the learned minister and his brother believed in this woman's powers, enough people in the town were convinced to keep the story alive. Again, the suspected witch was an old woman who stepped out of aged women's ordinary position to threaten those who had power over her, in this case her landlords. The townspeople believed that this old woman had the ability to gain revenge through black magic, and she probably did nothing to dispel their beliefs. Kicked out of her residence, this old woman may have found it useful to have the reputation of someone who should be treated kindly.

Another case demonstrates that a woman who sought to achieve power through gender inversion could be accused of witchcraft. This occurred in 1725 in Kittery, Maine, when weaver John Spinney publicly accused an old widow named Sarah Keene of being "a Damn'd witch." Keene sued Spinney for slander but lost the case in the Court of General Sessions of the Peace. Many of Keene's neighbors suspected that she was a witch: in depositions they asserted that she could transport her victims a great distance before injuring them, that she once inflicted bodily harm on someone by striking at the fire in a hearth, and that a third nipple indicated her association with the Devil. But in addition to these conventional descriptions is evidence of tension about Keene's tendency to invert ordinary gender relations. Paul Williams, one of Keene's neighbors, described a scene that added to Keene's reputation as a woman who transgressed societal bounds. The previous month, Williams had been at Keene's house with Spinney. The suspected witch and Spinney were "having Some Difference" when Keene, "haveing a Bridle in her hand Said She Could not find her mare and She Would Ride the Said John Spinney Down to Collonel Pepperells." Keene's daughter Esther then joined in mocking Spinney, "Saying She would make the head of the Bridle Shorter and fit it for Said Spinneys head, and ride him her Selfe."[40] Sarah Keene symbolically strove to set herself on top of her male harasser in an inversion of gender relations, an act that eventually caused a court to declare that a witchcraft accusation was not slanderous.

Others attempted to gain their ends by exploiting the fear of witchcraft and the penchant for spreading rumors in eighteenth-century New England.[41] One example occurred in 1718, when a man accused his mother of witchcraft before the church in Milton, Massachusetts. This man attempted to besmirch his mother's reputation, knowing that rumors of witchcraft circulated far and wide in his largely oral society. But his plan to manipulate popular opinion backfired, and he was charged with violating the fifth, sixth, and ninth commandments.[42]

Some people tried to gain attention and power by pretending to be bewitched, like the girls who were the primary accusers in Salem in 1692. An example from 1720 comes from a long manuscript written by Rev. Ebenezer

Turell of Medford but never published in his lifetime. In Littleton three young sisters aged five, nine, and eleven for eight months exhibited behaviors that made them seem bewitched. The eldest, Elizabeth Blanchard, not only tore her clothes and bit and spit upon those who tried to help her, but also engaged in magical practices. As Turell described, "she made an unlawful use of sieves, eggs, and other things, to shew tricks and tell futurities; a practice which many foolish people run into."[43] The three girls accused a local woman of "afflicting" them, and as soon as this woman died the strange behaviors of the girls ceased. Turell learned the details of this story because Elizabeth confessed to him a decade or so later that the guilt of having deceived her family and neighbors continued to torment her.

The significance of this example is revealed in laypeople's reactions to the girls' behavior. Jon Butler uses this case to show how local response "turned a modern corner" because people did not try to execute the suspected witch. Butler argues that this case reveals "the approach of modern sensibilities in an obscure prerevolutionary colonial village."[44] But the events in Littleton offer evidence of these people's distinctly early modern sensibilities. In this oral culture the case attracted wide notice, and the news of it "presently took air, and spread about the neighborhood, and also reached many places at a considerable distance; many went to visit them." Turell related the townspeople's views about the causes of the girls' actions, which reveal that most people suspected maleficium. According to Turell:

> some thought they labored of bodily maladies; others that their minds were disordered . . . Others, from some of their actions, (which were silly enough,) thought them to be underwitted; others that they were perverse and wicked children. But so far as I can learn, the greater number thought and said they were under an evil hand, or possessed by satan.

Indeed, many "seemed fully persuaded the children were bewitched." The eldest girl told Turell a story that portrays the locals not as people at the dawn of the Enlightenment but at the tail end a period populated by witches practicing the black arts:

> Elizabeth told me she once in company pinched her forehead, and then immediately complained of a violent pain in her head, and desired one to hold it, which was done; and all the while the person held it she complained she was pinched, and when the hand was taken away the plain mark of a pinch appeared, which confirmed her being bewitched to all present.[45]

No one thought to ask Elizabeth if she had pinched herself, a question that now seems obvious. But many people believed witchcraft caused physical harm they could not otherwise explain. Elizabeth and her sisters perceived this, which allowed them to gain attention by pretending to be bewitched.

Turell's use of this case as a caution against dabbling in magic reveals the extent of occult practices. Turell warned, "Young people would do wisely now to lay aside all their foolish books, their trifling ballads, and all romantick accounts of dreams and trances, senseless palmistry and groundless astrology." He also cautioned young people against trying to learn the secrets of the future, urging them, "never use any of the devil's playthings; there are much better recreations than legerdemain tricks. Turn not the sieve, &c. to know futurities." Turell's advice was not aimed merely at the youthful. For adults he offered,

> The horse shoe is a vain thing, and has no natural tendency to keep off witches or evil spirits from the houses or vessels they are nailed too [*sic*] . . . 'Tis an evil thing to hang witch papers on the neck for the cure of the agues, to bind up the weapon insted of the wound, and many things of the like nature, which some in the world are fond of.[46]

Turell repeated the typical ministerial injunctions against magically trying to protect oneself from witches or disease. Ultimately, the case of Elizabeth Blanchard and her sisters reveals on the one hand three girls manipulating the popular susceptibility to believe accusations of witchcraft and on the other hand a minister trying to use the case to further the clerical cause against lay interest in the occult.

The Littleton case is exemplary also in its demonstration of ministerial watchfulness for cases of witchcraft. Throughout the eighteenth century members of the clergy remained on the lookout for practitioners of magic and opportunities to inveigh against their activities. It is apparent in the following letter that ministers talked among themselves about cases of witchcraft, perhaps to demonstrate to their colleagues that they were vigilant regarding magic. In this letter from Rev. Eleazer Wheelock to Rev. Stephen Williams in 1737, Wheelock mentioned a story told by Thomas Clap, the future president of Yale. "It is common talk at Windham," wrote Wheelock, "that old Goody Fullsom . . . is a W—ch & indeed there are many Stories which Mr. Clap has told me of her that Look very Dark."[47] Similarly, in the middle of the eighteenth century Rev. Josiah Cotton observed that "there are but few towns, if any, but at one time or other have not had one or more in suspicion for witchcraft, as if the place were not complete in its inhabitants without some well-versed in that occupation." Although Cotton's words imply that suspicion of witchcraft remained widespread in the eighteenth century, when ministers discovered it in their parishes they continued to remark on it and attempt to suppress it, as in this example from Hopkinton, New Hampshire:

> there were at least two great witches in town. They were "witch Webber" and "witch Burbank" . . . It were impossible to tell how much harm might have resulted from witchcraft in Hopkinton, had it not been for the Rev. Elijah Fletcher. He was minister of the town from 1773 to 1786. When "witchcraft" threatened the community, he referred the matter to Rev. Timothy Walker of Concord. The Rev. Mr. Walker told the people that "the most they had to fear from witches was from talking about them; that if they would cease talking about them and let them alone they would soon disappear."[48]

This shows ministers collaborating against the specter of witchcraft in their parishes. However, Walker's condescending advice merely to ignore the suspected witches could not have been very comforting to those laypeople who feared the witches' malevolent powers. Cases such as this, with ministers revealing how fundamentally out of step they were with their parishioners who believed in magic, probably led numerous laypeople to continue to use countermagic against the power of suspected witches.

One final example demonstrates the power of witches in the eighteenth century, and especially how magic could be used to increase the power of women and the elderly. John Perkins, whom we have already met, had an attitude toward magic typical of the educated in the late eighteenth century. This world view allowed for the possibility of supernatural occurrences, but held that common people were too apt to ascribe magical causes to events that could be explained rationally by science. In his memoirs, written in 1777, Perkins offered several examples of witchcraft that he had been careful to examine rationally, searching for natural explanations to no avail. In his descriptions of these cases he "took all possible care not to be in any part of them mistaken, and in relating them shall take the same care not to exagerate or inhance the ideas."[49]

One such event occurred in 1722, when Perkins was a surgeon to the troops waging war against the Indians in Maine. At this time Perkins was staying in a large fortified house where eleven families had sought refuge from the Indians. According to Perkins, "in one of the apartments was a Woman who had many years been reputed a dealer in Witchcraft and frequently charg'd with injuring such as any ways offended her." One day this woman interrupted Perkins, who was in the middle of treating another patient, and told him of her "great pains and lameness," which Perkins took to be rheumatic, and "for which she desir'd me to give her some medicinal relief." Perkins thought it would be easiest and cheapest for her to pick some herbs and apply them herself, but this "she declin'd doing and insisted on my giving her something of my own medicines." This exchange grew ever testier, until Perkins gave up in anger and murmured, "the woman is a simpleton." As he began to leave he heard her say, "Better you had not said so." Wondering what she meant Perkins turned to find two men who had witnessed the scene, one of whom, Nathaniel Wheelwright, said, "I am sorry Doctor you had any words with her for she will certainly serve you some ugly trick." The young man of science, however, could not be bothered with such foolishness, and breezily dismissed Wheelwright: "if she does, she does; but I am not concerned about it." Perkins promptly forgot the incident and went about his rounds.

That night Perkins went to sleep at eleven o'clock and locked his door as usual. Just as he was falling asleep he heard some strange noises, like a person walking barefoot outside his door and "jumbling" with his lock. By the light of a nearly full moon he could see that nothing was in his room when suddenly his candlestick was thrown off the chair by his bed. Frightened, he got up and looked around but nothing seemed amiss, until he spied "a number of bright spots struck up on the Chimney Back, two of them as big as the top of a large coffee-Cup, others as big as english Crowns, shillings, &c." Putting these strange lights to a scientific test in order to "know whether any foreign light could shine in" Perkins "pass'd two or three times close to the chimney acrose from the fireplace but nothing altered them." Lighting his candle he "found nothing in the room but a Cat under the bed, try'd to frighten her out but she would not goe; on this looking about found a Curtain Rod standing up in a corner of the room and design'd to give it a swoop under the bed to drive her out, but saw no more of her." Significantly, Perkins assumed that this cat, an animal long associated with witches, was female. He may have thought it was the witch in spectral form.

Perkins's night of horrors continued with more strange sounds and violent crashes, until he finally decided to leave. His final observation came when "a great spot, as big as a hat crown, & near as bright as the moon, started up on the front Wal of the Room. I put on my cloathes & took a turn near it to see if it was any thing natural, which it evidently was not." Perkins could take it no longer: "I went down with as little noise as possible not to disturb any bodie, took my horse & rod[e] a mile and half to another garrison'd house where I was acquainted, the Watch let me in and thus for the present ended this unlucky affair."

This strange night reveals a number of dynamics typical to the eighteenth century. Witches in this period were more likely than their earlier counterparts to be engaged (or suspected to be engaged) in what might be called "mischief," relatively harmless tricks, rather than maleficium, which typically included bodily harm.[50] In addition, this case demonstrates the attitude of an educated layperson toward magic: a degree of skepticism and a desire to debunk most suspected cases of witchcraft, but ultimately a willingness to accept as supernatural events subjected to rigorous scientific scrutiny. Most importantly, this example shows how an old woman, doubly marginalized by her society and unable even to receive adequate medical care, was able to use magic (and the threat thereof) to increase her power. Nathaniel Wheelwright and the other residents of this garrison knew of this woman's powers and probably did their best to avoid angering her. Indeed, Wheelwright expressed his sorrow that the doctor had unwittingly had an exchange with this powerful woman. Although in an earlier period the suspicion of witchcraft could find a woman hanging dead from the gallows, such was no longer the case post-Salem. An old woman could use her reputation as a dealer in magic to gain some respect, some power, and some medicine the next time she asked the doctor for it.

Overall, magical practice in eighteenth-century New England sought to answer questions of life and death, healing and protection. Not all laypeople turned to magic; some helped their ministers root out those who turned to conjurers and cunning men and magical healers. Others, like Samuel Sewall, engaged in practices such as driving a nail for luck or hanging a horseshoe over a doorway that were vestiges of an age of more widespread use of magic. But these quasi-magical activities—like the four-leaf clover I carry in my wallet—usually reflect more of an unthinking nod to the past rather than a conscious decision that a particular nail would have any real effect. Still others, in conscious opposition to the teachings of every minister in New England, employed the talents of or were themselves judicial astrologers, diviners, or conjurers. In the eighteenth century these people increasingly came from the lower strata of society. Despite the association of magic and marginalized groups, power struggles over magic persisted throughout the century. Ministers continued to see magic as a threat to orthodox religious belief, and some laypeople persevered in practicing magic in direct opposition to their ministers' teachings. Ultimately those who used magic—often women, the aged, people of color, and the poor—sought empowerment, whether that entailed finding, learning, protecting, or retaliating. Ministers spoke out against such practices and tried to offer their own version of empowerment

through orthodox religion. They were, to be sure, at least partially successful, but ministers could never fully eliminate lay recourse to magic.

Heterodoxy

Philip Gura, in his incisive account of early New England radicalism, argues
that seventeenth-century religious radicals came relatively close to creating
a commonwealth that conformed to their utopian ideals. Unlike their contemporaries in England, "New England's radical Puritans at least had
glimpsed Sion's glory."[51] If so, those who were religiously heterodox in the
eighteenth century not only glimpsed but gazed upon Sion's glory in all its
dazzling beauty.[52] According to Gura's model, there was a sharp disjuncture
between the radicals of the early seventeenth century, like Anne Hutchinson
and Samuel Gorton, and those of the post–Great Awakening period who are
examined in this section, Richard Woodbury and Sarah Prentice. Gura argues
that although never eliminated by the guardians of orthodoxy, "between
1660 and 1735 those who spoke for the traditions of Puritan radicalism were
driven underground."[53] Though heterodoxy declined between the Restoration and the Awakening, Woodbury and Prentice were the legacy of a tradition not as buried from view as Gura asserts.

Between 1660 and 1735, heterodox beliefs and practices occasionally sur-
faced. Perhaps more apt than Gura's underground metaphor is to describe
heterodoxy in this period as unorganized. Without charismatic leaders to
follow, those who expressed heterodox opinions did so individually, which
generally made these people easier for ministers to control. In 1698 Samuel
Sewall noted the death of John Ive, "a very debauched, atheistical man."[54]
Although Sewall did not elaborate on Ive's beliefs, they so clashed with orthodoxy that Sewall refused to attend Ive's funeral, even though he was the
son of a prominent Boston man. Similarly, Rev. John Comer, while minister
at Newport in 1727, encountered a man with heterodox views. The day after
Comer preached a sermon from Ezekiel 33:11, this Mr. Hull came to discuss
the sermon with Comer, who discovered that Hull "much faulted my sermon" and "was a very strange-principled man, and upon discourse I found
him a sad and dreadful *Antinomian*."[55] Like Sewall, Comer did not elaborate
on this heterodox man's theological views, but it is possible to speculate about
them. Ezekiel 33:11 contains the phrase "turn ye, turn ye from your evil ways;
for why will ye die, O house of Israel?" Comer likely used this text to make a
general plea for orthodox belief and practice and Hull felt attacked by this.
Comer's use of "antinomian" to describe Hull probably indicates that Hull

claimed direct revelation of God's will, Anne Hutchinson's one view that eighteenth-century ministers saw as her most disruptive and heterodox. A similarly heterodox character was Louis Piot de l'Angloiserie, a Canadian who taught French at Harvard. According to Timothy Cutler, an Anglican minister in Boston, the Canadian was reported in 1735 to be "an Arian, to believe two Messiahs, Ben David and Ben Ephraim, and to have given out that the World would come to an end within a year or two of that time."[56] Even more disturbing to Boston's ministers than the heterodox beliefs of a Canadian "refugee" was that "one of the Tutors of the College, with several of His Relations, who are Teachers, appeared much affected by it."[57]

A case from before the Great Awakening in which the heterodox beliefs were more carefully spelled out occurred in central Massachusetts. In 1725 ministers in this region formed the Marlborough Association, a disciplinary body aimed at providing the clergy with a more unified voice for fighting heterodoxy. Three years later Rev. Israel Loring of Sudbury initiated one of this group's first cases, which involved

> some *inorthodox* opinions, broached by one Clap, of [Loring's] church of West Sudbury; the said Clap imagining and believing that we are not beholden to our Lord Jesus Christ for any satisfaction made to God by his blood, except for the sins against God's first precepts to Adam, and the moral law; but, as for *our* sins under the gospel, they are freely forgiven of God without any satisfaction.[58]

This was a "very troublesom affair," as the Association termed it, for Clap denied fundamental orthodox teachings. Clap asserted, in effect, that sinners were saved irrespective of Jesus' crucifixion, that sins were forgiven without satisfaction.[59] As a result, Clap was suspended from receiving the sacrament. The Marlborough Association noted its approval of this action since Clap's beliefs were "doctrines tending immediately to subvert Christian religion." In all four of these pre-Awakening cases, heterodoxy was not underground. Rather, it was quite aboveground, as Hull confronted a minister directly and Clap's beliefs were widely known, which suggests he proselytized. These cases differ from their seventeenth-century antecedents, however, in their lack of organization. As far as one can tell, Ive, Hull, and Clap were solitary in their heterodoxy, and de l'Angloiserie had only two or three followers. If they attempted to spread their beliefs they do not seem to have succeeded. This does not diminish their importance; their existence demonstrates the persistence of religious beliefs unsanctioned by the ministerial elite.

But a change did occur after the Great Awakening. While there were still isolated heterodox individuals after 1740, there was also a rebirth of loosely organized heterodox groups. Two prominent leaders of such groups—Richard Woodbury and Sarah Prentice—are examined in detail here. These two lay prophets demonstrate the importance of the body, sexuality, and gender in heterodoxy; they display heterodoxy's intimate connections between motifs of death and life; and they bear witness to the possibility of adding scripts to the religious culture.

RICHARD WOODBURY

The Great Awakening was at first supported by most ministers but later denounced by many when it became apparent that a great deal of heterodoxy accompanied the movement. Clergymen who initially saw the revival as an answer to their prayers for increased church membership were soon disenchanted by the propensity of some laypeople toward "enthusiasm": the visions, trances, and crying out that seemed to denote a devilish influence. A handful of ministers—including Gilbert Tennent, James Davenport, Andrew Croswell, and Nicholas Gilman—tolerated and even promoted this enthusiasm. But none of these ministers was as far outside the mainstream of orthodoxy as an illiterate lay exhorter and associate of Gilman, Richard Woodbury. The unusual pairing of the Harvard-educated Gilman and the unlettered Woodbury sheds light on the complex lay-clergy relations involved in heterodoxy. Gilman's acceptance of Woodbury as a prophet surely allowed the layman to increase his following more than he otherwise would have been able.

Nicholas Gilman had been the pastor of Durham, New Hampshire, for several years when the Great Awakening began to be felt in 1742, about eighteen months after the first signs of revival in Boston. Some time in 1742 or 1743 Richard Woodbury arrived in Durham from Rowley, Massachusetts, perhaps after word had reached Woodbury's hometown of the religious excitement to the north. It seems that Gilman immediately believed Woodbury's claim to be a prophet who spoke the directly revealed words of God. Woodbury convinced others besides Gilman that he was a prophet; many of Durham's residents became Woodbury's followers as well. By 1744, when the Awakening had died out in just about every other New England town, Woodbury's following was so strong in Durham that he decided to itinerate in southern New Hampshire and northern Massachusetts, creating quite a stir and gaining converts wherever he went.

Before he even set foot in another town, Woodbury first composed letters (with Gilman's help) to the standing ministers in those towns. One letter that survives, in Gilman's hand and signed by Woodbury with a wax seal, reached Rev. William Parsons of South Hampton, New Hampshire, in May 1744. In this letter, Woodbury attempted to reach the usual New Light goal of convincing a skeptical minister of the blessed nature of the Awakening. But the letter's tone separated Woodbury from ordinary New Lights: his approach was not at all conciliatory, and he practically threatened ministers with divine retribution if they stood in his way. "If you are obstinate against the ways of God," Woodbury warned Parsons, "remember the day approaches when you must give account of your Stewardship & be no longer Steward." But Woodbury hoped that Parsons would be on his side in the religious fight, and the would-be itinerant used appropriately martial imagery when he exhorted Parsons, "if you are on the Lords Side see that you come forth as a Bold Soldier, one that is not afraid to Venture his life for the Vindication of the Honour & Glory of his King."

Woodbury linked death with life throughout his exhortations, and this theme seemed to impress his lay listeners. Woodbury's beliefs about religion and sexuality also set him apart from other New Lights. He asked Parsons, "Consider, as you have marry'd and are Settled in the world, whether you are indeed espoused to Christ as your Head and Husband." Like the biblical Paul, Woodbury (who seems to have been unmarried) argued that celibacy allowed for greater attention to religious matters and prevented one from becoming too ensnared in the cares of the world. New England ministers rejected this doctrine, seeing celibacy as a threat to the procreating family that was society's foundation.[60] Finally, Woodbury punctuated his plea to Parsons with a clause that revealed his belief in his own special relationship with God: "I can assure you Sir, *by the Grace given Me of God,* this is a glorious work of his grace that has been going on in the Land."[61] Woodbury must have aroused ministers' anger even before he arrived in their parishes by claiming divine knowledge of God's will.

An exception was in Ipswich, where Woodbury—who had been privately ordained by Gilman just before they began their itineration—got a warm reception from New Light ministers Nathaniel and Daniel Rogers, not to mention the local townspeople.[62] After a fast-day sermon, appointed "at the Desire of the people" due to a minor earthquake, Woodbury led a small band of people, including Gilman, the Rogers brothers, and some laypeople who had attended the sermon, from the meetinghouse to the residence of a man supposed to be possessed. This motley troop "went to one John F[ow]ler in this Town & told him that as the Devil had been in him for some years

Woodbury was come to drive him out and after some Ceremony they declar'd him out." This impromptu exorcism apparently pleased the crowd, for immediately "all stampt him [the Devil] down to Hell, with their Feet upon the Floor: and then pronounced that the Devil should never have power of him more, and that he was Blessed for ever." Observers likely approved this event because it had the appearance of a sanctioned ritual like baptism, in which the gestures and words of the minister combine to effect change.

Another aspect of Woodbury's ministry that always attracted comment was that much of it occurred at night: an observer noted that "they have not been in their Beds for 3 Nights together." Nighttime activity, with its connotations of loosened bonds of authority and hints of sexuality, never failed to alarm the representatives of orthodox religion, especially when Woodbury had such powers over his lay followers: "when Woodbury says Fall down ye servants of God, they all fall down flatt upon their Faces and there lye till he bidds them get up." These people (and the ministers who supported him) were "perswaded that he, the said Woodbury, is a Prophet sent from God to reveal to them by his Mouth His Will & what is to come to pass." In addition to claiming to know the future, Woodbury asserted that he had the power to curse and bless people. According to one witness, "he says that *whom he curses is cursed to all Eternity* & that to whomsoever he gives Eternal Life they receive it."[63] This was perhaps Woodbury's most controversial office, for in this he ceased to claim merely the powers of a prophet and claimed the power of God himself. It suggests a great deal about the excited state of religion in the wake of the Great Awakening that three ministers and a group of laypeople believed a man who purported to have divine powers. But in matters of life and death, blessing and damnation, some people suspended credulity when they seemed to find an answer to those questions.

From Ipswich, Woodbury traveled to several more towns, and by July, he and Gilman reached Boston. At this point Woodbury's reputation preceded him, and there was a great deal of talk in Boston and nearby towns about his "frolicks," as one opponent termed them. A conversation between Dr. Alexander Hamilton and Justice Stephen Sewall in Salem turned to Woodbury and the "strange madness" he caused among the laypeople of Ipswich. Among the "blasphemous and absurd" things Woodbury allegedly claimed was "that he was the same to day, yesterday, and for ever."[64] In other words, Woodbury asserted that he was immortal, his body impervious to physical corruption. This was a common theme among heterodox individuals after the Awakening, which flowed from a desire to exist out of time, in a place where religious ecstasy occurred without the taint of base corporeality. Likewise, a

Boston newspaper noted that "while [Woodbury] was in Ipswich, and before he came thither, he evidently arrogated to himself the Revelation of secret things, by pretended predictions and denunciation of temporal and eternal curses upon particular persons." When Woodbury got to Boston, reports of his predictions turned on questions of life and death, as when he said to someone "at whom he was enraged, that he should be dead, dead, and in Hell, in the space of an hour or two," and when he declared before a group "that unless they imparted of their substance to the maintenance of the Gospel, they and their money should burn in Hell together."[65] Although the newspaper probably chose these accounts to make Woodbury appear to be a manipulative charlatan, they were consistent with his general message that he not only knew whether people would be saved or damned but could actually cause their salvation or damnation.

This is the last evidence of Woodbury's itineracy; shortly thereafter he and Gilman returned to Durham to continue their regular ministry. Although one might imagine that the excitement caused by Woodbury's preaching quickly died down, since ecstatic movements rarely sustain their momentum for long, in fact it seems that Woodbury aroused the passions of the Durham townspeople for many more years. Two years after Woodbury first began preaching, Rev. Samuel Chandler of nearby York, Maine, visited Durham. In his diary Chandler recorded the extraordinary religious occurrences that persisted in Durham. By August 1746 Gilman had completely relinquished his pastoral duties to Woodbury and Joseph Prince (1723–91), a blind, uneducated man who assisted with preaching. At that time Chandler and Rev. Jeremiah Wise of Berwick, Maine, delivered a sermon in Durham at the invitation of some laypeople who did not agree with Gilman's acceptance of Woodbury as a prophet. The unusual behavior of Woodbury's followers was evident from the start, for as Wise began to preach,

> there were a number, 4 or 5, that were Extraordinarily Agitated, they made all manner of Mouths, turning out their Lips drawing their Mouths awry as if convulsed straining their eye Balls & twisting their bodies in all manner of unseemly Postures, some people falling down, people jumping up catching hold of one another extending their arms & clapping their hands, groaning & talking, some people aproving what was spoken & saying aye, so it is, that is true, tis Just so &c, & some people exclaiming & crying out aloud *Glory Glory Glory* it drowned Mr Wises Voice.

These physical gestures and verbal displays of religious ecstasy, reminiscent of those common during the Great Awakening, disturbed Wise, who "spoke to the people, entreated them, condemned the practice, but all to no purpose." In this frenzied state, experiencing the bodily expression of religious passions, Woodbury's followers did not allow an ordained minister's authority to daunt them.

When the sermon ended, Chandler, along with Wise and Gilman and Woodbury's followers, retired to a nearby house for refreshment. Shortly, the religious passions of Woodbury's followers reignited. In through the door flew "a number of these high Flyers raving like mad men," crying out and otherwise behaving boisterously. Again Woodbury's followers were not daunted by the presence of a standing minister: Hannah Huckins bucked gender norms and saucily informed Chandler that she had attained perfection on earth. When Huckins complained of being unable to remember certain things, Chandler attempted to catch her in a logical trap, pointing out that "she said she had attain'd perfection & yet had a bad memory."

Rational argumentation was not the spirit of these enthusiasts, however, so rather than dampen their ardor Chandler's gambit only increased it. Huckins began crying out in religious ecstasy and immediately "fell to dancing around the room & singing some dancing tunes, Jiggs & minuets, & keeping time exactly with her feet, presently 2 or 3 more fell in with her & the Room was crowded with applauders." To Chandler's disbelief the singing and stomping increased, "the house was full of confusion, some singing Bawdy songs others dancing to them & all under the pretence of Religion, it was all to praise God." This scene continued all day and into the night, when a little after dark the rowdy band "left the house & went out into the street where they held it till near Ten of the Clock."[66]

Several elements of this uncommon scene of religiously inspired passion are significant. First, Woodbury was not the only one to claim bodily perfection. At least one of his followers, Hannah Huckins, and probably others believed that they had attained perfection. Second, ordinary religious authority did not awe these people. Instead of trying to hide or moderate their heterodox views when confronted by a disapproving minister, they seem to have relished the challenge and attempted to put on a particularly striking show for their clerical observer. Finally, the repeated bodily expression of religious passions suggests a degree of sexual sublimation. During Wise's sermon bodies twisted and convulsed, eyes and mouths strained, and people groaned in a sexualized display of religious passion. Later in the day people danced to tunes with fast rhythms and sang songs with earthy lyrics. It seems that Woodbury, who urged celibacy among ministers (and possibly among his followers) hoped to channel sexual energies into expressions of pious delight.

The following day Chandler spoke with Gilman and hoped to talk some sense into this fellow Harvard graduate. Instead, Chandler learned that Gilman had proposed for prospective members of the Durham church "new & ungospell terms of communion which were that they received Mr Woodbury whome he accounts a prophet sent of God." Chandler also discovered that Gilman "says he cant receive those that dont receive Woodbury & these People in all their Extravagancies." Chandler then asked those who disapproved of Woodbury how many people comprised this heterodox band, and he received eight names, though it seems that more were attracted to the periphery of the group.[67] Finally, after two extraordinary days, Chandler and Wise rode away from this hotbed of heterodoxy and back to their own parishes.

This pattern repeated itself several times over the next few years; the intervention of outside ministerial authority could not quell the passions of Woodbury and his followers. In 1747 an ecclesiastical council strongly condemned the "vile and absurd things" practiced in Durham, but the council was powerless to stop them.[68] If this were an ordinary congregation a council could threaten its minister with sanctions, but since this group operated completely outside the mainstream of ecclesiastical discipline little could be done to restore traditional religious order. The final bit of evidence concerning this heterodox group is in Isaac Backus's diary. In 1751 Backus, on one of his many long-distance itinerations, spent several days preaching in Durham. Seven years after the start of Woodbury's ministry, and three years after the death of Gilman, the illiterate exhorter was still active. Backus noted, "People Seemed Conciderable stupid, and one Woodbury that has run into many awful wild extreams about religion was there. And he spake A few words which Seemed to have a very hurtfull Tendancy to poor Sinners and was a trial to my mind."[69] Backus spent most of his time in Durham denouncing Woodbury and his followers, seemingly to no avail. After 1751 this group's fate is unknown.

For at least seven years Richard Woodbury and his small band of religious zealots existed at the fringes of New England's religious culture. Taking some of the enthusiastic practices of the Great Awakening to an extreme, they presented the standing order with the challenge of a leader who claimed to speak the direct word of God and his adherents who claimed physical incorruptibility. This group demonstrates the ultimate inability of ordinary religious authority to control the beliefs and practices of laypeople empowered by a heady combination of sexual energy and charismatic leadership. Similar forces were at work in the heterodox trajectory of Sarah Prentice.

SARAH PRENTICE AND THE IMMORTALISTS

Unlike Richard Woodbury, Sarah Prentice was never the unquestioned leader of a heterodox group. Instead, she was one of the most prominent members of a loosely organized band in southeastern New England that I call the "Immortalists," for, similar to Woodbury, one of their most distinctive beliefs was that they were not subject to bodily decay.[70]

As with Woodbury, the question of representativeness comes up when examining Prentice. What can this small band, deemed fanatics at the time, teach us about religious culture in eighteenth-century New England? Although beyond the pale of even New Light piety, this group is emblematic of the tendency among those energized by the Great Awakening toward (a sometimes extreme) purity in worship.[71] Likewise, the Immortalists point to intimate connections between evangelical piety, sexuality, and the body. They also demonstrate how religion could be used to upset traditional gender norms, with Sarah Prentice the opposite of the conventional image of a woman having children, staying with her husband, and remaining relatively humble. Finally, as with Woodbury, the Immortalists demonstrate the relative openness of eighteenth-century culture and the possibility for creating heterodox beliefs and practices. Prentice and those in her circle brought unique ideas to New England's religious culture.

Sarah Prentice was born in 1716 to a wealthy family in Groton, Massachusetts. At sixteen she married Solomon Prentice, a minister eleven years her senior. The following year Sarah joined Solomon's church in Grafton and proceeded to bear five children over the next eight years.[72] At this point in 1742 the people of Grafton experienced the Awakening in all its power under the direction of Solomon, their radical New Light minister. Sarah had another conversion experience, even though she had joined the church almost ten years before.[73] Her reconversion experience as narrated by her husband was a typical, if somewhat more explosive than ordinary, tale of spiritual distress followed by spiritual emancipation: for about a month in early 1742, Sarah was in such soul distress that it "Much Effected her Body to that Degree that She was Scarce able to Stirr hand or foot for some few Minuits." At the end of this period she was "exceedingly humbled and bowed to the will of God," saying that she would suffer anything God did to her. Finally, she experienced delightful release:

And Now, her Nerves and Sinews are contracted, and her Tongue Stiff in her head: her Own Phrase was, it felt like an Iron bar in her Mouth, She begged of the Lord She might have the Liberty of her Tongue, that there with She Might

Shew forth the Wondras work of the Lord . . . At length her Stomack heaved, and, She broke forth—*its Lovely! its Lovely!*[74]

Sarah Prentice's reconversion experience illuminates the connection between evangelical spirituality and the body. In the throes of her experience Sarah's nerves, sinews, tongue, mouth, and stomach mirrored her own sensation of paralysis and release.

Soon events in Grafton moved from the ordinary to the uncommon. Solomon found himself isolated: too radical for the many Old Lights in his congregation, too conservative for his wife and others of a like mind. Nearby ministers reported unusual occurrences among the awakened in Grafton. In 1744 Ebenezer Parkman learned from a moderate New Light woman in Grafton of the "many things which she finds among her Neibours—regard to Dreams, and holding most sensible Communion with God in sleep, etc."[75] Apparently those in Sarah Prentice's circle had visions of God in their dreams and considered their nocturnal communications to be real.

More disturbing yet were accounts of spiritually inspired free love. In February 1747 Parkman cryptically noted that Sarah Prentice's group "Vindicated the Doctrine of Knowledge of one another by the union of Love etc. etc." Three months later Parkman confronted Sarah Prentice with these reports. During a long afternoon of discussions, Parkman "endeavour'd also to warn her against Defect in Relative Dutys in the House; and giving occasion to others to suspect criminal Freedoms with the other sex, under the splendid Guise of Spiritual Love and Friendship."[76] It is easy to see why Parkman felt these actions, if they were true, threatened the standing order. If Sarah Prentice and those in her circle were having sex with one another on the grounds that they were all spiritually "spouses," this obviously represented an inversion of traditional ideas about marriage. As we shall see below, the reality, at least a few years later, turned out to be the very opposite of these early reports, with Sarah opting for celibacy as a way to gain purity.

The reports of heterodoxy were not limited to Grafton. In the 1740s a number of communities throughout southeastern New England were sites of Immortalism. A group of Immortalists in Windham County, Connecticut, had at least one person who declared himself to be Christ.[77] Likewise, Sarah Prentice sometimes associated in the late 1740s with Nat Smith of Hopkinton, Massachusetts, who along with his four brothers considered himself to have achieved eternal life.[78] The Smiths were an extremely disruptive clan, with Richard Smith convicted in 1743 for disturbing a church meeting led by Rev. Samuel Barrett of Hopkinton. During this meeting Smith "did Scream & cry out with a very loud Voice, saying that the said Barrett had not right to speak while he the said Richard was speaking."[79]

In addition to verbally opposing the clergy, the Immortalists defied the ministry with their beliefs. In 1751 Isaac Backus described the views of Immortalists in Norton and Taunton:

> They hold that the union between two Persons when rightly married together is A Spiritual Union whereas God Says they Twain shall be one flesh:—they deny The Civil Authoritys Power in Marriage:—and they hold that they are Getting into a state of Perfection in this World so as to be free from all Sicknings And trouble, and so that they Shall Never Die, and many other corrupt things.[80]

Molly Bennet of Cumberland, Rhode Island, expressed this belief in spiritual union in 1749 when she stated "that Solomon Finney and she was man and wife Enternally [internally] but not Externally," that is, that they were spiritual spouses who did not engage in sexual intercourse. Although Bennet and Finney were not legally married, "she said that they was man and wife in the sight of the Lord and it was made known to them that it was so."[81] While the exact relationship between Sarah Prentice and these groups, or among these various Immortalist sects, is not clear, they were united by a relatively uniform set of beliefs, namely that there should not be sexual relations in marriage (a "spiritual union") and that they had reached (or were approaching) bodily incorruptibility. These beliefs so threatened the standing order that in 1749 the Rhode Island general assembly passed a law clarifying the illegality of "Adultery, Polygamy, and unlawfully marrying Persons."[82]

The uniformity of beliefs among Immortalist groups separated by dozens of miles suggests proselytization. Two people were likely leaders in this endeavor. One was Sarah Prentice, who moved to Easton with her husband in 1747 when he was made pastor there. The other was Shadrack Ireland, a pipe maker and leading Immortalist from Charlestown, Massachusetts, who was Sarah Prentice's spiritual partner. Ezra Stiles, writing in 1793 about the death of Immortalist Nat Smith, declared that "he was one of Old Ireland's Men & of the Company of a dozen or 15 wild Enthusiasts who about 50 years ago lived in & about Medford, Sutton, Uxbridge, & declared themselves *Immortals:* of which Rev. Mr. Prentice's Wife of Grafton was one. She used to lie with Ireland as her spiritual Husband."[83] It seems, however, that Stiles based his report of Ireland and Prentice lying together solely on rumor, for in 1748 and 1751 Sarah bore children by Solomon. Furthermore, Sarah had not yet fully embraced Immortalism. It appears that in the late 1740s and early 1750s

Ireland and Sarah Prentice were spiritual confederates, working to gain converts to their heterodox religiosity.

In 1753 Sarah Prentice experienced two important and related changes: an embrace of celibacy and a belief that she had become immortal. In June 1753 she told Isaac Backus "that this night 2 months ago She passed thro' a change in her Body equivalent to Death, so that She had ben intirely free from any disorder in her Body or Corruption in her soul ever Since; and expected she ever should be So: and that her Body would never see Corruption, but would Live here 'till Christs personal coming."[84] As in chapter 2 when Mary Reed had a deathlike experience that rendered her religiously powerful, Prentice claimed that a similar transformation caused her to become immortal.

In February 1773 Ebenezer Parkman visited the Prentices because Solomon was sick and feared his end was near. During that visit Prentice informed Parkman of her decision to become celibate. Due to her husband's weakness Sarah did most of the talking:

> She speaks of her Husband under the name of Brother Solomon: she gave me some account of the wonderful Change in her Body, her Sanctification, that God had shewn to her His mind & Will, she was taught henceforth to know no man after the Flesh, that she had not for above 20 years, not so much as shook Hands with any Man, &c. Then came in Mr Benjamin Leland & Mr Samuel Cooper whom she call'd Brother Benjamin & Brother Samuel, &c.[85]

According to Sarah Prentice, her celibacy was not merely a whim but the very will of God revealed directly to her.

Prentice and those of similar religious propensities maintained their beliefs for the next twenty-five or thirty years, occasionally appearing in the historical record. In 1756 Isaac Backus preached in Grafton and ran across some Immortalists. Likewise, Backus reported in 1764 that a handful of people in Norton and Easton still believed in "spiritual union" and had left their lawful wives "for a great while."[86] Shadrack Ireland lived in Harvard, Massachusetts, among his followers until 1778 when his death caused a crisis of faith for those who believed in his immortality: "And when he was suddenly seized with death, he said, 'I am going, but don't bury me; for the time is short; God is coming to take the church.' Therefore he was put into a large box filled up with lime, and laid in the cellar, where it continued from September, 1778 to July, 1779, when the body scented so much that it was carried out in the night and buried in a corn-field."[87] Sarah Prentice, who lived until 1792, maintained her convictions until at least 1773 and probably for the rest of her life, as Ebenezer Parkman noted in 1782 that "Madam Prentice of

Grafton has been with the *Shakers*."[88] Unfortunately there survives no context for this cryptic remark. It is unknown whether Prentice visited the Shakers merely to survey another celibate group or if she became a follower of Mother Ann Lee.

Whatever the case, it remains to be understood why Sarah Prentice and the Immortalists set aside ordinary sexual relations to become celibate. Several explanations may be offered. A long—though contested—Christian tradition saw celibacy as a way to clear the mind of earthly interference, allowing for heightened powers of spiritual perception. Hence Shakers demanded that members renounce sex: celibacy facilitated clear communication with God. For the Shakers, this was a gendered construct, as celibate women were seen to be particularly ready conduits for receiving revelations.[89] The contact between Prentice and the Shakers suggests that the Immortalists also held these beliefs. Furthermore, celibacy was one way to escape earthly temporality for a more spiritual temporality. Much Christian literature has portrayed the ability of the body to reproduce itself as a form of decay, and celibacy was a way to gain a sort of immortality. As Caroline Walker Bynum argues, "to medieval theorists, fertility was also decay; the threat lodged in the body was change itself."[90] Of course, the Immortalists were not medieval Catholics, but they got many of their ideas about sexuality and the body from the same source: the Christian Bible.

The Bible is an extremely multivocal text, written by dozens of authors over many centuries. It is the key to understanding the sources of the Immortalists' ideas, and as such it is the key to understanding early New England's flexible religious culture. It contains ideas about sexuality that are open to multiple and conflicting interpretations; Immortalists relied on a reading of the Bible that was radically different from that advocated by orthodox ministers in eighteenth-century New England.

The Bible includes numerous prescriptions and injunctions about sexuality. Famously, the Old Testament command to "be fruitful and multiply" (Gen. 1:28) is complicated by the New Testament teachings of St. Paul (especially 1 Cor. 7). Whereas the Old Testament puts reproduction in a positive light, Paul casts doubt on the worthiness of conjugal relations. Though Paul clearly says, "if you marry, you do not sin" (1 Cor. 7:28), he also says that married people are distracted by worldly affairs, and he seems to make perpetual virginity into an exalted state.[91]

Whereas Catholics, in general, favored a Pauline interpretation that praised sexual renunciation, Protestants downplayed the allure of celibacy. In New England, ministers were especially strident in condemning sexual renunciation as a threat to the social order. Although English Puritans like William Gouge claimed that a celibate life had value (even if it was not the preferred course),[92] New England ministers moved away from any exaltation of celibacy and held procreating marital sex in the highest esteem.[93] This was the direct result of the these ministers' celebration of the family—children and procreating parents—as the source of societal stability and the center of daily religious experience. Cotton Mather told women that virginity was not necessary to please God. Rather, the virtuous woman pleases God by pleasing her husband through moderate sexual relations.[94] Likewise, in the early eighteenth century Samuel Willard made the case that celibacy was contrary to nature, while marital sexuality was the natural result of God's design. Willard argued that "the *Conjugal* Relation" was based upon "the natural Inclinations of Men, of which [God] Himself is the Author." How could something instituted by God be sinful? Willard asked. In fact, Willard asserted, throughout history celibates had been among the most unchaste people: "too often, there are none more *Unchast[e]*, than such as boast themselves in *Cœlabacy*, who in the mean while nourish in them *Unclean* Lusts." Rehashing the standard Protestant propaganda that Catholics constrained by vows of celibacy were among the greatest sinners and hypocrites, Willard declared that celibacy had been the cause of "horrendous *Whoredoms*, and bloody *Murders*."[95]

Thus, ministers in seventeenth- and eighteenth-century New England were steadfast in their denunciation of vows of celibacy as unnatural and dangerous, which is why Ebenezer Parkman, on a visit to the Prentices in 1755, "enquir'd strictly into their Sentiments and Practices respecting their Conjugal Covenant."[96] Ministers like Parkman—as well as the vast majority of laypeople who accepted their teachings on this issue—could not countenance religious vows of celibacy.

These concerns about celibacy are corroborated by attacks on the Shakers published about twenty years after the Immortalists were most active. The similarities between these two groups allow the historian to understand contemporary fears about the meaning of celibacy. The minister Valentine Rathbun focused on the negative effects that the Shaker doctrine of celibacy had on families. Rathbun wrote, "the effect of this scheme is such, that men and their wives have parted, children ran away from their parents, and society entirely broke up in neighbourhoods." Rathbun also compared Mother Ann Lee to Eve, noting that "as [Satan] first deceived the woman, and made use of her to delude the man; so he is playing his old prank over again."[97] It is reasonable to assume that many people felt the same way about Sarah

Prentice, seeing her advocacy of celibacy as a delusion that threatened the order of family and society. Two years after Rathbun wrote, Benjamin West, another critic of the Shakers, made clear the threat he envisioned from a female-headed religious sect. Because the doctrine of celibacy demanded that husbands leave their wives and vice versa, it not only destroyed families, but "women become monsters, and men worse than infidels in this new and strange religion." The cause of all this subversion of order, West argued, could be found in the fact that a woman headed this group:

> when we consider from whence these new laws and rules originate, and who stands at the head of their discipline, the wonder may abate in some degree, for God placed the man next to himself in the creation, between the woman and himself, and enjoined the womans obedience to the man, and said the man should rule over her.

Thus, because among the Shakers "the men hold themselves in intire subjection to the woman,"[98] it was hardly a surprise to West and his orthodox contemporaries that a female-headed religious group would have the effect of destroying families and society by inverting the "natural" order of men being above women.

These concerns about the power of a female religious leader are emblematic of the two most significant lessons of Sarah Prentice's story. First, Prentice's beliefs and practices show how piety contained the potential for upsetting traditional gender roles. In a society where women were supposed to have children, Prentice opted for celibacy at age thirty-six; at a time when devotion to one's husband was of great importance, Sarah set in motion the chain of events that got Solomon dismissed from his job in Grafton; and in an era when women were not expected to speak their mind in public, Prentice traveled from town to town telling all listeners (including ministers) of her heterodox beliefs. One historian sums up Prentice's local reputation by noting that she "was a genius who knew most of the Bible by heart and could, it was said, preach as good a sermon as any man."[99] It is not surprising, given her abilities, that contemporaries compared Sarah Prentice's powers to those of a man.

The second significant point is that Prentice and the Immortalists existed at all and gained converts across southeastern New England. Although their numbers remained small, for thirty years they represented the potential for extremism and heterodox beliefs and practices in a culture where the dominant religious ideology was strong but never uncontested. Taking advantage of the corporeal religiosity that came into favor during the Great Awakening, the Immortalists' message of bodily purity resonated with a group of people for whom orthodox spirituality was not entirely satisfactory.

Both magic and heterodoxy existed at the margins of religious culture in eighteenth-century New England. Probably only a minority of laypeople sought the services of magical practitioners, fewer still actually used spells or created judicial astrology tables themselves, and no more than a few dozen declared themselves to be immortal. But the laypeople who have been the subject of this chapter have a historical significance beyond their numbers. In their desire for empowerment and their search for a meaningful piety they approached and crossed the outer boundary of what ministers considered appropriate.

Laypeople engaged in a wide range of magical practices in the eighteenth century, all of which their ministers staunchly opposed. For example, some people relied on judicial astrology to learn if their children would lead long and happy lives, while others used various forms of magical healing to cure intractable illnesses. Some laypeople visited diviners and conjurers when they lost something of value or when they wanted to learn whom they might marry. Others sought empowerment through religious means that the clergy condemned as heterodox. Denying the most fundamental precepts of reformed Protestantism, some people, for example, believed sinners would have been saved even if Jesus had not been crucified. Others accepted the teachings of prophets who claimed direct communication with God, while a few asserted that they had died and returned to life in an immortal state.

Through these various acts of boundary crossing, laypeople demonstrated that within the relatively open religious culture of the eighteenth century ministers stood more as supplicants than as commanders. Clergymen did their best to prevent people from engaging in magic and they denounced and ridiculed those who joined heterodox circles. But these laypeople—focusing on the powerful themes of life and death, health and sickness, sexuality and purity—created a comfortable space outside the dominant religious culture. On the one hand were laypeople whose piety largely drew upon ministerial teachings, such as John Barnard, as well as the people we will turn to in the next chapter who responded to mainstream revivalism. On the other hand were magical practitioners and the heterodox, who found power, sought purity, and upset gender norms in ways distinctly at odds with many aspects of the ministerial tradition. These latter laypeople developed cultural scripts that became an enduring part of New England's religious culture.

CHAPTER FIVE

Earthquakes and Great Awakenings

The Continuity of Revivalism

N ITINERANT MINISTER rides a dusty mare into town and de-
livers a hellfire and brimstone sermon. Citing evidence of God's
displeasure and hinting that Judgment Day may be near, the
preacher urges his listeners to reform their ways before it is too
late. During the sermon young women and men cry out in religious ecstasy, registering their assent with moans and groans and
shouts of hallelujah. Within weeks dozens have joined the church,
to the great delight of the established pastor, who feels that his
efforts of the past decades have been amply rewarded. But this
revival is not without controversy: a faction of the church accuses
the new converts of excessive enthusiasm in their worship, and
indelicate hints are made about the late nights ostensibly spent
in religious devotions.

While this may seem to be an account of the Great Awakening
of the early 1740s, it could just as easily describe the revivals of
piety that occurred in New England in the mid-1730s and in the
early 1760s. This reveals an important and often overlooked aspect of eighteenth-century religious culture: the continuity of
revivalism.[1] While most historians have written about the Great
Awakening as marking a decisive break in the patterns of New
England popular religion, in fact the Awakening was but the largest and most contentious of a series of revivals that punctuated
the eighteenth century.

These repeated "harvests of souls" have primarily been seen as
resulting from a ministerial strategy that encouraged revivalism.
According to these interpretations, many ministers in the early
eighteenth century implemented a new style of preaching and
developed a new theory of conversion: preaching focused more

on gaining new converts and conversion itself was reconceptualized as a brief moment rather than a protracted process. Both of these innovations aimed to bring members into moribund congregations.[2] Having failed to bolster clerical authority through an earlier strategy of consociations, ministers turned to revivals as the answer to their problems. Historians have argued that ministers—led by Solomon Stoddard—created revivalism to gain new converts and increase ministerial power.[3]

There is no doubt that ministers, starting with Stoddard in the last years of the seventeenth century, attempted to harvest souls through revivalist preaching. But this view must be supplemented by the recognition that revivals could not occur without lay participation. Numerous ministers preached a revivalist message over the course of a century, but only on four occasions—the Earthquake Revival of 1727, the Connecticut River Valley Revival of 1735, the Great Awakening, and the Seacoast Revival of the early 1760s—did laypeople respond to their ministers' urgings. Not only did laypeople largely determine the timing of revivals, they largely determined their extent, as private prayer meetings generated much of the momentum for conversion. In order to understand revivalism more fully, the laity's role must be examined.

For laypeople, revivals were part of the rhythms of piety that beat at different tempos at various stages of their lives. But in addition to this individual experience, revivals also reveal a communal side of popular religion. Historians have focused on the individualistic aspects of the rapid and convulsive conversions that occurred during the Great Awakening. This view, along with the general disorder of the Awakening, has led some to argue that the Awakening helped create Yankee individualism among previously community-oriented Puritans.[4] But while the new morphology of conversion promulgated by revivalist preachers had individualistic elements, focusing on the individual convert's progression from sinner to saint, laypeople experienced conversion within a communal framework. A new convert, awakened by a revival, might be one of dozens or even hundreds in a town to have a conversion experience. Moreover, the commonly expressed fear of being "left behind" during revival seasons shows that an individual's religious experience was influenced by the experiences of friends, family, and fellow parishioners to an even greater degree than usual. Indeed, revivalism was contagious: the greatest spur to conversion was not ministerial preaching but witnessing one's peers converting in great numbers.

But a communal experience is not necessarily one with commonly shared goals or expectations. Because revivals heightened religious passions, greater strife than usual often accompanied them. Specifically, during revivals the religious culture's gender tensions were visible. As converts became more "enthusiastic" in their devotional styles, crying out and swooning during religious meetings, many ministers and some lay antirevivalists denounced what they saw as excess emotions. Especially during the Great Awakening, but also during the other revivals of the eighteenth century, these attacks on emotionalism—reminiscent of the ministerial campaign to restrain the emotionalism of mourning for the dead—were conducted in gendered terms. Even though the proportion of male new members seems to have been higher during the Awakening than during nonrevival years,[5] these male converts were often described in feminized terms because of their tendency toward emotional displays. Antirevivalists feared that religion, rather than being infused with vigor by new male and female members, would become overly dominated by "feminine" emotion at the expense of "masculine" reason. The dynamics of the four major eighteenth-century revivals in New England, examined in turn, reveal that revivalism was both a product of the more open religious culture of the eighteenth century and helped sustain and even further that openness.

The Earthquake Revival, 1727

Without warning, houses shook and the earth trembled and it seemed that the pit of hell might open at any moment. At about 10:45 on the night of 29 October 1727, the greatest earthquake in memory rocked the colonies northeast of New Jersey. People ran into the streets, sought the comfort of family and neighbors, and began to pray in earnest. Miraculously, no one was killed, but much was destroyed: in addition to a great deal of property, the residents of New England found their sense of comfort was a casualty of the earthquake. The temblor awakened many laypeople's latent fear of damnation; they quickly joined their churches in record numbers. The religious revival spurred by the Great Earthquake of 1727 shows laypeople responding less to revivalist preaching and more to events that the clergy could not control.

Contemporary accounts reveal that many individuals viewed the earthquake as one of the most important events in their lifetime. James Jeffry of Salem kept a diary in a succession of interleaved almanacs for a number of years. Three are extant, covering 1724, 1727, and 1744. Jeffry wrote his entries in the common line-a-day format, with each day's weather and perhaps a notable event summed up in no more than a few words. By far the longest entry in any of his diaries is that for 29 October 1727:

> about half an hour after Ten a Clock There was the most Terrible Earthquake ever was known in New England. Continued about two minutes the first shock & had severall Small ones afterwards the same night & continued at Times all the Week afterwards. All the People in Town satt up most part of the night, [I] was at [Mr.] Plaisted's & Mr. Lynde's with great many of the Town. I was setting by the fire when it came.[6]

Typical is Jeffry's description of many townspeople gathering at the home of a prominent person (Benjamin Lynde was one of Salem's most distinguished residents and chief justice of the Massachusetts Superior Court) for prayer and discussion of the amazing event. The excitement generated by the earthquake carried over into the next day, when meetinghouses were filled to overflowing with people hoping to understand this frightening dispensation. Jeremiah Bumstead, an artisan in Boston, reported that "Dr. Mather had a full meeting at his church next morning; & Mr. Sewall & Mr. Foxcrafft att their churches next night by candle-light, for prayer & preaching."[7]

During the next year, the revival of religion inspired by the earthquake brought unprecedented numbers of new members into many churches, especially in northeastern Massachusetts, where the tremors were the strongest. For example, Rev. John Brown of Haverhill noted that "since the *Earthquakes,* I have admitted and propounded 154 Persons; 87 for the Lord's Table, the rest for Baptism, or the Renewing the Baptismal Covenant." Likewise, Cotton Mather recorded the most new members in his long career in 1727, with 71 people joining his church.[8] Nor were these areas simply more prone to revivalism than elsewhere; the First Church in Essex received 92 new members in full communion in the year following the earthquake, compared to only 41 new members for the Great Awakening years of 1741 to 1743.[9]

The mind-set of these earthquake-inspired converts is revealed in a set of extraordinary documents from Lynnfield, a town in the "rumbled-over" district of the North Shore of Massachusetts. Compared to some other parishes, Lynnfield did not experience a very large revival: eight women and two men joined the church following the earthquake. But these converts' feelings remain open to observation in the conversion narratives transcribed by their minister, Nathaniel Sparhawk.[10]

Much in these narratives is quite conventional; indeed, the testimonials' relative uniformity hints at the minister's greater than usual authorial presence. All ten converts began by asserting the reality of the Trinity and ended with an affirmation of the importance of baptism and the Lord's Supper. Despite these and other formulaic elements, however, much that is individual comes through. Jeremiah Eaton, twenty-nine years old in 1727, seems literally to have heard God's voice after the earthquake, declaring that "every time I heard his voice it seemed to me as if I heard a sound say, 'if yee will not beleive by his voice yee would not beleive if one rose from the dead,' as it is Said In Luke 16:31."[11] Thirty-three-year-old Mehitable Osgood offered a standard reason given during revivals for converting, saying that the moment of terror came at a time when she was particularly vulnerable to suggestion. Osgood stated, "while I was delaying a Serious and close prosecution of my resolutions, It pleased God to awaken me in an awfull and terrible manner by the late dreadfull earth-quake to put my resolution in practice."[12]

Perhaps most striking in these narratives is the lack of references to millennialism. Not one of the Lynnfield converts mentioned the end of the world in their narratives. Even the four new members who directly referred to the earthquake said nothing about Judgment Day. This contradicts the prevailing ministerial interpretation that the earthquake resonated with lay millennialism. Ministers asserted that "the earthquake was a warning from God that the Last Day was not far off."[13] In numerous sermons, clergymen claimed that during and immediately after the earthquake laypeople feared that Judgment Day had arrived. According to Christopher Sergeant, minister of Methuen, Massachusetts, "Many [had] fears that it was the Great Day of the Son of man's appearing in the clouds of heaven. People in general were in expectations of sudden destruction."[14] Rev. Samuel Wigglesworth wrote that "many" thought "the end of all things was come" when the earthquake hit.[15] Likewise, Rev. John Barnard, the eldest son of chapter 1's pious carpenter, urged his listeners that the earthquake should "mind you of the approaching Judgment."[16]

Like Barnard the housewright, however, Lynnfield's laypeople did not find millennialism a compelling reason to convert. Rather, fears of personal destruction, dying in a state of sin, and going to hell led the Lynnfield converts to join the church. Jeremiah Eaton related that the quake "made me have quick Apprehensions of my own Sins and guilt, which made me fear my Condition to be so Wofull that it brôt those words to me, 'hell is Naked before him, and destruction hath no Covering,' Job 25:6." In this personalized and individual formulation, Eaton expressed fears about his own sinfulness. The earthquake made Eaton realize that death could come suddenly and he should be prepared for it. Thirty-one-year-old Elizabeth Aborn like-wise credited the "late terrible & Surprizing Earth-quake" with awakening her to her sinful state. After the tremors Aborn prayed to God to "Save me from all my Sins and from eternall wrath." Aborn feared damnation would result not from the end of the world but from the end of her own life. Jonathan Pearson expressed similar sentiments:

> God has by the late amazing Earth-quake Layd open my neglect before me that I see no way to escape, but by fleeing to Christ for refuge. God in that hour Set all my Sins before me, when I was Shaking over the pit looking every moment when the earth would open her mouth and Swallow me up and then must I have been miserable for ever & for ever have been reaping the fruites of my repeated rebellions against him all my Life long.[17]

Pearson worried about roasting in hell as the result of his sinful ways. As opposed to the ministerial interpretation of lay reaction to the earthquake, Pearson and his fellow Lynnfield converts were animated more by a fear of hell than by a fear of Judgment Day. As the experience of John Barnard suggests, orthodox laypeople may have found ministerial millennialism to be too esoteric a concern for their everyday lives, even in extraordinary circumstances like a natural disaster. True, there were lay millennialists in the eighteenth century, but they mostly occupied the religious culture's margins. This tension between lay and clerical interpretations seems to have remained unrecognized by both parties, and it never emerged as open conflict.

Yet another difference between lay and ministerial interpretations of the Earthquake Revival revolved around what caused great numbers of people to join churches after the quake. Ministers in northeastern Massachusetts took a great deal of credit for bringing new members into their churches. According to historian Michael Crawford, clergymen believed that "the revival of religion, no matter what the proximate cause, was the responsibility of themselves, who were entrusted with the preaching of the Gospel."[18] For example, Rev. William Williams, Jr., of Weston, claimed that conversions in his town resulted from hearing his earthquake sermons: "The Lord having opened their hearts . . . to give attention unto the *word preached*, which hath become powerful to the further awakening, and I hope conversion of some."[19] The laypeople quoted above, however, attributed their conversion to the earthquake itself and the fear of dying in sin it engendered in them. Not one of the ten Lynnfield converts mentioned ministerial preaching as a spur to conversion. Like millennialism, divergences in interpretation about the cause of conversions remained unspoken and never became sources of overt conflict.

In general, and despite these differing lay and clerical viewpoints, ministers were happy with the Earthquake Revival and hoped that its religious fervor would last for many years. But if most ministers were heartened by the revival of religion among their parishioners, some expressed concern that people claimed conversion when, in fact, all they had was a good scare. Samuel Phillips, among others, begged laypeople to have patience as they thought about coming forward for church membership. Phillips sermonized, "Don't look upon Conviction to be Conversion; but *wait* for the Lord, until He shall cause your Convictions to issue in a thorow and saving Conversion."[20] With so many people claiming to have been converted in the aftermath of the earthquake, ministers understandably feared that some of the conversions were insincere. According to most ministers, conversions were gradual and could not occur during the two minutes of shaking that frightful October night.

As with all revivals, even if ministers were happy about their parishioners' increased piety, they could become upset when laypeople took their religious fervor too far. John Rogers cautioned against the "total despair" that some people experienced, the result of fears of dying in a sinful state.[21] In addition to despair, some people were so frightened by the earthquake that they did nothing for weeks but pray all day. Samuel Phillips reported, "I hear of some, who have been backward, since the *Earthquake* began, to attend the business of their secular Calling; thinking it a wrong Thing to Labour." Phillips imagined these zealots responding to his criticisms by saying, "we are not Idle, but spend our Time in seeking and serving the Lord." Phillips answered that praying is a good thing, but people do not need to spend all their time in devotions.[22] Of course, such extreme behavior must have put these laypeople in a very small minority of those awakened by the earthquake. But this example is instructive nonetheless, for in later revivals extreme piety would become an even greater issue of contention. During revival seasons there was always the danger, from the ministry's point of view, that people might take the urge for religious devotions too far.

Thus the Earthquake Revival illuminates some of the themes common to revivals in eighteenth-century New England. Laypeople experienced the revival in a communal fashion, even if their conversions occurred individually. Some of the excitement of the night of the earthquake, with people meeting together and praying fervently in a group setting, continued for at least a year. And if ministers were generally happy with their flocks' greater piety, they also worried that some people might be taking their devotions a bit too seriously. Furthermore, just beneath the surface of revival-induced harmony existed conflicting interpretations of millennialism: the clergy believed that people feared the end of the world whereas laypeople actually feared more for their own sinfulness and the possibility of sudden death. Alternative interpretations of the same event would become even more visible in later awakenings.

The Connecticut River Valley Revival, 1735

Grandson of the first great New England revivalist, Solomon Stoddard, Jonathan Edwards was in a unique position to evaluate the revival of religion that swept up and down the Connecticut River Valley in 1735. His *Faithful Narrative* of the revival helped spread word of the religious fervor throughout America and even across the Atlantic to England and Scotland.[23] Because of the book's wide distribution, historians have credited the *Faithful Narrative* with structuring later revivals.[24]

One of the most striking things revealed by Edwards's account, however, is that Edwards and his ministerial colleagues seem to have been more observers than creators of the revival. Certainly Edwards's revivalist preaching, performed in the tradition of his grandfather, gave shape to the religious outpourings. But laypeople transformed this from a small local revival into one in which three hundred people were converted in Northampton alone and hundreds of others were awakened in dozens of towns. With their prayer meetings and religious societies, they spread the word of the revival and made it virtually impossible to ignore; like the Earthquake Revival, it was very much a communal experience.[25]

Edwards described the prerevival state of religion in Northampton as one of prevailing dullness, with youth attending frolics and paying more attention to worldly issues than to piety. As was so often the case, the revival began with young people's sudden deaths, which served to remind Northampton's youth how fleeting life could be. In April 1734 the "very sudden and awful Death of a young Man" and then the death of a young woman in great soul distress caused concern among many, especially in an area a few miles out of town called Pascommuck. The first few conversions did not seem that extraordinary, but when a young woman "who had been one of the greatest Company-Keepers in the whole Town" was awakened, people began to take notice. Young adults, who had previously been the most likely to disdain religion, now flocked to churches and prayer meetings. According to Edwards, concern became "universal" and was apparent "among Persons of all Degrees, and all Ages."²⁶ The spring and summer of 1735 were joyful seasons for Edwards and the ministers where the revival spread: South Hadley, Deerfield, and Hatfield, Massachusetts, and Windsor, Coventry, and Suffield, Connecticut, to name just a few. Edwards claimed that in Northampton alone three hundred souls were awakened in half a year.²⁷

One recurring theme in Edwards's *Narrative* is the role of peer pressure in the revival. Like its counterpart in 1727, this revival occurred within a communal context, with people's piety influenced by their neighbors and family members. When the excitement peaked it must have been difficult to scoff at the revival; even traditionally festive occasions like weddings had become, according to Edwards, times of spiritual conversation. Edwards reported that during this most fervent period it was "a dreadful Thing amongst us to lie out of Christ, in danger every day of dropping into Hell." Suddenly those who had been accustomed to a life in which religion played only a peripheral role found themselves the objects of scorn. Such people could also be ostracized: "A loose careless Person could scarcely find a Companion in the whole Neighborhood; and if there was *any one* that seemed to remain senseless or unconcerned, it would be spoken of as a *strange* Thing."²⁸ Even allowing for Edwards's hyperbole, during a revival of this intensity there were great pressures—especially on those in the most vulnerable age group of young adults—to join in the communal spirit of the revival.

In Edwards's account, enthusiastic excesses were kept to a minimum during the Connecticut River Valley Revival. As during the Earthquake Revival, however, some laypeople did become carried away with religious fervor and neglected their secular callings, to the dismay of Edwards and other ministers. "The *Temptation*," lamented Edwards, "now seemed to lie on that hand, to *neglect* worldly Affairs too much, and to spend too much Time in the immediate Exercise of Religion." Like the other harvests of souls in the eighteenth century, ministers attempted to rein in the laity's most extreme emotional tendencies, which the revival's communal nature exacerbated. Because so many people were fervent about religion simultaneously, all the usual tendencies of lay piety increased exponentially, including a tendency toward emotionalism. This inclination was manifested by a man in South Hadley who, during the revival's excitement, believed he had received direct revelation of God's will. According to Edwards, this man's "Delusion" was that "he thought himself divinely instructed to direct a poor Man in melancholy and despairing Circumstances, to say certain Words in Prayer to God, as recorded in Psalm 106:4, for his own Relief."²⁹ Although this unnamed prophet eventually repented of his sins, claiming that he was caught up in the revival's fervor and vulnerable to satanic temptations, his case reveals the extremes to which people could go amid a revival's group passions.

But the passions engendered by a revival were not always conducive to uplifting feelings about religion; indeed, the South Hadley prophet gave advice to a man who had become melancholy, a problem that was becoming widespread. In March 1735 one man slit his throat but lived to tell about it. Two months later Edwards's uncle, Joseph Hawley, became so engulfed by religious despair, fearing that he was damned for eternity, that he cut his throat and died. The temptation to suicide seemed contagious, and soon "multitudes in this and other towns seemed to have it strongly suggested to 'em, and pressed upon 'em, to do as this person had done."[30] Although Edwards did not report any more suicides, the fact that so many had suicidal thoughts disturbed him and opened him up to the charge that his brand of revival preaching, with its images of hellfire and brimstone, could lead people into dangerous religious despair. The salient point for this discussion is that revivalism worked to exaggerate the emotions involved in lay piety, both toward joy and despair.

Another perspective (although one equally self-serving as Edwards's claim that disorder was rare) on the revival's excesses is provided by Timothy Cutler, Anglican minister of Christ Church in Boston. In May 1739 Cutler wrote a letter to Edmund Gibson, bishop of London, describing in hostile terms the Connecticut River Valley Revival. Because of its critical tone, this letter helps balance Edwards's celebratory account of the revival. In addition, Cutler wrote the letter several years after the revival, so it was easier for him to obtain descriptions of the revival's excesses.

Along with reporting the suicide and attempted suicide in Northampton, Cutler described those behaviors that showed the residents of the Connecticut River Valley to be overly emotional in their religious practices (at least from an Anglican perspective). Cutler wrote to his superior, "I find that Children of about 12 years old would run about the streets, and say, they were *bound to Zion,* and would *enquire the way Zion ward,* that they would assemble to pray and sing in the Meeting-houses, and were admitted to the Communion." In addition to zealous children, Cutler described the tendency of some people to have visions. "Several inform me," Cutler reported, "That their Imaginations were much wrought [on,] some pretending to have seen very strange Sights, some surprizing Lights, and one an Hawk on a Stump of a Tree."[31]

Even more significant was Cutler's attempt to denigrate the revival by describing it in gendered terms. For Cutler, as for later critics of the Great Awakening, the emotions of revivalism conjured up frightening images of disorderly women and unleashed sexuality. Samuel Johnson, minister of the Anglican church in Stratford, Connecticut, provided a report to Cutler that linked the revival with female sexuality. Johnson claimed that in the North Parish of Stratford the revival "began with an old whimsical Maid, crazed with Love for a young man belonging to his (Mr Johnson's) Church." The old woman complained about the young man to Johnson, perhaps with the goal of gaining the man's attentions. In any case the Anglican minister "was not able to find any thing culpable in the man, and therefore dismissed the woman with some [s]erious suggestions and Exhortations." This rough treatment gave the old woman "a turn towards this imaginary [i.e., enthusiastic] Religion, and set her to crying for she knew not what, and thereby made others cry for they did not know what, especially little Girls."[32] According to Johnson and Cutler, both enemies of enthusiasm, the revival began with the cries of a sexually frustrated old woman whose hysterics then spread to young girls. Significantly, the old woman was described as "whimsical" while the minister was "serious," and such gendered constructions were, by extension, applied to the varieties of religion as well: revived piety was feminine and overly emotional while the religion of the standing order was masculine and sober.

In the eyes of its critics, enthusiastic religion was not only emotional but also sexual. One criticism frequently voiced during revivals was that the late nights given to prayer meetings and the participants' overwrought emotions led to sexual promiscuity. Cutler informed his superior of these further events in Stratford:

> In Mr Johnson's Parish the Humor [i.e., the revival] did not take with more than 4 or 5 young women, who in the time of it used to get together and cry, and they continue pretty serious, but two of them married soon after these religious Raptures, and had each of them a Child in 6 or 7 months.[33]

By implication these young women allowed themselves to be carried away by two distinct yet related forms of excess emotion: crying over revived religion and engaging in premarital sex. Despite Jonathan Edwards's attempts to defuse such explosive talk by asserting that this revival attracted as many male as female converts, unlike the earlier revivals under Solomon Stoddard when many more women were awakened,[34] critics continued to see the revival as a time when female passions were dangerously unfettered.

In both Edwards's and Cutler's accounts, the Connecticut River Valley

Revival was a communal experience whose very group focus served to exaggerate its emotionalism, which led to clerical fears of gender and sexual disorder. In this way one unintended result of lay activity was to challenge the sexual order of the period. These themes would be played out once again in a few years when the arrival of a theatrical preacher triggered an even larger and more divisive revival.

The Great Awakening

The Great Awakening began in the autumn of 1740 when a young English preacher named George Whitefield reached New England during his American tour. Whitefield's advance billing generated tremendous interest, as Boston newspaper accounts from Georgia and the Middle Colonies documented his electrifying preaching.[35] Crowds of up to five thousand flocked to see the man who spiced his sermons with histrionics, and when the churches could no longer hold the crowds he spoke outdoors. But the Awakening was not merely about Whitefield. Triggered by his arrival it soon took on a life of its own, spreading to areas where the young evangelist never preached. Through 1741 support for the revival remained high among New England's clergy, but by 1742 ministerial excitement began to wane. Accompanying the religious fervor in 1741 and 1742 were so-called excesses: visions, trances, discerning, and crying out. In addition, the traditional order seemed undermined by lay exhorters who were African Americans, women, or lower-class men. In 1742 and 1743 it was no longer merely Old Lights (lay and clerical opponents of the revival) who spoke against such practices: moderate New Light ministers soon joined the chorus of clerical voices inveighing against the excesses of revivalism. By 1744, the short-lived nature of revivalism became apparent. Like the Earthquake Revival and the Connecticut River Valley revival before it, the Great Awakening faded away, except for in some isolated areas such as Durham, New Hampshire, where radicals like Richard Woodbury kept the spirit of 1741 alive. The major long-term impact of the Awakening was institutional: many New Lights who separated from their churches, especially in Connecticut and Rhode Island, joined Baptist churches.[36] More broadly, the Awakening heralded revivalism's continuing presence in New England's religious culture.

Much ink was spilled during the Great Awakening: by its supporters, its detractors, and those who hoped to prove their moderation. Maintaining that tradition, historians have found the Awakening to be an irresistible topic. Curiously, while no full-scale monograph on the Awakening in New England has been written in over forty years,[37] virtually every historian of eighteenth-century religion, politics, or society has felt compelled to include this greatest of all colonial revivals in their accounts. I am no exception to this pattern. I hope to shed some light on this much discussed topic by finding a middle ground between the two competing schools of interpretation, one that sees the Awakening as having had widespread and long-term consequences for colonial society and culture, and the other that argues that the effects of the Awakening were much more limited. I contend instead that the Awakening was a period of substantial but ephemeral changes that reveal preexisting tensions in the religious culture, but in the end did not fundamentally alter lay piety or lay-clergy relations.

Historians who see great changes arising from the Awakening emphasize two themes. First, they focus less on the New Lights' theology than on their actions and highlight the activities of the revival's extremists.[38] This attention to the radical extreme can be useful, but it gives the impression that most new converts condoned the behavior of radicals, when in fact a large, moderate New Light majority favored revived religion without the histrionics of James Davenport or Gilbert Tennant.

This interpretation's second theme is that the revival changed the world view of New Lights. According to this line of thought, the Awakening caused laypeople to question authority, presumably for the first time. The revival, in these historians' account, stressed individualism over hierarchy.[39] It is certainly true that the Awakening was accompanied by a great deal of contention. Still, this analysis has several shortcomings. First, it is problematic to locate long-term social changes in "the revivalists" in general. Ministers who supported the revival, excepting the radical fringe like Davenport and Andrew Croswell, were very careful to embed their revivalist messages within calls for order and hierarchy. Furthermore, these authors write as if the Great Awakening were the first colonial revival of any importance, when in fact 1727 and 1735 both saw large regional revivals that generated their fair share of contention and antiauthoritarianism. Most importantly, this book has shown that laypeople did not challenge authority only during the Awakening. While the revival years witnessed greater strife, there had been and continued to be a lively tradition of lay questioning and individual critical thinking.

Jon Butler most cogently takes the opposite position and argues that the Awakening did not have long-term effects. Butler challenges virtually every point made by those historians who see the Great Awakening as a break with the past. He argues that "the revivals democratized relations between ministers and the laity only in minimal ways." In response to the claims that the revival had long-term effects, Butler asserts that "the congregations [that the revivals] occasionally produced usually blended into the traditional social system, and the revivals abated without shattering its structure."[40] These are convincing points, but Butler and those who share his position underestimate how revealing the events of the revival years were. Like a flash, the Awakening illuminated the tensions within New England's religious culture, if only briefly.

The patterns that emerge from the Awakening parallel those of the earlier revivals: laypeople experienced religion communally despite some individualistic tendencies in the new style of conversion; ministers attempted to rein in the emotions some laypeople exhibited in worship; and people expressed gender concerns, both in actual gender inversions where women preached and published, as well as more rhetorically and metaphorically, as the revival was attacked in gendered terms.

In almost all lay writings about the Great Awakening, the revival was portrayed as above all a group occurrence. Although people interpreted their spiritual distresses and delights individually, within their own minds, their experiences were shaped by their friends and family. During the Awakening, in fact, lay piety was even more communally oriented than usual. Normally solitary activities like reading godly books often took place in group settings. For example, in 1741 Nicholas Gilman reported that "in the Evening tho Dark and dirty a throng of people assembled at my House to hear Mr. Edwards's Narrative of Conversions at Northampton—read part of it, and made Some remarks to the people."[41]

Furthermore, going to sermons, which usually involved crowds of a hundred or so people, became something akin to going to a spiritual carnival, with throngs of people and the excitement that such large groups generated. Nathan Cole, in his well-known description of hearing George Whitefield preach in Middletown, Connecticut, estimated that "3 or 4000 of people Assembled together," not including the "steady Stream of horses" and the "ferry boats Running swift backward and forward."[42] Many sources reported crowds of up to five thousand people to hear preachers like Whitefield in the revival's early months.[43] Such large groups, since they fostered greater anonymity than in a typical congregation, leveled distinctions of rank among the participants.[44]

Moreover, people participated in group activities that had no counterpart in nonrevival periods. Some people became in effect revival followers, making pilgrimages to the places where religious fervor was the strongest. Even more impressive than Cole's twelve-mile sprint to Middletown was a journey taken by Joseph Goodhue and some companions in January 1741. Goodhue left his hometown of Newbury, Massachusetts, and "with others went to York [Maine] in which Place the Work of the Lord was marvelos to mee." There, Goodhue and his friends "went about frome hous to house" seeking spiritual comfort from anyone who might provide it.[45]

In addition to these sorts of group events, where people saw their neighbors and strangers exhibiting religious fervor, laypeople in their conversion narratives routinely discussed their companions' influence on their religious experiences. Although there is no collection of conversion narratives from the Great Awakening as there is from the Earthquake Revival, there are many lay accounts of conversion in diaries and reminiscences. In 1743 Sarah Prince, the spiritually precocious daughter of Boston minister and prorevivalist Thomas Prince, began keeping a diary after reading John White's *The Power of Godliness*, which urged good Christians to keep written records of their spiritual experiences.[46] Sarah Prince's first entry was an account of the first fifteen years of her life, including details about the Awakening and its effect on her piety, much of which was filtered through her encounters with her young companions. In her account, until she was twelve Prince did not greatly concern herself about religion. Then Whitefield arrived in 1740, and Prince was "something affected with his Ministery" but was not fully awakened until she began attending prayer meetings with her friends. "Some of my Acquaintance," wrote Prince, "were thotfull about their souls and we used to meet to Pray and conferr about spiritual things." Not only was Prince concerned about the state of her own soul, but she had "Longings for salvation of Others—I wanted all to tast[e] and see that God is Good." According to Prince, she even had a tendency to take the communal nature of her piety too far:

> And one Error that I went into was, Judging of my Experiences by those of others—whereas the word of God is the only standard . . . I particularly remember that many Persons whom I look'd upon to be Experienced Christians Invited that their must be a word of Promise bore in on the soul at the time of conversion and I not having any it greatly Perplex'd me.[47]

Thus, the adolescent Prince compared her own feelings and experiences against those who she felt were more knowledgeable. Prince viewed this common practice as an error, for her ministers (including, no doubt, her father) told her that the Scriptures were the only standard by which to measure her piety. But it was natural that Sarah Prince, in great distress and hoping that she was saved, would ask those around her how to know if she was converted.

Hannah Heaton was only slightly older than Prince when she set down her "Spiritual Exercises." Born on Long Island and residing in East Haven, Connecticut, Heaton was twenty when the Awakening began to affect some of her friends and her sister. Heaton first learned of the revival's effects among her companions back in Long Island while she was "at a tavern in a frolick." A young man from her home parish "told me how the work of god was carried on there and several of my mates that was converted." At roughly the same time Heaton received a letter from her sister Elizabeth documenting how "her spirit rejoysed in god." The lure of this news from home was too great for Heaton, who crossed the Sound a few days later, only to be besieged by those who hoped that she too would be awakened: "As soon as I got in to my fathers house young people come in and began to talk, sister Elisabeth began to cry over me because I had no interest in christ." This pressure immediately had an effect. The talk of revival "took hold of my heart, I kept going to meetings and was more and more concerned and o what crying out there was among the people, 'what shall I do to be saved?'"[48] In this case the passions caused by the revival increased exponentially as individuals were caught up in their peers' fervor.

A somewhat more mature version of the same dynamic is apparent in the conversion of thirty-two-year-old Sarah Edwards, wife of the Northampton revivalist. Her spiritual concern reached its height in January 1742, during a period when her husband was often away preaching in other towns. While Jonathan Edwards was preaching in Leicester, Sarah Edwards found the company of other godly men and women increased her piety. Following an afternoon lecture preached by Samuel Buell, Sarah Edwards lingered to enjoy the presence of those awakened by the revival. She reported that while she remained in the meetinghouse she was "from time to time overcome, and my strength taken away, by the sight of one and another, whom I regarded as the children of God, and who, I had heard were lively and animated in religion." After spending three hours in "very earnest" conversation in the meetinghouse, Sarah returned home to find a group of ministers and their wives at her house. This Christian community worked powerfully on her mind: "Seeing and conversing with them on the Divine goodness, renewed my former feelings, and filled me with an intense desire that we might all arise, and, with an active, flowing and fervent heart, give glory to God." The excitement proved to be too much for Sarah Edwards: she soon experienced one of her many fainting spells. Because of her piety's physical manifestations, with much swooning, Edwards often found herself being watched over by one or more women. Sarah particularly enjoyed discussions with these female caretakers, reporting in one instance, when she was "too much exhausted by emotions of joy, to rise and sit up," that "my feelings prompted me to converse very earnestly, with one and another of the pious women, who were present, on those spiritual and heavenly objects, of which I had so deep an impression."[49] As during nonrevival periods, laypeople experienced piety in a community context, but in the heat of a revival, that tendency increased greatly as one's network of pious friends grew. Of course, revivalist preaching was important during the Awakening, but these examples of communal piety offer a counterpoint to the overemphasis on such preaching. Much of the excitement created during this revival was spurred not by sermons but by the interaction of sensitive laypeople with their peers.

Is it a coincidence that these three examples of communal piety all involve women? To an extent it is. Men were, of course, part of the community awakened during the revival. And when men like Joseph Goodhue, Nathan Cole, and John Loring wrote about their experiences, they situated their piety in a group context.[50] But women were more likely to focus on the influence of their companions when describing their experience of the Awakening. This was related to women's somewhat different conception of community: women placed greater emphasis on female networks than men did on male networks. Not that there wasn't a male counterpart to the female communal culture surrounding private religious meetings and childbirth and quilting. As noted in chapter 1, prayer and reading groups were important sources of identity for pious men. In addition, men met on training fields for musters and in taverns for ale and thereby cemented their interpersonal ties. But women knew that as a group they could not vote in church affairs and that individually they should not speak unless spoken to. This may have led pious women to seek other women's company as a way to increase their religious experiences' legitimacy, both in men's and in their own eyes. And when women found their companions in a state of religious distress, this had a powerful effect on them, often inducing them to consider their own sinful states. During revivals this group dynamic was even more widespread, as women felt themselves under attack from antirevivalists who disparaged the Awakening in explicitly gendered terms.

Sarah Prince, Hannah Heaton, and Sarah Edwards experienced the Awakening in a group setting. For these three, this helped to heighten the revival's emotions, causing Heaton to contemplate suicide in her distress and Edwards to have repeated fainting spells. But these three women, though they approached the edge of ministerially sanctioned behavior, never let their passions overtake them to the extent that they became the objects of clerical attacks on revivalism's excesses. Others, however, urged on by the group mentality of revivalism, especially in the most frenzied years of 1741 and 1742, engaged in behaviors that provided arguments for antirevivalists. But the activities that Old Lights criticized during the Awakening did not spring from thin air. Rather, these behaviors were consonant with the prerevival context of lay piety.

When historians document the Awakening's excesses, they usually turn to the writings of Charles Chauncy and other Old Lights to find the most lurid quotes and most extreme anecdotes. Such biased sources need to be used extremely carefully; often they are not used with caution and a distorted view of the revival is presented.[51] Ironically, these partisan antirevivalist sources are not necessary to use: even those in favor of the Awakening deplored its excesses and documented them carefully, and these moderate New Lights are much more credible witnesses.

Although it may at first glance seem counterintuitive, prorevivalists like Jonathan Edwards described at great length new converts' dangerously enthusiastic activities. Moderate revivalists like Edwards did not want the Awakening to be tainted by the behaviors of an enthusiastic and seemingly sinful fringe. For example, Edwards worried that the tendency of some laypeople during the revival to claim divine inspiration would sully the revival's reputation. According to Edwards, "one erroneous Principle, than which scarce any has proved more mischievous to the present glorious Work of God, is a Notion that 'tis God's Manner, now in these Days, to guide his Saints, at least some that are more eminent, by Inspiration, or immediate Revelation."[52] Eleazer Wheelock, minister in Lebanon, Connecticut, also attested to such activities. Scarcely another clergyman in New England was as great a friend to revivalism as Wheelock; he traversed many miles in 1741 as an itinerant spreading the good word. But while in Voluntown, Connecticut, he reported "more of the footsteps of Satan than in any place I have yet been in. The zeal of some is too furious—they tell of many visions, revelations, and many Strong impressions upon their imagination."[53]

As with other offensive activities, claims of divine revelation were not new to the Great Awakening (as in chapters 2 and 4), they were merely more common. This was also true of lay exhorting. Edwards warned that "the common People in exhorting one another ought not to cloath themselves with the like Authority with that which is proper for ministers."[54] This issue did not suddenly appear in 1741: since Anne Hutchinson, ministers criticized laypeople who gave religious advice in a manner too much like a clergyman. Again, the revival years created an atmosphere that exaggerated these preexisting tendencies.

In response to these extreme behaviors, many ministers who had been wholehearted supporters of the revival began in 1742 and 1743 to warn the converted that their behavior endangered the revival. Ministers attempted to rein in the passions of the peak revival years because they believed that overly emotional piety could lead people into dangerous temptations. Jonathan Parsons, a strong supporter of the Awakening and minister in Lyme, Connecticut, tried to turn the revival's communal nature back on itself. While group passions had created some of the excesses in the first place, Parsons advocated group watchfulness to prevent errors. Emphasizing a community of Christians, Parsons argued in 1742 that laypeople needed to watch over their neighbors to make sure they did not stray from the path of legitimate piety. Parsons asserted that "'tis doubtless the important Duty of every Christian to *admonish, exhort, rebuke, instruct,* in his Place, according to his Opportunity: a straying Brother needs this kind Office from a gentle Hand, and sometimes he needs *sharp* Rebukes that he may be *sound in the Faith.*"[55]

Likewise, Jedidiah Jewet, New Light minister of Rowley, Massachusetts, urged his parishioners to avoid overly emotional expressions of their piety. "*My Brethren,*" Jewet declared, "I beseech you all, and particularly those, who think they have, in these late Times of uncommon Awakenings, been brought to believe . . . to shew Men that you do indeed believe, by a fruitful holy Life agreeable to the Gospel."[56] Jewet's concern that converts "shew Men" that their faith was legitimate indicates that he worried how others perceived the revival. Jewet and other New Light ministers realized by 1742 that they must try to temper their parishioners' most radical and emotional activities.

Published in 1743 by Boston's Thomas Prince as a moderate chronicle of the Awakening, *The Christian History* continued this strategy of New Light ministers trying to distance themselves from and halt the revival's most outrageous excesses. John Rogers, Jr., minister of the First Congregational Church in Ipswich, was seventy-seven years old and the elder spokesman of New Light ministers in northeastern Massachusetts when he submitted a letter to *The Christian History* in 1743. Rogers affirmed that he was generally delighted by this "*most powerful and clear Work of Grace* (according to our Apprehension) wrought in the Hearts of Multitudes, from one End of the Land to the other." But Rogers also worried that errors were likely among laypeople when they imbibed the spirit of the revival. Therefore, like Parsons before him, Rogers urged Christian watchfulness to stem the tide of errors, warning that "we must at the same Time carefully watch, and bear due *Testimony* against all *Errors* and *Disorders* that have or may arise." In a more authoritarian vein, Rev. John White of Gloucester, a friend of the revival but avowed enemy of disorder, declared his sentiments in an open letter to *The Christian History*. He made it clear that many ministers viewed their role in the Awakening, at least once it had begun, as one of repression: "As to *Visions* we had enough of them, until such Time as in a Lecture Sermon I declared my Sentiments concerning them; and so far as I can understand, there has never been one since. Our Congregation has been disturbed by *Outcries*, but I laboured to suppress them."[57] White believed it necessary to "suppress" the most emotional tendencies of his flock. His mistake, however, may have been in attributing too much success to his campaign. A key phrase in his testimony is that there were no more visions among his people "so far as I can understand." It seems likely that once White's parishioners realized his hostility to the revival's emotional trappings, they did their best to hide such behaviors from him.

Such critiques of emotion, even by those ministers who generally supported revivalism, were entwined with gender anxiety, which gave these attacks an even greater sense of urgency. This gender anxiety was not merely a product of reflexive misogyny. Rather, it was a response to the very real activities of women during the Awakening.[58]

For example, an anecdote related by Sarah Pierpont in her diary reveals the connections between women, evangelical religion, and sexuality. In February 1743 Pierpont described a "wed[d]ing in the Eastern Part of the Colony where the Lord Jesus Christ condescended not only to be a Guest (but oh astonishing) was Himselfe the Brid[e]groom and seized the bride for himselfe." Language equating Christ with a bridegroom and a new convert with a bride had been conventional in New England for over a century. Unusual in Pierpont's account was the connection with an actual earthly wedding. The bride had been affected by the religious fervor that peaked in 1742: "She had been in Distress about her soul for some Time, instead of being divorced by temporal Things as is too often the Case she grew more & more distressed to have her soul espoused to Jesus Christ." Pierpont expressed surprise that this woman's impending wedding did not decrease her spiritual distress, as most people had a tendency to be distracted by their worldly affairs. But for this woman the approach of the wedding coincided with an increase in her concern:

Her Distress now came to such a Degree that she fell down while the Minister was at Prayer but then recovering so as to joyn Hands with her Companion (who was a Christian) the blessed Jesus at that Instant broke in upon her soul so that the Minute she joyn'd Hands with an earthly Husband her soul clos'd with the Lord Jesus Christ as her Spiritual & Eternal Husband.[59]

Even allowing that Pierpont recast the story to make for a more dramatic telling, this wedding represents a number of the Awakening's themes. Like Sarah Edwards and Hannah Heaton, this bride experienced her conversion corporeally, falling down as the minister prayed. The clergyman may have been skeptical when the woman reported that she had her conversion experience at the moment she joined hands with her new husband since many ministers were wary of conversions that seemed to be brought on by emotional strains. Certainly as a bride-to-be this woman would have been feeling anxiety and excitement in the weeks leading up to the wedding; in this case during the heat of the Awakening she (and likely those around her) interpreted these feelings as indicative of spiritual distress. Though seen favorably by Pierpont (and in fact mirroring her own ecstatic experiences during these years), this was the very sort of emotionally induced conversion that made antirevivalists scoff.

Even more threatening to the standing order than emotionally vulnerable young women were those women who engaged in activities outside their traditional roles. During the Awakening, a number of women published poems and other accounts of their views on the revival. Publishing women's words was not unprecedented: as we have seen, women's dying words were occasionally printed and several volumes of pious poetry by Elizabeth Singer Rowe and Anne Bradstreet had appeared by the Awakening. But women's printed poetry during the revival was more controversial, appearing at a time of great partisanship in religious discourse and taking sides in that debate.

Into this fray in 1742 stepped Sarah Parsons Moorhead, boldly declaring her sentiments as a New Light. Her lengthy published poem gently criticized James Davenport for being too extreme, especially in denouncing other ministers. But Moorhead's perspective was as a supporter of the revival, which she made clear in the first lines of her poem. Moorhead did not mince words with the opponents of the Awakening, threatening them with divine justice:

Now let the Scoffers at the Word of God
Tremble, for *Gabriel* brandishes his Sword
Your raging Hearts shall feel the burning Steel
And God his Terrors in your Soul reveal.

These were not the words of a woman adhering to the doctrine of "speak when spoken to," but the clarion call of a soldier engaged in a religious war. Not only did Moorhead have the temerity to challenge antirevivalists on their own turf—the polemic pamphlet—she evinced the very emotional and sexualized interpretation of revived religion that made them the most nervous. Witness Moorhead's passionate account of her reaction to the radical New Light, Andrew Croswell:

My Soul by you it's glorious Power has felt,
My Bosom warms all my Affections melt:
I should not think a thousand Winters long,
While Jesus Love sounds sweetly from your Tongue.
Many such Times has Sovereign Love return'd:
By many Instruments my Heart has burn'd;
Then blame me not if I should take the Part
Of all, whom God has made to reach my Heart.[60]

With bodily images of tongue and bosom and heated words like warm, melt, and burn, Moorhead made it clear that revival preaching had touched her physically as well as emotionally. Surely her entry into the male-dominated world of print led antirevivalists to see this as one more example of gender inversion caused by the Awakening.

Likewise, in a poem honoring George Whitefield an unnamed "Gentlewoman" forcefully offered her opinions about revivalism and the controversial young itinerant. The Gentlewoman was an unabashed partisan of Whitefield, calling him the "Couragious Soldier of the God of Hosts." Like Moorhead, this poet used martial imagery, warning opponents of the revival that "Justice is pay'd in Streams of heav'nly Blood." Toward the end of this poem the Gentlewoman made her boldest argument, calling on the ministers of New England to imitate Whitefield:

May *Levi's* sacred Tribe that round him wait,
Dear *Whitefield's* zeal and plainness imitate;
Lay moral Themes, scholastick Terms aside;
And sin-sick Souls, by Faith to Jesus guide.[61]

In this passage the poet criticized the New England clergy for their sermons' lack of excitement and accessibility. For a woman publicly to air this complaint was an astounding inversion of ordinary power relations. Of course, the discursive space created by these two poems should not be overstated; after all, both authors felt compelled to write under the cloak of anonymity. But that fear of attributing their names to their works indicates just how much they breached the tenets of female decorum.

A final example of the gender inversions that so worried antirevivalists is the case of Bathsheba Kingsley of Westfield, Massachusetts.[62] Jonathan Edwards pithily described Kingsley as "a brawling woman," and this she indeed was.[63] Subverting gender, family, and religious hierarchies, Kingsley took advantage of the excitement and flux generated by the Great Awakening to become an itinerant lay preacher. The ecclesiastical council that attempted to thwart her ministry observed in 1743 that, like many lay prophets, Kingsley "has for many years in her conduct been almost wholly under the government of a series of dreams and imaginations and sudden impulses, supposing them to be immediate revelations from heaven."[64] The authority she claimed from these direct revelations led her to challenge the power of her husband and the local ministers.

Although ostensibly convened to rein in Kingsley's subversive religious practices, the ecclesiastical council was greatly concerned with Kingsley's neglect of her family duties. Their reasoning was clear: the family was the wellspring of orthodox religion, and disruption in one sphere was as dangerous as in the other. "We judge she has exceedingly departed from the way [of] her duty," Edwards wrote for the council, listing her numerous domestic indiscretions. According to the ministers, "her behavior has in general been exceeding contrary to that Christian gentleness and meekness that becomes a follower of the Lamb of God, especially in the treatment of her husband." In his notes, Edwards cryptically remarked that Kingsley was guilty of "praying that her husband might go quick to hell." Although it is unclear in what context this occurred, it may have been uttered during one of the couple's numerous disputes. Bathsheba's husband Hains did not support his wife's ministry; in fact, the council censured her for "often disobeying her husband's commands in going abroad and often stealing away privately and taking her husband's horse to go away to other towns contrary to his mind." Since all the property owned by the couple legally belonged to Hains, he thought he could forbid her from taking his horse. But he must not have realized what he was up against. Bathsheba did not acquiesce and instead became even more hostile, "commonly talking in a very severe, harsh, and reflecting manner to her husband before the rest of the family and others, without any restraint."

These actions struck the council's ministers as directly counter to the behavior "that becomes a Christian woman in her place." In her place, a woman should uphold the order of families within her home, something Kingsley rebelled against as the result of her status as deliverer of God's word. This galled Jonathan Edwards, who transcribed the council's report. Edwards, like his colleagues, held traditional notions about gender roles within marriage. In an unpublished sermon Edwards argued that women are "weaker" than men, and that "when a woman is married to an husband she receives him as a guide, as a protector, a safeguard and defense." Because of this, claimed Edwards, "it's against nature for a man to love a woman as a wife that is rugged, daring and presumptuous, and trusts to herself."[65] Kingsley was surely daring and trusted in her own abilities, and as such must have struck Edwards and the other ministers as somewhat "against nature" in her domestic relations.

But if Bathsheba Kingsley had not also attacked the power of other townspeople and the local ministers an ecclesiastical council probably would not have been convened. Because her attacks were not confined to her husband, the ministers agreed something had to be done. Kingsley was charged with "making almost a constant business of talking against others wherever she goes, freely at all times and before all sorts of persons censuring others." But Kingsley was not merely a quarrelsome person, she had a religious mission, and her "talking against" others occurred in the context of her "declaring her judgment and suspicions of others as to their souls' state." According to the ministers Kingsley spent a great deal of her time "setting forth others' vileness and wickedness." As part of her itinerations, Kingsley claimed the power to tell who was and was not saved, one of the "excesses" that most vexed the standing ministry.[66]

Finally, and most challenging to traditional hierarchies, were Kingsley's practices that implicitly, and sometimes even explicitly, set her in a superior position to ministers. Kingsley's direct revelations from God made her very confident in her abilities to preach and thus she was "apt to think her knowledge to be very eminent and superior to that of others," which led her to "think that [she] was a proper person to be improved for some great thing in the church of God, and that in the exercise of some parts of the work of the ministry." This reveals why ministers were so concerned about people, like Anne Hutchinson and Bathsheba Kingsley, who claimed direct knowledge of God's will: revelation led to a very self-assured prophet, one who could not be easily dissuaded from his or her views. Because she believed she spoke God's words, Kingsley spent a great deal of time delivering her important message. The council reported that she was a "great part of her time gone from home, almost perpetually wandering about from house to house, and very frequently to other towns, under a notion of doing Christ's work and delivering his messages." Unlike a typical itinerant, who usually spoke in large open-air gatherings, Kingsley preached at least part of the time on a personal level, visiting people in their houses to convince them of the need to be converted. But like other itinerants, Kingsley implicitly attacked the theory and practice of Congregational clericalism, in which the standing minister was the ultimate religious authority in his town or parish. The most grievous charge leveled by the council, however, was that she was inclined "to go reprove and warn her own ministers and denounce the judgments of God against 'em under a notion of delivering messages from God to 'em." Empowered by God's words, Kingsley directly challenged her ministers—Nehemiah Bull until 1740 and John Ballantine beginning in 1741—and even threatened them with God's wrath. And despite their efforts and stern pronouncements, the ministers were ultimately unable to stop Kingsley: several weeks after the council Kingsley was suspended from the Lord's Supper by her church.[67]

Clearly, Bathsheba Kingsley represented gender disorder of the first degree. Not only did she challenge her husband's authority within their home (his home, legally), and not only did she talk back to those townspeople who disagreed with her on religious matters, she claimed an authority equal to and even greater than local ministers. To the clergy who composed the council, she must have also represented the gender disorder possible when a revival got out of control. As this book has shown, eighteenth-century religious culture was suffused with latent gender anxieties, which could become explicit during liminal moments such as deathbed scenes and rituals. Although the Awakening was not precisely a liminal moment in the anthropological sense, it was a time of great flux. The uncertainty generated by this revival allowed for the activity of some antiauthoritarian women and consequently led to efforts to rein in that gender disorder. For the most part the ability of women like Moorhead and Kingsley to offer critiques of hierarchy faded with the Awakening's fervor. A few radicals like Sarah Prentice, however, continued their activities beyond the revival years.

Although she was unique, Bathsheba Kingsley represented the extremes of gender disruption that antirevivalists feared as a result of the Awakening. These concerns led lay and ministerial opponents of the Great Awakening to discuss the revival in gendered terms, rhetorically casting it and its converts as feminized. For example, Charles Brockwell, an Anglican missionary for the Society for the Propagation of the Gospel (SPG) living in Salem, wrote a letter to the secretary of the SPG in February 1742 describing what he saw as the unsavory elements of the colonial revival. Brockwell focused on such lower-class characters as "one Elvins a Baker," who "tho' a fellow of consummate ignorance is nevertheless followed by great multitudes and much cried up." In addition to overturning class hierarchies, the revival in Salem disrupted race, gender, and age hierarchies as well: Brockwell reported that "Men, Women, Children, Servants, & Nigros are now become (as they phrase it) Exhorters."[68] Brockwell hinted at the sexuality of revived religion when he claimed that "their works may justly be called the works of darkness as acted in the Night & often continued to the noon of the next day."[69] Thus for Brockwell the disruption of traditional order led to the sexualization of religion.

Similarly, Nathan Bowen, a forty-five-year-old lay antirevivalist in Marblehead, painted the revival in powerfully gendered terms. At every turn he saw gender disorder in the Awakening. In January 1742, during the most radical phase of the revival, Bowen complained that "some of the fisherman & others of the like powers pretend to Extreordinary Gifts!" More worrisome for Bowen than the class inversions implicit in fishermen preaching were the gender inversions it created: "One of [the fishermen] (namely F. Salter) has Set up a Meeting for Evening Devotion & is attended by Crowds of women &c." Bowen's "&c" indicates that for him, those who attended these meetings were, no matter their sex, so many women.[70] This and another "womans meeting" had the tendency "to subvert the Good order in society."[71] Thus, not only ministers but some laymen worried about gender inversions infringing on their patriarchal authority.

For Bowen this subversion was the result of people "of the meanest Capacity ie women & even Common negros" who "take upon them to Exhort their Betters even in the pulpit, before large assemblys." These meetings usually "drew together the Giddy Mob & of silly women in great Multitudes." In such scenes where women dominated, Bowen argued, emotions were likely to run high. At a revival meeting led by one Crocker, Bowen attested that "the old women were affrighted in to Fits of Schreeching; & the utmost Confusion." Finally, making it crystal clear that he believed the revival's gender disorder infected all new converts, regardless of their sex, Bowen described in July 1742 the reception Gilbert Tennant's preaching received. In a sermon Tennant spoke with great ferocity "'til he had wrought effectually on the old women of both Sexes."[72] To Bowen all those who responded to the passions of a Tennant or Davenport (or a lesser-known local preacher), whether men or women, were rhetorically feminized.[73]

Old Lights in Lyme, Connecticut, used a similar strategy when they focused on an alleged incident of homosexual display between two men during a revivalist church service. According to Jonathan Parsons, the New Light minister of Lyme, "one thing complained of as an indecency was, that two men embraced each other in their arms before the blessing was given." Parsons did not deny this charge, but asserted that it was not "so very indecent, as some would represent it."[74] Spreading rumors of homosexual conduct was one sure way for opponents of the revival to shine a harsh light on the gender transgressions of the awakened. In this way antirevivalists like Bowen and Brockwell and the Old Lights in Lyme saw the abundant gender inversions taking place during the Great Awakening and subsequently attempted to denigrate the whole revival by describing it, and its supporters, as feminized.

Old Light ministers such as Charles Chauncy also attempted to portray the revival as appealing primarily to the effeminate, emotional portion of the population. In a patriarchal society this strategy aimed to make revivalism seem marginal. According to Chauncy, "the *Subjects* also of these *Terrors* may lead us to make the like Judgment about them; and these are *Children, Women,* and *youngerly* Persons . . . whose Passions are soft and tender, and more easily thrown into a Commotion."[75] This attempt to feminize and marginalize the revival was part of the Old Light strategy of controlling emotionalism.[76] Although this campaign was not the major reason the Great Awakening ended—the fickle and unsustainable nature of revivalism had more to do with that—it certainly did not help that in the waning years of the revival there was such concerted opposition to the emotions that had attracted so many laypeople.

Thus the Great Awakening came and went from New England, differing from the two preceding revivals mainly in size and scope. During the revival years the religious culture's dynamics were laid bare: laypeople experienced piety in a communal context, some people exhibited a tendency toward great emotional extremes, many ministers attempted to control those seemingly excessive emotions, participants expressed gender tensions, and critics inveighed against gender inversions. But after the Awakening, as before, people feared death, expressed those fears on their deathbeds, partook in religious rituals, quarreled with their ministers, prayed, read godly books, and met in small groups to discuss the Bible. In some ways the religious landscape had been changed: the Baptist denomination grew as it absorbed many Separate New Lights, and organized heterodoxy spread. But laypeople had not suddenly embraced a new antiauthoritarianism that would lead them to the Revolution and beyond. Rather, the Awakening shined a spotlight on some of lay piety's antiauthoritarian tendencies that had existed before the Awakening.

The Seacoast Revival, 1763–1764

From October 1763 until the end of 1764, there occurred yet another harvest of souls in New England. This time participants lived within twenty miles of the seacoast from East Hampton, Long Island, to Newburyport, Massachusetts. Within this broad swath two centers of revivalism existed: one in Providence, Rhode Island, and the other in the Chebacco Parish, Ipswich. It had been over twenty years since the Great Awakening and numerous young men and women, some not even born when Whitefield first arrived in Boston, were receptive to this latest outpouring of religious fervor. The Seacoast Revival, as I have termed it, reveals as clearly as any other revival just how contagious and communally generated revivalism was.[77]

In 1763 John Cleaveland, the author of one of only two Seacoast Revival narratives,[78] invited Francis Worcester to preach in his parish. Worcester was not quite an itinerant but neither was he a standing minister: he had been ordained in Sandwich, Massachusetts, in 1735 as pastor of the Separatist Church at Scusset but was dismissed in 1749. Subsequently, Worcester lived in the North Shore region of Massachusetts and occasionally accepted the invitations of local standing ministers to ease their preaching burdens. Somehow, the sixty-five-year-old Worcester managed to touch the hearts of Chebacco Parish's young residents to a degree unknown in two decades.

In the conversion narratives copied down by church elders several months later, many of the awakened pointed to Worcester's week of preaching as the start of the revival. Thomas Story, only seventeen years old, remembered that "the first that bro't me under concern was hearing Mr Worcester say that young people would tell Lyes to make sport of it."[79] Sixteen-year-old Nathan Burnam elaborated on this theme by narrating that "I was under some checks of Conscience some Time before Mr. Worcester came to Chebacco, but should stiffle convictions by being in rude company: but Mr. Worcesters preaching bro't me under concern again, his saying that young people wo'd tell Lies to make Sport."[80] Two dynamics are revealed here. First, as during the Great Awakening, new converts credited revivalist preaching with planting the first seeds of concern. Second, the very similar accounts, with several mentioning Worcester's sermon that chastised youth for lying, suggest how much in lockstep were these late adolescent experiences of revival.

After this first week, the revival took on a life of its own, fueled by the group dynamics of Chebacco's youth. By November a number of young people had been awakened, and they began to hold private meetings. Perhaps to check their potentially sexualized nature, these meetings—attended by several dozen young, unmarried, and emotional men and women—were often conducted at the home and under the supervision of an adult, including occasionally Cleaveland. One such meeting, at Deacon Eleazer Craft's house the day after Thanksgiving in late November, took on almost legendary proportions in the revival accounts.[81] At least six of the fifty-three surviving testimonials mention this gathering. Collectively they indicate that the presence of some youth under concern served to heighten the spiritual distress of virtually all present. Hannah Low, only twenty, remembered that "I saw I was lost and a perishing Sinner, that Justice was out against me that friday night after the Thanksgiving—and was bro't to cry for Mercy—and when one was bro't into the Light by [i.e., near] me and I perceived it, it was like a Dart cast into my Soul."[82] Later that night, excited by the passions evident around her, Low had a conversion experience. Similarly, Thomas Story found that night's excitement too much to resist. "At Deacon Craft's," Story related, "seeing persons under concern and Jacob Choate struck under concern and hearing Mr Cleaveland talking to little Betty Perkins struck my Mind under convictions of my actual Sins, I see I had sinned against the Great God and tho't I was agoing to hell."[83] At this meeting impressionable young men and women became concerned about their spiritual state through a sort of peer pressure.

Soon word began to spread throughout the region of the religious excitement in Chebacco. Several people in nearby towns heard about the revival and came to see for themselves, like Mary Woodbury, who in 1766 recalled that "when I heard of the work of God in this Place about two years ago, and heard some say one Thing and some another about it, some saying it was the work of the Devil, I had a great Desire to come and see and hear for myself."[84] Although in his narrative Cleaveland attempted to downplay the disruptive nature of this harvest of souls, this quote demonstrates that talk about the revival was not all favorable along the North Shore. Negative publicity did not stop Hannah Bear of Newbury from making the ten-mile trek to Chebacco to participate in the revival: "when I heard of this work in Chebacco I was much affected with the news, and was persuaded that it was a glorious work of God, and was put into such distress of Soul that I could not sleep quietly anights."[85] The case of one pilgrim to Chebacco demonstrates how revivalism could undercut the authority of ministers unsympathetic to awakened laypeople's concerns. According to Cleaveland, one unnamed man came from a distance to experience the revival and upon meeting the Chebacco pastor the stranger said, "'O Sir, my Minister says there is no *original Sin*.'" To this Cleaveland replied, "'Well, what do you think? Do you think you have any?' 'O yes, (said he) enough to damn me to all Eternity!'"[86] As during the Great Awakening and increasing throughout the eighteenth century, laypeople's mobility and the availability of information about nearby religious happenings sometimes weakened the power of a minister to prevent his people from taking part in a revival.

Though most people who heard of the revival lived too far away to come all the way to Chebacco, this did not deter them from converting. Their hometowns became additional sites of revivalism starting in January 1764. At least thirteen towns in northeastern Massachusetts reported revival activity in this period.[87] Samuel Chandler, the Gloucester minister with revivalist leanings during the Great Awakening, did his best to support his parishioners' increasingly zealous piety. At the desire of Hubbard Haskell, a Gloucester resident awakened by the events in Chebacco, Chandler preached a sermon at Haskell's house, where "a Great throng of People crowded." Soon the youth of Gloucester experienced a revival of piety, with ever younger children being awakened; following a Sabbath sermon, Chandler reported that "after meeting came in Peter Livers age 8 years under convictions." If that was not enough to raise Chandler's suspicions that people were becoming a little too frenzied, his parishioners' crying out during sermons did. Perhaps as a result of these concerns, Chandler decided that he had been presented with at least one case of false assurance. Chandler wrote that "in the Evening came in Naby Davis, seems to be easy & pretend she does believe. I am doubtfull of the case fearing the evill one is presenting some false joys" to her.[88] Again it seems that gender anxiety raised its head during a revival. Compare Chandler's accounts of young people (predominantly women) crying out and being "in very great Distress"[89] with this description of a sober male convert: "In the Evening came in Mr Saltor who is a sensible understanding man seriously enquiring & seeking after God. I had much conversations with him. He well observes the workings of his mind & gives a very clear account of his convictions."[90] Saltor emerges from this description as the very antithesis of enthusiastic revived religion, being "sensible," "understanding," and "serious," as his pastor described him in the masculine language of rationality and reason. Although John Cleaveland argued that the Seacoast Revival bred none of the contention of the Great Awakening,[91] it seems that in some parishes generally sympathetic ministers became concerned with converts' female-gendered expressions of piety.

Beginning in February, reports of religious revival began to be heard from East Hampton, Long Island; Norwich and Plainfield, Connecticut; Providence, Rhode Island; and Rehoboth, Massachusetts.[92] Like the revival a generation earlier, ministers expressed the deepest satisfaction when the newly converted came from the ranks of "backsliders," "deists and cardplayers, and many frolickers."[93] In late February the revival reached new heights of intensity in Chebacco. The elders of the Chebacco church met in Cleaveland's house "to hear and take down in Writing, the gracious Experiences of such as had a Mind to be admitted Members of this Church."[94] Later that week the relations were read in the meetinghouse.

This reification of the conversion experience had a profound effect on some who still remained unconverted. Mary Rust, one of the older participants in the revival at thirty-five, recalled how she went to the first meeting where the relations were read: "I went to the Meeting but had no great sense till the last Relation was read, and then I was moved something and I was filled with earnest desires to God that he would appear for me before I left the [meeting]house."[95] Indeed, Rust's prayer was answered, and before the service was over she had been convinced of Christ's love. Similarly, John Cheever had been somewhat awakened in the early phase of the revival, "but my concern abated 'till I heard some relations of experience read, which raised my concern. I tho't God was calling in his chosen and I was likely to be left."[96] These statements demonstrate revivalism's self-perpetuating nature. The harvest of souls in Chebacco had seemingly come to an end when the very process of admitting recently converted members caused others to be awakened. This accounts for the ministerial eagerness to have conversion narratives read in meetings, so they would serve as inspiration for the converts' peers.

But by the summer of 1764 the revival began to wind down and passions began to subside. Across the region, the number of new members was large, but not on the level of the Great Awakening. For example, fifty were converted in Rehoboth, forty in Providence, fifty in Newburyport, thirty in Rowley, and ninety in Chebacco (where about two-thirds were women).[97] Despite its relatively modest size, the Seacoast Revival's dynamics resembled those of the three previous New England revivals. Most notably, this revival followed and enhanced the pattern of revivalism as encouraged by peer pressure, especially in Chebacco. There, although Francis Worcester's preaching helped spark the revival, as had Whitefield's itineracy a generation earlier, the revival fed upon the momentum generated when a large number of young men and women saw their peers being converted and feared they were being "left behind."

Historians of eighteenth-century religion and society in New England have focused too much on the Great Awakening at the expense of other eighteenth-century revivals. Seeking the roots of the popular antiauthoritarianism evident in the American Revolution, scholars have turned to the Awakening, with its very visible struggles between some ministers and their parishioners, as the wellspring of challenges to orthodoxy of all kinds. But historians have not adequately viewed the Awakening within the context of eighteenth-century revivalism and, even more broadly, within the context of popular religious culture. Such a broader view reveals the Awakening as one, albeit the largest and most contentious, of a series of revivals that would continue into the nineteenth century. Before George Whitefield was out of short pants the Earthquake Revival of 1727 revealed the laity's independence of thought, as men and women largely ignored their ministers' millennial warnings and responded to their own fears of death and hell. Eight years later, even according to the account of the greatest American-born revivalist preacher, ministers could not compete with the communal religious momentum generated in their parishioners' prayer meetings. Jonathan Edwards could only watch, amazed, as virtually everyone in his town embraced revived religion. Woe to those who scoffed at the revival, for the awakened majority ostracized them. And ministers who despised the revival and feared its passions, like the Anglican Samuel Johnson, were powerless to stop members of their churches from drinking the heady wine of revivalism.

Likewise, from the perspective of popular religious culture, the Great Awakening appears as a moment when latent tensions became manifest, not as a moment when the laity challenged authority for the first time. During the Awakening, Old Lights and moderate New Light ministers fretted about such potentially subversive lay activities as respecting the validity of visions, believing in the power of divine revelations, and the exhorting performed by women, African Americans, and lower-class men. True, these behaviors were evident more during the Awakening than ever before, but they had also been present throughout the previous century, often expressed during moments of flux or in highly emotional contexts such as the deathbed. Gender tensions, especially, permeated the religious culture, and it should come as no surprise that they emerged during the Awakening, as women who may have been individually weak were communally strong. Consonant with the themes of lay piety, the Awakening illuminated preexisting tensions among laypeople and between people and their ministers.

On the other hand, this perspective also modifies the argument that would dismiss the Awakening as "interpretative fiction." If anything, the Awakening reveals itself as a singular moment of interpretative importance, when ministers worked overtime trying to define rhetorically and metaphorically the parameters of orthodoxy. Presented with the reality of emotions unfettered and gender boundaries transgressed, almost every minister in New England by 1742 and 1743 attempted to squeeze the genie of revivalism back into the bottle of orthodox practice. But clergymen could not be successful in this. Although the revival and its attendant excesses began to wane by 1743, laypeople had proven themselves, once again, able to contribute beliefs and practices to the culture even as they responded to revivalist preaching. During the Awakening, as during the other three revivals of the century, laypeople largely determined the scope and dynamics of the religious fervor.

CHAPTER SIX

The Piety of Experience Richardson

Religion, Politics, and Gender

*I*N APRIL 1775 the first military engagement of the Revolutionary War took place less than ten miles from Experience Richardson's Sudbury residence. The Shot Heard Round the World sounded nowhere louder than in Richardson's home, for her son Josiah placed his life on the line in the battle. Richardson described in her diary her worries and later her relief when she learned that Josiah was, with God's help, "preserved." This moment, at the intersection of religion, politics, and the family, illustrates the central concerns Richardson expressed in her diary, where she detailed her spiritual state and described the major events in her life between 1742 and 1782. For forty years Richardson created a record of spiritual joy and anguish that reveals the inner world of a pious New England layperson.[1]

After several chapters in which the heterodox, the marginal, and those in contention with their ministers have taken the spotlight, it is useful to turn to an in-depth study of a woman of orthodox faith. This is not to say that Richardson accepted everything her minister said: she largely ignored Israel Loring's advice about mourning and she did not pay attention to the wider ministerial attempt to have women avoid emotional extremes as they practiced piety. But Richardson was very orthodox on most matters of faith, and she avoided the contention of the Great Awakening and the other divisive issues of her day. Richardson generally partook of those aspects of religious culture that New England's ministers heartily endorsed.

Richardson also provides a useful comparison with John Barnard. In many ways Barnard's piety represents the generation that was dominant in 1700, while Richardson was part of the generation dominant in the latter decades of the eighteenth century. This comparison reveals that the themes and forms of lay piety remained largely the same throughout the eighteenth century. Barnard and Richardson both had providential outlooks, they worried about their salvation and their submission to God's will, and they drew religious inspiration from their family and their community of pious friends.

Some issues, however, interested one more than the other: Richardson, unlike Barnard, was practically obsessed with Satan's power to deceive and tempt. Furthermore, as I argued in chapter 1, a layperson's age, sex, occupation, and family position shaped his or her piety. Thus, Richardson's sex inflected her spirituality in a way different from Barnard. While Barnard's sex made him the patriarch in his home, Richardson had other concerns: she feared childbearing in a way no man could and her emotionalism was a contested issue as ministers after the Great Awakening attempted to rein in the passionate piety that clergymen increasingly associated with women. Finally, as war was waged first with France and then with England, Richardson combined her religious concerns with political events in a way that Barnard never did. Like many laypeople in the 1760s and 1770s, Richardson's piety became politicized, a development of paramount importance in the definition of the new nation. The America in the minds of New England's laypeople became a chosen land, a view that would have wide ramifications—for good and ill—in the first century of the new republic.

The Continuity of Lay Piety

Experience Richardson practiced piety much as it had been done in New England for generations. Both in the themes stressed—providentialism, submission to God's will, concern for the family—and in the forms and rituals of piety—daily private prayer, family reading and singing, the Lord's Supper—Richardson's diary provides evidence of a style of religiosity remarkably resilient and slow to change, despite the religious, economic, and political upheavals of the eighteenth century.

Like Barnard and most other laypeople in early New England, providentialism was central to Richardson's piety. Despite the rise of Enlightenment rationalism among the elite,[2] Richardson did not believe natural occurrences could simply be explained by natural laws; rather, they were evidence of God's pleasure or displeasure with his people. Because she and her neighbors lived in a rural setting, dependent upon the land for sustenance, Richardson viewed drought and other extraordinary weather patterns as portentous events. For example, the summer of 1761 was remembered as one of the driest in a generation. As Richardson noted in her diary in July, "it is as big a drought now as ever I knew it, I think the pasters [pastures] look burnt & dry." Richardson compared this natural state to her spiritual state, lamenting, "but O! how dry & dead is my heart, O Lord rain down Righteness upon my sould [*sic*]" (8 July 1761). A month later the drought continued and Richardson hoped that a reformation of behavior would save New England's residents from God's wrath. "The drought [grows?] sharper, a terrible time it is—O that we lay thing[s] to hart that are of an afflictive nature & turn from our evel ways" (2 Aug. 1761). While early New Englanders interpreted natural disasters as signs of divine displeasure, the providential outlook could also lead people to see mercy in the wake of destruction. In January 1751, Richardson noted "we had the Dradfullest storme of wind & Rain from the Southeast as ever was known in this country, it is generally said." This remarkable storm "blue down our stable at the meeting house and blue down our privi house." Despite the havoc wreaked by the tempest, Richardson interpreted it as a signal of mercy: "It semed as if we all should be destroyed but God preserve our Lives. O I might take a Due Notic[e] of it" (22 Jan. 1751). Richardson, in a very typical manner, saw the events around her reflecting God's deliberate intervention into the natural world.

In Richardson's world view, however, people were not merely pawns, buffeted about by tempests of divine creation. Prayer and supplication were ways people could implore God to spare them and their families. When Richardson's son Gideon, a minister in Wells, Maine, was extremely ill and near death in 1757, she received word that "he is no worse but some better which seems very strainge & I cant but think it is an answer of prayer" (12 Mar. 1757). That God would pay attention to ordinary people like herself sometimes amazed Richardson. "This day I think I have ben senseable of a remarkable answer of prayer," she wrote. "I cannot but wonder that the great God of Heven and Earth should Regard the prayers of such a vile wrech as I am" (28 Nov. 1755). Despite the self-deprecating tone of this statement, Richardson repeatedly turned to prayer when distressed, and she often was rewarded with answered prayers. Richardson's frequent recourse to supplication must have pleased her minister, who often preached on the importance of secret prayer.[3]

But for pious New Englanders like Richardson, religion was not just a source of comfort. Prayers were occasionally left unanswered, and the act of praying itself could be fraught with tension, as people felt they might be making selfish requests. Richardson worried about her prayers for her son,

Gideon: "I have been afraid of being too earnest in asking for his life I think all along, but yet God knows I have longed very much he should live . . . I was afraid to ask for his life for fear of offending God but would say to God help me to say thy will be done" (28 Jan. 1758). According to Richardson, one could offend God with importunate pleas. Though a central component of lay piety that often brought comfort and a sense of empowerment, prayer could also bring worry and fears of asking for too much since it entailed such an intimate interaction with God.[4]

An act more completely comforting than prayer was reading the Bible, so when she needed comfort, Richardson turned to Scriptures as a source of wisdom and strength. During a time of personal "troubles," Richardson frequently read her Bible and reported that it helped ease her mind. In February 1752 she wrote, "this day I feel very heavy, my afflictions very great and ill in body, took a bible went to bead . . . Reading in the last Chapter of Hebrews part of 5 & 6th varses did quiet me so that I think I felt quiet [quite] easy for a while" (1 Feb. 1752).

Reading the Bible was an exercise Richardson could control, so when she felt distressed she could search for particularly soothing passages. In this case, Paul's letter to the Hebrews reminds the reader, "be content with such things as ye have: for he hath said, I will never leave thee, nor forsake thee." While prayer involved assuming the position of a supplicant, which could lead to worries about being importunate with one's requests, reading the Bible involved seeking truths already disclosed, which seemed less risky. Hence Richardson read the Bible when her troubles continued two months later: "being much cast down it seemed to me I had lost my hope in God and all was Gone, took a bible and Read in it and I think I may say the word was made a comfort word to me, I thot I may all ways have my dependence upon God for then I am strong" (14 May 1752).[5] In the language pious New Englanders had been using for generations, Richardson gained strength through reading the Bible because it reminded her of her dependence upon an all-powerful force.

In addition to solitary activities like reading the Bible, the piety of laypeople like Richardson was shaped by their interactions with a community of religious friends. As she aged Richardson looked forward to these meetings to help relieve her isolation, as in August 1772 when "some of my Dear friends & old acquaintance came to see me & was very Refreshing to my spirits to see the faces of old Christian friends & we had a plesent meeting but o that we may all meet in heaven" (31 Aug. 1772). Sometimes, however, these meetings were not as pious as Richardson would have liked. Apparently discussions sometimes turned to earthly subjects at the expense of more pious topics. After one such occasion in 1758 Richardson wrote, "This day I made a visit to some of my friends which I think was my duty to do but we had not so much Religious descourse as we used to have" (9 Jan. 1758). Although Richardson expressed guilt after the meeting, it is likely that she enjoyed the discussion while it was occurring.

In contrast, the discourse was almost always pious in the meetinghouse, and Richardson was a steady presence there on Sabbath days. Surrounded by friends and relatives, Richardson heard the word preached and discussed it during the break between sermons. Israel Loring was her minister for almost her whole life, and she seems to have greatly enjoyed his preaching. Throughout her diary Richardson remarked on Loring's sermons favorably, most often calling them "profatable" or "pleasant."[6] Richardson was especially delighted when she went to meeting feeling burdened by a particular concern and Loring preached a sermon that seemed suited to her situation. These moments were more than coincidence in Richardson's opinion: "I Pleaded with God that I might have a sutable word for me at meeting & when I came there I was surprised to hear the minister preach so sutable to my condition, the text was the very varse that suported me the week be fore" (3 Nov. 1754). These "sutable" sermons made Richardson feel that Loring spoke directly to her. Unlike a number of the laypeople who have appeared in this book, Richardson never complained about her minister's sermons regarding doctrine or delivery, and when Loring died at the advanced age of ninety, Richardson expressed sincere regret at losing "one of the Best of minesters" (9 Mar. 1772).

The meetinghouse was also the site of several rituals in which Richardson participated. Although some historians have seen the Great Awakening as the end of the sacramental renaissance,[7] this point may be more valid for ministers publishing sacramental manuals than for lay practice. Despite the growth of the Baptists in the wake of the Great Awakening and their anti-pedobaptist views, baptism and especially the Lord's Supper continued to have powerful meanings for New England's saints long after the Awakening had run its course.

Throughout her diary, Richardson recorded numerous intense experiences during the Lord's Supper. Like Barnard, Richardson's experience of communion did not diminish with age; if anything, it grew stronger. Two years after her husband's death, when she was sixty-seven years old, Richardson recorded one of the most intimate and moving communion experiences she had ever had:

in sacrament time I semed to be wonderfully caried out to lay hold of Christ, I think if I Remember Right I felt my self Lye down at Christ feet as it ware & Laid hold on his feet & told him I would not let his Go except he would apear for me some way or other under my destrissing difecilties. (9 Aug. 1772)

Similar to many lay saints in early New England, Richardson experienced the actual presence of Christ during communion.[8] She felt the presence with such intensity that she was able to recount holding on to Christ's feet during the ritual, pleading with him to aid her in her distress, telling her savior that she would not let go of his feet until he helped her. Though not nearly as Christocentric as the German-American pietists of Pennsylvania, orthodox New Englanders throughout the colonial period had a piety suffused with vivid images of Christ, especially when they partook in the Lord's Supper. As with most other pious laypeople, the ritual was not always so powerful; Richardson occasionally noted after communion that "in sacrement time I was very dull" (7 Oct. 1759). But in general the Lord's Supper and the intense and personal communion with Christ it entailed were central to Richardson's piety.

Richardson also engaged in a number of rituals outside the meetinghouse, following a program of ritualized daily prayer that many ministers promoted. First coined by the English minister John Flavel, the phrase "spiritualizing the creatures" was appropriated by New England ministers such as Cotton Mather to denote the process by which people should invest their ordinary activities with religious significance. For example, Flavel urged the farmer with a full barn but no faith to pray as follows: "How have I rejoyced in a thing of nought, and pleased my self with a vanity? God hath blessed me in my Fields, and in my Stores; but not with Spiritual Blessings in heavenly places in Christ."[9] Richardson, showing a great deal of initiative and creativity, devised her own ritual of daily prayer centering on dressing herself, noting that because "it may help my memory I will make use of all my cloaths as I put them on." Her elaborate ritual, with prayers appropriate for each garment, is worth quoting at length:

First when I am fastting my petecoats about my waste pray that my Lines [loins] may be Girt about with truth & when I put on my stays pray that I may put on the breastplate of Righteousness & when I put on gound [gown] pray above all to take the shield of faith wherewith I may be able to qu[e]nch all the fiery darts of the wicked, & when I dress my head pray I may take the helmet of salvation & when I put on my nackcloath pray I may take the sword of the spirit whith the word of God & when I dress my feet pray I may have my feet shod with the preparation of the Gospel of peace. (28 Jan. 1762)

As a woman, with a more elaborate dressing ritual than a man, Richardson had a wide range of prayers she could offer as she got ready to face the day. While this was the most complex of her daily rituals, it was by no means the only one. Richardson also prayed as she lay in bed before day break and as she lay down to sleep in the evening. She also had several times set aside each day during the course of her activities for reflection and prayer (28 Feb. 1776). These private rituals structured her daily life around acts of piety, in ways typical of, if more complex than, many pious lay New Englanders.

But as with John Barnard, there were distinctive aspects of Richardson's piety, themes she focused on more than other people, issues she deemphasized in her daily prayers. Compared to Barnard, a notable component of Richardson's piety was her focus on Satan's power.[10] Unlike Barnard, who almost never mentioned Satan in his religious writings, Richardson continually commented on the power of the devil. Richardson's concern about Satan resembled that propounded by her minister, Israel Loring. One of the most prominent themes in Loring's sermons was Satan's power and the horrors of hell that awaited the unrepentant. In *Serious Thoughts on the Miseries of Hell*, Loring advised his flock to ponder frequently the terribleness of hell.[11] In other sermons he asserted that those who refused to believe in Christ would go to hell and suffer "an extremity of torment."[12] Loring argued that Satan tried to ensnare the unwary by causing them to doubt their faith.

Richardson took heed of her minister's warnings about Satan's power. Many times she briefly mentioned her fear of Satan's powers, such as "Lord keep me from being deceved by Satan" (8 Aug. 1752) or "God seems to leave me to my self and Satan, strainge sinful thoughts come into my heart which seemes imposeble to keep out" (21 Mar. 1755). Richardson had a tendency to blame Satan for troubling thoughts, unlike Barnard who was more likely to blame himself. Richardson once wrote, "O Lord I pray thee & keep Satan from temp[t]ing me to have hard thoughts of thee & of they [thy] word which is dreadfull for me to bare" (2 May 1758). Richardson also feared that Satan would trouble her family, and she often prayed that they would be protected from evil. In 1763 after a morning spent in prayer, Richardson noted, "I was much carri[e]d out in prayer for all that live in this house that Satan might be keept from us" (8 Mar. 1763).

Part of Richardson's concern may have sprung from a very real sense of Satan's presence. Just as she had a very personal sense of Christ's physical reality in the Lord's Supper, she occasionally wrote as if Satan appeared as a physical reality to her. For example, on a fast day in 1756, Richardson had the following unnerving experience: "A lettel before sun down, want [went] to the barn & went in there to pray but I was so afraid Saittan would apear to me I Gave out & went out of the barn to pray. Thus for Sattan was two [too] hard for me at this time but I hop[e] to overcome him" (22 July 1756). It is hard to know what Richardson meant when she wrote that she worried that Satan might "apear" to her, but it is possible she referred to his actual presence. Though she wanted to pray in the isolation and quiet of the barn, those very features led her to fear that Satan might appear there and tempt her. This is a very different attitude toward Satan than John Barnard had, demonstrating again that laypeople did not share a monolithic piety, but emphasized different, personally relevant issues.

Despite this variability, however, Richardson's diary shows the rough continuity in the forms and practices of lay piety in the eighteenth century. Richardson's providentialism, concern for her family, and attitudes toward God's power were standard for pious laypeople for the whole eighteenth century. Likewise, her practices of prayer, Bible reading, sermon attendance, communion, and spiritualizing the creatures show just how slowly lay piety changed in early New England.

Aspects of Female Piety

While typical of many broad patterns of eighteenth-century lay piety, Richardson also represented more particularized aspects of lay beliefs and practices. As a woman, Richardson experienced certain things, such as childbearing, that no man could. Her role as bearer of fragile life shaped Richardson's piety and her very outlook on life. Furthermore, Richardson engaged in certain activities that, while not unique to women, were inflected by her femaleness. For example, her encounters with her female friends were analogous to male social gatherings, but the specifics of those encounters differed. As a female slave owner, Richardson had interactions with her female slave that may have differed from the way male slave owners related to their female slaves. Likewise her spiritual highs and lows: while men sometimes experienced religion as a series of ups and downs, this emotional pattern was increasingly likely to be gendered as female in the eighteenth century. Many ministers saw female emotions as a problem and tried to urge their parishioners to avoid such extremes. Thus, Richardson's fluctuating piety was in some ways oppositional to the ideal of female religiosity outlined by the clergy.

Richardson's female friends were the center of her social and religious life.[13] Indeed, social and religious functions were intertwined and inseparable in these meetings. One day in 1761 Richardson "visited Mrs Esterbrooks, a gentelwoman in hir eighty seventh year." The two women talked about the health of Esterbrooks, who had been lame but was now better, and Esterbrooks showed off that she had "two teeth that are newly cut a growing" (24 Aug. 1761). The visit's sociability mixed with a more religious function, as it spurred the fifty-six-year-old Richardson to hope for a long life and to reflect on her own mortality. Likewise, one day in 1773 Richardson reported, "this day I made a viset to Mrs Wheler & Mrs Rice & was kindly entertained by them." In this case Richardson did not mention any overtly pious facet of the meeting, and her use of the phrase "kindly entertained" suggests a gathering devoted to talking and socializing. Nonetheless, Richardson drew spiritual significance from the encounter, writing "Blessed be God for this & all mercies of this day for I thought I could lay my self and my other destress down at Gods feet & I felt very comfortable the most of the day" (15 Feb. 1773). A pleasant meeting with her female friends could remind the aging Richardson that she had a great deal for which to be thankful.

Sometimes, however, Richardson could be caught in the snares of sisterhood. When women came together on a festive occasion such as a childbirth, the gathering's merriment could lead the women to behave in ways inconsistent with their desires for pious carriage.[14] In 1760 Richardson noted one such occasion:

> this day I was at a groaning [childbirth] & I was not so carefull to keep up my watch against sin as I should have been. One would think such times might be profortable to qu[i]cken us—but I let down my watch & so fell into sin—I find merry company is a snare to me but I hope I shall take better care another time. (9 Apr. 1760)[15]

Richardson had hoped this would be a pious occasion, a time to reflect on the meaning of life, the mysteries of birth, and the responsibilities of the older generation to the new one. Instead, she found herself enjoying the raucous atmosphere of this quintessentially homosocial environment, undoubtedly imbibing some of the liquor that flowed freely to dull the pain of the new mother and to celebrate the occasion of a successful birth. Pious women who were more self-righteous than Richardson, such as Hannah Heaton, could be put off by this rowdy atmosphere. When Heaton gave birth to her son Nathan in 1744, her pain was eased by the words of God coming to her, "I will be with you in six troubles yea in seven." Heaton attempted to relate these holy words to the gathered women but they rebuffed her: "I spoke and told them of it but the midwife chid me and said she did not love to hear folks talk so."[16] When pious women gathered for a birth they generally hoped that religious reflections would dominate the occasion, but the freedom accorded by this female sphere sometimes led to worldly excess. Whereas Hannah Heaton disparaged this atmosphere, Richardson enjoyed it, if guiltily.

The celebration of a "groaning" resulted from childbirth's dangers and the sense of relief when a woman made it through her travail safely. As described in chapter 2, childbirth may not have been as dangerous as women in the eighteenth century believed it to be.[17] Nonetheless, women thought there was a good chance they would die due to complications associated with giving birth.[18] This is poignantly revealed in the months leading up to the birth of Richardson's last child, Luther, in 1748. Experience and her husband had not been as fertile as most couples in early America. In the twenty years of fertility between her marriage at age twenty-three in 1728 and the birth of Luther, she gave birth only three times (including Luther). At first, Experience proceeded along the normal course of procreation, bearing Gideon in 1729 and Josiah Jr. in 1733. But then fifteen years passed without a birth or even a pregnancy, as far as the records reveal. Looking back on this period years later, after Luther's death, Richardson remembered, "this child I prayed for as Hannah did for Samuel, before I was like to have him I had been marr[i]ed so long I was afraid I should have none but God Graciously answered my prayer & gave me a man child & I have given him to the Lord" (3 Mar. 1756). Though comforted by the biblical story of Hannah (1 Sam. 1–2), who had been infertile for many years before praying that she would devote her child to God if he gave her one, Richardson remembered the anguish of those infertile years in a culture where procreation was a woman's primary duty to her family and society.[19]

Despite praying to overcome her barrenness, Richardson was not fully prepared for the dangers of a late pregnancy. In December 1747, at the age of forty-two, Richardson was two months pregnant but not completely sure of it; she wondered if her menses stopped due to menopause or pregnancy. As she noted, "If I be with child, O my courig fails me." She was aware that she was "got in to years" and as a result "many dangers threten me." These dangers increased her piety, as she prayed, "Lord strengthen me & give me courig & patience to go through bringing a child into the world" (22 Dec. 1747).[20]

As the months went by and she realized she was, in fact, pregnant, Richardson became increasingly worried that she might die in childbirth. To compound her woes, Richardson felt guilty that she was not more resigned to dying, if it was God's will. "My Spirit much sunk this day," she wrote in the fifth month of her pregnancy, "fearing I was two [too] desi[r]ous to Live and not willing to submit to God's will" (19 Mar. 1748). Richardson's worries about death and guilt about those worries got so bad that they interfered with her ability to participate in some of the pious rituals she normally enjoyed. In the eighth month of her pregnancy there was a general fast on account of the drought. Ordinarily Richardson found such fast days to be important components of her piety, observing them carefully. In her agitation about her approaching childbirth, Richardson complained about the fast, noting "o how poorly did I keep it." She lamented, "how dul I felt and do feel now and the [h]our of my travel [travail] drawing nigh." She expressed her deepest fear at this moment: "O Lord I pray thee not to for sake me then" (10 June 1748). Her next entry shows that she had been freed from her fears by the safe birth of her son. In July Richardson wrote that "I was brought to bead I was much afraid of my travel which I had to pass through." Despite these fears, "God hath d[e]alt wonderfully with me," in allowing her to survive (14 July 1748). Thus Richardson passed through this trial much as other pious women did: with an ever increasing fear of death, with a desire to live that caused them to question their commitment to accepting God's will, and finally with a thankfulness that they were still alive. In this manner childbirth often profoundly strengthened the piety of those who survived it.

But the months of pregnancy and the hours of childbirth were not a mother's only anxious times. With her offspring routinely encountering childhood diseases and dangers, a mother could not relax for long. Sadly, Luther lived only four years before he succumbed to the perils of childhood. Richardson first noted an inkling of danger in early October when she wrote in her diary that "it has been a dredful time in our neabourhood for sikness and death." Despite the dangers to her and her family, Richardson confessed, "I feel very dead in Relegon" (2 Oct. 1752). Just three days later the local sickness reached into her own home. Richardson's entry is unusually brief: "this day my son Luther died which was four yrs and two months and eleven day old according to old stile" (5 Oct. 1752).

The brevity of her entry recording the death of her youngest son—poignant as she counted up how many, or more precisely how few, days he lived—should not be read as indicating fatalism or lack of concern, for over the course of the next year Richardson was subject to some of the worst spiritual depression of her life in response to Luther's death. One week after her child's death the grieving mother noted, "This day much sunk under my trouble." She comforted herself by trying to convince herself that she had Luther only for God and not for her own happiness, even though the long period of infertility that preceded her pregnancy with Luther clearly upset her. She opined, "I think I was willing to have this child I have lost for God, tho I had no mind to have it for my own pleasure." She also tried to comfort herself by thinking about all the snares Luther would have faced had he lived to adulthood: "if my heart dont deceve me I was made more contented still by haveing two men come here which [i.e., whom] I Looked upon very wicked, thinking how dreadfull it would have been if he had lived to have been a man grown and been like them" (12 Oct. 1752).

Richardson's heart may have deceived her a bit on this point because thinking that Luther was better off in heaven did not remove her troubles. This strategy of thinking what an evil man he might have grown into may have eased her pain somewhat, but it was not enough. Richardson realized that she would have preferred her child to live so she could exercise the guidance that might have spared him the fate of growing up godless.

The depth of Richardson's grief was evident four months after her child died, when she began to worry that her continued grieving was a sin against God, as the standard ministerial interpretation of grieving maintained.[21] Specifically, Richardson's minister stressed the importance of not grieving to excess. Israel Loring preached that people should not "murmur" under bereavements, but should bless God's name for all he had done for them. Furthermore, he directed those who had lost children to bear it in silence.[22] This advice distressed Richardson, but it did not prevent her from mourning her loss at great length. In February 1753 she wrote, "I fear I have sin[n]ed against God in destreesing myself about the state of my child that is dead, but I pray to God to give me a right sperit about this thing" (Feb. 1753). Only after grieving for a year was Richardson able to feel less consumed by her worries. As she noted on the anniversary of her son's death, "this day is a year sence my son Luther died, I have met with many troubles this year but I am carried along and upheld" (6 Oct. 1753). In a period of high fertility combined with high childhood mortality, when virtually all parents witnessed at least one of their offspring die during childhood, female piety was structured by fear of dying in childbirth, worries that children would succumb to disease, and long periods of grief—up to a year or more—for those children who died. As opposed to those who would argue that high infant mortality led parents to distance themselves emotionally from their fragile children,[23] the bitter pain of Experience Richardson and those like her displays a tight bond of love between parent and child in the early modern world. That bond, with the fears and hopes it engendered, was central to the meaning laypeople drew from their religion.

But the cares and responsibility of a family did not lead directly to increased piety for women. In fact, because women with large families were so busy, they often could not engage in as much prayer and pious reading as they wanted.[24] This even held true for Richardson, who had a very small family. Numerous times in her diary she recounted periods of pious activity when the rest of her family left her alone, implying that when the men were around, she had to deal with tasks like cooking and mending to keep the household economy in smooth working order. The annual militia muster was an occasion for Richardson to enjoy some privacy in her home. As she wrote in 1756, "this was trooping day, Stayed at home a lone, I spent a few hours in Reading and praying for revi[v]al of religon" (1 June 1756). Likewise, the following year found Richardson savoring some quiet time during a muster: "this day is training day, My family being all gone from home I spent a fuw hours in Reading & prayer that I might be prepared to Receive the sacrament the next Lords day" (1 June 1757). Ironically, on a day of male conviviality noted for excessive drink and the inebriated discharge of weapons, Richardson found time for the solitary reflection she craved but which housework often prevented her from enjoying.

Even though Richardson often complained that she felt burdened by the duties of running a home, it is likely that she actually had fewer responsibilities than most other New England women. Partly the result of having only three children, mostly this was because the Richardson family included several slaves. In noncoastal towns like Sudbury this was rare, evidence that the Richardsons were better off than most. Although the middle of the eighteenth century was the peak of African-American population density in colonial New England, even at that point blacks made up only 3 percent of the population.[25] Furthermore, slaves were not scattered randomly throughout New England, but concentrated in seaports like Boston, Newport, and New London. Only the very well-off in places like Sudbury owned slaves.

As a member of this rural elite, Josiah Richardson owned three slaves at the end of his life: his "negro man," Francis Benson; his "negro girl," Dinah; and Dinah's son, the "negro boy" Caesar.[26] Though Dinah legally belonged to Josiah, she was Experience's personal servant, probably spending most of her time helping with domestic chores. Dinah had been married to a slave named Caesar, who belonged to Mrs. Love Flint in nearby Lincoln (23 May 1762). Dinah gave birth to the younger Caesar in May 1762, only to witness her husband die unexpectedly four days after the birth. This was by no means the only family tragedy Dinah would endure; her only son would not live past his eleventh birthday (1 Jan. 1774). As another woman who had witnessed her share of family deaths, Richardson may have been able to empathize with Dinah's pain. When Dinah's husband died, Richardson wrote, "I pray God to santifi it to us all," expressing her wish that the meaning of Caesar's death would not be lost on the living (27 May 1762). Despite this sentiment, Richardson was probably not very close to her domestic slave: there is ample evidence that slave women and their female owners did not usually establish bonds of sisterhood.[27]

Buttressing this latter point, these slaves—or "servants" as Experience Richardson preferred to call them—were not a focus of Experience's piety, even though they were an integral part of the Richardson household economy. Only rarely did Richardson mention her slaves in her prayers, as when she asked "God that he would give conveying grace to me to my husband my children and my servants" (14 Mar. 1754). It does not seem that Richardson ever prayed with her slaves, as did the owners of Phillis Wheatley and as ministers like Cotton Mather advised.[28] In addition, only oblique evidence survives that Richardson actively worked to Christianize her slaves. On December 9, 1776, Richardson wrote laconically, "this day my servant Diner had hir freedom." Richardson joined those New Englanders who manumitted their bondspeople as revolutionary calls for liberty made slavery seem incongruous. It is unclear what emotions this manumission stirred in Richardson, though it is easier to imagine Dinah's happiness.[29] The prayer Richardson offered on this occasion was: "O that she may Devote hir self to the Service of God all the days of hir Life" (9 Dec. 1776). Thus it seems that Dinah was a Christian, though whether this was through Richardson's efforts is unclear. The best guess is that even though Richardson differed from most New England women as the owner of slaves, this fact did not alter her piety or experience of religion in any substantial way. In any case, when Dinah received her freedom Richardson was more alone than ever since Josiah Richardson had died six years earlier.

As noted above, it seems that Richardson may have enjoyed being alone earlier in her life, as solitude gave her the time to pray and read. Perhaps Richardson also enjoyed being alone because her husband was a stern taskmaster; unfortunately, her diary contains almost no hint of the Richardsons' marital relationship. Although her husband appears more frequently in her diary than John Barnard's spouse did in his, Josiah Richardson remains a shadowy figure. Perhaps the best guess is that the Richardsons enjoyed a marriage of average intensity: without the effusiveness of some and without the abusiveness of others.[30] When Experience prayed for her husband, it was usually for his health and occasionally that he would receive "converting

Grace."[31] Upon Josiah's death Experience expressed sadness, but she had clearly resigned herself to the death of her elderly husband. She wrote, "this day my Dear husband died, Oh may it be sanctified to me and to us all, I thank God I am not a mother without hope and now I bege of God that my maker may be my husband" (18 Oct. 1770). Richardson's request that God be her husband may provide a hint to the seeming lack of passion between Experience and her husband. Long before Josiah died, Experience expressed the fairly conventional opinion that God (or Jesus, depending on her prayer) was her husband. To cite just one example, Richardson once noted in her diary that "I keep trying to clame God the father for my father and God the son for my husband and God the holy ghost for my comforter, and where can I find a better father or a better husband or a better comforter" (21 Mar. 1770). Indeed, how could Josiah have competed as a provider with the omnipotent, as a companion with the omnipresent? I do not mean to suggest that pious New Englanders did not love their spouses, but it seems possible that these people's intensely personal relationship with their God provided some of the emotional outlet that they otherwise might have sought from their marital relationship.

Religion as an emotional outlet was a contested issue in the eighteenth century. For centuries reformed Protestant ministers had warned against the "enthusiastic" emotional excesses to which some laypeople were prone. But during the eighteenth century—and especially after the Great Awakening—ministers gendered emotional religious experience as female. Whereas seventeenth-century clergymen who described ecstatic religious experience were as likely to discuss men as women, by the eighteenth century the dominant cultural image of "excessive" piety or enthusiasm came to be female. This tendency gained force during the Great Awakening, when clergy described even male New Lights in feminized terms, especially when these new converts participated in particularly frenzied styles of worship.[32]

As a result of this new rhetorical link between gender and enthusiasm, the piety of people like Experience Richardson became suspect in the eyes of some ministers if it became too emotional. Indeed, Richardson's piety was extremely unstable. In the forty years covered by her diary, Richardson's piety was a roller-coaster of emotions. At times she went for days or weeks with positive feelings toward religion. In other periods she labored for weeks or even years under feelings of despair. These swings demonstrate that people did not always gain comfort from their religion and that personal piety became increasingly contested as ministers cautioned their parishioners to avoid religious turbulence.

Sometimes Richardson's most rapturous religious experiences occurred during or immediately after the Lord's Supper. Once, during a sermon after the sacrament, Richardson reported that "I was so over come with a sense of Christ welcoming me in to heaven at death that it was almost to[o] hard for my strength" (8 Aug. 1756). Another time this feeling of rapture washed over Richardson at home after Sabbath services. "After meeting when at home," she wrote, "I think I felt almost over come in singing God's praise" (4 June 1752). Other times something outside the meetinghouse caused Richardson to rejoice and made her feel very positive about religion. In 1756 this excitement derived from the spiritual progress made by her eldest son, Gideon. She noted in her diary, "Oh I feel rejoyed for the hope I have that my oldest son is borne again" (3 Mar. 1756). Finally, in certain cases her diary itself could be a source of delight to her, as she occasionally read over her entries and was happy for what she saw there. Following a day of fasting and prayer, Richardson read her diary and it made her glad: "This day lo[o]king over what I write yesterday it filled me with Great desire to Bless God that he would be so formilyer with me, that he would Let me have so much of his holy spirit" (2 July 1757). In all these cases, Richardson's religion made her feel a variety of positive emotions: rapture, delight, hope, and self-assurance.

But more often, Richardson felt religious despair. Despite ministers' warnings to avoid religiously induced melancholy, many lay saints like Experience Richardson felt the weight of their religion bear down on them, sometimes for very long periods of time without a respite.[33] For about two years, from 1750 to 1752, Richardson lived through some of her worst despair. Paradoxically, there was no discernible reason for her anguish: this period did not follow the death of a child and it does not seem to have been a difficult time financially. For two long years, though, virtually every entry in Richardson's diary displays grief and sadness. In June 1750 Richardson wrote that she felt "as dead and dul as ever I was in my life I think" (11 June 1750). Several months later she reported, "this day much sunk in spirit, O that God would help me to cast my care on him who careth for me" (18 Jan. 1751). A year later every single diary entry revolves around despair. Richardson began to describe her feelings in increasingly dramatic language: "my troubles increese, trouble upon trouble, things looke dreadful darke but I follow near after God, I hope God will hear me" (29 Jan. 1752).

By this point Richardson was so distressed that she began to wander around aimlessly, distracted from her daily chores and thinking about her pain. In February 1752 she noted, "this day felt very much sunk about my Great afflections, went into the cornhouse for something there, so destressed I walked back wards and foreward praying to God for help" (28 Feb. 1752). Eventually Richardson began to recover from her bout of melancholy, gradually entering more positive thoughts in her diary. But for nearly two dark years Richardson had displayed the symptoms of someone on the verge of suicide. Clergymen increasingly linked this pattern of religious melancholy to women's susceptibility to emotionalism. Perhaps this led to greater distress for Richardson, as she may have felt unable to take her concerns to her minister without seeming to be overly emotional; she did not mention Israel Loring once during those two years of concern, an unusually lengthy lapse. In any case, Richardson's gender inflected her despair, as ministers asserted that women should strive to avoid religious melancholy.

The Politicization of Religion

While many of Experience Richardson's beliefs and practices reflect the fundamental continuity of lay piety in the eighteenth century, one development in the 1760s and 1770s signals a new direction: the politicization of religion. The French and Indian War, the English imperial crisis, and the American Revolution caused New England's laypeople to combine religion with politics to an unprecedented degree.[34] Of course, laypeople noticed political events before the 1760s and incorporated them into their prayers and their public and private religious rituals. One could even argue that political concerns fundamentally structured the Puritan migration since many of the migrants of the 1630s opposed the policies of King Charles I and hoped to use Massachusetts Bay as a stage to display a "due form of government," in John Winthrop's words.[35] But for most laypeople, migration's overtly political motivations slowly slipped into memory and for much of the colonial period people generally ignored politics when they practiced piety.

This changed with the start of the French and Indian War in 1756. Historians have seen this war, a conflict with the "papists" and the "Antichrist" (to use some New Englanders' words), as an important moment for the development of American ideas at the intersection of religion and politics. Nathan Hatch, for example, has discerned in the war with France the origins of "civil millennialism" in America. According to Hatch, in the 1760s an older Puritan millennialism, which focused on the conversion of all nations to Christianity, was replaced by the newer civil millennialism, which saw America as a "new seat of liberty."[36]

While Hatch's interpretation is convincing for the ministers he studies, it is less so for New England's laypeople. Ordinary men and women frequently discussed war with France and later the American Revolution in their spiritual journals, but almost never in terms of an impending apocalypse. Richardson, for example, never described the French and Indian War in millennial terms or mentioned the possibility of Judgment Day, even though she wrote about the war in dozens of entries from 1755 to 1763 and described such seemingly portentous events as two earthquakes (1755 and 1761) and two severe droughts (1761 and 1762). Likewise, Richardson's many entries about the Revolution are devoid of apocalypticism. Instead of evincing a new civil millennialism, Richardson and laypeople like her discussed politics within traditional religious paradigms: providentialism, the desire for religious revival, and the fear of divine retribution for sinful behavior. But the very combination of religion and politics was novel, a linkage that opened an avenue for women to participate in the discursive reimagining of America in the years prior to and immediately following revolution.

Until relatively recently, historians of women and the American Revolution have largely ignored the role of religion. The founding texts of this subfield were more concerned with women's "public" actions and with the images of women in the revolutionary period than with more "private" expressions of female piety.[37] More recent scholarship has focused on religious women's contributions to the Revolution.[38] These works make it clear that pious women engaged in public and political acts—such as attending spinning bees or collecting money for the revolutionary cause—that flowed directly from their participation in organized religion.[39] I will demonstrate that in addition to these public acts, the private piety of women just before and during the American Revolution had important ramifications for the meaning of the new nation.

Specifically, female piety played a role in the gender politics of the revolutionary era. Several historians have argued that the democratic revolutions in America and France were fundamentally gendered. Central to the revolutionary project in these two countries was the replacement of the metaphor of king as father with the image of a fraternity of independent male subjects as the locus of political power.[40] According to this interpretation, women were the losers in a discursive battle over the meaning of the new political order. With politics defined as specifically masculine, women were now "explicitly denied" the "new political identity as citizens" that was held out to (white, property-owning) men.[41] This argument is persuasive, but in its focus on "public" acts and images it overlooks an important site of female agency:

in the politicization of personal piety women found an arena where they reimagined the new nation. Women like Experience Richardson participated in creating an image of America as a nation, as opposed to merely a collection of local interests. Central to this conception was the belief that America was a land of faith, with God on America's side in the Revolutionary War. As expressed by women like Richardson, if faith was paramount to the American political project, women were therefore also central as they embodied faith in the new nation.[42]

Before the French and Indian War, Richardson occasionally noticed political events, but only rarely. Only twice did she write about such events before 1755. Once was when the French fort at Louisbourg on Cape Breton Island fell to the English in 1745 during King George's War: "I have heard that Cap[e] Briton is taken by our English men." In this era of widespread oral information networks, Richardson did not need to read a newspaper to learn of important events like the fall of Louisbourg. Most likely she "heard" this stunning news in conversation with friends and family. Richardson's response to this information was standard for the period, thanking God in prayer. "I pray the Lord," Richardson wrote, "to enlarg[e] my heart to Love him for so great a mercy" (8 July 1745). As part of her providential world view, Richardson saw in Louisbourg's fall the deliberate actions of an omnipotent God.

Such mentions of political events were rare in lay spiritual journals before 1756. But as war with France loomed, men and women like Richardson found themselves increasingly concerned with the operations of the empire. As Richardson's minister Israel Loring taught her and her fellow parishioners, France was a country of papists who believed in justification by works, a "grand Error and Heresy."[43] These religious concerns mingled with political concerns, and in 1755, as hostilities mounted but before war was declared, Richardson noted that "we are threatned with a War" which she felt was "a sore jugment." God was meting out this "jugment" because of the sinfulness of New England's people. "We are grown so wicked," Richardson lamented, "that makes me fear we are to fall by our enemy." The only hope was for a general revival of piety: "O that God would Reclaim me first and then every body els[e]" (11 Apr. 1755). Though only ten years after the Great Awakening, Richardson felt that public piety had declined to such a level that they were threatened with divine destruction in war. Interestingly, Richardson desired that she would be "reclaimed" first: she was not afraid to place her own spiritual claims above the rest of New England.

Although war would not be formally declared until May 1756, by the autumn of 1755 men were being sent from New England to Albany and points west. At this point the conflict was transformed from a distant event to something with powerful local ramifications.[44] Richardson called it "a time of great destress in Newingland" because "we have sent out a great many men to defend us from the french and indians." Significantly, the operative regional distinction in Richardson's thought was New England, and not America as it would become during the Revolutionary War. People mostly viewed the war with France from a local perspective, and as local men entered the conflict, the possibility of their death was brought home to their friends and family. Experience's worries temporarily diminished because her family had the means to avoid service, at least in this early stage of the war. As she noted in her diary, "My husband has hired a man to go in my Son Josiah's place to do his turn." As the conflict worsened and the need for manpower increased, however, the Richardsons were no longer able to buy their son out of service, and within eighteen months Josiah Jr. trudged off to war. But even before her son was involved, Richardson was concerned for the well-being of New England's people and through frequent supplications she attempted to enlist God as an ally. She prayed, "Oh may we humble ourselves before God that he may turn away his wrath from us and subdue the enemies for us" (22 Sept. 1755). As a woman, Richardson could not fight in the war, and as a parent she did not want to see her son die for the cause. But Richardson could offer prayers, and she did so frequently. New Englanders' supplications that France be subdued were not answered, but prayers to spare men's lives seemed to gain a response, as early winter snows allowed most of the men to return home. In her neighborhood the good news circulated: "We hear the sholders are a coming home and about five hundred to stay and keep the fort and so to do nothing this year" (4 Nov. 1755).

Richardson was not deeply concerned with the war again until 1757. In the two years since 1755, she had prayed and occasionally held private fasts or joined in public fasts about the war. But not until August 1757 did she receive significant news. The information was not good: "O the terrible nuse I hear, our upper fort [Fort William Henry] is taken and the lo[w]er fort is beset." This was a particularly troublesome report since the previous year's campaign had not gone very well. According to Richardson, "the enemy gain ground upon us every summer, It looks as if we are to fall into their hands." This bad news caused Richardson to question her faith, as she wrote, "Now I want to trust in God but I think I can't" (13 Aug. 1757). Richardson's surprising lack of faith was the potentially negative side to a providential world view, for if God continued to heap judgments and suffering upon a people, it could be interpreted as a sign that God was not on their side and that their prayers might never be answered. Just as victories over the French helped convince people like Richardson that God was their ally, defeats at the hands of the enemy could cause them to question if they were on the side of righteousness. In fact, the local perspective on the war with France was revealed as Richardson and her neighbors continued to receive bad news from the front lines. "This day we have the mallancoly nues," wrote Richardson, "that Cap [Samuel] Dakin with about 26 more men are killed by the enemy four of which belong to the East side of the River." Four men from the east side of the Sudbury River, where Experience and her family lived, had been killed by the enemy, reminding Richardson that it could have just as easily been Josiah Jr. Despite her doubts and lack of faith, Richardson tried praying once more, asking God to "cause our enemy to bear peace with us again" (5 Aug. 1758).

Peace was not forthcoming, but a reversal of fortunes was. Shortly after Richardson's prayer for peace she noted, "this day we hear Cape Britton is taken by our English Army" (15 Aug. 1759). After a few years without any significant news, Spain entered the conflict on the side of France and Richardson learned the following: "We have Great cause to Bless God for the nuse we have from the Havana that it is taken." This turn of events surprised Richardson, who wrote, "I cant but wonder God will do such Great things for us when we are such a sinfull peopel" (8 Sept. 1762). And then, finally, word that the war was over. In February 1763 Richardson received "the nuse of a General peace between the nations" that was notable since it was "upon so good tarns [terms] Especially in these parts of the world" (14 Feb. 1763). The "heathen," as Richardson called them (14 Feb. 1763), had been defeated, yet at no point did her exultation arouse millennial expectations. During the war's bleakest years and during the celebration following France's defeat, Richardson never ventured the ideas so prominent among ministers, that victory over the Antichrist would allow the model of American liberty to begin the millennial reign. Rather, Richardson's newly politicized piety during the French and Indian War revolved around traditional lay concerns: the providential view that God's will could be discerned in the victories and defeats of the battlefield, worries about the safety of family and neighbors, and the hope that personal and public attempts to reduce sinfulness might win God's sympathy. To these traditional themes people added a new layer of political concerns, as they saw New England as a distinctive regional entity fighting an outside foe.[45]

This regional concern expanded into a national vision during the Revolutionary War. Richardson was a keen and interested observer of the events of the revolutionary years, and her diary offers numerous insights into the way laypeople interpreted that era's political events in religious terms.[46] Because Richardson's husband died in 1770, these years also demonstrate that she did not gain her political knowledge solely from him. Instead, Richardson learned about the Revolutionary War from other family members, her friends, and probably her minister. She gathered information from these people and then formulated her own interpretations of events.

As tensions mounted between England and the colonies and war seemed imminent, Richardson made a significant linguistic shift in her diary. For the first time in late 1774, she referred to herself belonging to a political entity larger than New England. After a "thanks Giveing day" in December, she noted that "things looks very Dark in our nation, we Go on without our King or Govenor" (15 Dec. 1774). Two weeks later she repeated this phrasing, writing that "our nation is in a terrible condition, O Reforme all that is a miss in our nation I pray thee for Christ Sake I pray thee" (1 Jan. 1775).[47] This shift to seeing America as a nation, distinct from England, was crucial for the next important development: people believing that America had God on its side.

Richardson sought divine guidance in this trial because she was almost literally in the middle of the conflict. She lived less than ten miles from the first military engagement of the Revolutionary War at Concord. Not only physical proximity tied Richardson to the events at Concord; her son Josiah was there as well. Richardson's diary entry is a rare surviving female account of this famous battle:

> This day our men are alarmed to go down to Concord to fight with the army that is come to take our Stores. There not only one minnet men but almost all our [minute men] took up the[i]r armes and marched there & a Dreadful fight they had & drove them [the British] back again & killed a great many of them but how many we cannot tell & some of our men wear killed, it is said about forty in all & two that belong to this part of our town, Dea[c]en Haynes & Asel Reed, & Joshua Haynes was wounded. (19 Apr. 1775)

Interestingly, at this moment of extreme tension, Richardson uncharacteristically offered no prayer or religious interpretation. Perhaps she was too overcome with emotion, worrying about her son and others she knew, to commit what must have been her private prayers to paper.

Richardson recorded her prayers about her son in the next week, as she passed from happiness that he was home from battle to sadness as he returned to war. She noted in her diary, "My only child went with the rest & fitt [fought] & was preserved & is now come home upon a fourlow but he must Go again I sopose." Her prayer at this moment took a form unusual for her, as she asked, "O King Jesus help us I pray thee" (25 Apr. 1775). It may be significant that Richardson prayed to "King Jesus," a phrase she almost never used, at a time when she felt "without our King," as she wrote several months prior to this. As people who had been raised in a monarchy tried to imagine another possible political system, it may have helped them to imagine Jesus as their new king, much the same way that Richardson upon her husband's death prayed that God would be her new husband. In this way religious faith served as a familiar paradigm while other paradigms shifted rapidly.

This reliance on God's power, combined with the new view that America was a distinct political entity, helped create the conception that America was a chosen nation, with divine support. Richardson ascribed numerous victories and positive events to God's direct intervention. At one point in the war "five Briggad[e]s of Hasengs [Hessians] and waldichers [Waldeckers] marched throw our town to the camps to be sent home, all under oath not to come out against us again." Richardson attributed the deportation of these German mercenaries fighting for the British to the fact that "God is Showing mercy to us" (5 Nov. 1777). Similarly, when the blockade of Boston's port was ended "by our enemys being drove of[f] by our own men," Richardson drew the lesson that God was aiding the Americans in their struggle against the British. "It apears plain," Richardson asserted, "that God has caused them Great men of war to be afraid of our small vessels" (14 June 1776). This theme of David versus Goliath, of the smaller and weaker but holier nation versus the larger and stronger but more wicked nation, would become a predominant theme in the early years of the new republic. In this ministers and laypeople largely agreed, and this would become one of the issues that helped lessen the tensions between laity and clergy in the first decades of the nineteenth century.

The Revolutionary War years passed by and Experience Richardson savored snatches of good news and endured hard times. She rejoiced when Burgoyne surrendered at the Battle of Saratoga and suffered when the price of beef rose to fifteen shillings a pound and butter fetched twenty shillings a pound. Though she occasionally had her doubts, Richardson largely maintained her faith through these years by writing in her diary, and in the process she participated in creating a new image of the relation between religion and politics. During the French and Indian War laypeople connected the politics of empire with religion to an unprecedented degree, though without their pastors' millennial overtones. In the revolutionary era these politicoreligious concerns grew as laypeople thought in terms of "America" for the first time. Women like Experience Richardson only rarely entered the battlefields of war, but they repeatedly entered the arena in which this new American nation was imagined. In their private religious journals and their private prayers, these women used their religious culture's traditional themes as they participated in creating the new language of American exceptionalism, in which an undersized David took on the Philistines in various guises. This would become the culturally dominant role of pious women in the new republic, a role not bereft of power and influence though centered on the private world of faith.

In many ways, religion was a private matter in eighteenth-century New England. People engaged in secret, or "closet," devotions, held private fasts, and wrote in their spiritual journals in the quiet hours of dawn and dusk. But in other important ways, piety was also a public affair. Pious laypeople attended public worship, read and prayed and sang outside the home with friends and family members, and in the last third of the eighteenth century they increasingly tied their piety to the very public matters of empire and nationhood. In these ways a woman like Experience Richardson, who did not hold a paid job outside the home or even belong to the sort of female church organization that would become ubiquitous in the nineteenth century, participated in the public life of revolutionary New England.

But even before war with England and France, Richardson's faith tied her to the public life of the colony. Richardson shared with virtually every other resident of New England the basics of reformed Protestant faith. Even though she was more pious and more orthodox (as defined by ministers) than many, and even though her age, sex, family relations, and personal inclinations led her to focus on some things—like Satan's power to tempt and delude the incautious—more than other people, Richardson shared the providential world view and the emphasis on family concerns that united New England's laypeople. These cultural scripts changed extremely slowly, despite the political and economic and even religious changes that occurred in the eighteenth century. In fact, even when piety was mobilized in the cause of politics in the 1760s and 1770s, this occurred within the dominant themes of popular religious culture. Innovations like a new civil millennialism, so eagerly embraced by the clergy, were virtually nowhere to be found in the faith of the people.

Religious Culture and the Origins of the American Revolution

*I*N THE LAST DECADES of the eighteenth century New England's religious culture consisted of a bounteous and almost bewildering variety of beliefs and practices. There was no single "lay" interpretation of religion as opposed to a "clerical" one: as much (or more) distance separated laypeople like Experience Richardson and Sarah Prentice as separated ministerial foes Charles Chauncy and Jonathan Edwards. Such factors as age, sex, and occupation led individuals to emphasize certain ideas at the expense of others. Despite this variety, one thing is clear: laypeople both drew on the religious culture and occasionally had the power to contribute ideas to that culture. Since about 1700 a cultural and institutional gap had arisen and grown between ministers and their parishioners as a result of clerical initiatives to increase their power. This resulted in a culture more open than in the seventeenth century; now laypeople found it easier to add cultural scripts of their own creation. The beliefs and practices laypeople created and sustained sometimes contradicted ministerial interpretations. Especially in liminal moments—times when the ordinary rules of society were suspended, such as during rituals, on the deathbed, and during revivals—some lay men and women offered constructions of their faith based on their own readings of the Bible and their own imperatives.

Sometimes these differing interpretations caused little or no strife, as when John Barnard emphasized the communal aspects of the Lord's Supper rather than its individualistic elements, as his ministers Increase and Cotton Mather did. Because Barnard expressed his beliefs in his private spiritual journal, the Mathers never saw how their deacon's musings differed from their own.

Likewise, when the Lynnfield converts of the 1727 Earthquake Revival ignored the apocalyptic warnings of their minister, Nathaniel Sparhawk, the pastor did not notice. Urging his parishioners to convert because the earthquake signaled the impending beginning of Christ's reign on earth, Sparhawk overlooked the Lynnfield converts' quiet assertions that the tremor reminded them more of their own sinfulness than of the unlikely possibility that the millennium was at hand. Thus the cultural distance between laity and clergy could, ironically, sometimes work to smooth over differences that might have caused trouble if they became public.

At other moments, however, disagreements between laity and clergy caused contention. Historians have shown that a bedeviling issue in the eighteenth century was the ever increasing taxes to pay ministers' salaries,[1] and certainly these squabbles occurred in many eighteenth-century parishes. But theological concerns more commonly caused strife. Thus, the picture of lay-clerical disputes in the eighteenth century outside the Great Awakening—of stingy Yankee farmers balking at pay raises for financially strapped pastors—is but a detail of a much larger canvas. As this book has shown, many disputes between laity and clergy revolved around theological issues or different interpretations of the same ritual. For women, in particular, the suspension of ordinary societal norms during religious rituals allowed them to express notions that diverged from ministerially defined orthodoxy. These conflicts reveal the laity's creativity and independent-mindedness.

For example, the deathbed was a liminal site where laypeople sometimes gained the power to express their beliefs in ways that upset their ministers. When some people asserted that deathbed visions had convinced them they were going to heaven, ministers quickly pointed out that visions were not reliable sources for learning whether one was saved. And when some laypeople used the power they gained on the deathbed to criticize or even swear at their ministers because they wanted to hear more comforting words, ministers believed this was the height of arrogance. Similarly, disputes over the meaning of the Lord's Supper were consistently troublesome in the eighteenth century. Although much of the time ministers and pious New Englanders agreed on the importance of attending communion, occasionally disputes broke out that revealed a gulf between lay and clerical understandings of the ritual. While ministers preached that people should attend the Lord's Supper even if they were embroiled in a quarrel with other churchgoers, most people refused to partake in the ritual under those conditions, using the Lord's Supper symbolically to dramatize their dispute.

This willingness to question authority—in certain circumstances and when the issues at stake were important enough—was a significant element in the culture of ordinary New Englanders throughout the eighteenth century. The importance of this streak of potential antiauthoritarianism became clear when it was mobilized to help break with England's patriarchal authority. Historians have offered two different interpretations of the links between religion and the American Revolution. One school has attempted to show how the doctrines and organizational structure of specific denominations led them to become vigorous supporters of the revolutionary cause.[2] A second school has sought to link the separations and strife of the Great Awakening with the coming of revolution.[3]

My interpretation is both broader and less causal than these two models. It is broader because I am not arguing that a particular denominational or religious "style" was crucial for revolution; rather, the willingness to challenge authority was deeply rooted in popular religious culture, not simply the result of being an evangelical or a separate or a member of some other specific group. It is less causal because I agree with Jon Butler that "the Revolution was a profoundly secular event."[4] Although New Englanders drew on the antiauthoritarianism that had been shaped in relations with their ministers during the eighteenth century when they challenged English authority, their concerns were more political and ideological than religious. The politicization of lay piety in the 1760s and 1770s was a response to the struggles of empire, not the cause of separation.

Despite the Revolution's secular origins, laypeople interpreted the imperial crisis through the prism of popular piety. A broadside published in 1774 under the pseudonym "The Watchman" characteristically expresses these concerns. The Watchman was a low-ranking town official in Boston who somehow discovered the British plans to quarter troops in the Massachusetts capital city. Reporting these plans to his fellow citizens, the Watchman offered a providential preface that sums up the prevailing attitude toward the relationship between religion and politics: "Whoever has candidly traced the rapid Growth of these Colonies from their little Beginnings to their present flourishing State in Wealth and Population, must eye the distinguished Hand of Heaven, and impress every Mind with a humble Confidence, that 'no Design formed against us shall prosper.'"[5] Significantly, the author referred to "these Colonies," broadening his horizons to include all of America in his providential world view. For him, the evidence that God was on America's side was apparent in the colonies' history and burgeoning population.

A pamphlet published two years later, in 1776, combined the Watchman's providentialism with the lay belief in the predictive abilities of dreams and visions. According to this pamphlet, a man in Swansea, Massachusetts, dreamed in 1732 that an angel appeared with an important message. The angel, "cloathed in White, his Garments very plain, and fair as Alabaster," delivered a message so momentous that the man transcribed it verbatim. Samuel Clarke discovered this "ancient Manuscript" and was astounded to find that it "exactly prophecies and foretells the dreadful Judgments and Calamities that are now come to pass in North-America."[6] Hence Clarke offered it to the Massachusetts reading public.

The angel's story was a cryptic tale in which God made New Englanders his chosen people, later plunged them into war due to their irreligion, but then brought them to triumph as a result of their religious reformation. According to the angel, God "visited a People . . . whom he chose as his peculiar People." Because this dream occurred in 1732, when lay political horizons did not include all of America, the chosen people inhabited only New England. The angel then predicted the French and Indian War, saying "Oh! New England, will he threaten thee with his Rod! Ah! with an Over-throw!" But at the last moment, the angel foretold, God would save the chosen New Englanders: "Then will your Deliverer deliver you from the Hands of merciless Men, not by an Arm of Flesh, but by his Arm of mighty Power. He will turn your Enemies back again without so much as striking one Blow."[7]

Describing the twelve-year period between the French and Indian War's end and the Revolution's beginning, the angel predicted "then shall the Nations have Quiet a small Space." Shortly, however, because of "Irreligion," God will "arise again and shake terribly the Earth" with the start of the Revolutionary War. The angel foretold war's terrible tidings: "Oh! New England, thy Distress shall be great! Thou art full of Oppression. Thy Sons shall be oppressed and slain in Battle." The only solution was a religious reformation. "One continued Trouble shall follow another," proclaimed the angel, "until the Inhabitants bow in Reverence and true Humility of Heart and Mind, with Cries to their Helper." The angel's message ended on a positive note, predicting the successful conclusion of the Revolutionary War. Ordinary people's newly invigorated piety would compel God to "raise up the Powers of the Earth to help his Children and his Church, and deliver his Servants."[8]

The publication of this dream in 1776 ties together many of the themes of lay piety as practiced throughout the eighteenth century and as it became more politicized in the revolutionary era. Despite ministerial cautions to the contrary, laypeople placed a great deal of stock in dreams and visions.

For this reason it is virtually inconceivable that the man who transcribed this dream was a minister: clergymen were interested in dreams, and would occasionally describe their dreams in their private journals, but I know of no case in the eighteenth century when a minister published his dream to demonstrate the truths it revealed. All the published works in this genre were laypeople's handiwork.[9] Ministers felt that dreams could be used metaphorically, but never to reveal the actual words of God or an angel.[10]

Furthermore, this pamphlet reveals the shift over time in lay attitudes toward religion and politics. The author of the 1732 transcription saw no further than New England as a political entity, while the man who offered this dream to the public in 1776 saw in it a prediction of the recent events in "North-America." But the man in 1732 would have agreed with the man in 1776 on one issue, despite their differing political horizons: God had chosen a people long ago as his "peculiar People," and these were the ordinary men and women of America (in 1776) or New England (in 1732). God would occasionally use wars and famines to convince these chosen people of his displeasure, as they became smug or irreligious, but inevitably he would cause them to reform, embrace religion "in its primitive Beauty and Purity" as the angel said,[11] and then he would intervene and destroy any enemy.

This view became the foundation of the increasingly congenial relations between laity and clergy after the Revolutionary War and into the nineteenth century. After the Revolution a new generation of preachers paid greater attention to their audiences' desires. In addition, as denominations outside Congregationalism gained strength and the system of state-supported churches weakened, ministers needed to compete for parishioners.[12] This greater religious choice helped defuse some of the laity's anticlerical tendencies: if people disagreed with a particular minister, it was now easier to find one with more acceptable views. These changes accompanied a return to simpler preaching as the more ornate eighteenth-century style fell out of fashion. One prominent theme in these sermons—as popular among ministers as among laypeople—was the "evangelical civic piety" created during the revolutionary era.[13] According to this civil religion, which would eventually give rise to the doctrine of Manifest Destiny, America's religious and political missions were inextricably intertwined. This view seems less charming to modern eyes, however, as the David of the revolutionary era became the Goliath of the industrial era.

Despite these changes in the nineteenth century, the forms and structures of Protestant piety would remain largely the same, with prayer, churchgoing, and religious reading still occupying a central position in the practice of lay piety. And lay expressiveness, creativity, and independent-mindedness would not die in nineteenth-century New England, as attested by the "antebellum spiritual hothouse": the myriad religious outlets enjoyed by laypeople.[14] Lay creativity would simply become more fully incorporated by ministers as they strove to appeal to their parishioners. The occasionally contentious relations of the eighteenth century, which had replaced the more shared culture of the seventeenth century, were ultimately succeeded by the democratic religious culture of the nineteenth century.

Notes

Abbreviations

AAS   American Antiquarian Society, Worcester
BPL   Boston Public Library, Boston
CHS   Connecticut Historical Society, Hartford
CSL   Connecticut State Library, Hartford
HL   Houghton Library, Harvard University, Cambridge
IPL   Ipswich Public Library, Ipswich
MHS   Massachusetts Historical Society, Boston
NEHGS New England Historic Genealogical Society, Boston
PEM   Peabody Essex Museum, Salem
SL   Sterling Library, Manuscripts and Archives, Yale University, New Haven

Preface

1. David D. Hall, *Worlds of Wonder, Days of Judgment: Popular Religious Belief in Early New England* (New York, 1989), 1–2. This is similar to the models in Carlo Ginzburg, *The Cheese and the Worms: The Cosmos of a Sixteenth-Century Miller,* trans. John Tedeschi and Anne Tedeschi (London, 1980; Baltimore, 1992); and Roger Chartier, *The Cultural Uses of Print in Early Modern France* (Princeton, 1987).

2. This concept of "structured agency" is discussed in the literature on "practice theory," including Sherry B. Ortner, *High Religion: A Cultural and Political History of Sherpa Buddhism* (Princeton, 1989), 3–18, 193–202; Pierre Bourdieu, *Outline of a Theory of Practice* (New York, 1977); and Marshall Sahlins, *Historical Metaphors and Mythical Realities: Structure in the Early History of the Sandwich Islands Kingdom* (Ann Arbor, Mich., 1981).

3. This spectrum from "open" to "closed" is found in T. J. Jackson Lears, "The Concept of Cultural Hegemony: Problems and Possibilities," *American Historical Review* 90 (1985): 567–93, esp. 573–74. Lears does not use the term "scripts"; I have adopted that language to make the discussion more parallel with Hall. Of course,

the "pure" ends of the spectrum do not describe real societies but rather serve as a heuristic device.

4. A whole secondary literature has arisen delineating this fascination. To name only the most important works: James West Davidson, *The Logic of Millennial Thought: Eighteenth-Century New England* (New Haven, Conn., 1977); Ruth H. Bloch, *Visionary Republic: Millennial Themes in American Thought, 1756–1800* (Cambridge, Mass., 1985); and Nathan O. Hatch, *The Sacred Cause of Liberty: Republican Thought and the Millennium in Revolutionary New England* (New Haven, Conn., 1977).

5. Mark A. Peterson, *The Price of Redemption: The Spiritual Economy of Puritan New England* (Stanford, 1997); Jon Butler, *Awash in a Sea of Faith: Christianizing the American People* (Cambridge, Mass., 1990); Patricia U. Bonomi, *Under the Cope of Heaven: Religion, Society, and Politics in Colonial America* (New York, 1986).

Introduction

1. M. Halsey Thomas, ed., *The Diary of Samuel Sewall, 1674–1729* (New York, 1973), 440.

2. Because of the contention surrounding the term "Puritan" (both today and three centuries ago) I avoid that term in favor of others, including "Congregational," "reformed Protestant," and "orthodox," depending on the context. Reformed Protestantism in colonial New England included an emphasis on the authority of scripture (Sola Scriptura); a belief in the Calvinist doctrines of justification by faith alone and predestination; and participation in only two sacraments, baptism and the Lord's Supper.

3. For example, in Marblehead. See Christine Leigh Heyrman, *Commerce and Culture: The Maritime Communities of Colonial Massachusetts, 1690–1750* (New York, 1984).

4. See, for example, James W. Schmotter, "Ministerial Careers in Eighteenth-Century New England: The Social Context, 1700–1760," *Journal of Social History* 9 (1975): 249–67.

5. The phrase is from David D. Hall, *Worlds of Wonder, Days of Judgment: Popular Religious Belief in Early New England* (New York, 1989), 245. Agreeing with this perspective are Charles E. Hambrick-Stowe, *The Practice of Piety: Puritan Devotional Disciplines in Seventeenth-Century New England* (Chapel Hill, N.C., 1982), vii, 4, 50, 88, 223, 287; George Selement, *Keepers of the Vineyard: The Puritan Ministry and Collective Culture in Colonial New England* (Lanham, Md., 1984); and Stephen Foster, *The Long Argument: English Puritanism and the Shaping of New England Culture, 1570–1700* (Chapel Hill, N.C., 1991), 289. Historians who disagree with the "shared culture" thesis include Carla Gardina Pestana, *Quakers and Baptists in Colonial Massachusetts* (New York, 1991); and Paul R. Lucas, *Valley of Discord: Church and Society Along the Connecticut River, 1636–1725* (Hanover, N.H., 1976).

6. Hall, *Worlds of Wonder*, 241, 12.

7. Virginia DeJohn Anderson, *New England's Generation: The Great Migration and the Formation of Society and Culture in the Seventeenth Century* (New York, 1991), 12–46.

8. David D. Hall, *The Faithful Shepherd: A History of the New England Ministry in the Seventeenth Century* (New York, 1974), 199–205; Edmund S. Morgan, *Visible Saints: The History of a Puritan Idea* (Ithaca, N.Y., 1965), 132–36.

9. Hall, *Faithful Shepherd*, 204.

10. Richard Godbeer, *The Devil's Dominion: Magic and Religion in Early New England* (New York, 1992), 122–52.

11. Richard P. Gildrie, *The Profane, the Civil, and the Godly: The Reformation of Manners in Orthodox New England, 1679–1749* (University Park, Pa., 1994), 19–40.

12. J. William T. Youngs, Jr., *God's Messengers: Religious Leadership in Colonial New England, 1700–1750* (Baltimore, 1976), 30–38; Horton Davies, *The Worship of the American Puritans, 1629–1730* (New York, 1990), 223–28; Hall, *Faithful Shepherd*, 221–22; and David Harlan, *The Clergy and the Great Awakening in New England* (Ann Arbor, Mich., 1980), 35–36.

13. Hall, *Faithful Shepherd*, 220; Morgan, *Visible Saints*, 141–43; Youngs, *God's Messengers*, 66, 69–78; Harlan, *Clergy and the Great Awakening*, 37; Lucas, *Valley of Discord*, 87–103; Harry S. Stout, *The New England Soul: Preaching and Religious Culture in Colonial New England* (New York, 1986), 107–8; Jon Butler, *Awash in a Sea of Faith: Christianizing the American People* (Cambridge, Mass., 1990), 98, 117; and James W. Schmotter, "The Irony of Clerical Professionalism: New England's Congregational Ministers and the Great Awakening," *American Quarterly* 31 (1979): 148–68, esp. 151–58.

14. See Foster, *Long Argument*, 277.

15. Michael P. Winship, *Seers of God: Puritan Providentialism in the Restoration and Early Enlightenment* (Baltimore, 1996).

16. Anglicization's religious implications are best analyzed in Stout, *New England Soul*, 127–47. See also Hall, *Faithful Shepherd*, 272.

17. Hall, *Worlds of Wonder*, 243.

18. Contrast this with Charles Hambrick-Stowe, who sees private devotion as "the very heart of New England spirituality." Hambrick-Stowe, *Practice of Piety*, 156, and more generally, 156–93.

19. Quoted in ibid., 140–41.

20. Nathan O. Hatch, *The Democratization of American Christianity* (New Haven, Conn., 1989), 17–46.

21. Gordon S. Wood, *The Radicalism of the American Revolution* (New York, 1991), 329–33. This dynamic began earlier outside of New England. See Annette Susan Laing, "'All Things to All Men': Popular Religious Culture and the Anglican Mission in Colonial America, 1701–1750" (Ph.D. diss., University of California, Riverside, 1995).

22. Richard Rabinowitz, *The Spiritual Self in Everyday Life: The Transformation of Personal Religious Experience in Nineteenth-Century New England* (Boston, 1989), xxviii, xxix–xxx.

23. Nathan O. Hatch, *The Sacred Cause of Liberty: Republican Thought and the Millennium in Revolutionary New England* (New Haven, Conn., 1977), 140, 174–75.

24. "Extracts from the Diary of Rev. Samuel Dexter, of Dedham," *New England Historic Genealogical Register* 14 (1860): 109–11.

25. "Westborough Church Records, 1724–1818," AAS, 23 November 1735, photocopies of originals held in Westborough Public Library.

26. Works that rely almost solely on sermons include Laurel Thatcher Ulrich, "Vertuous Women Found: New England Ministerial Literature, 1668–1735," in *Women in American Religion*, ed. Janet Wilson James (Philadelphia, 1980), 67–87; Mary Maples Dunn, "Saints and Sisters: Congregational and Quaker Women in the Early Colonial Period," in ibid., 27–46; Lonna M. Malmsheimer, "Daughters of Zion: New England Roots of American Feminism," *New England Quarterly* 50 (1977): 484–504; and Amanda Porterfield, *Female Piety in Puritan New England: The Emergence of Religious Humanism* (New York, 1992).

27. Ulrich, "Vertuous Women Found," 69–73.

28. Paul Donald Marsella, "Criminal Cases at the Essex County, Massachusetts, Court of General Sessions, 1700–1785" (Ph.D. diss., University of New Hampshire, 1982), 68, 73.

29. Francis G. Walett, ed., *The Diary of Ebenezer Parkman, 1703–1782* (Worcester, Mass., 1974), 158.

30. Diary of Ebenezer Parkman, AAS, 10 May 1766. See also Walett, *Diary of Ebenezer Parkman,* 236. For an example involving Rev. Samuel Cooper, see Joshua Green, "Notes of Sermons Heard, 1768–1775," NEHGS, 6 November 1768.

31. Laypeople were not only concerned that their religion provide them with comfort; justification by faith alone can be a terrifying doctrine, as human agency to effect salvation is largely denied, but many laypeople objected if their minister seemed to stray from that doctrine.

32. Samuel E. Morison, ed., "The Commonplace Book of Joseph Green," *Colonial Society of Massachusetts Publications* 34 (1937–42): 252.

33. Eighteenth-century examples written by men include Edward Goddard, Sermon Notes, c. 1709, Nathan Stone Papers, MHS; Diary of Benjamin Woods, 1726–1730, Diaries (Miscellaneous) Collection, box 18, SL; Edmund Quincy, Sermon Notes, 1722–1724, Belcher-Jennison-Weiss Papers, MHS; Anonymous Notes of Sermons Heard, 1723, NEHGS; Samuel Sewall, Jr., Notes of Sermons Heard, 1724–1725, BPL; and "Boston, Mass., Church Records" collection at AAS (four volumes of anonymous notes). At least one example written by a woman survives: Diary of Lucinda Howe, 1776–1780, CHS. This 148-page manuscript consists almost exclusively of sermon notes kept by Howe in her late teens and early twenties, ending three months before her marriage.

34. For example, Hambrick-Stowe, *Practice of Piety,* 116–17.

35. Diary of Joseph Brewster, AAS, 26 February 1757.

36. Green, Notes of Sermons Heard, 21 August 1768. See also 7 October 1770, when Green accused a minister of "impiety."

37. On Fitts, who was born in 1736, see Sylvia Fitts Getchell, *Fitts Families* (New-market, N.H., 1989), 112–14.

38. Diary of Abraham Fitts, AAS, 9 December 1764, 10 March 1765, 10 January 1773, 13 March 1763. See also 20 March and 1 August 1763 for further examples of active thinking on doctrinal matters.

39. For a discussion of ministerial ambiguity regarding culpability for sin, see Godbeer, *Devil's Dominion*, 85–106.

40. Wood, *Radicalism of the American Revolution*, 11–92.

41. "The Charges aledged against the Rev'd Mr Elisha Marsh," undated ms in Nathan Stone Papers, MHS. This dispute was not a result of the Great Awakening since, as a frontier town, Westminster did not experience the revival's divisions and in fact did not have a church until 1742.

42. William Baldwin to Elisha Marsh, October 1747, Nathan Stone Papers.

CHAPTER 1 *The Spiritual Labor of John Barnard*

1. This artisanal metaphor is similar to the Lévi-Straussian concept of *bricoleur*, the jack-of-all-trades who creates a discourse out of the "materials at hand." Claude Lévi-Strauss, *The Savage Mind* (Chicago, 1966), 16–33.

2. Roger Chartier, "Introduction," in Chartier, ed., *The Culture of Print: Power and the Uses of Print in Early Modern Europe* (Cambridge, 1989), 4; Henry Abelove, *The Evangelist of Desire: John Wesley and the Methodists* (Stanford, 1990).

3. Ned Landsman, "Evangelists and Their Hearers: Popular Interpretation of Revivalist Preaching in Eighteenth-Century Scotland," *Journal of British Studies* 28 (1989): 120–49.

4. E. Brooks Holifield, *The Covenant Sealed: The Development of Puritan Sacramental Theology in Old and New England, 1570–1720* (New Haven, Conn., 1974).

5. Carlo Ginzburg, *The Cheese and the Worms: The Cosmos of a Sixteenth-Century Miller*, trans. John Tedeschi and Anne Tedeschi (London, 1980; Baltimore, 1992).

6. Harry S. Stout, *The New England Soul: Preaching and Religious Culture in Colonial New England* (New York, 1986), 4.

7. John Barnard, Journal, MHS, 124; hereafter in this chapter, pages for this source are cited in the text within parentheses. Barnard's journal was to a great degree sacramental, largely devoted to recording his preparations for the Lord's Supper. The journal also contains some nonsacramental entries, primarily descriptions of unusual events, abstracts from godly books, and notices of deaths. Because the journal is the only extant source for analyzing Barnard's piety, I occasionally argue from silences in the text, a somewhat problematic but in this case necessary strategy. In such cases I offer my interpretations tentatively to compensate for the lack of corroborating evidence.

8. Holifield, *Covenant Sealed*, 197–224; David D. Hall, *The Faithful Shepherd: A History of the New England Ministry in the Seventeenth Century* (New York, 1974), 250–57.

9. Hall overstates his case when he argues that laypeople "sought baptism for their children but rejected the Lord's Supper because it added to the risk of judgment." David D. Hall, *Worlds of Wonder, Days of Judgment: Popular Religious Belief in Early New England* (New York, 1989), 242.

10. Sewall mentioned taking the Lord's Supper seventy-three times in his diary, often noting how important it was to him. See, for example, M. Halsey Thomas, ed., *The Diary of Samuel Sewall, 1674–1729* (New York, 1973), 139, 161, 258, 349, 351, 528, 779, 827, 894, 971. Sewall's and Barnard's life spans were strikingly similar, as Sewall lived from 1652 to 1730 and Barnard from 1654 to 1732. They were acquainted with one another and Sewall mentioned Barnard several times in his diary: four times in Barnard's capacity as a housewright (310, 314, 561, 694) and five times as a deacon (487, 782, 898, 924, 1059).

11. Cotton Mather, *A Companion for Communicants* (Boston, 1690), 85.

12. "Second Church of Boston Records, 1689–1717," 25 May 1690, MHS. This was twelve years after Barnard joined the church.

13. Richard F. Lovelace, *The American Pietism of Cotton Mather: Origins of American Evangelicalism* (Grand Rapids, Mich., 1979), 127–28.

14. Mather, *Companion for Communicants*, 91, 92. See also Cotton Mather, *The Retired Christian; or, The Duty of Secret Prayer* (Boston, 1703), 33; Increase Mather, *Practical Truths Tending to Promote the Power of Godliness* (Boston, 1682), 117–59; Increase Mather, *The Blessed Hope* (Boston, 1701), 115–16.

15. Hall, *Worlds of Wonder*, 156–61.

16. See also 150.

17. Holifield, *Covenant Sealed*, 76; also 4–26, 75–108, 169–96.

18. Compare this with Mather's similar formulation that "a *Sacrament* is a *Sign* and *Seal*," *Companion for Communicants*, 2.

19. Mather, *Companion for Communicants*, 4, 3–4.

20. Cotton Mather, *Bonifacius: An Essay upon the Good*, ed. David Levin (Cambridge, Mass., 1966), 27; also 19.

21. See also 18, 146.

22. Mather, *Bonifacius*, 37, 39, 63.

23. See Norman Pettit, *The Heart Prepared: Grace and Conversion in Puritan Spiritual Life*, 2d ed. (Middletown, Conn., 1989).

24. Holifield, *Covenant Sealed*, 10–11, 20–22.

25. Lovelace, *American Pietism of Cotton Mather*, 136.

26. Holifield, *Covenant Sealed*, 222.

27. Mather, *Companion for Communicants*, 60. Quoted in Holifield, *Covenant Sealed*, 222.

28. Increase Mather, *Practical Truths Tending to Promote the Power of Godliness* (Boston, 1682), 117–59; Increase Mather, *The Blessed Hope*, 115–16; M. G. Hall, ed., *The Autobiography of Increase Mather* (Worcester, Mass., 1962), 316–18.

29. Mather, *Companion for Communicants*, 141.

30. Seventy-four of 167 pages were devoted to preparing for the Lord's Supper. Mather, *Companion for Communicants,* 81–133, 140–62.

31. This point resonates with Hambrick-Stowe's use of Sewall to suggest the "popular belief in the literal presence of Jesus Christ in the meetinghouse during the Sacrament." Charles E. Hambrick-Stowe, *Practice of Piety: Puritan Devotional Disciplines in Seventeenth-Century New England* (Chapel Hill, N.C., 1982), 125.

32. Lovelace, *American Pietism of Cotton Mather,* 138.

33. Robert Middlekauff, in *The Mathers: Three Generations of Puritan Intellectuals, 1596–1728* (New York, 1971), asserts that Cotton Mather's attention to individualistic spirituality "implies a recognition that his culture by the early years of the eighteenth century had relegated religious experience to a private realm" (319). Perhaps a more accurate assessment would be that Mather relegated religious experience to a private realm while most laypeople maintained a communally oriented piety.

34. Compared to the seventy-four pages devoted to self-examination, only three pages were spent placing the ritual in its community context. Mather, *Companion for Communicants,* 57–58, 126–27.

35. David Warren Sabean, *Power in the Blood: Popular Culture and Village Discourse in Early Modern Germany* (New York, 1984), 41; Paul S. Seaver, *Wallington's World: A Puritan Artisan in Seventeenth-Century London* (Stanford, 1985), 36.

36. Lovelace, *American Pietism of Cotton Mather,* 138.

37. See also 4, 5, 13, 21, 74.

38. Hall emphasizes this point in his portrait of Sewall. Hall, *Worlds of Wonder,* 217–19, 229–34.

39. This contrasts with Cotton Mather's eulogies, which focused on the exemplary piety of "vertuous" women. See *Eureka; or, A Vertuous Woman Found* (Boston, 1703); *Monica Americana: A Funeral-Sermon Occasioned by the Death of Mrs. Sarah Leveret* (Boston, 1705); and *Victorina: A Sermon Preach'd, On the Decease, and at the Desire, of Mrs. Katharin Mather* (Boston, 1717).

40. John Barnard [Jr.], "Autobiography of the Rev. John Barnard," *Massachusetts Historical Society Collections,* 3d ser., 5 (1836): 179, 178.

41. In general, female diarists mentioned their husbands more than Barnard mentioned his wife. See, for example, Ellen Richardson Glueck and Thelma Smith Ernst, eds., "Diary of Experience (Wight) Richardson, Sudbury, Mass., 1728–1782," MHS; "Experiences or Spiritual Exercises of Hannah Heaton," CHS; and Thomas Eliot Andrews, ed., "The Diary of Elizabeth (Porter) Phelps," *New England Historic Genealogical Register* 118 (1964): 110–25.

42. For a similar point, see Charles Lloyd Cohen, *God's Caress: The Psychology of Puritan Religious Experience* (New York, 1986), 173–74.

43. See, for example, Mather, *Bonifacius,* 64.

44. See also 158–59 for a similar incident.

45. The shared culture of providentialism was a characteristic of the seventeenth century; see Hall, *Worlds of Wonder,* chap. 2, esp. 77–80. After 1700, ministers placed

less emphasis on this cultural script. Michael P. Winship, *Seers of God: Puritan Providentialism in the Restoration and Early Enlightenment* (Baltimore, 1996). Barnard and other laypeople, however, continued to invoke this world view throughout the eighteenth century.

46. Maris A. Vinovskis, "Angels' Heads and Weeping Willows: Death in Early America," in *Religion, Family, and the Life Course: Explorations in the Social History of Early America*, ed. Gerald F. Moran and Maris A. Vinovskis (Ann Arbor, Mich., 1992), 209–31.

47. See Hambrick-Stowe, *Practice of Piety*, 157–61, on devotional reading and study.

48. The historian who pays most careful attention to the gap between the printed word and lay interpretations thereof is Ginzburg, *The Cheese and the Worms*, xxii–xxiv, 27, 33–61. For a more theoretical account of the interaction between readers and texts, see Susan R. Suleiman and Inge Crosman, eds., *The Reader in the Text* (Princeton, 1980), esp. 106–19.

49. Hall, *Worlds of Wonder*, 32. For the importance of reading to one pious laywoman, see Barbara E. Lacey, "The World of Hannah Heaton: The Autobiography of an Eighteenth-Century Connecticut Farm Woman," *William and Mary Quarterly*, 3d ser., 45 (1988): 288–90.

50. Mather, *Bonifacius*, 77.

51. For example, Brian V. Street, *Literacy in Theory and Practice* (New York, 1984), 4.

52. Cotton Mather, *A Midnight Cry* (Boston, 1692), 65.

53. Ibid., 28.

54. Ibid., 57.

55. Lovelace, *American Pietism of Cotton Mather*, 65, 66–72, 245–47; Middlekauff, *The Mathers*, 320–49.

56. Mather, *Midnight Cry*, 21.

57. Kenneth Silverman, *The Life and Times of Cotton Mather* (New York, 1984), 303 and quote on the same page.

58. Cotton Mather, *Shaking Dispensations* (Boston, 1715), 42–48. Other millennial sermons by Cotton Mather include *Things to be Look'd For* (Cambridge, Mass., 1691); and *Things for a Distressed People* (Boston, 1696).

59. Reiner Smolinski, ed., *The Threefold Paradise of Cotton Mather: An Edition of "Triparadisus"* (Athens, Ga., 1995), 5; also 6, 31, 65.

60. Michael G. Hall, *The Last American Puritan: The Life of Increase Mather, 1639–1723* (Middletown, Conn., 1988), 325; also 76–78, 274–75. See also Middlekauff, *The Mathers*, 179–87; and Hall, *Faithful Shepherd*, 238–39.

61. Increase Mather, *A Dissertation Concerning the Future Conversion of the Jewish Nation* (London, 1709), 1, 24–27. Increase Mather's earlier chiliastic sermons include *The Day of Trouble is Near* (Cambridge, Mass., 1674); and *The Mystery of Israel's Salvation* ([London], 1669).

62. Increase Mather, *A Discourse Concerning Faith and Fervency in Prayer* (Boston, 1710), 83.

63. This set Barnard apart from Samuel Sewall, who was very concerned with the millennium; see Hall, *Worlds of Wonder,* 222–23. Barnard was probably more typical of the average layperson than the Harvard-educated Sewall.

64. Richard Godbeer, *Devil's Dominion: Magic and Religion in Early New England* (New York, 1992), 99. See also Silverman, *Life and Times of Cotton Mather,* 134. For more on Cotton Mather's demonology, see Middlekauff, *The Mathers,* 159–60; Silverman, *Life and Times of Cotton Mather,* 88, 135; and Lovelace, *American Pietism of Cotton Mather,* 130, 192–97. A good example of Mather invoking Satan's seemingly independent power is *Silentarius* (Boston, 1721), 7–8, 11, 26.

65. Mather, *Midnight Cry,* 10. See also Mather's story about devils, "of whom doubtless there are many present," who visit a congregation, 43.

66. See also 18, 47, 158.

67. The quote refers to Cotton Mather. Lovelace, *American Pietism of Cotton Mather,* 80. For Increase Mather, see his *Autobiography,* 279–80.

68. Perry Miller, *The New England Mind: From Colony to Province* (Cambridge, Mass., 1953), 282, Stoddard quoted on the same page.

69. Quoted in Thomas A. Shafer, "Solomon Stoddard and the Theology of the Revival," in *A Miscellany of American Christianity,* ed. Stuart C. Henry (Durham, N.C., 1963), 357.

70. Solomon Stoddard, *Three Sermons Lately Preach'd at Boston* (Boston, 1717), 85, 86.

71. Ibid., 87.

72. Stoddard, *Three Sermons,* 89. Emphasis added.

73. William Beveridge, *Private Thoughts Upon Religion, Digested into Twelve Articles, with Practical Resolutions form'd Thereupon,* 2d ed. (London, 1709), 60, 65. This may not have been the edition that Barnard read, as eight editions of this work were printed by 1715.

74. Ibid., 52, 53.

75. Barnard condensed this passage from John Flavel, *Pneumatologia: A Treatise of the Soul of Man* (London, 1685), 248–50.

76. This passage was copied from Flavel, *Pneumatologia,* 464–65.

77. Emphasis added.

78. David D. Hall, "The Uses of Literacy in New England, 1600–1850," in *Printing and Society in Early America,* ed. William L. Joyce et al. (Worcester, Mass., 1983), 23–24.

79. Richard Steele, *A Plain Discourse Upon Uprightness, Shewing the Properties and Privileges of an Upright Man,* 2d ed. (London, 1672), ix.

80. Ibid., 22.

81. As in *Bonifacius,* 19–20, 27.

82. Steele, *Upright Man,* 58.

CHAPTER 2　*"She Died Like Good Old Jacob"*

1. Diary of Ebenezer Parkman, 1742, AAS, 9 February and 11 February 1742.
2. Philippe Ariès, *The Hour of Our Death*, trans. Helen Weaver (New York, 1981), 95–139; T. S. R. Boase, *Death in the Middle Ages: Mortality, Judgment, and Remembrance* (New York, 1972); and Mary Catherine O'Connor, *The Art of Dying Well: The Development of the Ars Moriendi* (New York, 1942).
3. The phrase is from David E. Stannard, *The Puritan Way of Death: A Study in Religion, Culture, and Social Change* (New York, 1977). This chapter also modifies Stannard's chronological model, in which the Great Awakening is a turning point. I argue that deathbed dynamics held constant throughout the eighteenth century.
4. Gordon E. Geddes, *Welcome Joy: Death in Puritan New England, 1630–1730* (Ann Arbor, Mich., 1981); Peter Gregg Slater, *Children in the New England Mind: In Death and Life* (Hamden, Conn., 1977); Stephen C. Messer, "Individual Responses to Death in Puritan Massachusetts," *Omega: The Journal of Death and Dying* 21 (1990): 155–63; and James J. Naglack, "Death in Colonial New England," *Historical Journal of Western Massachusetts* 4 (1975): 21–33.
5. Slater notes that "the major obstacle to a more definitive presentation [of Puritan attitudes toward death and dying] is the scantiness of direct information on the response of Puritan women to bereavement." Slater, *Children in the New England Mind*, 32.
6. This tendency was roughly equal for men and women: 25 percent (27 of 107) of women and 23 percent (12 of 52) of men linked death with piety. The narratives in this sample are Kenneth P. Minkema, ed., "The East Windsor Conversion Relations, 1700–1725," *Connecticut Historical Society Bulletin* 51 (1986): 9–63; Kenneth P. Minkema, ed., "The Lynn End 'Earthquake' Relations of 1727," *New England Quarterly* 69 (1996): 473–99; J. M. Bumsted, "Emotion in Colonial America: Some Relations of Conversion Experience in Freetown, Massachusetts, 1749–1770," *New England Quarterly* 49 (1976): 97–108; Ebenezer Parkman Papers, box 2, folder 2, AAS; John Cleaveland Papers, PEM; Conversion Narratives of Nathaniel Brown, Mary Brown, James Stewart, and John Stewart, NEHGS; Relations of Isaac and Anna Farnsworth, IPL. My thanks to Anne Brown for transcriptions of the Farnsworth narratives.
7. Minkema, "East Windsor Conversion Relations," 24.
8. Relation of Eleazer Beeman, Ebenezer Parkman Papers, box 2, folder 2, AAS. See also relation of Elizabeth Ingersol, John Cleaveland Papers.
9. Confession of Hannah Wadsworth, November 1754, Massachusetts Colonial Manuscripts, AAS. I am indebted to Ross Beales for this citation. See also Rev. Israel Loring's description of a person who was "under great Convictions, occasioned by his beholding the dead body of one Pierce Drowned Sometime Since in Watertown River." Louise Parkman Thomas, ed., *The Journal of the Rev. Israel Loring (1682–1772) of Sudbury, Massachusetts, Covering His Early Life and the Years 1704–1745* (typescript at University of Michigan Library, 1983), 14 May 1741.

10. Diary of Lydia Prout, NEHGS, 12 February 1715.

11. [Cotton Mather], *Wholesome Words: A Visit of Advice Given unto Families that are Visited with Sickness* (Boston, 1713), 23.

12. Samuel Willard, *The Mourners Cordial Against Excessive Sorrow* (Boston, 1691), 39; also 32–33. See also John Barnard, *Two Sermons: The Christians Behavior under Severe and Repeated Bereavements* (Boston, 1714), 5–6; and Henry Gibbs, *Bethany; or, The House of Mourning* (Boston, 1714), 5, 9–10.

13. Gibbs, *Bethany,* 12.

14. Jonathan Parsons, *A Funeral Sermon . . . of Ebenezer Little* (Boston, 1768), 15. See also Cotton Mather, *Silentarius* (Boston, 1721), 13–17; and Thomas Skinner, *The Mourner Admonished* (Boston, 1746), 20–23.

15. Barnard, *Two Sermons,* 20. See also Willard, *The Mourners Cordial,* 119–21; and Benjamin Colman, *The Father's Tears over his Daughter's Remains* (Boston, 1735), 42–47.

16. Cotton Mather, *Right Thoughts in Sad Hours* (London, 1689), 18.

17. Diary of Rev. Samuel Chandler, PEM, 22 May 1746.

18. James P. Lane, *Lane Families of the Massachusetts Bay Colony* (Norton, Mass., 1886), 51.

19. Diary of Ebenezer Storer, NEHGS, 16 August 1755 and 12 March 1761.

20. Osborn quotes from this letter in Sarah Osborn to Rev. Joseph Fish, 10 December 1755, AAS, Sarah Osborn Papers.

21. Francis G. Walett, ed., *The Diary of Ebenezer Parkman, 1703–1782* (Worcester, Mass., 1974), 10–11.

22. Diary of John Gates, MHS, 1 May 1757 and 3 April 1757.

23. "Deacon John Paine's Journal," *Mayflower Descendant* 9 (1907): 99.

24. Diary of Daniel King, PEM, 1 September 1738.

25. Ellen Richardson Glueck and Thelma Smith Ernst, eds., "Diary of Experience (Wight) Richardson, Sudbury, Mass., 1728–1782," MHS, 23.

26. Diary of John Gates, 17 November 1756; Diary of Lydia Prout, 12 February 1715.

27. John Demos, ed., *Remarkable Providences: Readings on Early American History,* rev. ed. (Boston, 1991), 195.

28. Diary of Samuel Chandler, 8 November 1749.

29. See, for example, "Deacon John Paine's Journal," *Mayflower Descendant* 9 (1907): 137; and Diary of Mary Dodge, PEM, 28 December 1742.

30. "Diary of Experience (Wight) Richardson," 82.

31. Diary of Benjamin Lyon, CHS, 16 May 1764.

32. Rebecca Husman, ed., "Diary of Sarah Prince Gill," typescript at Kellogg Library, Bard College, 19–20.

33. Thomas Prince, *Dying Exercises of Mrs. Deborah Prince* (Newburyport, Mass., 1789), 49, 51.

34. Work Projects Administration, *Diary and Journal (1755–1807) of Seth Metcalf* (Boston, 1939).

35. "Experiences or Spiritual Exercises of Hannah Heaton," CHS, 225.

36. Diary of John Gates, 13 August 1758.

37. Slater, *Children in the New England Mind*, 49–90. I place the term "infant damnation" in quotes since it implies that all infants were damned, while ministers' actual position was that infants were not automatically saved.

38. Cotton Mather, *Small Offers Towards the Service of the Tabernacle in this Wilderness* (Boston, 1689), 59. Quoted in Stannard, *Puritan Way of Death*, 50.

39. Cotton Mather, *Cares About the Nurseries* (Boston, 1702), 32. Quoted in Stannard, *Puritan Way of Death*, 51.

40. Willard, *The Mourners Cordial*, 76; also, 78.

41. Jonathan Edwards, *Some Thoughts Concerning the Present Revival of Religion in New England* (Boston, 1742), 163–64.

42. David D. Hall makes a similar point in *Worlds of Wonder, Days of Judgment: Popular Religious Belief in Early New England* (New York, 1989), 209.

43. Diary of Lydia Prout, 20 October 1716.

44. "Diary of Experience (Wight) Richardson," 25. See also James P. Lane, *Lane Families of the Massachusetts Bay Colony* (Norton, Mass., 1886), 51.

45. Diary of Aaron Bull, CHS.

46. "Diary of Cotton Mather, 1681–1708," *Massachusetts Historical Society Collections*, 7th ser., 7 (1911): 180–81.

47. Kenneth A. Requa, ed., *Poems of Jane Turell and Martha Brewster* (Delmar, N.Y., 1979), 15.

48. Walett, *Diary of Ebenezer Parkman*, 124. See also Diary of Josiah Thacher, MHS, 22 January 1763.

49. M. Halsey Thomas, ed., *The Diary of Samuel Sewall, 1674–1729* (New York, 1973), 731.

50. Ebenezer Clapp, *The Clapp Memorial* (Boston, 1876), 378.

51. Relation of Ruth Hassock, John Cleaveland Papers, box 1, folder 1b.

52. Relation of Abigail Giddinge, John Cleaveland Papers. These women expressed their fears in the 1760s, a generation after the Great Awakening. Again, Stannard's model should be revised. Instead of the postrevival optimism about death that he predicts, these people—members of a New Light church—and many others like them retained a fear of death.

53. John Barnard, Journal, MHS, 169.

54. "Diary of Experience (Wight) Richardson," 105, 27.

55. Laurel Thatcher Ulrich reports that in midwife Martha Ballard's meticulous notes the rate of maternal death was only about 6 deaths per 1000 births. Ulrich, *A Midwife's Tale: The Life of Martha Ballard, Based on Her Diary, 1785–1812* (New York, 1990), 173.

56. This is quoted in Sarah Osborn to Joseph Peabody, 3 October 1762, Sarah Osborn Papers, AAS.

57. Quoted in [Cotton Mather], *Memorials of Early Piety, Occurring in the Holy Life & Joyful Death of Mrs. Jerusha Oliver* (Boston, 1711), 28.

58. "Experiences of Hannah Heaton," 71.

59. Thomas Eliot Andrews, ed., "The Diary of Elizabeth (Porter) Phelps," *New England Historic Genealogical Register* 118 (1964): 121.

60. Diary of Lydia Prout, undated entry between 1712 and 1714, page 5.

61. Gerald F. Moran, "'Sisters' in Christ: Women and the Church in Seventeenth-Century New England," in *Religion, Family, and the Life Course: Explorations in the Social History of Early America*, ed. Gerald F. Moran and Maris A. Vinovskis (Ann Arbor, Mich., 1992), 85–108.

62. Caroline Gardiner Curtis, ed., *The Cary Letters* (Cambridge, Mass., 1891), 60; Andrews, "Diary of Elizabeth (Porter) Phelps," 121. See also the case of Eunice Andrews of Ipswich, who linked her conversion with her "lying-in." Anne S. Brown, "'Bound Up in a Bundle of Life': The Social Meaning of Religious Practice in Northeastern Massachusetts, 1700–1765" (Ph.D. diss., Boston University, 1995), 78–79.

63. Curtis, *Cary Letters*, 61.

64. Diary of Daniel King, 15 September 1749.

65. This character is found in both the popular mind and the scholarship on early New England child rearing. John Demos, *A Little Commonwealth: Family Life in Plymouth Colony* (New York, 1970), 100–106; Philip Greven, *The Protestant Temperament: Patterns of Child-Rearing, Religious Experience, and the Self in Early America* (New York, 1977), 22, 28, 32–35.

66. Diary of John Gates, 30 March 1757 to 1 January 1758.

67. Victor Turner, *The Ritual Process: Structure and Anti-Structure* (Ithaca, N.Y., 1969), 97. Caroline Walker Bynum argues that Turner's model of liminality is not applicable to women, at least in the Middle Ages, because female saints described their lives more in terms of continuity than "climax" and "conversion." Whatever the merits of Bynum's argument for the Middle Ages, I do not believe it works for colonial America, when women routinely described in conversion narratives lives punctuated by climactic turning points. Bynum, "Women's Stories, Women's Symbols: A Critique of Victor Turner's Theory of Liminality," in *Fragmentation and Redemption: Essays on Gender and the Human Body in Medieval Religion* (New York, 1991), 27–51.

68. This scene is a composite based on hundreds of approvingly noted deathbed scenes that appear in sermons, ministerial diaries, and lay diaries.

69. Cotton Mather, *The Thoughts of a Dying Man* (Boston, 1697), 9, 12, 16, 17, 14.

70. Benjamin Colman, *Dying in Peace in a Good Old Age* (Boston, 1730), 10, 11.

71. Diary of Benjamin Lyon, CHS, 15 August 1763. The book was John Willison, *The Afflicted Man's Companion* (Boston, n.d.). Willison was a Presbyterian minister in Scotland.

72. Ibid., 25 December 1763, 9 March 1764, and 31 March 1764. Lyon refers respectively to Richard Baxter, *Richard Baxter's Dying Thoughts* (London, 1683); Edward Pearse, *The Great Concern; or, A Serious Warning to a Timely and Thorough Preparation for Death* (London, 1678); and Isaac Watts, *The Watchful Christian Prepared for Early Death* (London, 1732). That these four books were all originally written in Great Britain suggests the transatlantic nature of the ministerial model.

73. Thomas Foxcroft, *A Sermon . . . After the Funeral of Mrs. Elizabeth Foxcroft* (Boston, 1721), 40.

74. [Cotton Mather], *Memorials of Early Piety, Occurring in the Holy Life & Joyful Death of Mrs. Jerusha Oliver* (Boston, 1711), 49.

75. Diary of Samuel Chandler, 1 January 1746.

76. Walett, *Diary of Ebenezer Parkman*, 76.

77. Abigail Cleaveland to John and Ebenezer Cleaveland, 2 March 1751, John Cleaveland Papers.

78. Tarrant Putnam to Elijah Putnam, 28 March 1763, Putnam Family Mss 1749–1808, AAS.

79. Ibid. For the sixteenth-century antecedents of this belief, see Richard Wunderli and Gerald Broce, "The Final Moment before Death in Early Modern England," *Sixteenth Century Journal* 20 (1989): 268–69. Wunderli and Broce argue for an early modern popular belief that one's final moments *determined* whether one went to heaven or hell. If correct, this would differ from the eighteenth-century dynamic I am describing, where one's final moments merely *signified* one's final destination.

80. Mather Byles, *The Character of the Perfect and Upright Man; His Peaceful End Described* (Boston, 1729), 15.

81. Willard, *The Mourners Cordial*, 21; also, 71, 104.

82. "Deacon John Paine's Journal," *Mayflower Descendant* 9 (1907): 98.

83. Diary of Jonathan Willis, MHS, 21 July 1744.

84. Rebecca Husman, ed., "Sarah Prince Gill Diary," typescript at Kellogg Library, Bard College, 14–15. For another account of this deathbed scene, written by Sarah's father, see Thomas Prince, *The Sovereign God Acknowledged and Blessed, both in Giving and Taking Away* (Boston, 1744), 31–32.

85. Diary of Elizabeth Craft White, MHS, 15 January 1771 and 26 December 1770.

86. "French and Indian War Diary of Benjamin Glasier of Ipswich, 1758–1760," *Essex Institute Historical Collections* 86 (1950): 72.

87. Thomas, *Diary of Samuel Sewall*, 282, 391, 599.

88. David Hall argues that observers of lay deaths did not record anguish on the deathbed. According to Hall, "Out of [the deathbed] ritual emerged peace, or at least the strength to face the King of Terrors." Hall, *Worlds of Wonder*, 209–10. The reality, however, was more complex. While Hall's interpretation holds true for a majority of cases, some deathbed scenes did not adhere to the model of a hopeful death and the dying person expired fearing Satan, hell, or simply death itself.

89. Diary of Samuel Chandler, 21 January 1746.

90. William G. McLoughlin, ed., *The Diary of Isaac Backus* (Providence, R.I., 1979), 304, 427, 630.

91. Walett, *Diary of Ebenezer Parkman*, 169. Dying without comfort did not only happen to laypeople: Increase Mather, for example, died in a great deal of anguish. See Thomas, *Diary of Samuel Sewall*, 1007; Cotton Mather, *Parentator* (Boston, 1724).

92. Thomas, *Journal of Rev. Israel Loring*, 6 March 1728.

93. Walett, *Diary of Ebenezer Parkman*, 24–25.

94. "Journal of the Rev. John Ballantine, 1737–1774," AAS, 23 February 1767.

95. Walett, *Diary of Ebenezer Parkman*, 262.

96. Mather, *Thoughts of a Dying Man*, 40–41. See also [Cotton Mather], *Wholesome Words: A Visit of Advice, Given Unto Families that are Visited with Sickness* (Boston, 1713), 17.

97. Thomas Foxcroft, *A Sermon . . . After the Funeral of Mrs. Elizabeth Foxcroft* (Boston, 1721), 47.

98. Diary of Ebenezer Parkman, AAS, 27 September 1756. See also "Extracts from the Diary of Rev. Samuel Dexter, of Dedham," *New England Historic Genealogical Register* 14 (1860): 112; and Diary of Samuel Chandler, 29 February 1752.

99. Diary of Daniel King, 15 September 1749.

100. Walett, *Diary of Ebenezer Parkman*, 78.

101. Diary of Daniel King, 15 September 1749. Emphasis added.

102. Walett, *Diary of Ebenezer Parkman*, 119–20.

103. Diary of Ebenezer Parkman, AAS, 2 March 1761 and 13 September 1760. See also Diary of Ebenezer Parkman, AAS, 28 June 1742.

104. McLoughlin, *Diary of Isaac Backus*, 364.

105. Ibid., 585. A few ministers, however, overlooked their teachings when their own loved ones were dying. See, for example, Diary of Rev. Jonathan Mills, MHS, 20 July 1747, for a minister who believed his dying wife would surely go to heaven.

106. Diary of Ebenezer Parkman, AAS, entries of 9 February 1742 and 11 February 1742. For another minister cautioning against "dreams in which are divers vanities," see William Cooper, *The Beatifick Vision Productive of Likeness to Christ* (Boston, 1734), 21.

107. "Experiences or Spiritual Exercises of Hannah Heaton," 11 February 1778.

108. McLoughlin, *Diary of Isaac Backus*, 641. See also Caroline Hazard, ed., *John Saffin, His Book (1665–1708)* (New York, 1928), 21–22.

109. Joseph Emerson, *Early Piety Encouraged* (Boston, 1738), 22–23.

110. Diary of David Hall, MHS, 14 October 1752.

111. McLoughlin, *Diary of Isaac Backus*, 384.

112. Diary of Ebenezer Parkman, AAS, 7 October 1756.

113. Thomas, *Diary of Samuel Sewall*, 479. See also diary of Moses Prince, HL, 28 October 1717.

114. Diary of David Hall, 5 September 1741.

115. Diary of Samuel Chandler, 27 March 1749.

116. Grace Smith, *The Dying Mothers Legacy* (Boston, 1712), 5.

117. Robert F. Trent, ed., "'The Deuil Came Upon me Like a Lyon': A 1697 Cambridge Deathbed Narrative," *Connecticut Historical Society Bulletin* 48 (1983): 119.

118. Reiner Smolinski, ed., *The Threefold Paradise of Cotton Mather: An Edition of "Triparadisus"* (Athens, Ga., 1995), 144.

119. Walett, *Diary of Ebenezer Parkman*, 202.

120. Charles Chauncy, *Early Piety Recommended and Exemplify'd* (Boston, 1732), 18. Price also used the power of the deathbed to invert conventional age hierarchies: "tho' but in her 17th year, she was enabled . . . to correct the excessive sorrow of her distressed parents: minding them of the sovereignty of God; and . . . recommending to them the duty of submission." Ibid.

121. "Journal of the Rev. John Ballantine," 8 April 1762. For further examples see Thomas Skinner, *The Mourner Admonished* (Boston, 1746), 36–37; Thomas Foxcroft, *Sermon . . . After the Funeral of Mrs. Elizabeth Foxcroft*, 45; and a woman "tak[ing] up King David's Language" in Diary of Elizabeth Craft White, 26 December 1770.

122. Diary of Rev. John Walley, MHS, 20 January 1748. For a similar example, see Cotton Mather, *Light in Darkness* (Boston, 1724), 19.

123. McLoughlin, *Diary of Isaac Backus*, 388, 433–34, 350–51. See also Diary of Jospeh Pitkin, CSL, 45–47, for a dying woman giving counsel to men.

124. Phyllis Mack, *Visionary Women: Ecstatic Prophecy in Seventeenth-Century England* (Berkeley, Calif., 1992), 107–8; Clarke Garrett, *Spirit Possession and Popular Religion: From the Camisards to the Shakers* (Baltimore, 1987), 22.

125. Kidder, "Diary of Nicholas Gilman," 256–58.

126. Diary of Lucinda Howe, CHS, October 1776.

127. Diary of Ebenezer Storer, NEHGS, 16 August 1755 and 12 March 1761.

CHAPTER 3   *The Performance of Piety*

1. Daniel Scott Smith and Michael S. Hindus, "Premarital Pregnancy in America, 1640–1971: An Overview and Interpretation," *Journal of Interdisciplinary History* 5 (1975): 537–70.

2. New Salem Unitarian Church Records, PEM, 29 January 1743, in section headed "Confessions."

3. Nicholas B. Dirks, "Ritual and Resistance: Subversion as a Social Fact," in *Culture/Power/History: A Reader in Contemporary Social Theory*, ed. Dirks, Geoff Eley, and Sherry B. Ortner (Princeton, 1994), 486. For a similar interpretation, see E. Brooks Holifield, "Peace, Conflict, and Ritual in Puritan Congregations," *Journal of Interdisciplinary History* 23 (1993): 551–70.

4. David D. Hall argues that ritual practice "is the loving, unselfish community from which anger and greed have been displaced" and that ritual served to "express a conception of community." Hall, *Worlds of Wonder, Days of Judgment: Popular Religious Belief in Early New England* (New York, 1989), 20, 19. Charles Hambrick-Stowe

defines a ritual as an "activity that a society establishes to celebrate and renew commonly held perceptions." Hambrick-Stowe, *The Practice of Piety: Puritan Devotional Disciplines in Seventeenth-Century New England* (Chapel Hill, N.C., 1982), 51; also 100–103.

5. Max Gluckman, quoted in Dirks, "Ritual and Resistance," 485.

6. Greg Dening, *History's Anthropology: The Death of William Gooch* (Lanham, Md., 1988).

7. Robert St. George, "'Heated' Speech and Literacy in Seventeenth-Century New England," in *Seventeenth-Century New England,* ed. David D. Hall and David Grayson Allen (Boston, 1984), 279.

8. Horton Davies, *The Worship of the American Puritans, 1629–1730* (New York, 1990), 158–59, 165–66.

9. On the growing number of sacramental manuals after 1690, see E. Brooks Holifield, *The Covenant Sealed: The Development of Puritan Sacramental Theology in Old and New England, 1570–1720* (New Haven, Conn., 1974), 197–206.

10. Relation of Sarah Eveleth, box 1, folder 1b, "Testimonials," John Cleaveland Papers, PEM. All conversion narratives quoted in this section may be found in this collection.

11. For two excellent accounts of narrative self-creation, see Stephen Greenblatt, *Renaissance Self-Fashioning: From More to Shakespeare* (Chicago, 1980); and Michael MacDonald, "*The Fearefull Estate of Francis Spira:* Narrative, Identity, and Emotion in Early Modern England," *Journal of British Studies* 31 (1992): 32–61.

12. The theoretical backbone of this section is provided by Roy A. Rappaport, "The Obvious Aspects of Ritual," in Rappaport, *Ecology, Meaning, and Religion* (Richmond, Calif., 1979), 173–221. I agree with Charles Lloyd Cohen that conversion was an empowering experience for the saints. Cohen, *God's Caress: The Psychology of Puritan Religious Experience* (New York, 1986). Complementary to his psychological approach, I locate the power of conversion in the ritual structures in which it occurred.

13. For the strengths and weaknesses of this genre of sources, see Erik R. Seeman, "Lay Conversion Narratives: Investigating Ministerial Intervention," *New England Quarterly* 71 (1998): 629–34; and Cohen, *God's Caress,* 138–40.

14. Edmund S. Morgan, *Visible Saints: The History of a Puritan Idea* (Ithaca, N.Y., 1963), 80–112.

15. Perry Miller, *The New England Mind: From Colony to Province* (Cambridge, Mass., 1953), 226–47; Paul R. Lucas, *Valley of Discord: Church and Society Along the Connecticut River, 1636–1725* (Hanover, N.H., 1976), 169–87.

16. See below, chapter 5.

17. For example, Kenneth P. Minkema, "The East Windsor Conversion Relations, 1700–1725," *Connecticut Historical Society Bulletin* 51 (1986): 9–63; J. M. Bumsted, "Emotion in Colonial America: Some Relations of Conversion Experience in Freetown, Massachusetts, 1749–1770," *New England Quarterly* 49 (1976): 97–108; and Ebenezer Parkman Papers, box 2, folder 2, AAS.

18. John Cleaveland, *A Short and Plain Narrative of the Late Work of God's Spirit at Chebacco in Ipswich, in the Years 1763 and 1764* (Boston, 1767), 14.

19. Seeman, "Lay Conversion Narratives."

20. Christopher M. Jedrey, *The World of John Cleaveland: Family and Community in Eighteenth-Century New England* (New York, 1979), 117–19.

21. Rappaport, "Obvious Aspects of Ritual," 182.

22. The phrase "more or less" denotes that ritual can never be absolutely invariant but can come very close.

23. For more on Phillis Cogswell, see Erik R. Seeman, "'Justise Must Take Plase': Three African Americans Speak of Religion in Eighteenth-Century New England," *William and Mary Quarterly*, 3d ser., 56 (1999): 393–414.

24. For anthropological accounts of ritual's efficacy, see John L. Austin, *How To Do Things With Words* (Oxford, 1962); Ruth Finnegan, "How To Do Things With Words: Performative Utterances Among the Limba of Sierra Leone," *Man* 4 (1969): 537–52; and S. J. Tambiah, *A Performative Approach to Ritual* (London, 1979).

25. M. Halsey Thomas, ed., *The Diary of Samuel Sewall, 1674–1729* (New York, 1973), 39.

26. Anne S. Brown, "'Bound Up in a Bundle of Life': The Social Meaning of Religious Practice in Northeastern Massachusetts, 1700–1765" (Ph.D. diss., Boston University, 1995), 69 n. 79. See also Hall, *Worlds of Wonder*, 152–55. In general, people either had to join the church as a full member or renew their baptismal covenant in order to have their children baptized.

27. This section only considers conflicts within the pro-pedobaptist community. The disputes between pro- and anti-pedobaptists are amply described in William G. McLoughlin, *New England Dissent, 1630–1883* (Cambridge, Mass., 1971).

28. Except for some Lutherans who observed penance as a sacrament.

29. Holifield, *Covenant Sealed*, 4–6, 14–17, 178, 186–93; Morgan, *Visible Saints*, 121, 145.

30. John Graham, *The Duty of Renewing their Baptismal Covenant Proved and Urged upon the Adult Children of Professing Parents* (Boston, 1734), 1.

31. Benjamin Wadsworth, *The Bonds of Baptism* (Boston, 1717), 10.

32. See, for example, Wadsworth, *Bonds of Baptism*, 9–10; Cotton Mather, *Baptismal Piety* (Boston, 1727), 30. As David Hall has written, "no New England minister regarded the sacrament [of baptism] as efficacious." Hall, "Introduction," in Norman Pettit, *The Heart Prepared: Grace and Conversion in Puritan Spiritual Life*, 2d ed. (Middletown, Conn., 1989), xvii.

33. Diary of Joseph Goodhue, PEM, 23 March 1746.

34. Diary of Ebenezer Storer, NEHGS, 29 February 1756.

35. Thomas, *Diary of Samuel Sewall*, 133, 264, 497.

36. In Beverly, Massachusetts, for example, "more than twice as many mothers as fathers timed their decisions to join the church to coincide with the baptism of children." Brown, "'Bound Up in a Bundle of Life,'" 81.

37. [Ann Fiske], *A Confession of Faith; or, A Summary of Divinity* (Boston, 1704), 8.

38. Diary of John Gates, MHS, 5 January 1763.

39. Diary of Mary Dodge Cleaveland, PEM, 17 October 1751 and 26 August 1760. Men did occasionally use similar language to describe their children's baptism. See, for example, Diary of Benjamin Bangs, MHS, 15 August 1762.

40. Quoted in Anne S. Brown and David D. Hall, "Family Strategies and Religious Practice: Baptism and the Lord's Supper in Early New England," in *Lived Religion in America: Toward a History of Practice,* ed. David D. Hall (Princeton, 1997), 54.

41. Francis G. Walett, ed., *The Diary of Ebenezer Parkman, 1703–1782* (Worcester, Mass., 1974), 111–12.

42. William G. McLoughlin, ed., *The Diary of Isaac Backus* (Providence, R.I., 1979), 570.

43. See, for example, Westborough Church Records, 1724–1818, AAS, photocopies of originals held at Westborough Public Library, 18 and 19 May 1729.

44. Diary of Ebenezer Parkman, AAS, 17 December 1756.

45. "Journal of the Rev. John Ballantine," AAS, 3 July 1769.

46. Walett, *Diary of Ebenezer Parkman,* 62.

47. "Journal of the Rev. John Ballantine," 28 October 1770.

48. Ibid., 30 October 1770. For a similar example of lay precisianism about baptism, see Louise Parkman Thomas, ed., *The Journal of the Rev. Israel Loring (1682–1772) of Sudbury, Massachusetts, Covering His Early Life and the Years 1704–1745* (typescript at the University of Michigan Library, 1983), 19 February 1738.

49. Holifield, *Covenant Sealed,* 19, 55–56, 197–206.

50. Rebecca Husman, ed., "Sarah Prince Gill Diary," typescript at Kellogg Library, Bard College, 103.

51. For example, Hall, *Worlds of Wonder.*

52. See, for example, Vernon L. Parrington, *Main Currents in American Thought: The Colonial Mind, 1620–1800* (1927; New York, 1954), 11–15, on Calvinism's terrors.

53. Ellen Richardson Glueck and Thelma Smith Ernst, eds., "Diary of Experience (Wight) Richardson, Sudbury, Mass., 1728–1782," MHS, 16–17, 25.

54. Diary of Jonathan Willis, MHS, 30 June 1744 and 6 September 1746.

55. Kenneth A. Requa, ed., *Poems of Jane Turell and Martha Brewster* (Delmar, N.Y., 1979), 112.

56. Benjamin Colman, *The Father's Tears over his Daughter's Remains* (Boston, 1735), 52.

57. Requa, *Poems,* 113.

58. William Cooper, *The Beatifick Vision Productive of Likeness to Christ* (Boston, 1734), 9.

59. Ebenezer Parkman, "Memoirs of Mrs Sarah Pierpont," AAS, n.d., pages unnumbered.

60. Diary of John Gates, MHS, 6 June 1756.

61. Diary of Daniel King, PEM, 3 May 1730.
62. Diary of Mary Dodge, PEM, 10 April 1743. See also Diary of Benjamin Woods, Diaries (Miscellaneous) Collection, box 18, SL, 18 and 26 February 1727.
63. Cooper, *Beatifick Vision*, 9.
64. John Barnard, Journal, MHS, 12.
65. Diary of Lydia Prout, NEHGS, 20 October 1716.
66. Diary of Moses Prince, HL, 2 March 1718.
67. Diary of Lydia Prout, undated entry in 1714, page 6.
68. "Diary of Experience (Wight) Richardson," 50.
69. Ibid., 54, 63.
70. Diary of Benjamin Bangs, MHS, 20 January and 6 July 1760.
71. Diary of Ebenezer Storer, 3 February 1751 and 7 December 1755.
72. Parkman, "Memoirs of Mrs Sarah Pierpont," entry between 1734 and 1736.
73. Husman, "Sarah Prince Gill Diary," 29 January 1757.
74. McLoughlin, *Diary of Isaac Backus*, 191.
75. Diary of Samuel Chandler, PEM, 2 April 1749.
76. William Kidder, ed., "Diary of Nicholas Gilman" (master's thesis, University of New Hampshire, 1972), 243.
77. See, for example, I. M. Lewis, *Ecstatic Religion: An Anthropological Study of Spirit Possession and Shamanism* (Baltimore, 1971), 34.
78. Thomas, *Diary of Samuel Sewall*, 349.
79. Thomas Eliot Andrews, ed., "The Diary of Elizabeth (Porter) Phelps," *New England Historic Genealogical Register* 118 (1964): 116.
80. Diary of Jonathan Willis, 5 October 1746.
81. Diary of John Gates, 3 August 1766.
82. Diary of Lydia Prout, undated entry 1714, p. 4.
83. Diary of Benjamin Bangs, 18 May 1760.
84. Diary of William Cooper, MHS, 4 November 1764.
85. Diary of Benjamin Bangs, 18 May 1760; Diary of Jonathan Willis, 5 January 1745.
86. Thomas, *Diary of Samuel Sewall*, 161.
87. Husman, "Sarah Prince Gill Diary," 101.
88. Diary of Daniel King, PEM, 5 August 1739.
89. Parkman, "Memoirs of Mrs Sarah Pierpont," 9 October and 28 February 1736. This language recalls the story of doubting Thomas, John 20:24–29.
90. Stephen L. Longenecker, *Piety and Tolerance: Pennsylvania German Religion, 1700–1800* (Metuchen, N.J., 1994), 76–80; Jacob John Sessler, *Communal Pietism Among Early American Moravians* (New York, 1971), 97–114.
91. This suggests that while ministers may have used less sensual imagery to describe communion with Christ after 1700, as argued in Michael P. Winship, "Behold the Bridegroom Cometh! Marital Imagery in Massachusetts Preaching, 1630–1730," *Early American Literature* 27 (1992): 170–84, many laypeople continued to use such tropes.

92. On the sexualized nature of religious writings in early New England, see Richard Godbeer, "'Love Raptures': Marital, Romantic, and Erotic Images of Jesus Christ in Puritan New England, 1670–1730," *New England Quarterly* 68 (1995): 355–84; Walter Hughes, "'Meat Out of the Eater': Panic and Desire in American Puritan Poetry," in *Engendering Men: The Question of Male Feminist Criticism,* ed. Joseph A. Boone and Michael Cadden (New York, 1990), 102–21.

93. Parkman, "Memoirs of Mrs Sarah Pierpont," undated entry.

94. Requa, *Poems,* 114.

95. Diary of Ebenezer Storer, 7 December 1755.

96. Cooper, *Beatifick Vision,* 12.

97. Diary of Jonathan Willis, 3 January 1747.

98. Hambrick-Stowe, *Practice of Piety,* 125. Emphasis added by Hambrick-Stowe.

99. "Diary of Experience (Wight) Richardson," 112.

100. Husman, "Sarah Prince Gill Diary," 3–4.

101. Hall, *Worlds of Wonder,* 156.

102. "The Diary of John Comer," *Collections of the Rhode Island Historical Society* 8 (1893): 112.

103. See also Charles Cohen's analysis of the performative and public nature of piety in early New England. Cohen, *God's Caress,* 159–60.

104. Journal of Joseph Goodhue, 13 April 1746.

105. Diary of William Cooper, 4 August 1765.

106. John Tucker's Book, PEM, 21.

107. Diary of Benjamin Bangs, 6 September 1761.

108. Ibid., 19 July 1761.

109. Diary of William Cooper, 14 September 1766. See also 3 November 1765.

110. Diary of Jonathan Willis, 1 February 1747.

111. An important chronological point must be noted: most of these cases occurred after the Great Awakening. The Awakening may have emboldened some parishioners to take action against clergy by whom they felt wronged.

112. Interesting parallels in early modern Germany may be found in David Warren Sabean, *Power in the Blood: Popular Culture and Village Discourse in Early Modern Germany* (New York, 1984), 37–60.

113. See also Hall, *Worlds of Wonder,* 159–60.

114. Clifford K. Shipton, *Sibley's Harvard Graduates* (Boston, 1958), 10: 86.

115. *A Council of Churches met . . . at Duxboro Oct 4, 1742.*

116. John Bass, *A True Narrative of an Unhappy Contention in the Church at Ashford* (Boston, 1751), 7, 4. Though a partisan, Bass was a fair narrator.

117. Ibid., 4–5.

118. Diaries of Rev. Justus Forward, AAS, 14 January 1762, 4 April 1762, 13 January 1766, and 19 January 1766.

119. Quoted in Shipton, *Sibley's Harvard Graduates,* 10: 177, 10: 178–79. Shipton calls this a "revolutionary document."

120. Ibid., 11: 44.

121. Records of the Second Church in Lancaster, 1744–1813, AAS, 1 November 1772, 31 August 1773.

122. Ibid.

123. Unlike when people avoided the Lord's Supper during controversies with their ministers, abstentions resulting from conflicts among laypeople were as prevalent before the Great Awakening as after.

124. *Records of the First Church at Dorchester in New England, 1636–1734* (Boston, 1891), 135.

125. "The Records of the Transactions of the Second Church in Ipswich," PEM, 5 June 1754.

126. Quoted in McLoughlin, *Diary of Isaac Backus,* 436–37, 455, 495, 513.

CHAPTER 4   *Alternative Practices*

1. Francis G. Walett, ed., *The Diary of Ebenezer Parkman, 1703–1782* (Worcester, Mass., 1974), 288.

2. Exceptions include Herbert Leventhal, *In the Shadow of the Enlightenment: Occultism and Renaissance Science in Eighteenth-Century America* (New York, 1976); John L. Brooke, "'The True Spiritual Seed': Sectarian Religion and the Persistence of the Occult in Eighteenth-Century New England," in *Wonders of the Invisible World: 1600–1900,* ed. Peter Benes (Boston, 1995), 107–26; Jon Butler, *Awash in a Sea of Faith: Christianizing the American People* (Cambridge, Mass., 1990), 67–97; and Douglas L. Winiarski, "'Pale Blewish Lights' and a Dead Man's Groan: Tales of the Supernatural from Eighteenth-Century Plymouth, Massachusetts," *William and Mary Quarterly,* 3d ser., 55 (1998): 497–530.

3. A small sample: Richard Godbeer, *The Devil's Dominion: Magic and Religion in Early New England* (New York, 1992); Richard Weisman, *Witchcraft, Magic, and Religion in Seventeenth-Century Massachusetts* (Amherst, Mass., 1984); and David D. Hall, *Worlds of Wonder, Days of Judgment: Popular Religious Belief in Early New England* (New York, 1989), 7, 19, 98–100, 238.

4. Godbeer, *Devil's Dominion,* 123, 85, 6.

5. Butler, *Awash in a Sea of Faith,* 83.

6. There is evidence of magical belief among the broad middle stratum of eighteenth-century society. Winiarski, "Pale Blewish Lights," 521–22.

7. Butler, *Awash in a Sea of Faith,* 96. This description seems more appropriate for the nineteenth century, when local historians and folklorists published picturesque tales of magic in Olde New England.

8. Keith Thomas, *Religion and the Decline of Magic* (New York, 1971), 159–66, 277–79.

9. Kenneth A. Lockridge, *Literacy in Colonial New England: An Enquiry into the Social Context of Literacy in the Early Modern West* (New York, 1974), 88.

10. On this increased ministerial attack on magic, see Godbeer, *Devil's Dominion,*

188–222; and Richard P. Gildrie, *The Profane, the Civil, and the Godly: The Reformation of Manners in Orthodox New England, 1679–1749* (University Park, Pa., 1994), 157–81.

11. Godbeer, *Devil's Dominion*, 56; Hall, *Worlds of Wonder*, 71–116; and Michael P. Winship, *Seers of God: Puritan Providentialism in the Restoration and Early Enlightenment* (Baltimore, 1996).

12. Walett, *Diary of Ebenezer Parkman*, 89, 90.

13. "Experiences or Spiritual Exercises of Hannah Heaton," CHS.

14. John Perkins, "The Life, Writings, and Opinions of John Perkins Physician lately of Boston. Begun March 1777 and continued in 1778," AAS, 351.

15. "Extracts from Interleaved Almanacs of Nathan Bowen, Marblehead, 1742–1799," *Essex Institute Historical Collections* 91 (1955): 166, 179.

16. Diary of Samuel Chandler, PEM, 17 and 25 July 1753.

17. "Journal of the Rev. John Ballantine," typescript in AAS, 11 February 1762.

18. Ballantine once wrote in his diary, "Heard yesterday and today an unusual noise like the ticking of a watch, there were long intermissions after 2 or 3 strokes. It exercises my mind, it may be owing to weakness or superstition, but it occasioned thoughts not profitable." 27 May 1762.

19. M. Halsey Thomas, ed., *The Diary of Samuel Sewall, 1674–1729* (New York, 1973), 277, 317, 500, 529, 639, 822, 831, 895, 902.

20. Hall, *Worlds of Wonder*, 238.

21. Thomas, *Diary of Samuel Sewall*, 822.

22. "Journal of the Rev. John Ballantine," 1 August 1759.

23. Walett, *Diary of Ebenezer Parkman*, 163.

24. Leventhal, *Shadow of the Enlightenment*, 6.

25. Brooke, "The True Spiritual Seed," 115, 116, 118.

26. John D. Champlin, Jr., "Belief in Astrology in New England," *New England Historic Genealogical Register* 35 (1881): 276–77.

27. Cotton Mather, *The Angel of Bethesda*, ed. Gordon W. Jones (Barre, Mass., 1972), 297, 295.

28. Benjamin Franklin, "The Busy-Body, No. 8," in *The Papers of Benjamin Franklin, Volume I*, ed. Leonard W. Labaree (New Haven, Conn., 1959), 137, 138.

29. Quoted in Butler, *Awash in a Sea of Faith*, 88.

30. "Second Church of Boston Records, 1689–1717," MHS, 8 April 1694.

31. "Diary of Rev. Joseph Green, of Salem Village," *Essex Institute Historical Collections* 8 (1866): 221.

32. Butler, *Awash in a Sea of Faith*, 94.

33. Jon Butler, "The Dark Ages of American Occultism, 1760–1848," in *The Occult in America: New Historical Perspectives*, ed. Howard Kerr and Charles L. Crow (Urbana, Ill., 1983), 58–78.

34. Peter Benes, "Fortunetellers, Wise-Men, and Magical Healers in New England, 1644–1850," in Benes, *Wonders of the Invisible World*, 127.

35. Quoted in Leventhal, *Shadow of the Enlightenment*, 100.

36. Franklin Bowditch Dexter, ed., *The Literary Diary of Ezra Stiles* (New York, 1901), I: 386.

37. Diary of David Hall, MHS, 6 December 1745.

38. Perkins, "Life, Writings, and Opinions," 348.

39. William Waldron to Richard Waldron, undated letter in Waldron Papers, MHS, with a group of other similar letters from 1723 and 1724.

40. Neal W. Allen, Jr., "A Maine Witch," *Old-Time New England* 61 (1971): 76, 77. This article is based mostly on court depositions.

41. On the prevalence of rumormongering, see Helena M. Wall, *Fierce Communion: Family and Community in Early America* (Cambridge, Mass., 1990), 30–48.

42. Leventhal, *Shadow of the Enlightenment*, 85.

43. E. T. [Ebenezer Turell], "Detection of Witchcraft," *Massachusetts Historical Society Collections*, 2d ser., 10 (1823): 6–22, 8. In "Satan Dispossessed: Women and the Devil in Littleton, Massachusetts, 1720" (paper presented at the Institute of Early American History and Culture Conference, June 1996), Elizabeth Reis speculates that Turell concocted this story. Certainly the tale served his rhetorical purposes well, but I see no reason why Turell would go through the trouble of making up this story and then not publishing it.

44. Butler, *Awash in a Sea of Faith*, 84–85.

45. Turell, "Detection of Witchcraft," 10, 11, 12.

46. Ibid., 19–20.

47. Quoted in Leventhal, *Shadow of the Enlightenment*, 99.

48. Quoted in John Putnam Demos, *Entertaining Satan: Witchcraft and the Culture of Early New England* (New York, 1982), 387, 388.

49. All quotes relating to this example are from Perkins, "Life, Writings, and Opinions," 344–48.

50. Demos, *Entertaining Satan*, 390.

51. Philip F. Gura, *A Glimpse of Sion's Glory: Puritan Radicalism in New England, 1620–1660* (Middletown, Conn., 1984), 328.

52. I prefer the term "heterodoxy" over "radicalism" because the latter term is apt to cause confusion when these people attempted the conservative return to a pure apostolic church. "Heterodoxy" comes from the Greek *heterodoxos,* to think differently, as opposed to *orthodoxos,* to have the correct opinion. I use the term to refer to Christian beliefs and practices (as opposed to magical practices) wildly at odds with the range of opinions accepted by the vast majority of ministers and laypeople in eighteenth-century New England. Ordinary New Lights such as Jonathan Edwards and John Cleaveland were, under this definition, orthodox.

53. Gura, *Glimpse of Sion's Glory*, 326.

54. Thomas, *Diary of Samuel Sewall*, 396. It is difficult to know what Sewall meant by "atheistical" since that term referred to a wide range of heterodoxies in the early modern period. See David Wootton, "Lucien Febvre and the Problem of Unbelief in the Early Modern Period," *Journal of Modern History* 60 (1988): 695–730.

55. "The Diary of John Comer," *Collections of the Rhode Island Historical Society* 8 (1893): 43.

56. Arians believe that Jesus was not the son of God, but merely the most perfect human.

57. Douglas C. Stenerson, "An Anglican Critique of the Early Phase of the Great Awakening in New England: A Letter by Timothy Cutler," *William and Mary Quarterly*, 3d ser., 30 (1973): 482.

58. Joseph Allen, *The Worcester Association and its Antecedents: A History of Four Ministerial Associations* (Boston, 1868), 10–11.

59. Clap's views are further described in Louise Parkman Thomas, ed., *The Journal of the Rev. Israel Loring (1682–1772) of Sudbury, Massachusetts, Covering His Early Life and the Years 1704–1745* (typescript at the University of Michigan Library, 1983), 10 March 1729 and 21 March 1730.

60. Erik R. Seeman, "'It Is Better To Marry Than To Burn': Anglo-American Attitudes toward Celibacy, 1600–1800," *Journal of Family History* 24 (1999): 397–419.

61. Richard Woodbury to William Parsons, 23 May 1744, Nicholas Gilman Papers, MHS. Emphasis added.

62. This visit is described in Mrs. C. Wainwright to her sister Dudley at Roxbury, June 1744, folder 2, Parkman Family Correspondence, AAS. Wainwright's letter is corroborated by an account in the *Boston Gazette*, 24 July 1744.

63. Emphasis in original.

64. Carl Bridenbaugh, ed., *Gentleman's Progress* (Chapel Hill, N.C., 1948), 119–20, quoted in William Kidder, ed., "The Diary of Nicholas Gilman" (master's thesis, University of New Hampshire, 1972), 394.

65. *Boston Evening Post*, 30 July 1744, quoted in Kidder, "Diary of Nicholas Gilman," 392.

66. Diary of Samuel Chandler, PEM, 20 August 1746. A published version of this event may be found in Joshua Coffin, ed., "Religious Excitement One Hundred and Odd Years Ago," *New England Historic Genealogical Register* 15 (1861): 23–24. I have relied on my own transcription.

67. Ibid., 21 August.

68. Kidder, "Diary of Nicholas Gilman," 50.

69. William G. McLoughlin, ed., *The Diary of Isaac Backus* (Providence, R.I., 1979), 149–50.

70. A more detailed account of Prentice may be found in Erik R. Seeman, "Sarah Prentice and the Immortalists: Sexuality, Piety, and the Body in Eighteenth-Century New England," in *Sex and Sexuality in Early America*, ed. Merril D. Smith (New York, 1998), 116–31.

71. On the desire for religious purity, see Theodore Dwight Bozeman, *To Live Ancient Lives: The Primitivist Dimension in Puritanism* (Chapel Hill, N.C., 1988).

72. Ross W. Beales, Jr., "The Ecstasy of Sarah Prentice: Death, Re-Birth, and the

Great Awakening in Grafton, Massachusetts," *Historical Journal of Massachusetts* 25 (1997): 103–5.

73. Ross W. Beales, Jr., "Solomon Prentice's Narrative of the Great Awakening," *Massachusetts Historical Society Proceedings* 83 (1971): 130–47. Although Sarah Prentice is not mentioned as the subject of the conversion story on pages 134–36, Beales convincingly argues that the person's demographics indicate that it could be no one else. Beales, "Ecstasy," 107.

74. Beales, "Prentice's Narrative," 135.

75. Walett, *Diary of Ebenezer Parkman*, 101.

76. Ibid., 150, 154. Parkman did not describe Sarah Prentice's reaction to these warnings.

77. Francis G. Walett, "Shadrack Ireland and the 'Immortals' of Colonial New England," in *Sibley's Heir: A Volume in Memory of Clifford Kenyon Shipton* (Boston, 1982), 543. See also Isaac Backus, *A History of New England with Particular Reference to the Denomination of Christians Called Baptists,* 2d ed. (Newton, Mass., 1871), 2: 88.

78. Walett, "Shadrack Ireland," 545–46. For further incidents involving the outrageous Nat Smith, see Thomas, *Journal of Rev. Israel Loring,* 2 November 1743; Walett, *Diary of Ebenezer Parkman,* 91, 197–98.

79. Middlesex County General Sessions of the Peace, Record Books, 1686–1748, Massachusetts Archives, 338.

80. McLoughlin, *Diary of Isaac Backus,* 141.

81. Quoted in William G. McLoughlin, "Free Love, Immortalism, and Perfectionism in Cumberland, Rhode Island, 1748–1768," *Rhode Island History* 33 (1974): 75.

82. Rhode Island Colony, *Acts and Resolves, March 1749* (Newport, 1749), 53.

83. Dexter, *Diary of Ezra Stiles,* 418.

84. McLoughlin, *Diary of Isaac Backus,* 294. Backus's report was corroborated by Ebenezer Parkman in 1755. Walett, *Diary of Ebenezer Parkman,* 292.

85. Diary of Ebenezer Parkman, MHS, 23 February 1773. Shadrack Ireland also urged his followers in Harvard to be celibate: "Ireland forbade them to marry, or to lodge with each other, if they were married." Backus, *History of New England,* 2: 462.

86. McLoughlin, *Diary of Isaac Backus,* 430, 570–71.

87. Backus, *History of New England,* 2: 462.

88. Diary of Ebenezer Parkman, MHS, 11 October 1782. Quoted in Beales, "Ecstasy," 101.

89. Sally L. Kitch, *Chaste Liberation: Celibacy and Female Cultural Status* (Urbana, Ill., 1989), 168.

90. Caroline Walker Bynum, *The Resurrection of the Body in Western Christianity, 200–1336* (New York, 1995), xviii.

91. See also Paul's writings in Rom. 8:1–17 and Gal. 5:13–26.

92. William Gouge, *Of Domesticall Duties* (London, 1622), 212.

93. Seeman, "'It Is Better To Marry Than To Burn.'" Kathleen Verduin, in "'Our

Cursed Natures': Sexuality and the Puritan Conscience," *New England Quarterly* 56 (1983): 220–37, argues that New England ministers were wary about marital sexuality, seeing it as unclean. I agree that the clergy saw conjugal relations as *potentially licentious,* but I contend that they did exalt "chaste," that is moderate, marital sexuality.

94. Cotton Mather, *Ornaments for the Daughters of Zion* (Cambridge, Mass., 1692), 77.

95. Samuel Willard, *A Compleat Body of Divinity* (Boston, 1726), 675, 674. This sermon was originally delivered in 1704.

96. Walett, *Diary of Ebenezer Parkman,* 292.

97. Valentine Rathbun, *An Account of the Matter, Form, and Manner of a New and Strange Religion* (Providence, R.I., 1781), 12, 20.

98. Benjamin West, *Scriptural Cautions Against Embracing a Religious Scheme* (Hartford, Conn., 1783), 7.

99. Clifford K. Shipton, *Sibley's Harvard Graduates,* 8: 249.

CHAPTER 5   *Earthquakes and Great Awakenings*

1. Jon Butler makes a similar point but does not fully explore its implications. Butler, *Awash in a Sea of Faith: Christianizing the American People* (Cambridge, Mass., 1990), 177.

2. J. William T. Youngs, Jr., *God's Messengers: Religious Leadership in Colonial New England, 1700–1750* (Baltimore, 1976), 109–13.

3. Paul R. Lucas, *Valley of Discord: Church and Society Along the Connecticut River, 1636–1725* (Hanover, N.H., 1976), 200. See also Harry S. Stout, *The New England Soul: Preaching and Religious Culture in Colonial New England* (New York, 1986), 181.

4. This is a simplified version of the argument in Richard L. Bushman, *From Puritan to Yankee: Character and the Social Order in Connecticut, 1690–1765* (Cambridge, Mass., 1967). See also Patricia U. Bonomi, *Under the Cope of Heaven: Religion, Society, and Politics in Colonial America* (New York, 1986), 159.

5. Cedric Cowing, "Sex and Preaching in the Great Awakening," *American Quarterly* 20 (1968): 624–44; James Walsh, "The Great Awakening in the First Congregational Church of Woodbury, Connecticut," *William and Mary Quarterly,* 3d ser., 23 (1971): 544. According to Walsh, from 1702 to 1738, 44 percent of Woodbury's converts were male, compared to 56 percent between 1740 and 1742. But church admissions are not a perfect indicator of support of the revival because those previously admitted, who were predominantly female, could not be admitted again, even if their piety was reawakened.

6. Diary of James Jeffry, PEM, 29 October 1727.

7. "Diary of Jeremiah Bumstead of Boston, 1722–1727," *New England Historic Genealogical Register* 15 (1861): 314. For other dramatic contemporary accounts see M. Halsey Thomas, ed., *The Diary of Samuel Sewall, 1674–1729* (New York, 1973),

1055; Perry Miller, *The New England Mind: From Colony to Province* (Cambridge, Mass., 1953), 445; and "Extracts from the Diary of Rev. Samuel Dexter, of Dedham," *New England Historic Genealogical Register* 14 (1860): 202.

8. Quoted in Stout, *New England Soul*, 179, 355 n. 7.

9. Essex First Church Records, PEM, 21–22. In fact, the earthquake revival itself may have accounted for the paucity of Great Awakening converts in many northeastern Massachusetts congregations. Because most young adults converted in 1727, fewer joined in 1742.

10. All the narratives may be found in Kenneth P. Minkema, ed., "The Lynn End 'Earthquake' Relations of 1727," *New England Quarterly* 69 (1996): 473–99. I have changed Minkema's transcriptions to match my own style, changing "ye" to "the" and spelling out other abbreviations.

11. Minkema, "Lynn End Relations," 483. Michael Crawford disputes Ned Landsman's assertion ("Evangelists and Their Hearers: Popular Interpretation of Revivalist Preaching in Eighteenth-Century Scotland," *Journal of British Studies* 28 [1989]: 120–49) that laypeople in the Cambuslang revival in Scotland in 1742 heard voices. Crawford asserts that converts "tested their spiritual state by individual scriptural texts that came strongly into their minds, which is not the same as hearing voices." Michael J. Crawford, *Seasons of Grace: Colonial New England's Revival Tradition in Its British Context* (New York, 1991), 207. In general, I agree with Crawford, but Eaton's use of the words "voice" and "sound" in his narrative seems to indicate an aural experience.

12. Minkema, "Lynn End Relations," 486.

13. Peter Lockwood Rumsey, *Acts of God and the People, 1620–1730* (Ann Arbor, Mich., 1986), 129.

14. Quoted in Youngs, *God's Messengers*, 111.

15. Samuel Wigglesworth, *A Religious Fear of God's Tokens, Explained and Urged* (Boston, 1728), 4.

16. John Barnard, *Two Discourses Addressed to Young Persons; To Which is Added, A Sermon Occasioned by the Earthquake* (Boston, 1727), 96.

17. Minkema, "Lynn End Relations," 483, 491, 492, 490.

18. Crawford, *Seasons of Grace*, 116.

19. William Williams, *Divine Warnings* (Boston, 1728), iv. Quoted in Crawford, *Seasons of Grace*, 116.

20. Samuel Phillips, *Three Plain Practical Discourses* (Boston, 1728), 63, 135.

21. John Rogers, *The Nature and Necessity of Repentance* (Boston, 1728), 12.

22. Phillips, *Three Plain Practical Discourses*, 96.

23. Jonathan Edwards, *A Faithful Narrative of the Surprising Work of God*, 3d ed. (Boston, 1738). For the international influence of this tract, see Patricia J. Tracy, *Jonathan Edwards, Pastor: Religion and Society in Eighteenth-Century Northampton* (New York, 1979), 122.

24. Youngs, *God's Messengers*, 113; Crawford, *Seasons of Grace*, 125; Tracy, *Jonathan Edwards*, 109.

25. Harry Stout has likewise noted that the "primary momentum" for this revival was generated among laypeople. Stout, *New England Soul*, 188–89.

26. Edwards, *Faithful Narrative*, 5, 7, 8.

27. Ibid., 16. Patricia Tracy disputes the figure of three hundred, noting that Edwards recorded only half that number in the church records. Tracy, *Jonathan Edwards*, 113.

28. Edwards, *Faithful Narrative*, 9, 15.

29. Ibid., 8, 74.

30. Ibid., 73.

31. Douglas C. Stenerson, "An Anglican Critique of the Early Phase of the Great Awakening in New England: A Letter by Timothy Cutler," *William and Mary Quarterly*, 3d ser., 30 (1973): 486, 485. It is unclear what the hawk represented and why this struck Cutler as notable; perhaps the observer took the bird to be a messenger from God.

32. Ibid., 484–85.

33. Ibid., 485.

34. Edwards, *Faithful Narrative*, 16.

35. Harry S. Stout, *The Divine Dramatist: George Whitefield and the Rise of Modern Evangelicalism* (Grand Rapids, Mich., 1991), 113–25.

36. On the Separates, see C. C. Goen, *Revivalism and Separatism in New England, 1740–1800: Strict Congregationalists and Separate Baptists in the Great Awakening* (Middletown, Conn., 1987).

37. Since Edwin Scott Gaustad, *The Great Awakening in New England* (New York, 1957).

38. Harry S. Stout and Peter S. Onuf, "James Davenport and the Great Awakening in New London," *Journal of American History* 70 (1983–84): 556–78; Gary B. Nash, *The Urban Crucible: Social Change, Political Consciousness, and the Origins of the American Revolution* (Cambridge, Mass., 1979), 198–219; Leigh Eric Schmidt, "'A Second and Glorious Reformation': The New Light Extremism of Andrew Croswell," *William and Mary Quarterly*, 3d ser., 43 (1986): 214–44; and idem, "'The Grand Prophet,' Hugh Bryan: Early Evangelicalism's Challenge to the Establishment and Slavery in the Colonial South," *South Carolina Historical Magazine* 87 (1986): 238–50.

39. Bonomi, *Under the Cope of Heaven*, 147; Bushman, *From Puritan to Yankee*; and Harry S. Stout, "Religion, Communications, and the Ideological Origins of the American Revolution," *William and Mary Quarterly*, 3d ser., 34 (1977): 519–41.

40. Jon Butler, "Enthusiasm Described and Decried: The Great Awakening as Interpretative Fiction," *Journal of American History* 69 (1982): 314, 324–25. See also James P. Walsh, "The Conservative Nature of Connecticut Separatism," *Bulletin of the Con-*

necticut Historical Society 34 (1969): 9–17; Christine Leigh Heyrman, *Commerce and Culture: The Maritime Communities of Colonial Massachusetts, 1690–1750* (New York, 1984), 182–204; Anne S. Brown, "Visions of Community in Eighteenth-Century Essex County: Chebacco Parish and the Great Awakening," *Essex Institute Historical Collections* 125 (1989): 239–62; and James F. Cooper, Jr., "Enthusiasts or Democrats? Separatism, Church Government, and the Great Awakening in Massachusetts," *New England Quarterly* 65 (1992): 265–83.

41. William Kidder, ed., "The Diary of Nicholas Gilman" (master's thesis, University of New Hampshire, 1972), 230.

42. Michael J. Crawford, ed., "The Spiritual Travels of Nathan Cole," *William and Mary Quarterly*, 3d ser., 33 (1976): 93.

43. For example, Benjamin Colman, "Memorandum," 14 September 1740, Benjamin Colman Papers, MHS.

44. Stout, "Religion, Communications, and Ideological Origins," 525–26. On other effects of itinerancy, see Timothy D. Hall, *Contested Boundaries: Itinerancy and the Reshaping of the Colonial American Religious World* (Durham, N.C., 1994).

45. "Joseph Goodhue, his booke," PEM, 11–12.

46. Rebecca Husman, ed., "Sarah Prince Gill Diary," typescript at Kellogg Library, Bard College, 1. White's tract was a classic jeremiad. John White, *New England's Lamentations: Under Three Heads, The Decay of the Power of Godliness; The Danger of Arminian Principles; The Declining State of our Church Order, Government, and Discipline* (Boston, 1734).

47. Husman, "Sarah Prince Gill Diary," 2, 3, 4.

48. "Experiences or Spiritual Exercises of Hannah Heaton," CHS, 5–6.

49. Sereno E. Dwight, *The Life of President Edwards* (New York, 1830), 176, 178. See also 185.

50. See discussion of Goodhue above and n. 45; Crawford, ed., "Spiritual Travels," 93–95; and John Loring to Israel Loring, 9 December 1741 and 22 January 1742, Nathan Stone Papers, MHS.

51. An example of biased sources used uncritically is Nash, *Urban Crucible*, 209–12, 215–17, which relies on the rabidly antirevivalist *Boston Evening Post.*

52. Jonathan Edwards, *Some Thoughts Concerning the Present Revival of Religion in New England* (Boston, 1742), 226. See also 234, where Edwards describes laypeople who "have sought after a miraculous Assistance of Inspiration."

53. "Diary of Eleazer Wheelock," *Historical Magazine*, 2d ser., 5 (1869): 237.

54. Edwards, *Thoughts Concerning the Present Revival*, 307–8. See also Jonathan Parsons, *A Needful Caution in a Critical Day; or, The Christian Urged to Watchfulness* (New London, Conn., 1742), 47–49.

55. Jonathan Parsons, *Wisdom Justified of her Children* (Boston, 1742), 17.

56. Jedidiah Jewet, *The Necessity of Good Works, as the Fruit and Evidence of Faith* (Boston, 1742), 24.

57. Thomas Prince, ed., *The Christian History, Containing Accounts of the Revival*

and Propagation of Religion in Great-Britain & America, Vol. 1 (1743): 168, 169; Vol. 2 (1744): 45.

58. The next few paragraphs are indebted to Susan Juster, *Disorderly Women: Sexual Politics and Evangelicalism in Revolutionary New England* (Ithaca, N.Y., 1994). See also Heyrman, *Commerce and Culture*, 377–86.

59. Ebenezer Parkman, "Memoirs of Mrs Sarah Pierpont," AAS, 11 February 1743.

60. A Female Friend [Sarah Parsons Moorhead], *To the Reverend Mr. James Davenport on his Departure from Boston* (Boston, 1742), 1, 5–6, 8.

61. Gentlewoman, *A Poem in Honour of the Reverend Mr. Whitefield* (Boston, 1744). The only extant copy of this poem is in the Newberry Library, Chicago. I thank Professor Robin Bachin for kindly transcribing it.

62. Bathsheba Kingsley's age is unknown. Because her husband was thirty-three years old in 1743, it is likely that Kingsley was between twenty-five and thirty-two years old at that time.

63. All quotes in the following paragraphs come from "Advice to Mr. and Mrs. Kingsley," a draft, in Edwards's hand, of the findings of an ecclesiastical council called in early 1743 to deal with Bathsheba Kingsley. The ms is located at the Andover Newton Theological Seminary and will appear in a forthcoming edition of the Jonathan Edwards Papers. I am grateful to Ken Minkema for making this document available to me before press time. See also Catherine A. Brekus, *Strangers and Pilgrims: Female Preaching in America, 1740–1845* (Chapel Hill, N.C., 1998), 23–26.

64. Kingsley had been actively preaching since at least October 1741, when she was chastised by her church for "stealing a Horse [and] riding away on the sabbath without her husbands Consent." "The Publick Records of the Church at Westfield," Westfield Athenaeum.

65. Jonathan Edwards, "When Marriage is According to Nature and God's Designation," ms sermon in Beinecke Rare Book and Manuscript Library, quoted in Rosemary Radford Ruether and Rosemary Skinner Keller, eds., *Women and Religion in America: A Documentary History*, vol. 2 (San Francisco, 1983), 365–66. There is no date given for this sermon.

66. See, for example, Benjamin Bradstreet, *Godly Sorrow Described, and the Blessing Annexed Consider'd* (Boston, 1742), iii.

67. "Publick Records of the Church at Westfield," 1 March 1743.

68. For an African-American exhorter in Ipswich, see Erik R. Seeman, "'Justise Must Take Plase': Three African Americans Speak of Religion in Eighteenth-Century New England," *William and Mary Quarterly*, 3d ser., 56 (1999): 393–414.

69. David Lovejoy, *Religious Enthusiasm and the Great Awakening* (Englewood Cliffs, N.J., 1969), 65–66.

70. Amy Schrager Lang, *Prophetic Woman: Anne Hutchinson and the Problem of Dissent in the Literature of New England* (Berkeley, Calif., 1987).

71. "Extracts from Interleaved Almanacs of Nathan Bowen, Marblehead, 1742–1799," *Essex Institute Historical Collections* 91 (1955): 164.

72. Ibid., 169, 164, 165, 171.

73. On the feminization of male evangelicals, see Lang, *Prophetic Woman*.

74. Quoted in Philip Greven, *The Protestant Temperament: Patterns of Child-Rearing, Religious Experience, and the Self in Early America* (New York, 1977), 139.

75. Charles Chauncy, *Seasonable Thoughts on the State of Religion in New-England* (Boston, 1743), 104.

76. For the contrast between the rhetorical effeminacy of evangelicals and the "manly" piety of Old Lights, see Greven, *Protestant Temperament*, 124–25, 243–44.

77. This revival is mentioned in Christopher M. Jedrey, *The World of John Cleaveland: Family and Community in Eighteenth-Century New England* (New York, 1979), 116–17.

78. John Cleaveland, *A Short and Plain Narrative of the Late Work of God's Spirit at Chebacco in Ipswich, in the Years 1763 and 1764* (Boston, 1767), 5.

79. Relation of Thomas Story, 17 June 1764. All relations in this section may be found in John Cleaveland Papers, box 1, folder 1b, "Testimonials," PEM. These narratives are analyzed in chapter 3.

80. Relation of Nathan Burnam, 26 August 1764. See also the relations of Martha Burnam, Mary Cleaveland, and Mary Rust for very similar accounts.

81. Cleaveland, *Short and Plain Narrative*, 6.

82. Relation of Hannah Low, 26 August 1764.

83. Relation of Thomas Story, 17 June 1764. See also relations of Nathan Burnam, Susanna Low, Jacob Choate, and Elizabeth Perkins.

84. Relation of Mary Woodbury, 2 February 1766.

85. Relation of Hannah Bear, 26 August 1764.

86. Cleaveland, *Short and Plain Narrative*, 15.

87. Ibid., 13.

88. Diary of Samuel Chandler, PEM, 6 January 1764, 12 January, 17 and 26 January, 27 January.

89. The quote refers to Abigail Davis. Ibid.

90. Ibid., 19 February.

91. Cleaveland, *Short and Plain Narrative*, 31.

92. Samuel Buell, *A Faithful Narrative of the Remarkable Revival of Religion, in the Congregation of East-Hampton, on Long-Island, in the Year of our Lord 1764* (New York, 1766), 6–7; William G. McLoughlin, ed., *The Diary of Isaac Backus* (Providence, R.I., 1979), 549, 558, 563, 581.

93. McLoughlin, *Diary of Isaac Backus*, 549, 558.

94. Cleaveland, *Short and Plain Narrative*, 14.

95. Relation of Mary Rust, 26 August 1764.

96. Relation of John Cheever, 26 August 1764.

97. McLoughlin, *Diary of Isaac Backus*, 581, 558; Cleaveland, *Short and Plain Narrative*, 16.

CHAPTER 6   *The Piety of Experience Richardson*

1. A typescript of the diary, "Diary of Experience (Wight) Richardson, Sudbury, Mass., 1728–1782," compiled by Ellen Richardson Glueck and Thelma Smith Ernst, is located in the MHS; hereafter in this chapter, pages for this source are cited in the text within parentheses. Experience Richardson was born in 1705 and died in 1782. She married Josiah Richardson in 1728 and was widowed in 1770, never to remarry. She had three children: Gideon (1729–1758), Josiah (1733–?), and Luther (1748–1752). A genealogist erroneously claims that Experience Richardson had a daughter (also named Experience). This Experience (Richardson) Crossman was actually her grand-daughter, the daughter of Gideon. John Adams Vinton, *The Richardson Memorial* (Portland, Me., 1876), 215–16. Her pastor for most of her life was Israel Loring, who lived from 1682 to 1772 and was minister in Sudbury from 1706 until his death at the age of ninety. Her diary's first entry is dated 1728, but between then and 1742 Experience wrote in her diary only about a dozen times. Starting in 1742, however, she began to keep her diary more regularly.

2. On the rise of Enlightenment ideas among ministers in the eighteenth century, see Michael P. Winship, *Seers of God: Puritan Providentialism in the Restoration and Early Enlightenment* (Baltimore, 1996).

3. For example, Israel Loring, *The Nature & Necessity of the New-Birth* (Boston, 1728), 50.

4. This point differs from David D. Hall's reading of Samuel Sewall. Hall argues that for Sewall, prayer "functioned to transmute anxiety into assurance." Hall, *Worlds of Wonder, Days of Judgment: Popular Religious Belief in Early New England* (New York, 1989), 234.

5. For further examples see Richardson diary, 19 May 1753, 30 October 1757, 8 May 1760, and 3 March 1772.

6. For example, see Richardson diary, 13 March 1757 and 25 June 1758.

7. E. Brooks Holifield, *The Covenant Sealed: The Development of Puritan Sacramental Theology in Old and New England, 1570–1720* (New Haven, Conn., 1974), 229.

8. Charles E. Hambrick-Stowe, *The Practice of Piety: Puritan Devotional Disciplines in Seventeenth-Century New England* (Chapel Hill, N.C., 1982), 125.

9. John Flavel, *Husbandry Spiritualized; or, The Heavenly Use of Earthly Things*, 10th ed. (Boston, 1709), 167. See also Flavel, *Navigation Spiritualized; or, A New Compass for Sea-Men* (Boston, 1726). On Mather's use of this technique, see Robert Middlekauf, *The Mathers: Three Generations of Puritan Intellectuals, 1596–1728* (New York, 1971), 310.

10. For another woman deeply troubled by Satan, see "Experiences or Spiritual Exercises of Hannah Heaton," CHS.

11. Israel Loring, *Serious Thoughts on the Miseries of Hell* (Boston, 1732), 22.

12. Israel Loring, *Justification Not By Works, But By Faith in Jesus Christ* (Boston, 1749), 87–88. See also two other works by Loring: *The Duty and Interest of Young*

Persons to Remember Their Creator (Boston, 1718), 33–34; and *Three Discourses on Several Subjects* (Boston, 1731), 51.

13. On female piety in early New England, see Laurel Thatcher Ulrich, *Good Wives: Image and Reality in the Lives of Women in Northern New England, 1650–1750* (New York, 1980), 167–235.

14. Childbirth's celebratory nature is described in Laurel Thatcher Ulrich, *A Midwife's Tale: The Life of Martha Ballard, Based on Her Diary, 1785–1812* (New York, 1990), 188–90.

15. In the original Richardson crossed out the word "groaning" but it remains legible.

16. "Experiences of Hannah Heaton," 20.

17. Ulrich, *Midwife's Tale*, 169–83.

18. On the disjuncture between perceptions and reality of mortality, see Maris A. Vinovskis, "Angels' Heads and Weeping Willows: Death in Early America," in *Religion, Family, and the Life Course: Explorations in the Social History of Early America*, ed. Gerald F. Moran and Maris A. Vinovskis (Ann Arbor, Mich., 1992), 209–31.

19. For an example of the anguish caused by an infertile period of only twelve months at the start of a young couple's married life, see Diary of Joseph Pitkin, CSL, 38.

20. The transcription reads "____mber" for the month of the entry, which I have interpreted as December because in November Richardson would have been only one month pregnant. Similarly, see the case of Elizabeth Weston, who had her last child at forty-five and was extremely nervous about being pregnant so late. Ulrich, *Midwife's Tale*, 195–96.

21. See, for example, Samuel Willard, *The Mourners Cordial Against Excessive Sorrow* (Boston, 1691); John Barnard, *Two Sermons: The Christians Behavior under Severe and Repeated Bereavements* (Boston, 1714); Henry Gibbs, *Bethany; or, The House of Mourning* (Boston, 1714); and Thomas Skinner, *The Mourner Admonished* (Boston, 1746).

22. Israel Loring, *Two Sermons Preached at Rutland* (Boston, 1724), 8, 18.

23. For example, Lawrence Stone, *The Family, Sex, and Marriage in England, 1500–1800*, abridged ed. (New York, 1979), 54–66.

24. On the plethora of duties even elite women had in early America, see Jeanne Boydston, *Home and Work: Housework, Wages, and the Ideology of Labor in the Early Republic* (New York, 1990), 2, 18.

25. William D. Piersen, *Black Yankees: The Development of an Afro-American Subculture in Eighteenth-Century New England* (Amherst, Mass., 1988), 14.

26. These quotes are from Richardson's will, in Vinton, *Richardson Memorial*, 215–16. Josiah Richardson's estate was valued at £422 upon his death in 1770.

27. There has been little work on this subject in northern colonies, but it seems plausible to apply findings for the South to New England. See Joan Rezner Gundersen, "The Double Bonds of Race and Sex: Black and White Women in a Colonial Vir-

ginia Parish," *Journal of Southern History* 52 (1986): 351–72; and Elizabeth Fox-Genovese, *Within the Plantation Household: Black and White Women of the Old South* (Chapel Hill, N.C., 1988).

28. Julian D. Mason, Jr., *The Poems of Phillis Wheatley*, rev. ed. (Chapel Hill, N.C., 1989), 3–5; Cotton Mather, *The Negro Christianized* (Boston, 1706).

29. Although Dinah's age is unknown, since she gave birth in 1762 she cannot have been much older than fifty in 1776, and she might have been as young as in her early thirties. This was not an elderly slave being cast off when her productive years were past.

30. For an example of another marriage along these lines, see the relationship between Mary Fish and her first husband John Noyes. Joy Day Buel and Richard Buel, Jr., *The Way of Duty: A Woman and her Family in Revolutionary America* (New York, 1984), 26–50.

31. For example, see Richardson diary, 5 June 1765.

32. Amy Schrager Lang, *Prophetic Woman: Anne Hutchinson and the Problem of Dissent in the Literature of New England* (Berkeley, Calif., 1987), 105–6; Susan Juster, *Disorderly Women: Sexual Politics and Evangelicalism in Revolutionary New England* (Ithaca, N.Y., 1994), 4.

33. See especially sermons on excessive mourning and suicide. For example, Skinner, *Mourner Admonished*; and Samuel Phillips, *The Sin of Suicide* (Boston, 1767).

34. On religion and politics in the revolutionary era, see Patricia U. Bonomi, *Under the Cope of Heaven: Religion, Society, and Politics in Colonial America* (New York, 1986), 187–216.

35. The original statement of this argument is Perry Miller, *Errand Into the Wilderness* (Cambridge, Mass., 1956), 5–6.

36. Nathan O. Hatch, *The Sacred Cause of Liberty: Republican Thought and the Millennium in Revolutionary New England* (New Haven, Conn., 1977), 24.

37. Linda K. Kerber, *Women of the Republic: Intellect and Ideology in Revolutionary America* (New York, 1980), restricts her discussion of religion to two brief sections: 110–11, 260–63. See also Mary Beth Norton, *Liberty's Daughters: The Revolutionary Experience of American Women* (Boston, 1980).

38. Laurel Thatcher Ulrich, "'Daughters of Liberty': Religious Women in Revolutionary New England," in *Women in the Age of the American Revolution,* ed. Ronald Hoffman and Peter J. Albert (Charlottesville, Va., 1989), 211–43; and Elaine Forman Crane, "Religion and Rebellion: Women of Faith in the American War for Independence," in *Religion in a Revolutionary Age,* ed. Ronald Hoffman and Peter J. Albert (Charlottesville, Va., 1994), 52–86.

39. Ulrich, "Daughters of Liberty," 214–28; Crane, "Religion and Rebellion," 83–85.

40. Joan B. Landes, *Women and the Public Sphere in the Age of the French Revolution* (Ithaca, N.Y., 1988); Lynn Hunt, *The Family Romance of the French Revolution* (Berkeley, Calif., 1992); and Juster, *Disorderly Women.*

41. Juster, *Disorderly Women,* 143.
42. Similar views may be found in "Experiences of Hannah Heaton."
43. Loring, *Justification Not By Works,* 19.
44. On recruitment's local implications, see Fred Anderson, *A People's Army: Massachusetts Soldiers and Society in the Seven Years' War* (New York, 1984), 26–62.
45. The religious motivations of New Englanders who fought against France are discussed in Anderson, *A People's Army,* 155–57.
46. Mary Fish also showed "a growing interest in the discussion of current affairs" as the Revolution approached, and she combined religion and politics in a way similar to Richardson. Buel and Buel, *Way of Duty,* 68; also, 69–144.
47. Later Richardson referred to "our congress," 16 March 1775. Hannah Heaton made a similar shift in her diary. See "Experiences of Hannah Heaton," 22 April 1775 and November 1775.

Conclusion

1. For example, James W. Schmotter, "Ministerial Careers in Eighteenth-Century New England: The Social Context, 1700–1760," *Journal of Social History* 9 (1975): 249–67; J. William T. Youngs, Jr., *God's Messengers: Religious Leadership in Colonial New England, 1700–1750* (Baltimore, 1976), 102–8.
2. Perry Miller, "From the Covenant to the Revival," in *The Shaping of American Religion,* ed. James Ward Smith and A. Leland Jamison (Princeton, 1961), 322–68; Harry S. Stout, "Religion, Communications, and the Ideological Origins of the American Revolution," *William and Mary Quarterly,* 3d ser., 34 (1977): 519–41; Donald Weber, *Rhetoric and History in Revolutionary New England* (New York, 1988); and Alan Heimert, *Religion and the American Mind: From the Great Awakening to the Revolution* (Cambridge, Mass.,1966). On the changing reputation of Heimert's book within the historical profession, see Philip Goff, "Revivals and Revolution: Historiographic Turns since Alan Heimert's *Religion and the American Mind,*" *Church History* 67 (1998): 695–721.
3. Cedric B. Cowing, *The Great Awakening and the American Revolution: Colonial Thought in the Eighteenth Century* (Chicago, 1971); William G. McLoughlin, "The Role of Religion in the Revolution: Liberty of Conscience and Cultural Cohesion in the New Nation," in *Essays on the American Revolution,* ed. Stephen G. Kurtz and James H. Hutson (Chapel Hill, N.C., 1973), 197–255; Rhys Isaac, *The Transformation of Virginia, 1740–1790* (Chapel Hill, N.C., 1982); and Patricia U. Bonomi, *Under the Cope of Heaven: Religion, Society, and Politics in Colonial America* (New York, 1986).
4. Jon Butler, *Awash in a Sea of Faith: Christianizing the American People* (Cambridge, Mass.,1990), 195.
5. "Whoever has candidly traced . . . " (Boston, 1774).
6. Samuel Clarke, *The Strange and Remarkable Vision* (Salem, Mass., 1776).
7. Ibid., 4–5.

8. Ibid., 5–7.

9. See, for example, Ebenezer Adams, *True & Wonderful Relation, Of the Appearance of Three Angels* (Boston, 1761); *A Short Relation Concerning a Dream* (Boston, 1769).

10. William Cooper, *The Beatifick Vision Productive of Likeness to Christ* (Boston, 1734), 21. See also Diary of Ebenezer Parkman, AAS, 9 February and 11 February 1742.

11. Clarke, *Strange and Remarkable Vision*, 7.

12. Nathan O. Hatch, *The Democratization of American Christianity* (New Haven, Conn., 1989), 17–46; Gordon S. Wood, *The Radicalism of the American Revolution* (New York, 1991), 329–33.

13. The quoted phrase is from Nathan O. Hatch, *The Sacred Cause of Liberty: Republican Thought and the Millennium in Revolutionary New England* (New Haven, Conn., 1977), 140.

14. Butler, *Awash in a Sea of Faith*, 225–56.

Note on Primary Sources

WHEN I STARTED THIS PROJECT I was cautioned against expecting to find much written by laypeople, given that so little is extant from the seventeenth century. I was told it was particularly quixotic to hope to find sources written by women. These concerns turned out to be unwarranted. For a variety of reasons—an increasing population, the wider availability of cheap paper, the decreasing cost of publishing—an abundance of sources written by and about ordinary eighteenth-century New Englanders survives.

But writing a book like this requires more than finding documents: it means taking seriously writings that are not only hard to read but, more importantly, often seem at first glance to be formulaic, repetitive, and stylized. But beneath layers of conventional language, much that is individual shines through. Furthermore, formulaic language itself can offer insights into how religious culture is negotiated and reproduced.

Increasing numbers of scholars are paying attention to sources like these; the following guide is meant to aid those who wish to begin such an examination. In eighteenth-century New England (not to mention other regions of colonial America) much work remains to be done to understand the religion of ordinary people. We need more local studies that examine how lay piety interacted with the power dynamics of individual communities. We need more work on Baptists and Anglicans to see if the relations between laity and clergy in those denominations parallels the story for Congregationalists. And we need much more work on Christianized Indians and African Americans to learn how these individuals appropriated and shaped reformed Protestantism.

The obvious place to start is the Early American Imprints series, published by Readex and the American Antiquarian Society. Originally on an opaque medium called microcard, this series is now widely available on microfiche, which is much easier to read and photocopy. This extraordinary resource contains all extant titles published in America to 1820. Every published sermon may be found here, along with other ministerial sources (devotional guides, catechisms, and polemics written against ungodly behavior and heterodox beliefs). Several types of ministerial sources are particularly useful for examining lay piety. Funeral sermons often contain descriptions of a person's dying days and even sometimes include excerpts from the deceased's spiritual journal. Funeral sermons must be used carefully: the deathbed scenes they describe are almost always model scenes, as ministers chose to publish accounts of deaths deemed worthy of emulation. My sense, though, is that these model deaths were reported accurately. Some of the best examples of this genre are Amos Adams, *The Character of a Christian's Life* (Boston, 1756); Mather Byles, *The Character of the Perfect and Upright Man; His Peaceful End Described* (Boston, 1729); Charles Chauncy, *Early Piety Recommended and Exemplify'd* (Boston, 1732); Samuel Checkley, *Little Children's Being Bro't to Jesus Christ* (Boston, 1741); Benjamin Colman, *The Father's Tears over his Daughter's Remains* (Boston, 1735); William Cooper, *The Beatifick Vision Productive of Likeness to Christ* (Boston, 1734); Thomas Foxcroft, *A Sermon . . . After the Funeral of Mrs. Elizabeth Foxcroft* (Boston, 1721); Jason Haven, *A Discourse Occasioned by the Death of Mrs. Hannah Richards* (Boston, 1770); Ivory Hovey, *The Duty and Privilege of Aged Saints* (Boston, 1749); Cotton Mather, *Memorials of Early Piety, Occurring in the Holy Life & Joyful Death of Mrs. Jerusha Oliver* (Boston, 1711); Jonathan Parsons, *A Funeral Sermon . . . of Ebenezer Little* (Boston, 1768); Thomas Prince, *Dying Exercises of Mrs. Deborah Prince* (Newburyport, Mass., 1789); and Thomas Skinner, *The Mourner Admonished* (Boston, 1746).

Funeral sermons are not the only source for dying words. Ministers sometimes published batches of deathbed scenes to demonstrate a particular group's piety. See John Brown, *The Number of Deaths in Haverhil, and also Some Comfortable Instances Thereof Among the Children*, 2d ed. (Boston, 1738); and Experience Mayhew, *Indian Converts; or, Some Account of the Lives and Dying Speeches of a Considerable Number of the Christianized Indians of Martha's Vineyard, in New-England* (London, 1727). The latter book is not in Early American Imprints but is a rare source for understanding the piety of Christianized Indians.

Ministerial accounts of religious revivals are useful for understanding lay piety. These too must be used with caution, especially when the author was opposed to the revival he described. Antirevivalists had an incentive to exaggerate enthusiastic practices (though their fears illuminate the bounds of orthodoxy). Surprisingly, prorevivalist ministers also included descriptions of enthusiasm, to show the kinds of behaviors they hoped people would avoid. Some of the most important revival narratives include Samuel Buell, *A Faithful Narrative of the Remarkable Revival of Religion, in the Congregation of East-Hampton, on Long-Island, in the Year of our Lord 1764* (New York, 1766); Charles Chauncy, *Seasonable Thoughts on the State of Religion in New-England* (Boston, 1743); John Cleaveland, *A Short and Plain Narrative of the Late Work of God's Spirit at Chebacco in Ipswich, in the Years 1763 and 1764* (Boston, 1767); and Jonathan Edwards, *A Faithful Narrative of the Surprising Work of God*, 3d ed. (Boston, 1738). An invaluable compendium of ministerial revival narratives from around the Anglo-American world is Thomas Prince, ed., *The Christian History, Containing Accounts of the Revival and Propagation of Religion in Great-Britain & America*, 2 vols. (1743 and 1744).

Another type of helpful ministerial sources are published accounts of church disputes and the results of ecclesiastical councils. These sources often provide lengthy transcriptions of ostensibly verbatim testimony from laypeople and ministers. A few illuminating examples are *At a Council of Ten Churches Convened at Marlborough on February 4, 1734* (Boston, 1734); *A Narrative of the Proceedings of Those Ministers of the County of Hampshire* (Boston, 1736); *A Council of Churches met . . . at Duxboro Oct 4, 1742* (Boston, 1742); and John Bass, *A True Narrative of an Unhappy Contention in the Church at Ashford* (Boston, 1751).

Early American Imprints also includes a number of sources written by laypeople. One can find the occasional description of dreams with religious significance, visions, and visitations by angels. See Ebenezer Adams, *True & Wonderful Relation, Of the Appearance of Three Angels* (Boston, 1761); Anonymous, *A Short Relation Concerning a Dream* (Boston, 1769); and Samuel Clarke, *The Strange and Remarkable Vision* (Salem, Mass., 1776). Numerous lay poems appeared as broadsides and sometimes as longer pamphlets. These were especially common during the Great Awakening: *A Poem, Occasioned by the Spreading in this Province . . .* (Boston, 1742); A Female Friend [Sarah Parsons Moorhead], *To the Reverend Mr. James Davenport on his Departure from Boston* (Boston, 1742); and Gentlewoman, *A Poem in Honour of the Reverend Mr. Whitefield* (Boston, 1744). For other printed lay sources see, for example, Edward Goddard, *A Brief Account of the Formation and Settlement of the 2d Church and Congregation in Framingham* (Boston, 1750); Ebenezer Morton, *More Last Words to these Churches* (Boston, 1746); Daniel Parker, *A Perswasive to Make a Publick Confession of Christ and Come Up to All His Ordinances* (Boston, 1730); Grace Smith, *The Dying Mothers Legacy* (Boston, 1712); and Mercy Wheeler, *An Address to Young People* (Boston, 1733).

Many lay sources have been published in relatively accessible periodicals and books. The number of published lay diaries is nearly overwhelming. Useful guides include Laura Arskey, Nancy Pries, and Marcia Reed, *American Diaries: An Annotated Bibliography of Published American Diaries and Journals* (Detroit, 1983); and Joyce D. Goodfriend, *The Published Diaries and Letters of American Women: An Annotated Bibliography* (Boston, 1987). Diaries must also be used carefully, especially since they were not as private in the eighteenth century as today. They were quasi-public (family members often read them when the author died), so journals sometimes were attempts to fashion an image for posterity. The greatest lay diary of all is M. Halsey Thomas, ed., *The Diary of Samuel Sewall, 1674–1729*, 2 vols. (New York, 1973), but Sewall was not a typical layperson: highly educated, wealthy, and more orthodox than many. Some other helpful published lay diaries that range further down the social scale include "Diary of Jeremiah Bumstead of Boston, 1722–1727," *New England Historic Genealogical Register* 15 (1861): 193–204, 305–15; "Stow, and John Gates' Diary," *Worcester Society of Antiquity Proceedings* 16 (1897–99): 267–80; "Journal Kept by Lieut. Daniel Giddings of Ipswich During the Expedition against Cape Breton in 1744–5," *Essex Institute Historical Collections* 48 (1912): 293–304; "French and Indian War Diary of Benjamin Glasier of Ipswich, 1758–1760," *Essex Institute Historical Collections* 86 (1950): 65–92; "Journal of Captain Samuel Jenks," *Massachusetts Historical Society Proceedings*, 2d ser., 5 (1889–1890): 352–91; Fitch E. Oliver, ed., *The Diaries of Benjamin Lynde* (Boston, 1880); Work Projects Administration, *Diary and Journal (1755–1807) of Seth Metcalf* (Boston, 1939); *The Diary of Matthew Patten of Bedford, New Hampshire* (Concord, N.H., 1903); Thomas Eliot Andrews, ed., "The Diary of Elizabeth (Porter) Phelps," *New England Historic Genealogical Register* 118–22 (1964–68); Caroline Hazard, ed., *John Saffin, His Book (1665–1708)* (New York, 1928); "Extracts from 'Text Books' of Dea. Joseph Seccombe," *Essex Institute Historical Collections* 34 (1898): 23–39; and William Tudor, ed., *Deacon Tudor's Diary* (Boston, 1896).

Also invaluable for documents written by laypeople are genealogies and town and county histories. Many of these were published in the nineteenth century and often include long transcriptions of sources no longer extant.

To understand the piety of Christianized slaves, one could begin with Erik R. Seeman, "'Justise Must Take Plase': Three African Americans Speak of Religion in Eighteenth-Century New England," *William and Mary Quarterly*, 3d ser., 56 (1999): 393–414. This should be supplemented with Julian D. Mason, Jr., ed., *The Poems of Phillis Wheatley*, rev. ed. (Chapel Hill, N.C., 1989); Sondra A. O'Neale, *Jupiter Hammon and the Biblical Beginnings of*

African-American Literature (Metuchen, N.J., 1993); Graham Russell Hodges, ed., *Black Itinerants of the Gospel: The Narratives of John Jea and George White* (Madison, Wisc., 1993); and Richard Newman, ed., *Black Preacher to White America: The Collected Writings of Lemuel Haynes, 1774–1833* (Brooklyn, N.Y., 1990).

Ministerial sources published in more recent books and periodicals shed a great deal of light on lay piety. My debt to Ebenezer Parkman's querulous relationship with his parishioners is evident throughout my footnotes: Francis G. Walett, ed., *The Diary of Ebenezer Parkman, 1703–1782* (Worcester, Mass., 1974). In 300 double-columned pages this edition only gets to 1755; nearly thirty years of Parkman's diaries remain unpublished. I have also relied heavily on Isaac Backus and Ezra Stiles: William G. McLoughlin, ed., *The Diary of Isaac Backus*, 3 vols. (Providence, R.I., 1979); and Franklin Bowditch Dexter, ed., *The Literary Diary of Ezra Stiles*, 2 vols. (New York, 1901). Other published diaries include "Diary of Rev. Samuel Checkley, 1735," *Colonial Society of Massachusetts Publications* 12 (1908–9): 270–306; "The Diary of John Comer," *Collections of the Rhode Island Historical Society* 8 (1893): 3–132; "Extracts from the Diary of Rev. Samuel Dexter, of Dedham," *New England Historic Genealogical Register* 13–14 (1859–60); "Fragment of a Diary Kept by Rev. Samuel Fiske of Salem, 1719–1721," *Essex Institute Historical Collections* 51 (1915): 282–89; Samuel E. Morison, ed., "The Commonplace Book of Joseph Green," *Colonial Society of Massachusetts Publications* 34 (1937–42): 191–253; *Diary of Cotton Mather*, 2 vols. (New York, 1957); "Diaries of Rev. William Smith, 1738–1768," *Massachusetts Historical Society Proceedings* 42 (1908–9): 444–78; and *Diary of Rev. Daniel Wadsworth, Seventh Pastor of the First Church of Christ in Hartford* (Hartford, Conn., 1894).

Conversion narratives straddle the lay/ministerial distinction. The large majority of eighteenth-century narratives were written by ministers, who revised their parishioners' words to an unknowable extent. One surviving document includes two original lay narratives and the revised ministerial versions; I use this source to discuss some of this genre's potential problems in Erik R. Seeman, "Lay Conversion Narratives: Investigating Ministerial Intervention," *New England Quarterly* 71 (December 1998): 629–34. Despite their shortcomings, conversion narratives are important because they record the words of the illiterate and semiliterate (as opposed to diaries, written only by the literate). Published narratives may be found in Kenneth P. Minkema, ed., "The East Windsor Conversion Relations, 1700–1725," *The Connecticut Historical Society Bulletin* 51 (1986): 9–63; Kenneth P. Minkema, ed., "The Lynn End 'Earthquake' Relations of 1727," *New England Quarterly* 69

(1996): 473–99; and J. M. Bumsted, ed., "Emotion in Colonial America: Some Relations of Conversion Experience in Freetown, Massachusetts, 1749–1770," *New England Quarterly* 49 (1976): 97–108. Unpublished sources include Conversion Narratives of Nathaniel Brown, Mary Brown, James Stewart, and John Stewart, NEHGS; Relations of Isaac and Anna Farnsworth, IPL; box 1, folder 1b, John Cleaveland Papers, PEM; and box 2, folder 2, Ebenezer Parkman Papers, AAS.

Church records contain valuable information about lay piety. They include revealing disciplinary records and fodder for statistical analyses (dates of birth, death, baptism, and admission to full membership). Some of these sources have been published, but most remain in manuscript form. An indispensible guide to Congregational church records in Massachusetts is Harold Field Worthley, *An Inventory of the Records of the Particular (Congregational) Churches of Massachusetts Gathered 1620–1805* (Cambridge, Mass., 1970). This guide is necessary because Massachusetts church records are not gathered in a central repository, but scattered around the state in local archives, libraries, and church basements. Connecticut, in a boon to researchers, has gathered church records in the CSL. Virtually all colonial New England church records (and town records) are available through the massive genealogical microfilming project sponsored by the Church of Jesus Christ of Latter-day Saints. The microfilm reels are held in Salt Lake City and may be accessed for a small fee through Mormon Family History Libraries scattered across the country.

Finally, but most importantly, are unpublished sources. These documents are the hardest to work with since those written by laypeople are generally very hard to read. Handwriting is often shaky and idiosyncratic, spelling is almost always nonstandard, ink is usually faded. Furthermore, they can seem formulaic and conventional. But these sources reward careful readings, for in spiritual journals ordinary New Enlganders recorded their most powerful religious convictions. Typically, individual formulations are encased within a hard (but not impenetrable) shell of conventional language. A useful guide is William Matthews, *American Diaries in Manuscript, 1580–1954: A Descriptive Bibliography* (Athens, Ga., 1974). The most revealing lay diaries are Benjamin Bangs, John Barnard, William Cooper, John Gates, John Marshall, Experience Richardson, Josiah Thacher, Nathan West, Elizabeth Craft White, and Jonathan Willis in the MHS; Joseph Brewster, Jeremiah Bumstead, Abraham Fitts, Joseph Mason, and Edmund Williams in the AAS; Mary (Dodge) Cleaveland, Joseph Goodhue, James Jeffry, and Daniel King in the PEM; Aaron Bull, Hannah Heaton, Lucinda Howe, Alexander King, and

Benjamin Lyon in the CHS; Lydia Prout and Ebenezer Storer in the NEHGS; Joseph Pitkin in the CSL; Sarah Prince Gill, Kellogg Library, Bard College; and Moses Prince, HL.

Several manuscript diaries by ministers also shed light on lay-clergy relations, including David Hall, Nehemiah Hobart, Jonathan Mills, Ebenezer Parkman, and John Walley in the MHS; John Ballantine, John Emerson, Justus Forward, and Ebenezer Parkman in the AAS; Samuel Chandler in the PEM; and Jacob Eliot in the CHS.

Lay sermon notes are usually transcriptions of ministers' words, but they occasionally include editorial comments. These include Anonymous Notes of Sermons Heard, NEHGS; "Boston, Mass., Church Records," AAS (four volumes of anonymous notes); Edward Goddard, Sermon Notes, Nathan Stone Papers, MHS; Diary of Lucinda Howe, CHS; Edmund Quincy, Sermon Notes, Belcher-Jennison-Weiss Papers, MHS; Samuel Sewall, Jr., Notes of Sermons Heard, BPL; and Diary of Benjamin Woods, Diaries (Miscellaneous) Collection, box 18, SL.

Index

Abbot, Moses, 98, 99, 104
Aborn, Elizabeth, 152
African Americans, 84, 123, 192–93; as
    exhorters, 158, 172, 178
Alden, Samuel, 109
almanacs, 6, 121, 149–50
American Revolution, xiii, 180, 197–98, 200–
    203, 206–8; and nationalism, 201–2; and
    women, 197–98
angels, 207–8
anglicization, 7
Arianism, 132, 235 n. 56
Arminianism, 11
Ars Moriendi, 40, 44
assurance, 38, 40, 55–56; on deathbed, 62,
    70–71
astrology, 6; judicial, 121–22; natural, 121

Backus, Isaac, 138, 141, 142; on baptism,
    92; on Lord's Supper, 101, 113–14;
    prescriptions regarding death, 67–68,
    70–72, 75–76
Baker, Thomas, 27
Baldwin, William, 13–14
Ballantine, John, 68–69, 75, 120; on baptism,
    93, 94–95
Bangs, Benjamin, 100–101, 103, 107–8
baptism, 4, 88–95, 184, 216 n. 9; conflicts
    over, 79–80, 93–94; efficaciousness of, 20,
    91–92; and Halfway Covenant, 5–6
Barnard, John, 15–43, 180–81, 186, 204;
    attitudes toward death, 30–32, 35, 40, 55–
    56, 99; and baptism, 20; family roles of,

25–27; and Lord's Supper, 18–20, 22–24,
    28, 99; sacramentalism of, 17–25
Barnard, John, Jr., 48; on millennialism, 151
Barnard, Jonathan, 27
Barnum, Jane, 113
Barrett, Samuel, 140–41
Bass, John: and baptism, 109; and Lord's
    Supper, 110
Baxter, Richard, 62
Bay Psalm Book, 33
Bear, Hannah, 175
Beeman, Eleazer, 46
Belcher, Ruth, 113
Bennet, Molly, 141
Beveridge, William, 39–40
Bible, 11, 13, 32–34, 38, 50, 94, 143; lay reading
    of, 33–34, 183; version used, xiii
Billings, Jane, 54
Bissell, Esther, 46
Blanchard, Elizabeth, 126–27
Bonner, Mary Clarke, 74
Bowen, Nathan: and gender roles, 172; and
    influence of Enlightenment, 119
Bradish, Mary, 120–21; and popular parody,
    10
Bradstreet, Simon, 120
Brewster, Joseph, 12
Brewster, Martha, 53–54
Brockwell, Charles, 171–72; and sexuality,
    172
Brown, Anne, 89
Brown, Elisha, 119–20
Brown, John, 150

Bull, Aaron, 53
Bumstead, Jeremiah, 150
Burnam, Nathan, 174
Butler, Jon, 159–60, 206; on magic, 117–18, 126
Byles, Mather, 64
Bynum, Caroline Walker, 143, 223 n. 67

Calvin, John, 22, 89, 95
Cambridge Platform, 4, 5
Catholics, 89, 143–44; during French and Indian War, 196, 198
Cary, Margaret, 57
Cary, Mercy, 79–80, 91
celibacy, 134, 142–45; biblical teachings on, 143; views of, in England, 144; views of, in New England, 143–45
Champlin, Christopher, 121–22
Champlin, Elizabeth, 121–22
Chandler, Samuel, 101, 120, 136–38, 176; prescriptions regarding death, 48, 50, 63
Chauncy, Charles, 74–75, 164, 204; and gender anxieties, 173
Cheever, John, 177
childbirth, 188, 222 n. 55; fears of, 56–57, 189, 190
Choate, Abraham, 85–86
Christ. *See* Jesus
civil millennialism. *See* millennialism, civil
Cleaveland, Abigail, 63–64
Cleaveland, Ebenezer, 82
Cleaveland, John: and conversion narratives, 83, 86, 174–77
Cleaveland, Mary, 91, 99
clergy. *See* ministers
Cogswell, Phillis, 84
Cohen, Charles Lloyd, 227 n. 12
Cole, Ezekiel, 93
Cole, Nathan, 160
Colman, Benjamin, 62; on baptism, 91; on Lord's Supper, 97–98
Comer, John, 105–6, 131
comets, 118–19. *See also* astrology; magic
communion. *See* Lord's Supper
Connecticut River Valley Revival, 154–58; gendered accounts of, 157; visions in, 156

conversion experience, 82, 83, 139–40, 161–63, 177; assurance of, 37–38; eighteenth-century model of, 148; evidence for, 24
conversion narratives, 46, 55, 81–88, 161, 174–75; as sources, xi, 74, 83, 150–51
Cooper, William, 103, 107, 108
Cotton, John, 49
Cotton, Josiah, 127–28
Crawford, Michael, 152
Croswell, Andrew, 159, 168
cultural scripts, ix, x, 29, 146, 211 n. 3; of deathbed behavior, 44–45, 47, 62–63, 77–78; durability of, 203
culture: ambivalence of, ix, 17, 42–43; negotiations of, 5, 43, 77–78, 146, 204; open versus closed, ix, x, 15, 32, 78, 204; shared, 4, 6, 217 n. 45
Cutler, Timothy, 132, 156–58; on sexuality, 157

Davenport, James, 159, 167
Davenport, John, 5
Deans, Elizabeth, 75
death, 30–31, 45–60, 142; fear of, 31, 55, 67–68, 190; and Lord's Supper, 99–100; and magic, 122, 130; and piety, 46, 134, 154. *See also* deathbed scenes; mourning
deathbed scenes, 40, 44–45, 60–77; comfort gained by, 64–65; elements of model, 44, 61–63
Dexter, Samuel, 10
diaries. *See* journals, spiritual
Dill, Mary, 108
Dinah (slave), 192–93, 245 n. 29
Dirks, Nicholas, 79–80
divination, 53, 121, 123–24; and African Americans, 123; ministerial warnings against, 127
Dodge, Mary. *See* Cleaveland, Mary
dreams, 45, 53–54, 140, 207–8. *See also* visions
drought, 86–87, 197; and providentialism, 181–82
drunkenness, 105–6

Earthquake Revival, 149–54; and
millennialism, 151–52
earthquakes, 87, 134, 149–54, 197; and
millennialism, 151–52, 197
Eaton, Jeremiah, 151–52
Eaton, Mary, 76
Eddy, Priscilla, 67
Edwards, Jonathan, 154–58, 160, 164–65,
169–70; on gender roles, 170; on "infant
damnation," 52
Edwards, Sarah, 162–63
emotionalism, 155, 194–96; gendered aspects
of, 149, 166, 194; ministerial critique of,
149, 165–66, 194
Enlightenment, 117, 181; elite laypeople
influenced by, 119; ministers influenced
by, 7
Eveleth, Sarah, 81–82, 88

family, 46, 144–45, 160, 169, 191–92; and
piety of laypeople, 25–27, 46–47, 58–60,
89, 90–92, 169, 191–92; prayers for, 26, 27,
180, 201–2
fast days, 10
fatherhood, 27, 58–60
Fiske, Ann, 90–91
Fitts, Abraham, 12–13; on Satan's powers,
13
Flagg, Ebenezer, 12–13
Flavel, John, 39, 40–41; on "spiritualizing the
creatures," 185
Fobes, Esther, 113–14
Forbush, Thomas, 68
fornication, 79, 82, 85, 88; and revivalism,
157
Forward, Justus, 110–11
Foster, Bethiah, 87
Foxcroft, Elizabeth, 63, 77
Foxcroft, Thomas, 69
Franklin, Benjamin, 122–23
Franklin, James, 5
French and Indian War, 196–200; and
millennialism, 196–97
French Revolution, 197
Frothingham, Sarah, 74

Gates, John, 51; on Lord's Supper, 98, 102–3;
on mourning, 49, 59–60
Gates, Josiah, 59–60
gender, 8, 56–57, 157, 166–73; and magic, 119;
and sexuality, x. *See also* gender roles,
inversions of
gender roles, inversions of, 74–77, 125, 139,
145, 168, 169–73
"Gentlewoman" (fictional character), 168
Gibbs, Henry, 47
Giddinge, Abigail, 55
Gill, Sarah Prince. *See* Prince, Sarah
Gilman, Nicholas, 101, 133–38, 160; and lay
visions, 76–77, 138
Ginzburg, Carlo, 16
Glasier, Benjamin, 66
Godbeer, Richard, 37, 117
Goodhue, Joseph, 161; on baptism, 90; on
Lord's Supper, 107
Gorton, Samuel, 131
Goss, Thomas, 111–12
Gouge, William, 144
Graham, John, 89
Great Awakening, 9, 60, 85, 158–73, 180,
231 n. 111; and American Revolution,
206; communal piety in, 160–64;
conversion experiences during, 139–40,
161–63; "excesses" of, 76–77, 133–38,
164–66; gender anxieties in, 166–73, 178–
79, 194
Green, Joseph, 11, 123
Green, Joshua, 12
Gura, Philip, 131

Hacket, George, 72
Halfway Covenant, 5–6, 81, 89
Hall, David D., ix, 17, 224 n. 88, 226 n. 4; on
Lord's Supper, 105, 216 n. 9; on "shared
culture," 4
Hall, (Rev.) David, 72, 93; on witchcraft, 124
Hambleton, John, 69–70
Hambrick-Stowe, Charles E., 105, 226 n. 4
Harvard College, 5, 6, 132
Haskell, Hubbard, 176
Hassock, Ruth, 55

Hatch, Nathan O., 196–97; and civil
    millennialism, 196
Hawley, Joseph, 156
Hayward, John, 113–14
Heaton, Hannah, 119, 162; attitudes toward
    death, 51, 57; on childbirth, 57, 188–89
heaven, 52, 63, 191
hell, 52, 136, 175; fears of, 55, 151–52
heterodoxy, x, 8, 73–74, 92, 131–46;
    definition of, 234 n. 52; before Great
    Awakening, 131–32; in seventeenth
    century, 131
Hinckley, Mary, 49
Holifield, E. Brooks, 17
homosexuality, 172–73
Howe, Lucinda, 77, 214 n. 33
Huckins, Hannah, 137
Hull, Hannah, 88
Hutchinson, Anne, 4, 28, 164; heterodoxy of,
    131, 132

Immortalism, x, 135, 137, 140–43; ministerial
    criticism of, 141
Immortalists, 139–46
Indians, 123, 128
"infant damnation," 52–53, 60, 222 n. 37
infertility, 189, 244 n. 19
Ingersol, Elizabeth, 84
Ireland, Shadrack, 141–42
Ive, John, 131

Jeffry, James, 149–50
jeremiads, clerical, 6, 35
Jesus, 33, 38, 63–64, 100, 202; blood of, 50,
    100–101, 103–4; lay visions of, 44–45, 71–
    72, 101. *See also* Lord's Supper, Christ's
    presence at
Jewet, Jedidiah, 165
Job, 59–60
Johnson, Samuel, 68–69
Johnson, (Rev.) Samuel, 157, 178
journals, spiritual, 16, 62, 254–55
Judgment Day. *See* millennialism

Keene, Sarah, 124
Kendall, Samuel, 80

Keyes, Robert, 116
King, Daniel, 69, 70; and Lord's Supper, 98–
    99, 103, 104; and mourning, 49, 58–59
King, Nathaniel, 58–59, 69, 70
Kingsley, Bathsheba, 169–71; and direct
    revelations, 171; and disruption of family
    order, 169–70
Kinsman, Jeremiah, 85

laity. *See* laypeople
Laud, William, 5
laypeople: and baptism, 90–93; communal
    piety of, 8, 23–25, 28, 64, 106–14, 183–84,
    217 n. 33; and disagreements with
    ministers, 12–14, 22–24, 37, 69–73, 93–94,
    108–12; independent thinking of, 9, 13, 15,
    43, 159, 205; link between family and piety
    of, 25–27, 46–47, 58–60, 89, 90–92, 169,
    191–92; and magic, 121–30; and
    millennialism, x, 36–37, 151–52, 197, 200;
    orthodox views of, 16, 21, 43, 48, 92–93,
    180; prophecy by, 76–77; and respect for
    ministers, 5, 31, 184. *See also* assurance;
    conversion experience; emotionalism;
    men; providentialism; revivals, religious,
    communal piety of; women
Lears, T. J. Jackson, ix
Lee, Ann, 143; compared to Eve, 144; as
    threat to family order, 144–45
life course, piety over the, 30, 35, 56
liminality, 66, 171, 204, 223 n. 67; and
    inversions of power, 61, 80
literacy, 4, 17, 32–33; impact on lay piety of,
    34–42; near universality of, 33; and social
    control, 34–35
Long, Hannah, 26
Lord's Supper, 17–20, 47, 69, 95–114, 184–85,
    195; Christ's presence at, 22–23, 98, 105,
    185, 217 n. 31; communal piety in, 28, 104,
    106–8; fear caused by, 19, 102–3;
    preparation necessary for, 17, 18, 95–98
Loring, Israel, 132, 180, 184, 196, 198; on
    death, 68, 191; on Satan, 186
Louisbourg, fall of fort at, 198
Lovelace, Richard, 22
Low, Hannah, 175

Low, Rachel, 85, 87
Luther, Martin, 89
Lynde, Benjamin, 150
Lyon, Benjamin, 50, 62–63; spiritual journal of, 62

magic, 116–31; black, 124–25; "folklorization" of, 117–18; ministerial opposition to, 116–18; white, 116, 121–24, 130
maleficium. *See* magic, black
Mammon, 86
Manifest Destiny, 208
manumission, 193
Marlborough Association of Ministers, 49, 132
Marsh, Elisha, 13
Mather, Cotton, 17–25, 34–37, 40, 41, 118, 150, 185, 217 n. 33; on female piety, 8, 144, 217 n. 39; on good works, 20–21, 41; on Lord's Supper, 18–19, 22–24, 204; on magic, 53, 122, 123; prescriptions regarding death, 31–32, 47–48, 52, 62, 69, 74; on slavery, 193
Mather, Increase, 6, 22, 40, 41, 118, 123; on millennialism, 36
McKinstry, John, 48–49
Mede, Joseph, 36
Mellen, John, 111–12
memorialization, 50–51
men, 90, 163, 170. *See also* fatherhood; gender; homosexuality; patriarchy
Menocchio, 16
Metcalf, Seth, 51
millennialism, x, 8, 36, 151–52, 197, 200; civil, 196–97, 200
ministerial associations, 7
ministers: attempts to increase power of, 6–7; and baptism, 79, 89–90; jeremiads of, 6, 35; on Lord's Supper, 23–24, 96–97, 111–12; on millennialism, x, 36, 151, 196, 200; opposition to celibacy, 143–45; opposition to magic, 116–18; ordination ritual, 6–7; prescriptions regarding death, 44, 47–48, 52, 62, 64; role in revivals, 147–48, 152, 154, 158; and sacramental renaissance, 15, 17–18. *See also* anglicization; millennialism,

civil; mourning, ministerial prescriptions for; sermons
Moorhead, Sarah Parsons, 167–68
Moravians, 104
mourning: lay practices of, 47, 48–50, 58–60, 190–91, 194; ministerial prescriptions for, 47–48, 49–50, 191

Native Americans. *See* Indians
New England Courant, 6
New Lights, 158, 159, 167–68; importance of conversion for, 83
newspapers, influence of, 6, 15
Noyes, Mary, 56

Old Lights, 158, 164, 173, 178
Oliver, Jerusha, 56–57, 63
ordination, 6–7
Original Sin, 8, 109–10
Osborn, Sarah, 48
Osgood, Mehitable, 151

Paine, John, 49, 64
Parkman, Ebenezer, 10, 11, 118–19, 140, 142, 144; on baptism, 91–92, 93–94; on magic, 116–17, 120–21; prescriptions regarding death, 44–45, 54, 63, 68–73
Parsons, Jonathan, 47–48, 165; on homosexuality, 173
Parsons, William, 134
patriarchy, 26–27; lay questioning of, 13–14, 206
Paul, Saint, 134, 143
Pearse, Edward, 62–63
Pearson, Jonathan, 152
Perkins, John, 119, 124, 128–30; and influence of Enlightenment, 119, 128
Phelps, Elizabeth, 57, 102
Phillips, Samuel, 153
Pierce, William, 93–94
Pierpont, Sarah, 98, 101, 104, 166–67; sensual piety of, 104
Piot de l'Angloiserie, Louis, 132
Pratt, Isaiah, 44–45, 55
prayer, 8, 9, 26, 27, 57, 182–83. *See also* family, prayers for

predestination, 45, 51–52, 56
pregnancy, 57, 189–90, 244 n. 20
premarital sex. *See* fornication
Prentice, Sarah, x, 139–46, 204; on celibacy, 142–43; conversion experience of, 139–40; on Immortalism, 141–42
Prentice, Solomon, 139–42
Price, Elizabeth, 74–75
Prince, Deborah, 65
Prince, Joseph, 136
Prince, Sarah, 50–51, 65, 161; on Lord's Supper, 96, 104, 105
Prince, Thomas, 161, 165
print culture, 5, 6, 15, 80
Protestantism, reformed, 20, 22, 44, 51–52, 143; definition of, 212 n. 2; lay attachment to, 3; and magic, 117; resilience of, 208–9; sacraments of, 15–16, 89, 95–96; in seventeenth century, 4, 82
Prout, Lydia, 99, 100, 103; attitudes toward death, 46–47, 49, 52–53, 57
providentialism, 29, 30, 118–20, 199–200, 206; and connection to natural phenomena, 34, 54–55, 118–19, 181–82; waning influence on elite laypeople of, 119; waning influence on ministers of, 7, 217 n. 45
Psalms, 33–34
Puritanism. *See* Protestantism, reformed
Putnam, Molly, 64
Putnam, Tarrant, 64

Quakers, 4

Randal, Hannah, 91
Rathbun, Valentine, 144
reading. *See* Bible; literacy
Reed, Mary, 76–77, 142; visions experienced by, 76
Reforming Synod (1679), 6
Reis, Elizabeth, 234 n. 43
revivals, religious, 147–79; communal piety of, 148, 153, 155, 160–64, 175, 177; continuity of, 147–48; disorder during, 155–57, 164–73; and gender anxieties, 157, 166–73, 176

Revolutionary War. *See* American Revolution
Richardson, Experience, 180–203, 204; attitudes toward death, 49, 50, 52–53, 56, 182, 190–91; emotionalism of, 194–96; on Lord's Supper, 97, 100, 105, 195; and nationalism, 200–203; providentialism of, 181–82; views of Satan, 186–87
Richardson, Gideon, 182, 189
Richardson, Josiah, 192, 193–94
Richardson, Josiah, Jr., 180, 189, 199, 201–2
Richardson, Luther, 52, 189, 190–91
rituals, 79–115, 135; disorder created by, 79–80; efficaciousness of, 79, 80; invariance of, 83–85; performative nature of, 107
Robey, William, 28, 32
Rogers, Daniel, 134
Rogers, John, 153
Rogers, John, Jr., 165–66
Rogers, Nathaniel, 134
Rogers, Susé, 63
Rust, Mary, 177

sacramental renaissance, 15–16, 17–18, 19
Sambon, John, 71
Satan, 37, 43, 44, 164; people tempted by, 13, 181, 186–87
Saybrook Platform, 7
Seacoast Revival, 83, 174–77; conversion narratives from, 81–88
Second Coming. *See* millennialism
Second Great Awakening, 9
Sergeant, Christopher, 151
Sergeant, Hannah, 86–87
sermons, 11, 16, 151; lay notes of, 12, 214 n. 33
Seven Years' War. *See* French and Indian War
Sewall, Samuel, 3, 120, 131, 217 n. 31, 219 n. 63; attitudes toward death, 54, 66–67, 73; on baptism, 88–89, 90; on Lord's Supper, 17, 102, 103, 105, 216 n. 10
sexuality, x, 104–5, 108, 135, 140, 157; and piety, 137; positive views of, 144, 236 n. 93
Shakers, 143–45
shared culture. *See* culture, shared

Skinner, John, 112–13

slaves, 84, 192–93, 245 n. 29

Smith, Grace, 74, 77

Smith, Nat, 140, 141

Smith, Richard, 140–41

Smith, Thomas, 116

Smolinski, Reiner, 36

Sola Scriptura, 212 n. 2

Sparhawk, Nathaniel, 150–51, 205

Spinney, John, 125

"spiritualizing the creatures," 185–86

spoken word, power of, 80

Stafford, Joseph, 121

Steele, Richard, 39, 41–42

Stevens, Hubbard, 101

Stiles, Ezra, 124, 141

Stoddard, Solomon, 16, 37–39, 82, 148; on conversion, 37, 38

Stone, Nathan, 93–94

Storer, Ebenezer, 90, 101, 104; mourning practices of, 48, 78

Story, Thomas, 174, 175

suicide, 99–100, 156

Tennant, Gilbert, 159, 172

Thayer, Susanna, 54

Turell, Ebenezer, 126–27, 234 n. 43

Turell, Jane, 91, 97–98, 104

Upham, Abigail, 72

Veazie, Samuel, 108–9

visions, 164, 166; on deathbed, 44, 45, 71–72, 76–77; during Lord's Supper, 101–2. *See also* dreams

Wadsworth, Benjamin, 89

Wadsworth, Hannah, 46

Waldron, William, 124–45

Walley, Bethiah, 75

"Watchman, The," 206

Watts, Isaac, 63

West, Benjamin, 145

Wheelock, Eleazer, 127, 164

Wheelwright, Nathaniel, 129, 130

White, Elizabeth, 66

White, John, 161, 166

White, Samuel, 71–72

Whitefield, George, 158, 160, 161; lay support of, 168

Wigglesworth, Samuel, 151

Willard, Samuel, 52, 144; on mourning, 47; prescriptions regarding death, 64

Williams, Roger, 4

Williams, William, Jr., 152

Willis, Jonathan, 65; on Lord's Supper, 97, 102, 103, 104, 108

Willison, John, 62

Winthrop, John, 196

Wise, Jeremiah, 136–38

witchcraft, 124–30. *See also* magic, black

women, 10, 26, 45, 90–92, 163, 166–71, 187–96; deathbed words of, 73–77; images of, 10–11; and witchcraft, 124–30. *See also* childbirth; fornication; gender; pregnancy; sexuality

Wood, Gordon S., 13

Wood, Williams, 116

Woodbury, Mary, 175

Woodbury, Richard, 133–38, 158; on celibacy, 134, 137; on Immortalism, 135, 137

Worcester, Francis, 174, 177

Worcester Association of Ministers, 93

"world of wonders." *See* providentialism

Zwingli, Ulrich, 22, 89

Library of Congress Cataloging-in-Publication Data

Seeman, Erik R.
    Pious persuasions : laity and clergy in eighteenth-century New England /
Erik R. Seeman.
        p.   cm. — (Early America)
    Includes bibliographical references and index.
    ISBN 0-8018-6208-6 (alk. paper)
    1. New England—Religious life and customs.   2. New England—Church
history—18th century.   3. Laity—New England.   I. Title.   II. Series.
BR520.S44   1999
277.4′07—dc21
                                                                        99-15429
                                                                        CIP